S0-BIP-194

Atlantic

ESSAYS

Atlantic

E S S A Y S

SAMUEL N. BOGORAD
The University of Vermont

CARY B. GRAHAM
Butler University

An Atlantic Monthly Press Book

D. C. HEATH AND COMPANY

BOSTON

ATLANTIC — D. C. HEATH BOOKS
ARE PUBLISHED BY
D. C. HEATH AND COMPANY
IN ASSOCIATION WITH
THE ATLANTIC MONTHLY PRESS

Library of Congress Catalog Card Number: 58–5891

(5 L 7)

PREFACE

FOR a century *The Atlantic Monthly,* a magazine of literature, science, art, and politics, has provided the literate reading public with materials of lasting significance and interest. Named by Oliver Wendell Holmes, one of its early contributors, and edited successively by James Russell Lowell, James T. Fields, William Dean Howells, Thomas Bailey Aldrich, Horace E. Scudder, Walter H. Page, Bliss Perry, Ellery Sedgwick, and Edward Weeks, *The Atlantic Monthly* has numbered among its contributors distinguished authors, artists, journalists, and statesmen. Indeed, *The Atlantic Monthly* is virtually an indispensable source of study for an understanding of the national and international scene during the past century and in our own time.

In homes, schools, and colleges, indeed wherever a high premium is placed upon good writing, *The Atlantic Monthly* has been a source of thoughtful and provocative interpretations of the past, the present, and the future. Essays from *The Atlantic Monthly* have been widely reprinted in anthologies compiled for college classes in English. Instructors and students alike have found these essays effective materials for teaching and study. The long history of classroom usefulness of such essays encourages the belief that a book of essays compiled exclusively from *The Atlantic Monthly* will satisfy a genuine need for those courses in which a collection of essays is in demand for the teaching of reading and writing.

All of the essays in this collection have, of course, already undergone the rigorous scrutiny of *The Atlantic Monthly* editors. Our own standards of effective writing have been the fundamental criteria in the selection of these particular essays. Keeping in mind that this collection is designed primarily for college freshmen, we have excluded essays which, though interesting and important, depend for full understanding upon knowledge or information which it would be unreasonable to expect of first-year college students.

In selecting the essays, we have sought to include those which not only are effectively written but also are readily adaptable to classroom discussion. Most of the essays are drawn from recent or relatively recent issues of *The Atlantic Monthly.* The essays have a broad range of style, from the plain to the sophisticated, but the over-all stylistic level is that of contemporary writing. Those using this collection will, after all, be engaged in the effort to help college students understand and achieve the level of writing proficiency which is expected of them as educated men and women.

The essays have been arranged in eight groups. This arrangement is intended simply to bring together for the sake of convenience those essays which have obvious relations in subject matter and thus to facilitate cross-reference of ideas. Each of the essays has been chosen for its intrinsic values and not to fit any preconceived groups or divisions; nor have the essays been arranged according to any preconceived levels of difficulty. Although we have included essays of varying subject matter and difficulty, we have not tried to represent all areas of knowledge or experience. There is nothing sacred about our grouping, and the essays may be freely used in whatever order suits the needs and convenience of the instructor.

In the study questions we have sought to provide a valid rhetorical basis for helping students to improve their skills in reading, writing, and thinking. We believe that rigorous analysis of an author's purposes, methods, and results is an effective tool in pursuing this aim. Hence our questions constantly emphasize *why? how?* and *what?* In finding answers to these questions, the student is led to evaluate what he is reading, to discover useful writing techniques for himself, and to think critically as he reads and writes. This emphasis on purpose in the questions not only tests the student's understanding of what he has read and illustrates methods which may be useful to him in his own writing, but also helps to reveal to the student the inseparableness of reading, writing, and thinking, as well as the relationship of author, essay, and reader. The study questions are of such a nature that this collection of essays can be especially useful in connection with the handbook or rhetoric that most students use.

We have scrupulously avoided study questions which are merely triggers to set off indiscriminate discussion. The questions are, rather, an integral part of the total design of the book: to place upon the student the responsibility of understanding the purposes of expository prose, through analysis of structure, diction, theme, mood, and tone. In addition, the questions encourage the student to determine the relation between these elements, on the one hand, and the intellective and emotive purposes of the essays, on the other. To this end we have excluded the what-is-your-opinion-of-this and do-you-agree-with-the-author type of question, which we regard as a serious shortcoming of the editorial apparatus of many anthologies. Nor have we included questions which focus attention on tangential subject matter.

We recognize, of course, that discussion of the subject matter of the essays is a vital part of critical reading and thinking. Indeed, our choice of essays has been strongly determined by their value for discussion of ideas and varied points of view. But we have not included questions directly related to this activity, preferring instead to allow the instructor complete freedom in developing his own procedures in this area where individual teaching techniques are so important. Needless to say, although our questions are primarily related to the principle of analyzing purpose, they lead to and are ultimately inseparable from the consideration of ideas. We have made no attempt to be exhaustive in providing study questions. Instead we have tried to indicate certain lines of analysis and inquiry which the instructor and student can pursue in further detail as required.

Theme topics and writing assignments have not been included in the editorial apparatus, our belief being that instructors prefer to make up their own. It should be noted, however, that many of our questions lend themselves to written assignments and can be profitably used in this manner. Convinced as we are that a student should never read without a good dictionary at hand, we have not supplied footnotes to provide information that is readily available in *The American College Dictionary* or *Webster's Collegiate Dictionary*. Where the context does not make clear the force and meaning of allusions, we have supplied clarifying footnotes. The brief biographical headnote preceding each essay is intended chiefly to point out the qualifications of the author to write on his particular subject and to suggest something of his achievements.

There remains the pleasant obligation of thanking those who have helped us to bring this book to publication. We are especially grateful to the field representatives of D. C. Heath and Company, whose inquiries among teachers of freshman English indicated that a book of essays from *The Atlantic Monthly* would find a welcome reception. The publishers of *The Atlantic Monthly* have rendered us valuable aid in securing permission to use copyrighted materials. The editorial advice and counsel of Mr. John R. Walden, Head of the College Department of D. C. Heath and Company; of Mr. Charles F. Weden, Associate Editor; and of Mr. Robb Harvey of the same company have been enormously helpful. To our colleagues in The University of Vermont and Butler University, as well as to our friends in other institutions, who have aided, abetted, and criticized our efforts, we express our gratitude. We need hardly add that although we are grateful to all these persons, we are alone responsible for the finished product.

Samuel N. Bogorad
Cary B. Graham

Burlington, Vermont
Indianapolis, Indiana

CONTENTS

Education in College

GEORGE F. KENNAN
Training for Statesmanship 3

HOWARD MUMFORD JONES
Undergraduates on Apron Strings 12

OSCAR HANDLIN
Yearning for Security 20

LYNN WHITE, JR.
Educating Women in a Man's World 27

ALLEN JACKSON
Too Much Football 36

HAROLD W. STOKE
College Athletics: Education or Show Business? 52

Language and the Arts

JACQUES BARZUN
English as She's Not Taught 65

ALICE HAMILTON, M.D.
Words Lost, Strayed, or Stolen 76

E. M. FORSTER
The Ivory Tower 81

W. T. STACE
The Snobbishness of the Learned 94

GEORGE F. WHICHER
Out for Stars: A Meditation on Robert Frost 105

AL CAPP
The Comedy of Charlie Chaplin 114

EDWARD WEEKS
The Meaning of Literary Prizes 125

Personalities

BERTRAND RUSSELL
Mahatma Gandhi 139

GAMALIEL BRADFORD
Mark Twain 150

C. W. CERAM
The Man Who Found Troy 166

JUDGE CHARLES E. WYZANSKI, JR.
Brandeis 180

ROLLO WALTER BROWN
" Kitty " of Harvard 195

A Touch of Humor

RICHARD GORDON
The Common Cold 209

ROBERT LYND
Objections to Laughter 215

PHILIP WYLIE
Science Has Spoiled My Supper 229

Social Patterns and Problems

RALPH BARTON PERRY
Domestic Superstitions 239

DAVID L. COHN
Do American Men Like Women? 249

JAMES HOWARD MEANS, M.D.
Government in Medicine 259

JUDGE ELIJAH ADLOW
Teen-Age Criminals 269

ALBERT JAY NOCK
Utopia in Pennsylvania: The Amish 280

As the Scientist Sees It

GEORGE R. HARRISON
Faith and the Scientist 295

VANNEVAR BUSH
As We May Think 308

HARLOW SHAPLEY
A Design for Fighting 327

STANLEY CASSON
Challenge to Complacency: What Future Archaeologists Will Think of Us 346

Freedom of Thought and Expression

WALTER LIPPMANN
The Indispensable Opposition 363

ZECHARIAH CHAFEE, JR.
The Encroachments on Freedom 371

HOWARD MUMFORD JONES
How Much Academic Freedom? 384

JAMES S. POPE
The Suppression of News 395

GERALD W. JOHNSON
The Monopoly of News 406

Values

IRWIN EDMAN
A Reasonable Life in a Mad World 417

ARCHIBALD MacLEISH
Humanism and the Belief in Man 424

VANNEVAR BUSH
Can Men Live Without War? 438

CLARENCE B. RANDALL
Free Enterprise Is Not a Hunting License 446

CURTIS CATE
God and Success 455

Atlantic

E S S A Y S

Education in College

GEORGE F. KENNAN

HOWARD MUMFORD JONES

OSCAR HANDLIN

LYNN WHITE, JR.

ALLEN JACKSON

HAROLD W. STOKE

GEORGE F. KENNAN entered the Foreign Service in 1926, following his graduation from Princeton. For the next quarter of a century he had assignments in many countries of Europe. One of the few American diplomats who speak Russian, he was appointed "Diplomatic Chief of Staff" to Secretary of State Marshall in 1947 and Ambassador to the Soviet Union in 1952. However, the Kremlin declared him *persona non grata* and he was expelled from Moscow. At present he is a member of the Institute for Advanced Study at Princeton. He has published three books: *American Diplomacy* (1950), *Realities of American Foreign Policy* (1954), and *Russia Leaves the War* (1956). The present essay was originally delivered as a speech to the Princeton alumni, in February, 1953.

TRAINING FOR STATESMANSHIP

by GEORGE F. KENNAN

ONE can hardly complain today about the time and effort devoted in American colleges and universities to instruction in foreign affairs. I doubt whether there is a liberal arts curriculum in the country which does not offer courses or activities in this field, and many of the technical institutions also are beginning to include such courses.

There are people, I am sure, who would feel that the high volume of instruction in this field is in itself the guarantee of a fairly respectable measure of achievement. These people would argue that some instruction in international affairs is obviously better than none at all, and that therefore this impressive volume of activity must produce useful results, regardless of the content of the courses.

About this I have my doubts. I am not certain that there is any virtue in teaching people about international affairs — aside from such virtue as may reside in the tenor of the teaching itself. Since the amount of relevant factual material is infinite, embracing in the last analysis practically everything there is to know about the human family, international affairs is a field in which the pursuit of knowledge without understanding is peculiarly pointless and useless. This being the case, mere volume of instruction does not guarantee anything at all in the way of desirable results. In fact, if instruction does not proceed from a realistic understanding of the subject, it can be worse than useless. I think anyone who has lectured extensively about foreign affairs will have had the same experience I have had — of noting that the questions asked by simple and relatively uneducated people are often more sensible and penetrating than those asked by people who have had a good deal of teaching on these subjects but have been taught the wrong way.

Instruction in international affairs can be given for two different purposes. The first is to instill into the student the type of understanding of the subject needed by the man who is not going to make participation in international affairs his business in life but who wants to acquit himself creditably of his duties of citizenship. A man who wants to be a good citizen needs to be able to judge men and issues in national life. But there are few important issues of national policy that can be understood today except in relation to our international position. And even the quality of the statesmanship of our national leaders often becomes manifest primarily in their reactions to problems that are at least partly problems of international life. The conscientious citizen therefore obviously requires as broad and enlightened an understanding of this subject as he can get.

The second purpose which instruction in international affairs can serve is to prepare men for service in the foreign field, either in governmental or in other positions.

It is a mistake to think of international affairs as anything outside the regular context of life — as anything which a man could hope to understand without having to understand things much more basic. There is no such thing as foreign affairs in the abstract. The relations between nations are part of the whole great problem of politics — of the behavior of man as a political animal. They are inseparably connected with the fundamental human problem of power that lies at the heart of all politics: the problem of how the freedom of choice of the individual, or of the organized society, is to be limited in order to repress chaos and ensure the good order necessary to the continuation of civilization.

We Americans have a strange — and to me disturbing — attitude toward the subject of power. We don't like the word. We don't like the concept. We are suspicious of people who talk about it. We like to feel that the adjustment of conflicting interests is something that can be taken care of by juridical norms and institutional devices, voluntarily accepted and not involving violence to the feelings or interests of anyone. We like to feel that this is the way our own life is arranged. We like to feel that if this principle were to be understood and observed by others as it is by us, it would put an end to many of the misunderstandings and conflicts that have marked our time.

But we ignore the fact that power underlies our own society as it underlies every other order of human affairs distinguishable from chaos. Order and civilization are not self-engendering. They do not flow from themselves or even from any universal and enlightened understanding of political institutions in the abstract.

In our country, the element of power is peculiarly diffused. It is not concentrated, as it is in other countries, in what we might call the "pure form" of a national uniformed police establishment functioning as the vehicle of a central political will. Power with us does exist to some extent in courts of law and in police establishments, but it also exists in many other American institutions. It exists in our economic system, though not nearly to the degree the Marxists claim. Sometimes, unfortunately, it exists in irregular forces – in underworld groups, criminal gangs, or informal associations of a vigilante nature – capable of terrorizing their fellow citizens in one degree or another. Above all, it exists in the delicate compulsions of our social life, the force of community opinion within our country – in the respect we have for the good opinion of our neighbors. For reasons highly complex, we Americans place upon ourselves quite extraordinary obligations of conformity to the group in utterance and behavior, and this feature of our national life seems to be growing rather than declining. All these things can bring us to put restraints upon ourselves which in other parts of the world would be imposed upon people only by the straightforward exercise of the central police authority.

Now I am not taking exception to this curious diffusion, within American life, of the power to make men conform to given patterns of behavior. It has both advantages and dangers. It represents unquestionably a manner of protecting the interests of the individual against the more dangerous and humiliating forms of tyranny and oppression in normal times. But we must not permit this advantage to blind us to the fact that such a thing as power does exist and is, indeed, a necessity of civilization, flowing from certain facts about human nature – certain imperfections if you will – that are basic and that are not going to be corrected by any man-made device, whether institutional or educational. These basic facts provide one of the main keys to the understanding of history. They lie at the heart of our problem of living together as human beings within the borders of this land. And they also lie at the heart of our problem of living side by side with other human societies within the broader framework of this planet.

Whoever would understand foreign affairs, therefore, cannot and will not do it solely by understanding the intricacies of tariffs or the various classifications of treaties or the ways in which the United Nations Charter differs from the Covenant of the League of Nations or the techniques of sampling mass opinion. International affairs are primarily a matter of the behavior of governments. But the behavior of governments is in turn a matter of the behavior of individual man in the political context, and of the workings of all those basic impulses — national feeling, charity, ambition, fear, jealousy, egotism, and group attachment — which are the stuff of his behavior in the community of other men.

Whoever does not understand these things will never understand what is taking place in the interrelationships of nations. And he will not learn them from courses that purport to deal with international affairs alone. He will learn them, rather, from those things which have been recognized for thousands of years as the essentials of humanistic study: from history and from the more subtle and revealing expressions of man's nature that go by the names of art and literature.

II

I WOULD say, therefore: Let the international affairs course stand as an addendum to basic instruction in the humanities. Let it stand as an exercise in which the student is told to take what he has already learned about the characteristics of the human animal and to note in what curious and marvelous ways they find their ultimate expression in the behavior of governments. Let foreign relations be viewed as one area — an extremely important one — in which these laws of nature work themselves out. But let the teaching of the subject not be permitted to obscure its basic components. Let no one be permitted to think that he is learned in something called a "science" of international relations unless he is learned in the essentials of the political process from the grass roots up and has been taught to look soberly and unsparingly, but also with charity and sympathy, at his fellow human beings. International affairs is not a science. And there is no understanding of international affairs that does not embrace understanding of the human individual.

Only if these principles are observed will we be able to free ourselves from the strain of utopianism that has been present in the teaching of international affairs in our country in recent decades. By this I mean teaching that portrays incorrectly the nature of our world environment and our relation to it and encourages students to disregard the urgent real requirements of international life in favor of the cultivation of artificial and impractical visions of world betterment. This argument about the philosophy of our approach to our problems of foreign relations is one that has been agitating our academic communities intensely in recent months. I am myself a partisan in the dispute. I shall only say here that further exposure to the bitter realities of the practice of international relations, in a place where these realities are about as bitter as they can conceivably be, has strengthened my conviction that the shortcomings in the teaching of international affairs, and primarily the leanings toward shallow and utopian interpretations, represent, in their ultimate effect, an important limitation of our ability to handle ourselves effectively in world affairs. Admittedly this is largely a question of general educational level, and not just of the philosophical tenor of courses on foreign affairs; but that is precisely my point. Until we can achieve a deeper and more realistic understanding generally, among the influential strata of this country, as to what is really involved in the process of international relations, I fear we shall not succeed in reducing appreciably the number of bewildering and painful surprises our people derive from the unfolding of international events.

If the young men of this day are to be trained to look clearly and intelligently on America's foreign relations, the teaching to which they are subjected must be stern and uncompromising. It must be founded in humility and renunciation of easy effects. It must exclude all that is Pollyannaish and superficial. It must reject utopianism and every form of idealism not rooted in an honest and unsparing recognition of the nature of man. It must free itself from the tyranny of slogans, fashionable words, and semantic taboos. It must proceed from a recognition that the understanding of this subject can never be more simply acquired than the understanding of its basic component, which is man himself.

III

SO MUCH for the teaching of the understanding of international affairs. Now a word about the teaching of the practice of it. There are a number of institutions in the country engaged, either entirely or partly, in this sort of teaching. I think they have done fine work. I think that they deserve every support. What I say is not in criticism of them but rather by way of defense of them against the pressures to which I know they must from time to time be subjected.

The participation of individual Americans in international activity takes a variety of forms, even within the framework of government work alone. The variety is so great that no institution could hope to give complete vocational training, in the strict sense of the word, for work in the international field. A man who enters the Foreign Service of the United States or who goes abroad in the employ of any great American concern, commercial or philanthropic, is apt to find himself dealing with the most amazing diversity of problems. This lies in the nature of international life and in the necessity — whatever the man's function — of reconciling conflicting national outlooks and customs.

As far as I can see, the qualities that enable people to measure up to these various functions are the general qualities of understanding, adaptability, tact, and common sense. Certainly that is true of the Foreign Service of the United States. To be useful in the tasks of service in the international field, a man requires dignity both of the intellect and of character. The two are linked in curious ways, but character, in my opinion, is unquestionably the more important.

As one who has been in charge of Foreign Service establishments at one time or another, I can say without hesitation that I would wish my subordinates to be well-disciplined both in mind and in character; but if I had to choose, I would take any day the man on whose character I could depend, even though I had to nurse him along in his thinking, rather than the man whose mind might have been trained but whose character was unformed or undependable.

The qualities of honor, loyalty, generosity, consideration for others, and sense of obligation to others have been the guts of usefulness and effectiveness in the Foreign Service as I have known it. This was true even in the more distant days when it was easier to be a part of government, when the relationship of the individual officer to his superiors rested on rather old-fashioned assumptions that made things simple and uncomplicated for both parties and permitted the officer to concentrate his attention almost entirely on the external aspects of his work. How much truer it is today, when so much more is asked of the individual and so little help is given him. In our present controversial age, when the growing awareness of the responsibilities of citizenship and the sudden impact of the hideous problem of human disloyalty are whipping our established institutions about like trees in a storm, the position of the professional civil servant can become the center of some of the most severe strains and tensions our society knows. In this day of bigness and impersonality, of security clearances and loyalty investigations, of swollen staffs and managerial specialists — in this day, in short, of the fading vitality of the individual relationship in government — it requires a special manliness and fortitude for the civil servant to stride confidently along the path of his duties, to retain his serenity of mind and confidence in the future, to find the deeper roots of understanding of his own country and the deeper sources of faith in the utility of what he is doing.

As I said in my talk before the Pennsylvania State Bar Association, there has been much discussion about Communist penetration into our government. But people seldom attempt to appraise the actual damage done thereby to our public policy. I have been fairly close to the policy-making processes in Washington for the past six years. With many of the decisions I have been personally in accord; with others, not. But I cannot recall a single major decision of foreign policy during that period which Communist influence could have had any appreciable part in determining. If, therefore, I were to be asked what part Communist penetration had played in creating our difficulties and perplexities of today in the field of foreign affairs, I would have to say that — as far as these past years are concerned — that part has been negligible, and I am sure it is negligible today.

On the other hand, I have seen serious damage done in these recent years to public confidence and to governmental morale by the mishandling of our own measures to counter precisely this problem of Communist penetration. Such damage has been done by the public discussion of things that should have been handled quietly and privately. It has been done by the inability of many people to distinguish between questions of loyalty and questions of opinion. It has been done by the workings of hastily devised and not fully appropriate procedures for testing and establishing the reliability of public servants. Finally, such damage has been done by the failure of many people to realize that what is important from the standpoint of personal loyalty is not the dusty record of actions committed ten to twenty years ago and now proven by hindsight to have been errors, but the picture of the living human being as he stands before us today, and the extent to which he now possesses wisdom and maturity and stability and all those other positive qualities which too often are acquired only through the process of painful error.

The result to date of all these deficiencies in the treatment of the subject of civic loyalty has been the creation of a situation which worries me precisely because it seems to me to play very dangerously into the hands of those men who have constituted themselves our adversaries in the international sphere. I can see no reason why malicious people should have any particular difficulty in rendering unavailable for service to this country almost any person whom they might select for this treatment. All that is necessary is to release a spate of rumors and gossip and demands for investigation. There are always tongues willing and eager to take up this cry and carry it further; something of it is bound to stick in the public mind; and in the end, if the public servant in question is not discouraged and demoralized, a portion of the public will at any rate have lost confidence in him, and his usefulness to the country will have been thereby reduced. Mind you, I am thinking here not only of the man's loss, which may be grievous. I am thinking of the country's loss, which is more grievous still. Are we so rich in talented public servants that we can afford to leave the ones we have vulnerable to this sort of danger?

In coping with the strains and trials that such conditions involve, the official will not be much helped by memorized facts or by acquired techniques. He will not be much helped by erudition, as distinct from understanding. He will be helped primarily by those qualities of courage and resolution that make it possible for men to have independence of character, to face the loneliness and opprobrium this sometimes involves, and to stand up for their friends and their beliefs and their sense of duty to the national tradition.

It is my impression, from the recollection of my days as an undergraduate, that understanding based on a firm grasp of the humanities, and character based on an uncompromising integrity in all personal associations, are the very essence of a liberal education and represent goals to which our colleges have clung in the face of very considerable pressures. This is my plea: Let those students who want to prepare themselves for work in the international field read their Bible and their Shakespeare, their Plutarch and their Gibbon, perhaps even their Latin and their Greek, and let them guard as the most precious of their possessions that concept of personal conduct which has grown up around the honor system, but of which the honor system is only a part and a symbol. Let them guard that code of behavior which means that men learn to act toward each other with honor and truthfulness and loyalty, to bestow confidence where confidence is asked, and to build within themselves those qualities of self-discipline and self-restraint on which the integrity of a public service must be founded.

If these things are clung to and cultivated, then our colleges will be doing what is most important to prepare their sons to confront the problems of international life, whether as citizens or as public servants. Whatever else can be taught them about the contemporary facts of international life will be a useful superstructure — but only that.

QUESTIONS

1. Why does Kennan not regard the widespread college and university instruction in foreign affairs as the "guarantee of a fairly respectable measure of achievement"? What does he regard as the indispensable supplement to knowledge of the field?

2. At the end of Paragraph 3, Section I, Kennan says that many people "have had a good deal of teaching on these subjects but have been taught the wrong way." Where else in the essay is this idea elaborated? Show that this statement is the key to one of Kennan's main aims in the rest of the essay.

3. Paragraphs 6–10, Section I, deal with "the fundamental human problem of power that lies at the heart of all politics." What significant difference does Kennan point out between the forces of power in America and those in other parts of the world? What is the relationship between this discussion of power and Kennan's principal purpose in the essay?

4. Considering the total organization of materials in the essay, point out the structural function of each of the three sections.

5. In the last sentence of Paragraph 1, Section II, Kennan says, "And there is no understanding of international affairs that does not embrace understanding of the human individual." Where else in the essay is this idea repeated? Why does the author repeat it so frequently?

6. In Section III, Kennan discusses the necessity of "dignity both of the intellect and of character." Point out the relationship between Kennan's preference for the man of character to the man of intellect, on the one hand, and the substance of Paragraphs 5–9, Section III, on the other.

HOWARD MUMFORD JONES was born in Michigan, grew up in Wisconsin, and holds degrees from the University of Wisconsin and the University of Chicago. His career as a teacher includes posts at the Universities of Texas, North Carolina, and Michigan. For more than twenty years he has been a professor of English at Harvard University, and was president of the American Academy of Arts and Sciences from 1944 to 1951. Well known as an editor, lecturer, author, and translator, he has been interested especially in American culture as reflected in history and literature. Among his books are *Education and World Tragedy* (1946), *The Theory of American Literature* (1948), *The Bright Medusa* (1952), and *The Pursuit of Happiness* (1953).

UNDERGRADUATES ON APRON STRINGS

by HOWARD MUMFORD JONES

I WISH to argue an unpopular cause: the cause of the old, free elective system in the academic world, or the untrammeled right of the undergraduate to make his own mistakes. Doubtless my case is one-sided and prejudiced, though it seems to me the case for controlled education is equally one-sided; nor does the fact that controlled education is just now in the ascendant make the present system eternal. Doubtless also there was a vast deal of waste in the old system. But as I have seen no study of waste under the present controlled system, I am prepared to hazard the guess that the present philosophy, though it produces bright, interchangeable students in quantity with almost no pain, is not inevitably the philosophy of education that will preserve this republic unto the latest generation.

I take it everybody knows what is meant by the old, free elective system. It was common in American colleges and universities in the last decades of the nineteenth century, and it lasted into the twentieth. In its time it was heralded as a tremendous advance over an older form of educational control. Theoretically everything was wrong with it, if you are to believe the twentieth-century diagnosticians. It was, they pontificate, the quintessence of laissez-faire. It encouraged individualism – rugged or otherwise. It let the student choose his courses and his instructors, something that he had come to college to do. It permitted the lazy man to be lazy and it permitted the student who had found, or thought he had found, his vocation, to concentrate on that vocation — that is, in the jargon of the present hour, to " narrow " his education by electing courses that seemed to him to fit his own particular case. The theory of the old, free elective system was a function of an obsolescent notion of the college and of the university, a notion advanced by Ezra Cornell, who wanted to found a university in which anybody could study anything. Nobody has ever made it clear to me why this idea is a product of the Old Nick himself.

Manifold objections were raised to the old, free elective system as practiced, for example, at Harvard under President Charles W. Eliot. It was argued that when an undergraduate could choose chemistry for fourteen out of his sixteen courses required for the bachelor's degree, he was not receiving a proper education. Whether the youth in question was merely eccentric I do not know — he may have been a genius, though I do not see how the authorities could tell; and all I can say is that, if you put college credits aside and look at the thing in terms of self-development, he was following the path originally trodden by persons like Thomas A. Edison, Henry Ford, John Stuart Mill, and Napoleon. The last was so bored by ordinary courses he showed no ability at Brienne * except in matters that had to do with his genius for war. I have sometimes speculated what another Napoleon or Edison would do in our carefully calculated courses in general education. Is it at all conceivable that in setting up these required patterns of instruction we are either postponing or obliterating the expression of talent? This is, of course, the century of the common man. But I wonder what Leonardo da Vinci would do in the century of the common man.

It is also argued that the old, free elective system was, as I have indicated, a godsend to the lazy. I do not dispute it. I only want to know what the lazy are doing in the present well-regulated systems of general education. Have they disappeared from the college campus? Are these courses — overviews of the history of Western Man, for the most part — so exciting that the lazy now automatically catch fire and kindle to intellectual challenge? Am I to infer that pedagogical skill has so vastly increased, the lazy have ceased to be? I have lately been rereading Vincent Sheean's † *Personal History*, including the wonderful passage in which he narrates how and why the University of Chicago taught him nothing in particular and taught it very well. But nobody later than Mr. Sheean seems to have confessed. All I know has to do

* A small town in France; Napoleon entered the military academy there when he was ten.

† Vincent Sheean (1899–), American journalist, foreign correspondent, novelist. *Personal History* was published in 1935.

with the complaints of English teachers about the indifference of students to ordinary requirements in prose.

Another customary charge against the old, free elective system is that it overcompensated the "popular" teacher and ignored the specialist who really knew. Perhaps it did. But has the situation altered under the present controlled system? As I watch the ebb and flow of enrollment in various courses nowadays, I wonder whether the world of the campus has changed. I seem to see, cynical fellow that I am, the same fashions at work – a surge into psychology or social anthropology, a surge into Russian, a surge into modern poetry. I see, or dream I see, the idols of the campus drawing their usual full houses while the classrooms of essential scholars have their modest quotas where the real work of the university is done. I venture to doubt that the "popular" teacher has somehow miraculously dissolved into the smooth, impersonal fabric of required courses in general education.

Products of the free elective system, graduating any year between 1895 and 1915 (my dates are approximate, or, as the New Critics would say, symbolical only), came into social or economic or cultural or political power in this republic some ten or twenty years after being graduated. They fought World War I. They carried forward the technological revolution that accompanied or followed that catastrophe. They were in the saddle during the administrations of Wilson, Harding, and Coolidge, and you can, if you like, say they are responsible for the twenties, for the stock-market crash of 1929, and for a variety of other sins. Perhaps I have no defense. All I can murmur is that American literature, American art, American music, American science, and American technology came of age during this quarter-century; and though I am as ready as the next historian to admit that 1929 was a catastrophic year, I am not persuaded that the world-wide depression setting in at the end of the twenties was the direct result of the old, free elective system.

It is also argued that the free elective system did not produce an informed citizenry, aware of the glorious history of the United States, alert to the significance of Western culture, and alive to the philosophic values of democracy. I dare say some part of the charge is true. But as I think of the careers of Robert M. La Follette,* Frederick

* La Follette, Turner, Norris, and Hart are identified in college dictionaries. Others in this group who are not listed there are Robert Morss Lovett (1870–1956), American educator and author, Professor of English, University of Chicago (1909–1936); Edward A. Ross (1866–1951), American educator, Professor of Sociology, University of Wisconsin and elsewhere; Charles E. Merriam (1874–1953), Professor of Political Science, University of Chicago (1911–1953), author of many books in political science.

Jackson Turner, Robert Morss Lovett, Edward A. Ross, Charles E. Merriam, Frank Norris, Albert Bushnell Hart, and a variety of other persons associated with education in those years, I wonder where these characters and others like them picked up their singular dedication to civic virtue, and I speculate also on the immaculate morality of American public life when, some twenty or twenty-five years from now, graduates of the present controlled theories of education shall have completed their labors in the way of loyalty oaths and filled all the key posts of the republic with pure and righteous men. I seem to recall that teachers such as Royce with his doctrine of loyalty to the Great Community,* James with his philosophy of the average man trying it on, and Dewey with his notion that if you want democracy you begin with the young—I seem to recall, I say, that these gentlemen had a particular knowledge of the democratic process. It would be vulgar of me to say that a crisp version of this philosophy may be found on the postcard which said: "Live every day so that you can look any man in the face and tell him to go to hell." On this assumption Mr. Lincoln Steffens seemed to think that there was something to be said even for the corrupt political boss, and Rev. Walter Rauschenbusch † seemed to believe there might be something that Christian ethics had to offer society. Nowadays we have the disciples of Freud and the neo-Calvinists.

II

WELL, it may be asked, what have we substituted for the old, free elective system? The substitution is not altogether bad. We have many, many more undergraduates in our colleges than we had in 1880 or 1900, and we have to do something with them; otherwise they will be disappointed of a degree, and the consequences may be disastrous for college financing. And inasmuch as ours is an excessively mobile population, we have invented for education what we invented for indus-

* Royce believed that in order to preserve the values of liberty and the dignity of the individual, the smaller units of society (provinces) must be re-vitalized. He wrote in his last book, *The Hope of the Great Community* (1916): "Therefore, while the great community of the future will unquestionably be international by virtue of the ties which will bind its various nationalities together, it will find no place for that sort of internationalism which despises the individual variety of nations, and which tries to substitute for the vices of those who at present seek merely to conquer mankind, the equally worthless desire of those who hope to see us in future as 'men without a country'. . . . There can be no true international life unless the nations remain to possess it."

† Rev. Walter Rauschenbusch (1861–1918), Professor of Church History, Rochester Theological Seminary; author of *Christianity and the Social Crisis* (1907), and other books.

try — a beautiful system of interchangeable parts. You may start your education in California and finish it in North Carolina, but it will not be much of a jar as you move, say, from Stanford to Duke. If Harvard has courses in general education, so do several hundred other colleges. If Wisconsin has a student radio, so do scores of other universities. If Iowa has a student theater, so do Michigan, Yale, Texas, and, for all I know, The Greater Southwest Teachers College State University. The philosophy of rugged individualism, which in its time gave a unique flavor to the new Johns Hopkins University, has now so far passed from favor that when they instituted Brandeis University in Waltham, Massachusetts, they ignored the opportunity to make an institution dedicated to intellectual excitement and created a school as much like the other schools around it as they could.

Putting intellectual matters aside, I submit that the motto of our present prevailing system of interchangeable parts is "adjustment." The freshman "adjusts" to his college. The sophomore "adjusts" to his professors, and by and by the senior is supposed to "adjust" to the outside world, nobody asks why. I doubt that "adjustment" would have made much sense to Emerson or Thorstein Veblen or Edgar Allan Poe or John Sloan or Jonathan Edwards or Frank Lloyd Wright or Carlson * of Chicago or Einstein of Princeton. In my observation the world adjusts to the genius, not the genius to the world; and if Woodrow Wilson was right in saying that the principal purpose of a liberal education is to enable you to know a good man when you see him, I doubt that psychological testing is a proper telescope. Of course it can be argued that the thousands who annually pass through the American college are not geniuses, and this is true. But what about the genius who would like to be trained in his calling? Are we keeping paths open for the lonely talents who really shape culture and who are not content to imitate culture in others? Or are we so universally bent on "adjustment," all in the interests of a smoothly running society, we propose to break or smother the John Reeds and the Thorstein Veblens before they develop into dangerous reds?

Adjustment operates, in the jargon of the day, on two levels: the intellectual and the personal. Intellectual adjustment begins as required courses for freshmen (and sometimes sophomores) who have commonly just escaped from a good many required courses in the secondary school. And these required courses are the products of the kindest thoughts and a considerable administrative skill. Their instructors are hand-picked and, being selected, brood conscientiously over

* Anton Carlson (1875–1956), eminent physiologist; taught for many years at the University of Chicago.

Great Books, The Development of Western Man, Humanism, and other well-meant exercises supposed to replace the old, pernicious survey course in English literature or the history of Europe. Commonly, however, inspection shows that the new required courses are simply the old courses blown up out of all manageable size. I may call them processing courses; and like all processing, they are directed at the average, the medium, the median, or the mean, whatever one's statistical philosophy devises. The difficulty is that in these enormous surveys instruction, like the radius vector of the planets, sweeps over equal areas in equal times. Meanwhile those who are not average are bored.

But the precious ointment in our sight is not intellectual adjustment but personal adjustment, and this is a sacred cause – so sacred that we have invented a weird and unique hierarchy of secular priests to see that the student forever " adjusts." There is on the face of the civilized globe no other group like it. We have deans, tutors, counselors, vocational guides, counselors on marriage, alumni advisers, medical men, and psychiatrists. We have orientation week, campus week, the reading period, religious retreats, and summer camps. I am not prepared to argue down the validity of any one of these inventions taken singly; all I am prepared to say is that, taken as a whole, they befog the idea that higher education is an intellectual exercise. Higher education becomes adjustment. And what these well-meant therapeutic devices do is to postpone decision-making. The symbol of this refusal to face the fact that in life as in war there are final occasions is the make-up examination.

Under the old, free elective system, when a youth went off to college, he went off to a mysterious place where he had to learn the rules by himself or suffer the consequences of not knowing them. This situation, however naïve in terms of " adjustment," had one big advantage: he was at last Away From Home. Going to college was like Bar Mitzvah in Hebrew tradition: once past it, you not only entered upon man's estate, but, moreover, there was no return. You had cut the leading strings; and the fiction of the nineties that pictures the Yale undergraduate with his bulldog and his pipe was true to the facts. Today we do not cut the leading strings, we merely lengthen them. It is not true that an American lad cannot make a significant mistake as a young collegian, but it is true to say that an entire battery of adjusters is happily at work to see that his mistakes shall never, never harm him. Mistakes should not be harmless. Experience, said Oscar Wilde, is the name we give to our mistakes. Take away the mistakes, and what good is the experience?

American college life is, or has become, a wan attempt to prolong adolescence as far as it can be stretched. If this seems excessive, look at any alumni reunion. To the intent of keeping the young idea in "adjustment" this regiment of supervisors dedicates a zealous professional activity. And their intent could not be more laudable. The intent is to promote the unalienable right to happiness. The intent is to do away with waste. The intent is, in the name of democracy, to see that the son or daughter of any or every taxpayer shall not fail. In order not to fail, the offspring must "get something" out of a college education. This, of course, puts an excessive strain upon the advisory staff, which forever demands more recruits, just as it puts an excessive strain upon the intellectual staff, and partly as a means of reducing this strain it has proved easier to channel young America into true and tried educational courses, usually set forth as required work in general education.

General education proves in fact to be a reduction in the classroom for average consumption of a certain average quantum of information about the behavior of Western Man. Why does this sort of thing represent an advance on my zealous scientific undergraduate who, inspired with enthusiasm for chemistry, took seven eighths of his work in what he came to college to find out? I cheerfully grant that, however superior as a chemist, he may have been a poor citizen, but are we turning out better citizens? The hope of the republic rests upon an informed citizenry. All the investigations into the book-reading habits of Americans, college graduates included, reveal that the reading of books drops sharply at the school-leaving age, and that we read fewer books in proportion to our population than does any other nation of the West.

The ancient fable of Mark Hopkins on a log is only a fable, and I do not favor the log. But I do favor Mark Hopkins. That is to say, I think there is a good deal to be said for the lopsided zealot, on fire with fanatical enthusiasm for the first crusade, aerodynamics, quaternions, the Federal Reserve system, or the superiority of William Butler Yeats to all other recent poets. I do not expect him to transmit this enthusiasm to the sad average, but I should like to give him the opportunity to collogue with his younger kind. In Blake's words, the way to the palace of wisdom leads through excess. I suggest that our well-meant hope that waste may be reduced may mean that excellence is reduced also. I suggest that the purpose of an academic institution is, or ought to be, to produce men of singular and exceptional talent, not merely conformable citizens. I am not quite clear, and never have been, why everybody has to be exposed to equal parts of Euripides and Beethoven, the Middle Ages and modern times, biology and mathematics. Like Mr. James Thurber,* all I could ever see in the microscope they gave me in botany was a reflection of my own eye.

But of course this is merely an exercise in dissent.

QUESTIONS

1. What, according to Jones, were the virtues of the free elective system? What were its faults?

2. What, according to Jones, are the main disadvantages of what he calls " controlled education "? What are its virtues?

3. Part of Jones's technique is to ask questions, the answers to which are either expressed or implied. What effect does this stylistic device have on the attitudes aroused in the reader? Is there any evidence of dogmatic assertion in the essay?

4. What is the author's attitude toward " adjustment "? What is his specific complaint against intellectual adjustment? What is his specific complaint against personal adjustment?

5. Why does Jones call his essay an *exercise* in dissent?

6. Does the value of the essay lie chiefly in its cleverness and caustic wit? What does the essay suggest about the breadth of the author's understanding?

* James Thurber (1894–), artist and writer; many of his stories, articles, and cartoons have appeared in *The New Yorker.*

OSCAR HANDLIN is the son of Russian immigrants who operated a grocery store in the Brooklyn area for many years. He was educated at Brooklyn College and Harvard University, where he received the doctorate in 1940. Under the influence of Arthur Schlesinger he became a specialist in American history. After occasional teaching assignments at Brooklyn College, he joined the Department of History at Harvard University in 1939. A recognized authority on American social and economic history, he is the author of *Boston's Immigrants* (1941), *Adventure in Freedom* (1954), *Chance or Destiny* (1955), and *Race and Nationality in American Life* (1957). In 1952 he received the Pulitzer Prize in History for *The Uprooted,* a study of American immigration since 1920.

YEARNING FOR SECURITY

by OSCAR HANDLIN

THE girls seem the more concerned. Where will all this leave them? The boys know the answer. It may be the draft will close in or else universal service will draw them away. There will be a job to do and they will do it competently. The thought of protest, even of questions, seems not to occur to them. This is the order of a world they accept.

We who remember another world, before the war, are uneasy in the face of their acquiescence. We expect of these young people something other than their complete passivity. But we look in vain for the gesture of resistance as they lose control of a good part of their lives.

Not that we are ourselves particularly eager to throw up the barricades. Indeed, as we move on toward our forties, the group of us seems to grow increasingly conservative. But that, we feel, is a prerogative of our advance into middle age. It is not right that these our juniors should surpass us in attachment to the status quo. We think nostalgically of our own stormy youth of fifteen years ago and shake our collective heads. We cannot understand why these boys and girls, as young now as we were then, pass by the excitement and risk – of experiment, of protest, of revolt.

I suppose we are uncomfortable partly by way of personal justification. If they are right now, does not that imply that we were wrong then? And since we retain an emotional attachment to that past of ours, we cannot admit that we were then wrong.

But there is also a deeper level to our uneasiness. For we grew up to think with Emerson that America is the country of young men. That was part of our heritage of optimism, of our faith in progress. A society that believed in inevitable improvement, that judged tomorrow always better than yesterday, necessarily ascribed a special virtue to youth, less constricted by the errors of the past, more responsive to the opportunities of the future. It was proper that the young should rise up against the old; experience would always justify the rebellion. In fact, the old rather expected that this would happen and could enjoy their own relaxed stability because they knew someone else labored under the burden of progress. Perhaps we in our group resent this present generation so much because we fear they are stealing from us the leisure of our conservatism. How can we sit by if they too accept the status quo, and if no one pushes forward?

I remember once in 1946, just after the veterans came back to the university in large numbers, we tried to put into words what seemed to us the dominant characteristics of this generation. Invariably our discussion took the form of a comparison with our own generation of the 1930s and with that which had preceded us ten years earlier.

Well, the lost generation of the first postwar years we knew through its impact upon us. In a sense that group of the early 1920s was disillusioned; it thought it had been betrayed, sacrificed for hollow slogans. It was very much aware of reality and of the limitations of its own powers. But nevertheless it held to kinds of faith that were very important to us who followed it.

The men of that generation had a great certainty as to the intrinsic worth of what they were doing. The artists and the novelists, like the teachers and physicians, like the businessmen even, then felt no need to justify their callings by any extrinsic standards; and that gave their work a sense of great authenticity. What they did, those people believed, was worth doing for its own sake, because their doing it expressed their own individuality.

In retrospect, that seemed to us to have been the unique quality of that earlier generation. It cherished its own personality, and for that reason it indulged in eccentricities of many sorts, trumpeted its own ingenuous discovery of sex, felt outraged by prohibition – indeed by any sham that seemed to derogate from the dignity of the individual. The surface disillusionment and the skepticism about forms concealed only dimly a genuine faith. It was no accident that the two books of great meaning for that generation — *Ulysses* * and *The Great Gatsby* † — both ended with a series of mighty affirmations.

In our own youth, we came to take those affirmations for granted — so much so that we then minimized the achievements of our predecessors and were more likely to criticize what they had left undone than to value what they had done.

Mainly, the burden of our complaint was that the men of the 1920s had been too much concerned with the isolated individual, too little with man as a social being. While we too cherished self-development, free expression, and personal dignity, we regarded a failure in the social system as the chief impediment to those ends, and we looked to planning as the corrective. The humanitarian energies on which the New Deal drew were generated by the confidence that men did have the power so to mold their social environment as to create an adequate setting within which they could attain full realization of their personal capacities. That was the meaning we then imparted to social justice.

In the generation of the 1930s as in that of the 1920s, the logic of their situation supplied young people with a drive that made them willing to struggle. They were realists all right, believed in economic determinism or dialectical materialism, in behaviorism or Freudianism. There was no inclination among them to accept any comfortable transcendentalism that offered man an easy nobility. But their realism left room for venturesomeness; indeed, realism seemed to demand experiment and nonconformity.

II

IT WAS against this image of ourselves that we were disposed to judge this present generation. We were at first well impressed. The veterans who returned to college struck us as mature and earnest; they worked hard and got good grades. (We tended to forget that they *were* older and that this was the pick of a five-year crop.) But we quickly came to realize that all this earnestness and effort was directed toward a very meager goal. Reluctantly but inexorably, we arrived at the conclusion that these young men and women were earnestly working toward a riskless security and, to attain it, were willing to sink into a dull conformity.

I remember being shocked when I caught a glimpse of their own

* "Stream-of-consciousness" novel by the Irish author James Joyce (1882–1941).
† A study of values in the "Jazz Age" by the American author F. Scott Fitzgerald (1896–1939).

visions of their futures. The lad who hoped to be a doctor looked forward to getting onto the staff of some institution, to live, as he said, without problems and with a salary. On a questionnaire, the graduate students put down what they expected to be after twenty years; with amazement we saw their ideal: the administrator-dean. The college, we discovered, was muggy with modest ambitions; the little dreams were not of wealth or fame or monumental accomplishments, but of bureaucrats' offices in government or the corporations.

In a way, we explained this poverty of aspiration as the product of a yearning for security. We could understand that. But we could not understand why these youngsters were all the time making matters more difficult for themselves. If they worried about the future, why did they take on obligations so casually? To us they seemed to marry, bear children, recklessly, without forethought or concern; and statistics which showed a steady drop in the age of marriage and a steady rise in the birth rate bore us out. The answer was, we concluded, that they did not regard these as obligations; somehow, someone would provide. Meanwhile, they settled easily into the ruts they dug for themselves, expecting to spend out the rest of their lives undisturbed.

Like everyone else. Not willing consciously to take on risks, the young people showed no inclination to deviate from established patterns. Their minds ran to motorcars and suburban bungalows. As students they read thoroughly what was assigned them, but were not inclined to be adventuresome or heretic. In discussion they were eminently docile.

Partly, they conformed because it was dangerous not to. They knew that those who dealt out the office space in government and industry were not likely to discriminate among types of radicalism, that a red glow was reflected from every heterodox idea. Still, there seemed to be no objection, certainly no rebellion, against these pressures toward like-mindedness.

On the contrary, this generation welcomed the shackles of orthodoxy — all those eager faces looking up at the platform, waiting to be told what to believe. There was a delight in dogma; know the authorities, accept the classics, and wash your problems away. What did youth say when it spoke up to the educators? In a broadcast last year the chairman of the *Yale Daily News* bemoaned his instructor's lack of enthusiasm for free enterprise. His warning was explicit: Stop stirring up those nagging doubts or we'll tell the trustees on you (and everyone knows where the money comes from).

When I hurled these charges at groups of them, they sat back complacently. What I intended as epithets, they took as compliments. Pleased, they would tell me they were so well adjusted because they were better brought up. Their parents read Gesell and saved them from frustrations.

Why was this generation which had been so ill used, which had so many grievances – why was it so lacking in youthful energies?

From time to time, in these years, various ideas have come to us. At first, when the shadow of the great war loomed largest, we ascribed these effects to the nature of the group's participation in the conflict. These boys had gone in and out of uniform with a curious sense of detachment.

About war in general, they had acquired no strong opinions, nor about the next war in particular. They were not convinced that another conflict was avoidable, nor that it was inevitable. They certainly had no feeling that they could do anything about it. They would take it if it came; meanwhile they wished to get as far with their personal lives as possible.

Korea came to them with the uneventfulness of a monthly bill in the mail. Those eligible for the draft or enrolled in the reserves felt more concern than the others whose obligations had already been cleared. But there was nowhere an expressed consciousness of the great social and intellectual issues involved, nowhere any insistence that youth had a special stake in the matter, a special claim to be heard.

We would not deny, as we discussed it, that a decade of involvement in war on these terms would generate apathy among the young. But we were not content to accept this as a total explanation. Granted that the years of conflict were such a decisive breach, were there no pre-war paths this generation could have taken up? In any case, why was it so inadequately prepared for today's great crisis?

With some reluctance we began to suspect there had been some original fault in the liberal tradition of our own times, some fault that accounted both for the inadequacies of youth and also for the slow death of that tradition itself since 1939. It became clearer, as we understood more of what had happened, that our own liberalism had not known how to face up to the challenge of totalitarianism. Japan, Germany, Italy, Spain, the war itself, were the evidence; and peace added the Soviet Union.

From the point of view of those who reached maturity in the years of our successive defeats, there was not much attractive in our liberalism. Our great victories had come in domestic policy, but events increasingly gave primacy to foreign affairs. And in foreign affairs was written only the record of our failures.

A fellow who came out of the army in 1945 would think of liberalism in terms of the struggle for the Democratic vice-presidential nomination of the year before; he would seek to take up the tradition in the pages of the *Nation* and *New Republic.* To chart the course those journals had taken in the ten years before would not inspire the veteran with enthusiasm; and to trace the eccentric gyrations of Mr. Wallace would lead no one to the conviction that in liberalism was any present saving grace.

The tragic divorce of youth from liberalism was illustrated for us by the decay of the organized youth movements. In our time, young people had been persons of consequence, courted by politicians, consulted by statesmen, active as auxiliaries in the labor movement. The organizations of greatest consequence had been controlled from within the age group. This favorable situation has now collapsed. Washington would be as little inclined to regard the ideas of youth as youth is to look for ideas in Washington. The old associations have fallen apart – some disrupted by Communist infiltration, others simply through the weight of their own inertia and their seeming lack of relevance to the times. Even the veterans of this generation seem disinclined to do much for themselves. The A.V.C. has not managed to evoke substantial response; generally the demobilized young man prefers to let the old-line hacks of the Legion and the V.F.W. do the job for him.

So, for a long time we said, Well, the war; and hoped that as the war receded, we would come back to where we were before. When the first group of nonveterans turned up and were the same, we said, Well, their education was skimped; after all, what perspective would they have acquired, going through high school in the war? But already before Korea, these explanations were sticking in our throats. Now certainly it's time, and more, that youth should have asserted itself.

Against our will, really, we are drawn to the conclusion that some deeper change is involved. We begin to fear the divide is deep, reaches down to some fundamental alteration in our society. Now and then, for instance, it occurs to us that there is something familiar about the call for security, about which we complain in them; we hear in it the echo of what we were ourselves saying fifteen years ago. Was this not a key word in the strivings of the New Deal in both domestic and foreign policy?

Only, we insist, to us this was not an end but a means. We never surrendered individualism to Mr. Hoover, but hoped, perhaps recklessly, that a foundation of security at the base of the social structure would unloose creative individual energies through the rest of it. If we fought for unemployment insurance or farm relief or industrial unionism, it was not to plunge a large part of the population into complacency, but to ease destructive fears so that men could turn their energies toward other ends.

Looking back now, we acknowledge that it may have been our fault that we thought so little of those other ends — so little that this generation, which was not immediately involved in our struggle, can see as ideals only the means for which we battled.

Yet they need not have fallen into that confusion. Our least certain speculations revolve about the question of why they did. Always we come back to an underlying doubt: perhaps it is not youth that has changed, but the situation of youth; not they, but the world we made for them.

If Emerson's America was the country of young men because it believed in progress and had faith in itself, has our America ceased to be the country of young men because it has lost confidence and no longer believes in itself?

QUESTIONS

1. What observations about the young men of the 1940s does Handlin use to lead into a comparison of them with the youth of the 1930s and the 1920s? What special distinction does he make between the two latter groups?

2. Paragraph 5, Section I, refers to a statement by Emerson. How is Emerson's belief connected with the controlling idea (main theme) of the essay? What additional use is made of Emerson's idea?

3. What is the difference between intrinsic worth and extrinsic worth, in the paragraph on page 21 beginning " The men of that generation . . ." in Section I? Consider the context, and use the dictionary if necessary.

4. In Paragraphs 2 and 3, Section II, what inconsistency in the younger generation does Handlin note? Is this only an apparent and not an actual inconsistency?

5. In Section II, point out the explanations for the " easy conformity " of the recent generation. Which of these does the author believe to be valid? Explain how Handlin places responsibility for this conformity upon the earlier generations (the 1930s and the 1920s).

6. How would you describe the attitude of the author toward those who " yearn for security "? For example, is he alarmed? sympathetic? scornful? angry?

LYNN WHITE, JR., a specialist in the history of the Renaissance and the Middle Ages, holds degrees from Stanford University, Union Theological Seminary, and Harvard University. After several years of teaching at Princeton and Stanford Universities, he accepted his present position, the presidency of Mills College in California. He is a close observer of contemporary problems, especially education and world affairs. The essay which follows was included in one of his books, *Educating Our Daughters: A Challenge to the Colleges* (1950). Recently, Dr. White has edited *Frontiers of Knowledge in the Study of Man* (1957), to which he also contributed a chapter.

EDUCATING WOMEN IN A MAN'S WORLD

by LYNN WHITE, JR.

WE IN the United States claim to be developing "complete" men and women—men and women so aware of the best that has been thought and felt by mankind, and so familiar with the path our race has traveled, that they are worthy members of our common pilgrimage. Yet in fact our colleges and universities have almost entirely disregarded the interests, aptitudes, and accomplishments of three vast and overlapping segments of mankind: (1) the Orient, (2) the nine tenths of humanity who until recently were socially submerged, and (3) women. To phrase the matter differently, our education has been designed for the Occidental male aristocrat. The geographic, democratic, and feminist revolutions, which have remade the world in which we live, have scarcely begun to affect our formal preparation to live in that world.

Global peace is not going to be had by setting American students to reading *Sakuntala* * and the *Tao Te King* * any more than our entry into war with Italy and Germany in 1941 was prevented by the high esteem in which Dante and Goethe are held among us. But it will hardly be denied that many of the miscalculations of our foreign policy towards Asia, blunders for which we have paid and shall continue to pay in blood and gold, are in part traceable to the fact that we Americans limit our horizon with the blinders of a North Atlantic

* *Sakuntala,* a famous drama in Sanskrit, by Kalidasa; *Tao Te King,* Chinese religious and philosophical classic, ascribed wholly or partly to Lao-tse.

education which gives us no understanding of the ancient, proud, and in many ways sophisticated peoples whom we face across the Pacific. If we insist on reading Great Books, possibly a list compiled from the non-Occidental traditions might do us more good at this particular moment of history when our power seems so greatly to have outrun our competence. Limitations of a student's time, and of the funds of most colleges and universities for curricular expansion, will make the process of change long and slow. But even a small college has a duty to break the shell of the Occident with a rich offering in either Islamic, Indic, East Asiatic, or Russian studies, and to encourage students to prepare themselves a bit better to become citizens of the world by taking a few courses outside the circle of their own cultural tradition.

It is ironic that the thin upper crust of cultivated Orientals is already getting a global education still unavailable to most Americans. The educated Syrian reads his Koran and Voltaire; the Chinese knows Mencius, Dewey, and Bertrand Russell; the Hindu is familiar with the Bhagavad-Gita and Dickens. At times this produces a mere glib cosmopolitanism, but those of us who are fortunate enough to meet a good many educated Asiatics often have an uncomfortable sense of being intellectually outclassed: they have encompassed more of human experience than we.

Until less than two hundred years ago a "liberal" education was valid in the sense that it was truly fitted to the pattern of life of the upper classes which monopolized it. But from the later eighteenth century onward there has come a seismic movement which Ortega y Gasset has called "the revolt of the masses." At its best it is democracy, but both fascism and communism are corrupt expressions of it, since both, like democracy, are anti-aristocratic.

We Americans have achieved so coherent a set of social attitudes and economic habits growing out of "the revolt of the masses," we have given every individual such status (or at least every white individual), that we recoil from such words as "the masses" and even from the hint of condescension in such phrases as "the common man." We have the world's oldest and most consistent equalitarian society.

But have we rethought our education in terms of our breach with the aristocratic tradition? In quantitative terms the answer is clear: we have made available all levels of education, and particularly that of the colleges and universities, to a larger part of the population than ever before enjoyed them in any nation. This has been done not merely by setting up a vast network of tax-supported institutions but also by establishing hundreds of independent colleges and universities. Their general endowments, which reduce the cost of education to all their students, are supplemented by special endowments of scholarships for needy persons, on a scale unknown elsewhere.

II

IN ONE sense, then, we have democratized higher education. But in another and more important way we have not done so. The "liberal" education which was worked out to meet the needs of the old aristocracy of priests and nobles was essentially contemplative, focused on understanding things rather than doing things. Such an education was fitted functionally to their position in the world: they gave orders, and to give clear and wise orders they needed "trained minds" — that is, minds trained to think clearly, weigh evidence, and grasp all aspects of a problem. Since, by and large, they did not have to carry out orders, training in the specific ways of doing things was irrelevant to them.

The democratic revolution, together with the growth of technology so intimately connected with it, has destroyed the old simplicities which made legitimate a sharp distinction between "liberal" and "vocational" education. The whole idea of a purely vocational education is aristocratic and patronizing because it implies that some people are fit for nothing but to be trained to work. But democracy is grounded in a bold faith that every man is capable of rising to the level of political judgment which once was expected only of the aristocracy. Moreover, while the old ideal of the "gentleman of leisure" has fallen into disfavor, the forty-hour week has given most Americans an amount of leisure which to former generations would have seemed as fantastic as our political responsibilities. A democratic education must therefore above all else try to develop those capacities for thinking, understanding, and enjoying which have been the goals of traditional "liberal" education; for the democratic revolution has ennobled us all.

On the other hand it has made workers of us all. Even men who might be able to live on their investments generally make at least a pretense of working, in order to avoid disapproval. But more important for our educational thinking than this new attitude towards work is the fact that jobs have become so specialized and intricate that increasingly the preparation for them is being transferred from the level of apprenticeship to that of formal schooling. What once were trades are becoming professions.

Indeed the three traditional "learned" professions of divinity, medicine, and law would seem to offer the pattern for a truly democratic higher education because they have always combined liberal education with vocational training, emphasis on skill in doing things with a sense of the importance of grasping the implications of what one is doing.

Now that we have abolished inherited class distinctions and functions, we are all masters and all servants. We must create, and indeed for the first time in history we are in a position to create, an education embracing and interpreting the entire experience of mankind, including that of labor.

This means that technology in the broadest sense must be included in general education and studied in a humanistic mood on a par with art, religion, science, politics, literature, and every other major concern of the race. It will not be easy, for the gulf between liberal and vocational education has been so deep that our technologists still normally have only the attitude of servants towards their work: that is, they are so involved in the immediate job to be done that they seldom ask the meaning of what they are doing, or speculate about its significance in the total framework of human life. Such narrowness impoverishes all of us.

To be as concrete as possible, we shall not have built a new liberal education in democratic terms until we can give in our colleges a course on the internal-combustion engine as humanely conceived as a course on Shakespeare's plays.

We must not neglect our Shakespeare, but the average American – even the average educated American – has far more frequent and intimate contact with automobiles and airplanes than with the theater. The people clustered around a new model of car parked by the curb, the way they lift the hood and peer at its entrails, show an instinctive grasp of the value of skill which has been omitted from the education they receive. If that education enabled us to see in every such engine a monument of an ongoing tradition, a record of human gropings, stupidities and genius, a symbol of our debt to a host of ancestors and a sermon on our duty to serve the age, humanistic attitudes might be more easily inculcated than at present.

The core of traditional liberal education has been the understanding and appreciation of the experience of values. In America we have made a gigantic effort to extend to all the people the liberal education which was once a perquisite of privilege, yet the degree of real personal cultivation which we have achieved is disappointing. We have failed because our humanism has not been humane enough to include the experience of the value of skill which has always been, and which remains, more vivid to the bulk of mankind than any other value, and which, if properly understood, would serve as guide to the other values cultivated traditionally in our schools. The democratizing of education is far more than a matter of sending everybody to school: it involves reshaping the educational inheritance from the aristocratic age and expanding both its content and its sympathies to meet the needs of our time.

III

IN addition to our educational neglect of the Orient and of the once voiceless masses of mankind, we have overlooked in our schools the specific interests and activities of women. Since it is to the advantage of men to live with women and learn to like them, the masculine bias of our education cheats men as well as women. But it is harder, much harder, on women than on men.

A woman must be educated to handle options more fundamental than any which ever confront a man. The pattern of a man's existence is fairly simple. He is born; he is educated partly to be a person and partly to earn a living; he earns a living, gets a wife, begets children, and works until he dies. The pattern of a woman's life today is essentially different. After she graduates from college she is faced with her first major choice: family or career (although "career" is a glamour word for the kind of jobs most women can get!). If a man marries he must work harder than ever at his career; there is no conflict. Yet, despite all the brave phrases which are currently fashionable, a married woman who tries to combine the two usually has either a token career or a token family, at least so long as her children are young.

Moreover, the woman who marries and takes her family seriously must be prepared to face a second distinctively feminine option. Twenty or twenty-five years after marriage, when normally she is in her forties, she may still have a husband about the house who needs some care and affection, but the children, who have taken the bulk of her time since she left college, have grown up and established their own homes. What is she to do with her released energies and intelligence during the next three decades? For the second time in her life she must choose as a man never chooses; for even to do nothing is to choose.

The failure of our educational system to take into account these simple and basic differences between the life patterns of average men and women is at least in part responsible for the deep discontent and restlessness which afflict millions of women. But this inadequacy in our schools presents merely one part of a much wider problem, the outline of which has only recently begun to be seen. We are learning that the leaders of the feminist revolution, which during the past three generations has so largely changed the way men and women think about each other and treat each other, did not understand the forces which led them to revolt. They refused to recognize that some of their weapons in the battle for reform were boomerangs. They failed — forgivably! — to foresee the less happy results of their enthusiasm.

American feminism has achieved much; but beneath the surface of the seeming freedom which women enjoy in the United States, there is in the hearts of millions of them a strange sense of bondage. Whether American women as a group are more unhappy than the women of other countries is a question which cannot yet be answered. But it is certain that American women are much more deeply discontented with themselves and their lives than are American men.

America's deepest spiritual malady is lack of respect among its women both for themselves as persons and for themselves as a group. We have accepted the theory of equality between women and men, but we are far from achieving the substance of it. The task will not be complete until women respect women as much as they do men, until women by achieving respect for themselves win the full respect of men, and until women are as glad to be women as men are to be men.

What has gone wrong in our own nation that so many of our women should doubt, resent, or repudiate their womanhood? The heart of the trouble lies in the fact that within the last one hundred fifty years industrialism and the urban growth which accompanies it have largely taken from women their former economic productivity and have forced upon them the pair of difficult choices mentioned above: first, of family or job; second, what to do when the children grow up.

In the pre-industrial world of peasant villages and of small towns serving an agricultural hinterland, a woman worked as hard as her husband and, like him, kept on working until death. Because the work was done at home, or nearby, there was no contradiction between rearing a family and laboring to feed and clothe it. Work was decentralized and therefore compatible with the family. When the children grew up and married, they usually lived close by, and the economic and social unity of the family remained unbroken.

The factory-and-office system of centralized labor, the feverish and infinitely wasteful rush and counter-rush of commuters from home to work and back again, have made it very hard for a married woman with children to add to the family purse as once she did habitually, even though she may have the best of will to do so. So much has been said in recent years of "career women" and "woman's increasing place in economic life" that the primary fact is overlooked that less of the world's work is done by women today than ever before in history. Until industrialism and the growth of cities prevented most women from working, every woman was a "career woman." In a pre-industrial society a man needed a woman economically as much as a woman needed a man, but under the conditions of modern mechanized city life this reciprocity between husband and wife has been unbalanced.

IV

THE differences between men and women are as significant as their similarities, and the two sexes cannot properly be measured with the same yardstick. Physically, this is obvious. To point out that many a high school boy has broken the women's international record for throwing the discus is like remarking that very few men nurse infants. Such observations have nothing to do with one's opinion regarding equality, or the lack of it, between the sexes. Even the assertion that women are physically "superior" to men because of their greater life expectancy may be rejected as putting too much stress on the mere durability of women. Most of us are prepared to accept the notion that in bodily structure and function women and men are incommensurable but equal in dignity. It would seem that if women are to restore their self-respect they must reverse the tactics of the older feminism which indignantly denied inherent differences in the intellectual and emotional tendencies of men and women. Only by recognizing and insisting upon the importance of such differences can women save themselves, in their own eyes, from conviction as inferiors.

What this conclusion implies for our present structure of women's higher education is obvious, and to many it will be painful. Both on coeducational campuses and in women's colleges we have assumed that for educational purposes a woman is a man in disguise. Our few women scholars have had to fight so hard for professional acceptance that as a rule they have passionately embraced the male standards of accomplishment according to which they were required to strive for recognition. So profoundly masculine is our whole tradition of higher education that at the present time a woman tends to be defeminized in proportion as she is educated.

Our women's colleges have done little more than our coeducational institutions to explore and develop a distinctively feminine higher education. Indeed, the women's colleges are a remarkable illustration of the pervasiveness of the masculine dominance in our society. It may have been necessary in the historical context of the past century to prove that women were intellectually tough enough to undertake the same studies men did, and certainly the proof was produced. But it is clear that the leaders of women's higher education on the northeast seaboard thought that they were doing their full duty in making women's colleges as much like men's colleges as possible. The symbol of this attitude is the blessed word *euthenics* (presumably a label for family studies – although no Greek would have understood it so!) behind which Vassar tried to conceal its belated and embarrassed recognition of the fact that it is girls who study at Poughkeepsie. That Radcliffe, which is in curricular bondage to Harvard and which got around only in the autumn of 1948 to appointing the first woman professor to its faculty, should be regarded by otherwise perspicacious women as anything but a piteous example of female docility, indicates how rudimentary our thinking in these matters remains.

Men and women are remarkably like each other, and remarkably unlike each other. Since men, often with malicious intent, have generally stressed the differences, the feminists battling against masculine domination naturally emphasized the identities. Surely if we are to achieve the American ideal of equality in dignity between men and women, it must be an equality of differences as well as an equality of identities. We must agree with the feminists that "women are people," yet hold to the supplementary truth that "people are either women or men." The sex differentiation is fundamental. If we are to rear our daughters to be proud that they are women, we must end our present peculiar habit of educating them as though they were men.

A higher education specifically designed for women would in no way limit the opportunities of the individual girl to learn and do what she wishes. The fact that she is a girl does not make her less an individual. Lise Meitner's calculations played a critical part in the release of atomic energy, and the Meitners of the future must be encouraged by every possible means. But the fact that there are, and (according to many psychologists) probably will always be, far fewer women than men in the ranks of great mathematicians should not lead a girl to esteem herself and her sex less highly. As a people we have vastly overrated cultural creativity. Our uncritical acceptance of "progress" as good in itself is the measure of the masculine dominance in our culture.

It is as important to cherish as to create, and the one takes as much intelligence as the other, although perhaps of a different kind. The Chinese, who have thought more deeply than we about such matters, and particularly about relations between the sexes, have abstracted these two life-permeating activities as the coequal principles of Yang and Yin,* which in turn they identify with man and woman. A steam

* *Yang* comes from a Chinese word meaning "the sunny side of a hill." The terms *Yang* and *Yin* indicate dual principles in Chinese thought, the former being the bright, active principle as contrasted with the latter, which is the dark, passive principle.

engine needs not only a boiler but a flywheel. Our higher education must redress the balance in its judgment of values. It must encourage those who wish to conserve, as well as those who wish to originate, what is good, true, beautiful, useful, and holy. Only in such an intellectual atmosphere will girls learn to accept themselves as fully the equals of men.

QUESTIONS

1. In Section I, in what ways does White suggest that we have disregarded two of the three "segments of mankind" mentioned in the opening paragraph? Which of the three segments is reserved for principal consideration in Section II?

2. In Section II, how does White modify the usual distinction between "liberal" and "vocational" education? What, in the author's opinion, should both kinds of education have in common? Does White depreciate vocational training?

3. Both Section III and Section IV deal with the third segment mentioned in the opening paragraph of the essay. Try to determine the main idea in each section and list the supporting or developing ideas.

4. In Section III, what distinctions are noted between the pattern of woman's life today and that of one hundred fifty years ago?

5. In Section IV, what change in higher education does the author suggest? What criticism of women's colleges does he make? In what way does the last paragraph recall a contention made in the early paragraphs of the essay?

ALLEN JACKSON, born in Chicago, acquired his education – athletic and academic – at Redford High School in Detroit and at the University of Michigan. In addition to playing football for four years at Michigan, he gained recognition for his work with the Student Players and for occasional cartoons in the *Michigan Daily* and *Gargoyle*. While spending a year in England after graduation, he played Rugby football and concluded ("Rugby is a Better Game," *The Atlantic Monthly*, November, 1952) that the ancestor of our American game has most of the virtues and few of the faults revealed in "Too Much Football." Since returning to the United States, he has worked in a copper mine and in a steel mill, and has taught in a private school in New Orleans. A more recent article, "Laugh for the Olympics," appeared in the June, 1956, issue of *The Atlantic Monthly*. In 1957, Mr. Jackson became an instructor in English at Temple University.

TOO MUCH FOOTBALL

by ALLEN JACKSON

FOOTBALL is a complicated game, and the intense competition fostered by the business practices of big-time college football causes this complication to be increased. The result is that the players, if they wish to play the game at all, must spend more time on the gridiron than they bargained for. However, any spectator will tell you there are certain benefits connected with playing college football, such as being part of a school's football tradition, learning fair play, having one's character built, traveling to different parts of the country, and being glorious. All of these compensate the athlete for the loss of school time. But after having played four years at guard for the University of Michigan, which possesses the largest college football stadium in the world, I can see that the supposed benefits of big-time football are either grossly exaggerated or completely imaginary, and it seems to me that most of the enormous amount of time I spent on the gridiron was wasted.

One of the most harmful aspects of the highly organized and regimented athleticism which is the result of a college sport having become "big time" is that the spontaneity has been taken out of the sport. In professional athletics the individual player expects to devote his whole person to his game because his livelihood depends upon consistent, "professional" performance. But the college athlete is primarily a student, not a professional, and when he is forced into the overorganization and overperfection which the big-time game demands, he can no longer decide for himself whether he should study or play football on a particular day.

Probably few of the freshmen who try out for the team realize how much of their time will eventually be exacted by football. I remember discovering with dismay, as a freshman, that if I were to keep up with the rest of the men who were competing for positions on the varsity I would have to report for spring practice. Practicing football for six weeks during the warm and budding spring did not strike me as being either a glorious or a worth-while occupation, but I needed to do it during both my freshman and sophomore years if I was to get in the line-up. I was engaged in actual practice on the field for about twenty hours a week during the spring semester, and during the fall my working week was boosted to about twenty-eight hours. Of course this includes only the time actually spent on the field, and does not include such things as evening movies of the next week's opponent, study time wasted because of fatigue, extra time demanded by game trips to other schools, and time spent in whirlpools and under heat lamps in the training room.

The four-year total actually spent on the field, counting three extra weeks of Rose Bowl practice, comes to about 1350 hours. Although it was hard for me to realize it at the sophomoric height of my athletic zeal, my reason now tells me that football is only a single, minor, and unacademic part of a college education, and that it should not be more important than other single parts of college — such as, for example, the study of history. At Michigan I took six courses in history, each of them meeting three times a week for fifteen weeks, and each requiring an average of two hours of study for each hour in class. The total number of hours here is 810, about half of the time that I spent on the gridiron.

Of course many of the men on the Michigan team receive excellent grades despite their football playing. Last year the team average was higher than the school average, and the two players with the highest grades were an engineer and a premedical student. But these very men have agreed with me that high grades do not mean satisfactory learning, and that football interferes with learning. Besides demanding that the student forego concerts, visiting lecturers, and outside reading during the football semester, big-time football also requires students with heavy loads to take part of their courses in summer school, and to skimp and cram their way through the fall semester as best they can.

A significant little adage which circulates in Michigan athletic circles says in effect that there are three aspects of college life at Michigan – intellectual, social, and athletic – but that the student has time for only two. This idea can circulate only where athletics have become, or are thought to have become, as important as the academic work of the University. The student who plays football is expected to sacrifice his studies for the sake of the game, and he is very darkly frowned upon if he misses practice for the sake of his studies. When after one Saturday game I limped off the field with a twisted ankle, I knew that I would be expected to spend a good deal of Sunday in the training room taking treatment for the injury. But since Sunday was the only time that I was able to study for a coming examination, I stayed away from the training room. As a result the ankle stiffened and on the practice field I was made to feel guilty for the rest of the week. The coaches are aware that in theory studies come first, but they are also aware that, in a big-time league, if studies actually come first, second-rate teams are likely to be the result.

One of my teammates, a philosophy student who at the time played fourth string, possessed a scholarship which would have enabled him to study in Europe. However, if he made use of this scholarship he would be unable to return in time to play football the following season. He asked the coaches' advice on this, hoping that they would tell him to go to Europe by all means, and come back and play for them when he was ready. But instead it was hinted that if he stayed he might well get to the " top " the next season, whereas if he took the scholarship it was quite possible that someone else would have his place when he got back. These suggestions were further implemented by numerous long-distance telephone calls from alumni who were amazed that anyone should consider taking a trip to Europe when there was a chance he might make the Michigan team. So he stayed, and the next season played third string.

Another teammate of mine decided during his junior year to use his GI Bill to cultivate a long-standing desire to study the piano. He had already earned a varsity letter as a sophomore center on Michigan's '48 National Championship team, and was looking forward to playing first string in his senior year, inasmuch as the man ahead of him was graduating. But during the following spring semester he became so engrossed in his piano playing that, although he still intended to play football in the autumn, he decided not to turn out for spring practice. Consequently, when he returned for practice in the fall of his senior year he was promptly and without explanation assigned to the fifth string. He was replaced by men who had practiced the previous spring and who because of this were evidently considered better gambles toward a winning combination.

The reasonable and sensible thing to do in such a situation would be to quit football because it was now obvious that he had fallen from favor and would never make the first team. But it is impossible to be sensible in the midst of people who are afflicted with football. Making what the fanatic football alumnus would call a courageous display of determination, he decided to try to win back his position, a decision which he now thinks foolish and wasteful. The result of his efforts was that by the end of the season he was still nothing more than a third-string center; and with the exception of two non-conference games and the waning, reserve-flooded minutes of the other games, he spent most of his time sitting on the bench.

II

WHILE examining the nature of big-time football it will be necessary for me at times to criticize the position of the coaches. I wish to make the point here that it is not the individual but the position with which I find fault, and that this position must be criticized because it is one of the major means through which big-time football accomplishes its distortion of the sporting spirit.

One of the ideas most thoroughly drummed into the heads of young Michigan football players is that it is a very valuable thing to be associated with Michigan football tradition. These men talk about Michigan's record, the fine men who have played for Michigan, in a manner almost liturgical, and the implication is that such things happen only at Michigan. Although much of this talk is sincere it is nevertheless misguided; it ignores the fact that Michigan tradition means basically that Michigan has always won more games than it has lost, and it means to keep on doing so.

At Michigan to win is of utmost importance; fair play and sportsmanship are fine, but to win is of utmost importance. Judging from the loud noises I have heard from chauvinistic, unathletic alumni from other big football schools, the Michigan people are not unique in proclaiming a "We're the best" athletic philosophy. But thanks to Fielding H. Yost and his point-a-minute teams of 1901 through 1905, the Michigan alumni have a better record to boast of than do the alumni of most other schools.

Yost was one of the first coaches to begin the custom of ensuring a winning record by encouraging large men to come to Michigan primarily to play football — a custom which is still zealously fostered. He was so successful in obtaining skillful players that between 1901 and 1905 his teams won 55 games in a row, and each year averaged 548 points to the opponents' 8 points. Most of the old-time Michigan alums will tell you that Fielding Yost was successful because he was ahead of his time as a coach, and this is certainly true. In pioneering player-recruitment and in consciously or unconsciously promoting a public acceptance of the idea that winning, and winning by a big score, is an end in itself, Yost acted in strict accordance with some of the most basic elements in modern football.

I do not quarrel with Yost's winning record as such, but I do quarrel with the tendency in modern football to *emphasize* winning as an end in itself, and the tendency toward a "kick him when he's down" attitude which such an emphasis fosters. Such an attitude, it seems to me, was more evident than the good sportsman's attitude when Yost's teams consistently ran up scores like 128 to 0, 88 to 0, and 130 to 0 against little schools without recruiting systems, such as Buffalo, West Virginia, and Ferris Institute. Such records, of course, are possible only when the public gives prestige to those who trample weak competition.

Whether big-time football distorts the values of the football-following public by its win emphasis or whether the public makes possible such emphasis by giving prestige to the teams which trample weak competition is a problem similar to the chicken and egg question. But whatever the cause, the result is that teams which feel the need of strengthening their reputation do so by keeping their reserves on the bench and running up the score on the first weak opponent encountered.

When the 1947 Michigan team went to the Rose Bowl there was a difference of opinion, among football experts, over whether Michigan or Notre Dame had the greatest team in the world. This controversy probably had much to do with the fact that most of the Michigan first team was kept in the Rose Bowl game until the latter part of the fourth quarter, by which time it had run up a score of 49 to 0 on the weaker Southern California team. But even with this large accumulation of points there was almost a full team of Michigan reserve players who did not get into the game or who played for only a few seconds – the reason being, clearly, that if Southern Cal was prevented from scoring, the record would look much more impressive, and it would be obvious to the football experts that Michigan undoubtedly had the greatest team in the world.

III

THE prestige which the college football business has succeeded in gaining for schools with winning records often produces an unsavory bigotry which goes beyond ordinary pride among both the players and students from a big football school. At Michigan one of those bigotry-fostering, tradition-conscious pre-game speeches which were impressive to sophomores but tiresome to seniors was to this effect: The men whom we were about to play would be battling *Michigan;* they would as a result be intimidated; and we should take advantage of this fine opportunity to dominate them. As a psychological device this idea was probably useful in giving confidence to sophomore players – but whether it worked or not, the point is that good sportsmen do not emphasize the use of their grandfathers' reputations to intimidate an opponent.

"When Michigan loses, someone has to pay." I heard the first of many repetitions of this illogical idea in 1949 when Michigan's 25-game winning streak was decisively broken by Army. Since then I have heard it repeated with dogged monotony by the coaches after each Michigan loss, including Michigan's loss to Michigan State last fall. During the practice week following this game I personally counted forty-three repetitions of the slogan. This one slogan symbolizes to me the perversion of the sporting spirit which has been produced by big-time football. The slogan not only implies that Michigan *shouldn't* have lost, but it also suggests that the loss was caused by something wrong somewhere – perhaps something shady on the part of the other team.

The point of view suggested by this slogan becomes positively unchristian in its implication that revenge will be sought at the expense of next week's opponent. This desire for revenge is doubly evil in that it cannot be directed at the people who seem to have inflicted the injury but must be spent upon the first innocent victim who happens along. But the brass-tack meaning of "When Michigan loses, someone has to pay" is simply that since Michigan prestige and Michigan gate receipts depend upon a spectacular winning record, a lost game must be counteracted, if possible, with a larger than usual winning score the following Saturday. And the slogan is successful in arousing these attitudes. Many of the players continue to deify the coaches long after they should have outgrown this, and to them everything said on the field is gospel. Those who do not care for much of what goes on are in the game too deep to get out, and if they wish to stay on the team they must close their minds to reason and allow themselves to be directed.

I do not wish to imply that the players are actually taught unfair tactics at Michigan: this is certainly not true. But the Michigan coaches find it necessary to emphasize winning to a much greater degree than is natural or reasonable, and in a game like football this sort of emphasis is bound to lead to unsportsmanlike conduct. Indeed, the feeling that it is terribly necessary to win is so strong, and the resultant feeling of relief after having won a game is so pronounced, that if any questionable tactics have been used by Michigan men during the game they are merely laughed off.

Virtually all of my teammates on last year's squad were very clean players, but the atmosphere of big football often turned team spirit into mob spirit when the group as a whole accepted actions which to the individual would seem unsportsmanlike. One of the key players on last year's team was noted for his feats in the boxing ring and for his quick temper. When on Monday afternoons the team would watch movies of the preceding Saturday's game, this player would occasionally be seen landing a seemingly accidental left-hook on an opposing player's chin. Of course the movies of any football game are likely to show up actions which appear to be underhanded; but the point here is that such actions – especially by the hotheaded boxer – would invariably strike the coaches as funny, and they would run the play over again in slow motion so that everyone could see and laugh.

The assembled players took their cues from the coaches and also laughed heartily to see such fun. Then, a few plays later on the screen, the coaches would solemnly draw our attention to the fact that the other team was "gang tackling," and that we would have to look for just "this sort of thing" from our next week's opponent because it was *that* kind of team. Michigan's maize and blue players are not encouraged to "gang tackle" of course; they are simply ordered to cover the opposing ball-carrier with "a blanket of blue."

IV

ANOTHER bromide which the big-time football votaries like to administer to promising young athletes is that there is something wonderful about being part of the "team spirit" found in big-name teams. Human beings have long since proved themselves social animals, and it seems reasonable that they should enjoy team games. But big football has perverted the team spirit as well as the sporting spirit.

In the first place the competition for individual positions on big teams is altogether too stiff, and this does more to break down than to build up team spirit. The bigness of the game, the publicity and prestige which go along with a first-team position, and the large number of grim and intense young athletes who are drawn to the gridiron by these abnormalities cause a spirit of internecine conflict to be as much in evidence as *esprit de corps.*

Besides this, the increasing specialization demanded by big-time football does nothing toward engendering social cohesion on the team. The compulsion to win generated by the game's big-business aspect demands that the individual players become precise and accurate in their various specialities to a degree unnatural in college athletics. On the Michigan practice field the ends, backs, and linemen all spend much of their time in separate corners of the field, performing their various specialties with monotonous repetition. During the week there are only one or two hour-long scrimmages, on the average, and the rest of the time is devoted to various forms of dummy practice, running of signals, and practicing specialties. All of this is necessary to produce a winning team in a big-time league, but it is not much fun. Any sport which requires a week's practice of specialties for each sixty-minute game has become too mechanized to allow the spontaneous sort of team spirit which would seem to be the special value of college football.

Everyone has seen football teams gather in the center of the field just before the opening kickoff for a last-minute handshake, and this sight, plus the stock sport page photographs of men on the bench who are "trying just as hard as the men in the game," seems to indicate that team spirit is an actual and worth-while reality in big-time football. I should like to state plainly and emphatically that much of the huddled handshaking and bench emotion is artificial. The players know that in order to win it is necessary to get "worked up" for the game, whether they feel like it or not. Also, the bigness and complexity of modern football produces a decrease in team homogeneity and a corresponding decrease in spontaneity. The players sense that they will be less effective without such homogeneity, and they attempt to regain this feeling on the practice field and in the big game by an artificial emphasis upon such devices as the pre-game handshake and the bench chatter.

My first experience with the automaton spirit which big-time coaches often find it necessary to enforce in order to make their teams efficient winning machines was when, as a freshman, I was used as a human dummy to test the proficiency of the '47 Rose Bowl varsity. Occasionally, when one of my freshman or reserve teammates would be laid out by the businesslike efficiency of the varsity, in such a way that play could not be resumed until the field was cleared, the coaches would promote big-time football's party-line attitude toward such a situation by reciting this slogan: "Well, move the ball or move the body." The varsity players, tickled by such wit, would then move the ball to an uncluttered part of the field and resume play.

When I became a varsity player I began to notice other evidences that big-time football cannot afford to depend upon spontaneous team spirit. At the training table on the Friday night before a game the Michigan players were expected to show that they were in the process of "storing it up" for the next day's contest by eating their meal with a quiet intensity which precluded laughter or any evidence of high spirits. Probably there were a few players who actually felt a sort of judgment-day taciturnity, but for many of the players it was an artificially imposed atmosphere, and bad for the digestion. If, as often happened, some of the lighter hearts would forget for a moment that they were supposed to be grim on Friday evenings, there would be ominous and foreboding looks from the coaches' table — and if the unwholesome gaiety persisted, the coaches would silence it by uttering with gloomy irony, "We hope you'll all be this happy tomorrow night."

Another instance in which the Michigan players had an attitude externally imposed upon them will serve also to exemplify the pernicious effect which big-time football has had upon the reputations of schools which sponsor big-name teams. A few days before we started on our Rose Bowl journey we were summoned for an orientation lecture, a surprising amount of which was devoted to our table manners and general deportment while in Pasadena. It seemed that many of the teams which had in the past gone to the Rose Bowl had been guilty of ungentlemanly conduct — one team, we were told, had been fond of throwing bread rolls the length of a table in the hotel dining room and flipping squares of butter against the ceiling, where they stuck. But Michigan, we were told, did not do that sort of thing. Although it was good to hear that Michigan did not do that sort of thing, neither I nor my teammates had ever been in the habit of throwing butter at the ceilings of plush hotels, and we wondered why we were being so energetically told to act in a normal manner.

The reason was that the big-time football system has unconsciously superimposed a mercenary stereotype upon the college football player, and people often *expect* a visiting football team to be rowdy; because of this, the coaches were at pains to impress us with lurid examples, of questionable authenticity, of how not to act. In Pasadena we conducted ourselves with a normal amount of gentility — neither better nor worse than the average of the teams which preceded us, a waitress told me. But the Michigan players heard themselves complimented profusely on their conduct.

The point of all this is that when an entire athletic group, like college football players, has such a reputation that players who conduct themselves with ordinary grace are looked upon as above average, there is something wrong with the system. Moreover, schools which sponsor big-name teams, and so associate themselves with this bad reputation, subtly lose prestige in the eyes of the general public. Big-time football has promoted a syllogism something like this: football players are something less than students; therefore, universities which sponsor big football teams, though famous, are something less than universities.

V

IN ORDER to exhibit one of big-time football's most unscrupulous practices, I shall have to explain the nature and function of the "red shirts," as they are called at Michigan. The generally used term is "cannon fodder." Because modern football is such a complicated game, the head coaches are able to attend to only the first two or three teams, called "blues" at Michigan. However, it is necessary to have at least two more teams, the red shirts, against whom the blues can scrimmage, or who can hold the dummies for the blues to block. The blues do not play amongst themselves because they are likely to hurt one another and be lost for the big game on Saturday. Also it is necessary for the varsity blues to feel their power and be able to march up and down the field through the weaker red shirts.

A few of the red shirts know that they will never rise in the varsity hierarchy, and they are still content to come out for practice season after season to be used by the blues. But there are not enough of these men. The rest of the red shirts are players who dream of making at least the third-string varsity one day, but whom the coaches are reasonably sure will never make the grade. Instead of telling these men that their chances of making the varsity are extremely small, the coaches, because they need men on whom their varsity can sharpen its claws, encourage the red shirts to return each year to try again. Of course all this is a matter of subtle suggestion; it is impossible to prove actual misrepresentation of facts, but I have spoken to and played against a number of disenchanted red shirts who for four years held dummies and waited their turn to be mashed by the blues, only because it was hinted that they might make it one day.

To a young boy who is fresh out of high school—where he was a big man because of his football playing—the slightest hint by a big college coach that he might make the varsity is enough to set the home town buzzing and to increase the player's illusion of prestige. When he fails to make the varsity team, it seems one of life's most terrible tragedies.

Two years ago, such a player came to Michigan. As a great high school star and a holder of state records in track he was looked upon by his friends and home-town supporters as a potential All-American, and when the Michigan coaches watched him operate on the freshman team they seemed to agree. The following season—last fall—the player's picture was in every sporting magazine in the country, and since such publicity could occur only with the coaches' sanction, it was assumed that he would do great things. Then the football season began, and game after game the highly publicized player was left sitting on the bench. Although he dressed for all the games, and made all the trips, for some reason unknown to himself or to his teammates he was never allowed to play, except for a few seconds in one game, and by the end of the season it was apparent that he would not make a varsity letter. When Michigan prepared to make its second trip to the Rose Bowl, a trip on which ten more than the usual number of players were taken, so that even some of the red shirts went along, the coaches refused to take him, and in so doing as much as told him that he would never play for Michigan.

To a boy who had been heralded as a second Tom Harmon this was a crushing blow, especially since any reasonable person would assume that the football system, after publicizing the player with such vigor, would feel honor-bound to take him along on the Rose Bowl trip. What happened to this boy represents in concentrated form what happens to most of the students who play big-time football. They are first deluded into thinking that they are great and that football is great; then they are used by the system and finally discarded with at best nothing to show but a scrapbook full of redundant and inaccurate clippings.

Of course such build-up and subsequent disappointment occurs elsewhere in life, particularly in a professional sport like baseball. But this is all part of the professional scene, and it has no place in college athletics. College football should have all the benefits of a strictly amateur sport; but it is losing these and acquiring the undesirable aspects of a professional sport.

VI

ANY accusation that football leaves the player with nothing but a scrapbook full of clippings will move the defenders of the game immediately to demand that some mention be made of the "character building" upon which football seems to have a priority. Aside from the probability that the coaches who direct uncommercialized college sports, such as track, wrestling, and gymnastics, could present good arguments showing these sports to be just as effective builders of character as football, it seems to me that anyone who assumes that athletics are an extraordinary factor in the development of an individual's character is guilty of ignoring the many forces which contribute to such development.

But in the football world there is great emphasis placed upon character development; and if, in the coaches' not infallible judgment, an individual player's character does not seem to be developing in the manner prescribed by the big-time football system, his position on the team will be endangered. Because all big-time football players and coaches have grown up with the idea that it is necessary to give your all for the alma mater, anyone who does not seem willing to do this is looked upon as a coward.

The importance of winning in big-time football makes it absolutely necessary to field the best team possible on important Saturdays, regardless of injuries. When the modern compulsion to win is superimposed upon the old give-your-all idea, the pressure on an injured player to play despite his injury is immense. No matter how many times a player proves himself in battle, the first time he decides that an injury should keep him off the playing field he is given the raised eyebrow and accusing stare by the coaches, trainer, and even some of his teammates. This subtle accusation is caused by the team's collective dread of weakening the winning combination, and it is especially acute if the injury is not obvious and the coming game is expected to be close.

Near the end of my junior year, when I was a first-string, battle-scarred veteran of many games, I received what I considered to be a very serious knee injury a week before Michigan was to play Ohio State for the conference championship. The knee was badly swollen, and it was impossible for the doctor who looked at it to make a valid diagnosis until the swelling subsided. But, since I could not walk, and since it was necessary for me to spend two days in the hospital, I assumed that I would not be expected to play in the big game.

However, the man who substituted for me lacked both my weight and experience. So I found to my dismay that as soon as I could walk I was expected to "gut it out," as the Michigan training-room slogan would describe it, by reporting to the practice field, having my knee trussed up with tape, and preparing to give my all for Michigan. Although I could feel loose things inside my knee, I was so intimidated by this frightening preoccupation with guts that I hobbled dutifully out onto the practice field.

On the field I found that my obvious inability to play was looked upon with suspicion, and I began to hear remarks that I was allowing the knee to get the better of me. Instead of being ordered back to my hospital bed for a thorough examination, I was merely told that whether I played or not was entirely up to me. At this point it was clear that I was expected to play, and if I did not I would be dubbed a quitter. Like everyone else, I think there are certain things for which it is worth while to give my all, but I decided then that the primitive alma-materism of an obsolete generation of college playboys was not one of them, and I did not play.

About a week later the knee became locked in a rigid position, and it was necessary for me to return to the hospital. It was now possible to see that a piece of cartilage had been torn in such a way that there was little chance of its growing back together, and an operation would be required. The operation did more than fix my knee, because now the coaches knew that I had not been faking and that I could once more be depended upon to give my all for Michigan. But the point had been made: big-time football has no respect for either the individual's word or his body.

VII

A WORD must be said about the rabid football alumni and the overzealous football fans. I find no fault with anyone who has a normal interest in athletics, but the perverted bigness of football produces people with a perverted interest in sport. Although the number of the most adhesive of these hangers-on to the football scene is not large, their presence is distressing because they are undoubtedly the articulate representatives of a much larger group whose interest in and attitude toward big-time football allow the unhealthy and prolonged hysteria which permeates the college football scene each fall.

Except for a fawning and familiar interest in a few backfield stars, many of the football alumni whom I met had no real interest in the players as individuals; indeed their interest in the stars was usually based only upon athletic reputation and seldom upon character. Many of the football alumni who help destitute athletes through school, from my observation, do this because of a selfish interest in the perpetuation of the school's winning record, with which they have identified themselves, and not because of a personal interest in the welfare of the particular athlete. It is this sort of person who exerts the pressure which fires coaches when the team has not won enough games to satisfy the alumni's collective ego. These are the men who are influential in promoting among young boys a distorted idea of what it really means to play big football; and these are the ones who think that other people's judgments of men are as superficial as their own when they say that football players will have no trouble finding jobs, because everyone is glad to hire a football player.

Concerning the finding of jobs, it would be my guess that largely because of *very* widespread recruiting practices, the term football player has become synonymous with ape, and because of this it is often better for the job applicant to save mention of his gridiron record until after he has become acquainted with a prospective employer. Concerning the meaty subsidization question, I am glad to say that the University does none of it. A few of the players receive help from alumni, but a school with Michigan's prestige and record can usually get all the football material it needs without such aid.

During my four years at Michigan I played in games which took me from New York to California, but I was never given the opportunity to meet or speak to an opposing player. If there is any value in having an intercollegiate schedule, it would seem that such value would come from the opportunity which game trips afford to become acquainted with men from other schools and other parts of the country. But big football has no time for palaver. Indeed, on almost every trip we took, we were cautioned to keep to ourselves — because, and this is another slogan that I unfortunately know by heart, "We are here for only one purpose, and that is to win."

Often during a game I would develop a genuine fondness for some of the players with whom I was exchanging blows, and I would have valued a friendly glass of beer with them after the game. But the visiting team was always whisked off to its train with businesslike alacrity; about the only thing I learned from traveling to other schools was that in every college stadium the grass is more or less green.

Nor did I learn anything from making the Rose Bowl trip — I merely verified my suspicion that of all the farces connected with big-time football, the Rose Bowl is the biggest. The so-called honor and glory of playing in the Rose Bowl is transient and meaningless, as is any glory and honor which is nothing more than the product of a publicity man's imagination; the three-week extra practice is not justified by the benefits of the game; and the trip to the coast is crowded and regimented. But the visiting team does at least get a trip out of it, and this is more than the host team gets. Of course I had no opportunity to speak to any of the California players, but it is impossible for me to understand how they, as Rose Bowl participants, could think of themselves as anything but extremely unlucky. For them there is no send-off, no cross-country trip, and no guided tours — nothing but three more weeks of drudgery under a southern California sun.

So, after four years of seeing everything there is to see in big-time college football — victories, defeats, publicity, hospitals, championships, and bowls — of being known as a "football player" rather than a human being, of seeing myself and my teammates misrepresented and misquoted by sportswriters who seldom attempted to know the players personally, of playing in a 97,000-seat stadium in which my nonpaying student friends were forced to sit in the end zone, of having my natural desire for physical exercise corrupted and commercialized, of giving up pleasant afternoons in favor of kicking and rolling in the dust and muck of the practice field — I have decided that big-time football is a poor bargain for the boys who play the game.

QUESTIONS

1. Comment on the effectiveness of the opening paragraph as related to the entire essay. Note especially the scope of the third sentence. What is the meaning of the word "sophomoric" in the second sentence of Paragraph 4? In simple terms, what is the idea developed in the last four paragraphs of Section I?

2. In Section II, what methods are used to define "Michigan football tradition"? Does the author suggest that the tradition is wholly bad? Where does he place the responsibility for the tradition?

3. Try to determine from the context the difference between "unsavory bigotry" and "ordinary pride" as used in Paragraph 1, Section III. To what sort of conduct, in Jackson's opinion, does the former lead? How is this point made clear in the last two paragraphs of this section?

4. In Section IV, point out the ideas which support Jackson's generalization about "team spirit." In what way do the last three paragraphs deal with a perversion of team spirit?

5. What “ values ” of intercollegiate football are discussed in Section VI? Explain how the last paragraph of this section helps to unify the essay without *merely* repeating what is said in the first paragraph of Section I.

6. How would you explain the attitude of this writer toward his subject? Is he bitter? disillusioned? resentful? Is he an “ extremist ” whose statements are not to be taken seriously? What do you think he intended the reaction of the reader to be?

Harold W. Stoke is particularly qualified to discuss college athletics and education, having spent all his adult life in academic positions as a teacher and administrator. Dr. Stoke has taught political science at Berea College and at the University of Nebraska. He has been Dean of the Graduate School at the University of Nebraska, Acting Dean of the Graduate School at the University of Wisconsin, President of the University of New Hampshire, 1944–1947, and President of Louisiana State University, 1947–1951. He is at present Dean of the Graduate School at the University of Washington. A scholar as well as a teacher and administrator, Dean Stoke has contributed to journals of political science, and is the author of *The Foreign Relations of the Federal State* (1931) and, with Norman L. Hill, of *The Background of European Governments* (1935).

COLLEGE ATHLETICS

Education or Show Business?

by HAROLD W. STOKE

On the morning of December 7, 1951, in the General Sessions Court in New York City, fourteen tall young men stood before Judge Saul S. Streit. The scene was the climax of the notorious basketball scandals in which players had been convicted of receiving bribes from professional gamblers for throwing basketball games in Madison Square Garden. The judge was stern, but for the culprits he tempered justice. Jail sentences and fines were few and light. Judge Streit then looked over the heads of the defendants and hurled angry words at the colleges and universities they represented. He charged that these institutions had so far forgotten their educational mission and had so overemphasized athletics that they themselves had made this scene in his courtroom all but inevitable.

Addressing himself to the colleges, Judge Streit demanded immediate and drastic reforms. Among these were the restoration of athletic responsibilities to faculties and to the academic administrative authorities; the revitalization of the National Collegiate Athletic Association; the establishment of an amateur code and of a capable, well-financed policing authority.

While there was some dismay (if little surprise) in university circles at the basketball scandals, there was genuine puzzlement about the judge's suggestions for reform. The point that had escaped him was that all his proposals had been tried for years — uniformly without success. If Judge Streit and the countless educators who have tackled this problem had asked themselves why Bradley University, Kentucky, New York University, North Carolina State, or any other university should ever play basketball in Madison Square Garden, they would have started on a line of inquiry which would have brought about a better understanding. Obviously it was no educational interest that brought the teams there, no huge concentration of alumni, no essential training program. It wasn't wholly a matter of money. They were there in response to a far more complex and subtle compulsion: to assist their schools as a part of the system of American higher education to carry out that system's latest and growing responsibility — namely, to provide public entertainment.

In our American society the need for entertainment is an inevitable consequence of the changing conditions of our lives — the lengthening life span, the shorter work week, speed and mobility, industrialization and prosperity. These changes create social vacuums, and for filling social vacuums the American system of education — and particularly higher education — is one of the most efficient devices ever invented. It is flexible, highly varied, and in touch with virtually the entire population; furthermore, it is characterized by a genuine spirit of service. It is manned by aggressive and accommodating people; it is suffused with a thoroughly practical philosophy. Hence, to its already great and growing array of services — its teaching, research, adult education, military training, and general public service — it has added another, public entertainment. This responsibility has been accepted in some instances eagerly, in some instances reluctantly, but nonetheless accepted. Drama, music, radio, and television widen the educational as well as the entertainment services of the universities; wherever these touch the public they possess more of the characteristics of entertainment than of education. Yet of all the instrumentalities which universities have for entertaining the public, the most effective is athletics.

What educational institutions thus far have not seen is that the responsibility for supplying public entertainment is a responsibility different in kind from those they have previously performed. The failure to understand this fact has led to endless strain in the management of athletics, to bewilderment among educators and the public, and even to outright scandal. Conceived as education, athletics is inexplicable, corrupting, and uncontrollable; as public entertainment, and even as public entertainment to be provided by educational institutions, athletics becomes comprehensible and manageable.

The most essential distinction between athletics and education lies in the institution's own interest in the athlete as distinguished from its interest in its other students. Universities attract students in order to teach them what they do not already know; they recruit athletes only when they are already proficient. Students are educated for something which will be useful to them and to society after graduation; athletes are required to spend their time on activities the usefulness of which disappears upon graduation or soon thereafter. Universities exist to do what they can for students; athletes are recruited for what they can do for the universities. This makes the operation of the athletic program in which recruited players are used basically different from any educational interest of colleges and universities.

The fundamental distinctions between athletics and education are somewhat obscured by several arguments frequently heard. The first is that athletics has "educational values." This is the familiar "character building," "team spirit," "sportsmanship" argument. Anyone who knows the actual operations of athletics will admit that such values could be realized far better if athletics were handled as recreation and physical education. The second argument is that many fine athletes make fine scholastic records — implying that there must not, after all, be any conflict between athletics and education. Again the answer can be short. Big-time athletics requires 20 to 28 hours per week of its devotees, aside from the time spent away from the campus; hence it is bound to detract from an athlete's education. But how can an impoverished athlete get a chance at a college education? I'll answer that question with another: Is he any more entitled to it than anyone else?

II

COLLEGE athletics *is* public entertainment. Last year football audiences numbered 40 million, and now basketball is outstripping football in attendance. It is estimated that the public pays $100 million a year to the colleges for admission tickets, and television has added enormously to the number of spectators and to the revenue. Public interest as measured in publicity, newspaper coverage, and attention is far beyond that given to any educational activity. In no major school does the attention given to the appointment of a president compare with that given to the appointment of a coach, and the general public can name many more coaches than presidents.

The organization of this public entertainment is intricate. Most of the larger colleges and universities, private and public, are organized into athletic conferences managed by highly paid commissioners. Through them, complicated athletic schedules are worked out with all the finesse of the international bargaining table, and considerations of finance, publicity, the prospective careers of coaches and even of presidents, are balanced in equations which would baffle electronic computers. Stadiums, field houses, and playing fields are constructed with the entertainment-seeking public primarily in mind. At the time the Yale Bowl was built it would have seated the entire adult population of New Haven, while Michigan could have put twice the population of Ann Arbor into its stadium. The University of Southern California and the University of California at Los Angeles are big schools, but even they would scarcely need the Memorial Stadium for their students and faculty. Obviously the real underwriters of bonds which build athletic plants are not students, but the public. Many an athletic director caught in a squeeze of high costs and inadequate gate receipts wishes to heaven he had all of the student tickets to sell to the people willing to pay more for them.

The same force lies back of the other feature of athletics – the numerous and high-priced coaching specialists, the elaborate half-time shows, the colorful bands (supported almost as completely by scholarships as are the athletes and for the same purpose), the frolicsome majorettes, the carefully planned and executed spontaneous student rallies and demonstrations, the food, drink, and program concessions. None of these could possibly serve any educational purpose for which a college or university exists, but they are wonderful aids to public entertainment.

Perhaps most significant of all is the fact that the rules of the games themselves are now constructed and reconstructed with their entertainment value uppermost. Like dramatic coaches and directors bringing into being a Broadway production, the coaches and athletic directors gather each year to adjust the rules of football and basketball for the purpose of heightening the dramatic and entertainment value. The substitution rule, who may run with the ball, what may be allowed to happen within the ten-yard line or within the last four minutes, the nature of the penalties, and, currently, the one- or two-platoon system in football are matters which are governed by their effect upon the entertainment and upon the welfare of the enterprise. In basketball, the rules have been changed to encourage high scoring, constant running and action, alternate chances at scoring in order to provide the murderously exciting finishes which now characterize the game. Revisions are made each year only after the most elaborate study and consideration and with a wariness which would do credit to the fuse workers in a munitions factory.

Consider the Bowl games. They are important influences on athletic policies and at the same time irrefutable evidence that athletics, so far as the Bowls are concerned, have no educational significance whatsoever. So far as I know, no one seriously claims that they do.

All of the Bowls for obvious reasons are located in the South or in winter vacation areas. They are immensely successful business promotions; there is nothing about them remotely related to education. As one man put it: "Rose Bowl, Sugar Bowl, Orange Bowl – all are gravy bowls!" A half-million people saw the games in the eight major bowls last January 1, and it is estimated 70 million more heard them on radio or saw them on television. Receipts were almost $2.5 million. The distribution of the money follows a kind of formula in each conference – a large percentage to each school participating in the Bowl, a smaller percentage to each school in the conference and to the conference treasury itself. A more subtle formula to ensure support for Bowl games could hardly be devised. Participation in one of the Big Four Bowls – Rose, Sugar, Cotton, and Orange – may bring each participating school as much as $125,000. Everyone profits – except the players, whose amateur status has thus far confined them to such grubby rewards as gifts of gold watches, blankets, free tickets which can be scalped, sometimes a little cash – the last usually secretly. Under pressure from the players and perhaps from a sense of institutional guilt at the indefensible exploitation, the rewards to players are improving, but they still are far below the A.S.C.A.P. and Equity pay scales for big-time entertainers.

III

How is all this to be made compatible with the nation's educational system? Most troubles arise from the failure of colleges to see that in supplying public entertainment they have embarked upon an operation which is different from their educational functions – and one that requires different management. Colleges have acted as if athletics were merely an extension of student recreation. Since athletes come from the same high schools as other students, are about the same age, and do get a kind of education, it has been assumed that the academic regulations applicable to the general run of students should also apply to athletes. We overlook completely the different reasons for which each is there. Hence schools have prescribed the same formal academic requirements for both the athlete and the nonathlete — a minimum number of hours must be taken, a certain number of courses must be passed, systematic progress, however slow, must be made toward a degree, and a host of other regulations must be followed.

Yet athletics, like a corrosive acid, has eaten through every academic regulation — to the great frustration, bewilderment, and cynicism of the educational community. It has defeated faculties, forced the resignations of presidents, wrecked coaches, and undercut the support of institutions where the efforts to apply academic regulations have been insistent. Where such regulations have been successfully applied they have all but killed the athletic programs, or put them in abeyance, as at New York University, Fordham, or Pittsburgh, until a more "understanding" attitude permits revival. There are, of course, many schools — Oberlin, Swarthmore, Haverford, Bowdoin, to name a few — that attract little attention from the entertainment-seeking public because they make little attempt to supply public entertainment.

The truth is that the appetite of the public cannot be satisfied by the quality of entertainment which can be provided by athletics governed by academic regulations. Consequently, at institutions which are meeting the public's demands, academic regulations must be ignored, compromised, or eliminated. Admission requirements for athletes have become less formidable than they used to be, and usually an arrangement can be made for the boys to make up high school deficiencies. The requirements as to courses, progress toward degrees, and even grades can generally be met by either a flexible elective system or the "tailored curriculum" leading to a highly specialized "degree" in which many hours of handball, swimming, and coaching can be included. Where this does not suffice, every athletic department of any size provides at its own expense counseling and tutoring service for any of its men likely to get into trouble. Not all athletes need these negations of educational regulations, but the point is that when required the negations must be available. How compelling the necessity is can be estimated by the situations which come to light when these compromises are not sufficient — the wholesale cheating at West Point, the alteration of records at William and Mary, special examinations, and countless other devices involving various degrees of accommodation or even fraud and misdemeanor. No matter what the regulation, if it prevents athletics from supplying the public entertainment for which it exists, a way around must be found. This has been the fate which has uniformly attended the regulative efforts of faculties, administrators, code committees, accrediting associations, and even the N.C.A.A. itself.

Why should this conflict be so irreconcilable? There are many reasons, but perhaps the most compelling is that adequate entertainment can only be provided by winning teams. No amount of gushy sentiment about "playing the game" will conceal the fact that the public wants its teams to win. Victory is a part of the total titillation. If the public can't have it from one source it will transfer its loyalties and money to some other. Chick Meehan filled Yankee Stadium with football fans roaring for N.Y.U., but when de-emphasis came, N.Y.U. found that 6000 was a good crowd to watch it play Fordham, the archrival. "When Michigan loses, someone has to pay" may be a slogan at Ann Arbor, but it sums up the attitude of all schools with athletic entertainment programs. This means that to supply the entertainment, the schools must get the entertainers.

The recruitment of players is the key to most of the athletic anxieties of college presidents, the desperation of coaches, the pressure of alumni, and the activities of outside influences, business and otherwise. A chain reaction of undesirable consequences follows. The school must get the player, and the best one; the player knows this, and the bidding starts. Sometimes negotiations are carried on by a parent or other relative in order that the player may be technically free of all nonamateur bargains; otherwise he becomes a part of a corrupt bargain about which, if questions arise, he must lie or forever keep silent. Gradually the "board, room, and tuition" formula – plus a little extra, if necessary – has won acceptance. Sometimes the myth of employment persists as the justification for such payments, but it is now generally acknowledged to be a myth. The effort to limit the number of such scholarships is actually an effort to equalize competition between schools. The conferences often set a limit – but there are ways around it, the junior college "farm system" for one.

The bidding, of course, is highest for the best. In this field rumor is rife. There is the cartoon of the coach who angrily turns to one of his players and says: "Jones, you're through! Turn in your suit and your convertible." The deal may have a hundred variations, from a pledge to help the ambitious athlete on through medical school to assistance to various relatives. My own experience leads me to believe that the bizarre bargain is less frequent than educators and the public think, but is crucial nonetheless. One or two stars can transform a team into a winner and are worth what they cost. Schools bargain with all kinds of appeals – the prestige of the Ivy League may appeal to the boy from the Middle West; religious affiliation may take a boy to Notre Dame; the lavish dormitory facilities for athletes may tip the scales for Louisiana State or Texas. Most conferences have rules which prevent an athlete who has signed with one school from leaving it to join another, even though he later discovers the immense advantages of the second school. Conferences resent scouts from outside their territory, yet raiding is universal. By a dozen devices high school coaches are encouraged to become feeders for particular colleges and universities, sometimes by the flattering appointment to a coaching school staff, support for a bigger job, or even cash. Thus the web of recruitment is widespread, subtle, and effective.

The services of the American educational system in the field of public entertainment cannot be taken lightly – least of all by the educational institutions themselves. It may not be an ideal use of an educational institution to supply public entertainment, but the public interest exists; and for the institutions, either the necessity or the willingness to supply it also exists. The schools which would like to refuse will be compelled to supply it to keep up with their willing rivals. Their only choice is whether they will manage the entertainment in such a way as to prevent damage to themselves as educational institutions – damage which the present methods certainly entail. These methods frequently create financial obligations which imperil educational development because they have contractual priority over educational budgets. Those who recruit players and the players who are recruited are too often corrupted not because of the bargains they strike, but because the bargains are in violation of pledges all have agreed to uphold. Influences outside universities are encouraged to seek control of educational operations – influences which are seldom willing to confine their interests to athletics. Athletics requires an atmosphere of academic accommodation to its necessities, to the great cynicism of faculties and students. It has bred a kind of humiliating schizophrenia in educational administrators who are compelled to defend with platitudes what they do not believe or to keep an uneasy silence. It has created a kind of amused tolerance toward institutions on the part of the very public which buys the entertainment – a tolerance which says that whatever the virtues and respectability of higher education on all other scores, it must be given the privilege of this secret sin.

IV

AT the risk of scornful disagreement let me outline how, it seems to me, the great strain in our educational institutions can be reduced.

The first and most crucial step is purely intellectual: to make the admission, both inside and outside the universities, that our programs of intercollegiate athletics are operated primarily as public entertainment and not as educational responsibilities. This will lay a foundation for entirely new solutions to the problem.

With the acceptance of this concept most of the undesirable stresses and strains will begin to disappear. Athletics — that is, *winning* athletics — now becomes a legitimate university operation. Recruiting becomes not only legal but justifiable. To get the best athletes becomes not only understandable but commendable in exactly the same way that one seeks for excellence in any department of the university. One gives the athlete what the resources will allow — just as Illinois offers the graduate assistant in history or chemistry what it can to attract the best. No one thinks the less of Illinois because it can outbid Montana for graduate students. In short, athletic practices which are not at all appropriate to "educational" activities become acceptable and legitimate as parts of a program of public entertainment.

The same principle clarifies the position and character of the coaching staff. Let it be the best that can be obtained, as large and specialized as the situation requires. Let it be freed to meet its obligations without the moral strain imposed by the necessity to circumvent impossible requirements. The financial situation likewise becomes manageable. Since athletics is to be managed as entertainment, it need not in logic or in fact be a charge on the educational budget; and just as no educational institution expects to support itself from athletics, so athletics should not expect to be a charge on education. Self-support for athletics as public entertainment is at once a financial liberation and a restraint.

And why should there be concern about the academic record of a young man who comes to a university primarily to play on a team and whom the university has brought for exactly that purpose? I submit that nothing is lost by relieving all athletes of the obligation to meet academic requirements, if they cannot or do not wish to do so. Let us be courageous enough to admit that the university's interest in them is that they be good athletes, not that they be good students. It is the insistence that they be students which creates the problem both for the faculty and for the athletic managers, and to the detriment of both. Of course, if a boy wishes to be a student as well as an athlete, by all means encourage him, but in that case the fact that he is an athlete need not enter into his status as a student any more than his grades as a student should be made to affect his effectiveness as an athlete. The athlete will then for the first time be on a par with every other student who works his way through school. His academic progress will be exactly proportional to the time and interest he has beyond the demands of his employment.

What if the athlete has no interest whatsoever in his further education? A team entirely made up of professionals is not the solution for the colleges. The best solution is a prescription of academic work suited to the tastes and talents of the athlete but with the clear understanding by professors and athletes alike that the record as a student will be neither a hindrance nor a help to athletic success.

What! someone says. Have unbridled bidding for athletes? No eligibility rules? No discipline? By no means — but let these things arise, as they will, from athletic and not from academic sources and necessities. Let eligibility rules be drawn and enforced by those who are most concerned about them — the athletic managements — not by faculties. Who can be counted on to expose infractions of eligibility rules? Opponents! Every roster of players is exchanged between coaches — why should a faculty committee bother? Who is hurt if the ineligible player plays? The opposition! Who is the best insurance that he won't? The opposition! No, faculties and administrators have gratuitously assumed a lot of unnecessary burdens — and to what purpose or to what effect it is hard to see.

The relinquishment of formal academic — not institutional — control over athletics will have very substantial advantages both for athletics and for education. The first is the restoration of institutional and personal integrity. Gone will be the necessity to keep up the pretense that at the present time suffuses the discussion of athletics as a part of an educational program. The establishment of single-mindedness will be the greatest advantage, for educational institutions are basically devoted to intellectual honesty. Such honesty will free athletics as well as education from the schizophrenia from which they both now suffer.

A very valuable outcome will also be the dissipation of the sentimentality which currently surrounds college athletics in the mind of the public. This myth is carefully preserved not for its truth but for its utility. Listen to any major coach talk about his team and you will see how little such sentimentality is justified. He refers to his "material," not to boys; he discusses weakness at end and tackle and backfield, completely oblivious of the feelings of his men. There is not a player whom he will not instantly displace if he can get a better one. One of the most unhappy tasks that athletic managements must perform is to get rid of players to whom scholarships have been given — commitments made — but who can't quite make the grade on the field.

Perhaps the public which sees the universities as operating departments of public entertainment and sees athletes as assistants in the department will come to think of the whole matter a little differently — to the great relief of everyone concerned.

When doctors find that a given treatment results in no improvement, they re-examine their diagnosis; when scientists find that experiments produce no anticipated results, they revise their basic hypothesis. Educators now find that what was once the recreation of students in school has been transformed into a responsibility of the educational system to supply the public with entertainment. It is essential that educators carry through a fundamental revision of concepts of athletic management appropriate to this transformation.

QUESTIONS

1. Why does Stoke begin his essay with the basketball scandals of 1951? What is the author's aim in making Paragraph 2, Section I, so short?

2. What type of response does the author intend the reader to have in Paragraph 4, Section I? Point out how irony is used in this paragraph to help achieve the author's intention.

3. What is the specific purpose of the next to the last paragraph in Section I? Point out how this specific aim relates to the main purpose of Section I.

4. At the beginning of Paragraph 3, Section II, Stoke says, " The same force lies back of the other features of athletics. . . ." Identify " the same force."

5. What is the function of the author's consideration of Bowl games? What conclusions seem to be implied in the last sentence of Section II?

6. What, according to Stoke, are the results of acting " as if athletics were merely an extension of student recreation "?

7. Summarize Stoke's recommendations in Section IV. What advantages does he say will result from his solution? What is the effect of the author's reference to doctors and scientists in the final paragraph of the essay?

Language and the Arts

JACQUES BARZUN

ALICE HAMILTON, M.D.

E. M. FORSTER

W. T. STACE

GEORGE F. WHICHER

AL CAPP

EDWARD WEEKS

JACQUES BARZUN was born in France, but came to the United States at the age of twelve. He received his higher education at Columbia University, graduating at the head of his class in 1927 and receiving the doctorate in 1932. He has been a professor of history at Columbia since 1945, has appeared frequently on the *Invitation to Learning* radio program, and has contributed articles to various magazines, including *The Atlantic Monthly, The Nation,* and *The Saturday Review.* Calling himself a "student of cultural history," he has written books on education, criticism, and musicology. These include the much discussed *Teacher in America* (1945) and *God's Country and Mine* (1954), the latter with the subtitle "A Declaration of Love Spiced with a Few Harsh Words."

ENGLISH AS SHE'S NOT TAUGHT

by JACQUES BARZUN

AT AN educational conference held in Vancouver last summer, leaders of the Canadian school system generally agreed that from half to three quarters of their students in the first year of college were incompetent in grammar, syntax, and analysis of thought. What was notable in the discussion was that nearly every participant used the English language with uncommon force and precision. Any looseness or jargon heard there came from the three American guests, of whom I was one. Most of our hosts – Canadian teachers, principals, supervisors, and university instructors – had obviously gone through the mill of a classical education; the chairman made a mild pun involving Latin and was rewarded with an immediate laugh. Yet they declared themselves unable to pass on their linguistic accomplishment to the present school generation, and they wanted to know why.

In the United States the same complaint and inquiry has been endemic, commonplace, for quite a while. You come across it in the papers. You hear parents, school people, editors and publishers, lawyers and ministers, men of science and of business, lamenting the fact that their charges or their offspring or their employees can neither spell nor write "decent English." The deplorers blame the modern progressive school or the comics or TV; they feel that in school and outside, something which they call discipline is lacking, and they vaguely connect this lack with a supposed decline in morality, an upsurge of "crisis." Like everything else, bad English is attributed to our bad times, and the past (which came to an end with the speaker's graduation from college) is credited with one more virtue, that of literary elegance.

The facts seem to me quite different, the causes much more tangled, and the explanation of our linguistic state at once more complex and less vague. For many years now I have been concerned with the art of writing and kept busy at the invidious task of improving other people's utterance, and I cannot see that performance has deteriorated. The level is low but it has not fallen. As a reader of history I am steadily reminded that the writing of any language has always been a hit-and-miss affair. Here is Amos Barrett,* our chief source on the battles of Concord and Lexington: "It wont long before their was other minit Compneys . . . We marched Down about a mild or a mild half and we see them acomming . . ." and so on. An illiterate New England farmer? Not so, since he could write; he had been taught and in some way represents "the past." The question he poses is, how do people write who are not professionals or accomplished amateurs? The answer is: badly, at all times.

Writing is at the very least a knack, like drawing or being facile on the piano. Because everybody can speak and form letters, we mistakenly suppose that good, plain, simple writing is within everybody's power. Would we say this of good, straightforward, accurate drawing? Would we say it of melodic sense and correct, fluent harmonizing at the keyboard? Surely not. We say these are "gifts." Well, so is writing, even the writing of a bread-and-butter note or a simple public notice; and this last suggests that something has happened within the last hundred years to change the relation of the written word to daily life.

Whether it is the records we have to keep in every business and profession or the ceaseless communicating at a distance which modern transport and industry require, the world's work is now unmanageable, unthinkable, without *literature.* Just see how many steps you can take without being confronted with something written or with the necessity of writing something yourself. Having been away for a couple of weeks during the summer, I find a bill from the window washer, who luckily came on a day when the cleaning woman was in the apartment. He has therefore scribbled below the date: "The windows have been cleaned Wed. 12:30 P.M. Your maid was their to veryfey the statement"—perfectly clear and adequate. One can even appreciate the change of tenses as his mind went from the job just

* A private in the Colonial Army, who wrote a memoir of his experiences.

finished to the future when I would be reading this message from the past.

Call this bad writing if you like, it remains perfectly harmless. The danger to the language, if any, does not come from such trifles. It comes rather from the college-bred millions who regularly write and who in the course of their daily work circulate the prevailing mixture of jargon, cant, vogue words, and loose syntax that passes for prose. And the greater part of this verbiage is published, circulated, presumably read. A committee won't sit if its drivelings are not destined for print. Even an interoffice memo goes out in sixteen copies and the schoolchildren's compositions appear verbatim in a mimeographed magazine. Multiply these cultural facts by the huge number of activities which (it would seem) exist only to bombard us with paper, and you have found the source of the belief in a "decline" in writing ability — no decline at all, simply the infinite duplication of dufferism. This it is which leads us into false comparisons and gloomy thoughts.

II

THE apparent deterioration of language is a general phenomenon which is denounced throughout Western Europe. One had only to read the Catalogue of the British Exhibition of 1951 to see the common symptoms in England. Sir Ernest Gowers's * excellent little book of a few years earlier, *Plain Words,* was an attempt to cure the universal disease in one congested spot, the Civil Service, which is presumably the most highly educated professional group in Britain.

In France, the newspapers, the reports of Parliamentary debates, and the literary reviews show to what extent ignorance of forms and insensitivity to usage can successfully compete against a training obsessively aimed at verbal competence. And by way of confirmation, M. Jean Delorme, a native observer of the language in French Canada, recently declared the classic speech "infected" on this side of the Atlantic too. As for Germany, a foreign colleague and correspondent of mine, a person of catholic tastes and broad judgment, volunteers the opinion that "people who cultivate good pure German are nowadays generally unpopular, especially among the devotees of newspaper fiction and articles. The universal barbarism of language has already gone well into the grotesque."

So much for the democratic reality. But great as has been the effect of enlarged "literacy," it does not alone account for what is now seen

* English lawyer, born in 1880, who held various civil service and other governmental posts.

as linguistic decadence. The educated, in fact the leaders of modern thought, have done as much if not more to confuse the judgment. For what is meant by the misnomer "pure speech" is simply a habit of respect toward usage, which insures a certain fixity in vocabulary, forms, and syntax. Language cannot stand still, but it can change more or less rapidly and violently. During the last hundred years, nearly every intellectual force has worked, in all innocence, against language. The strongest, science and technology, did two damaging things: they poured quantities of awkward new words into the language and this in turn persuaded everybody that each new thing must have a name, preferably "scientific." These new words, technical or commercial, were fashioned to impress, an air of profundity being imparted by the particularly scientific letters *k*, *x*, and *o* = Kodak, Kleenex, Sapolio. The new technological words that came in were sinful hybrids like "electrocute" and "triphibian," or misunderstood phrases like "personal equation," "*n*th degree," or "psychological moment" — brain addlers of the greatest potency.

The passion for jargon was soon at its height, from which it shows no sign of descending. Every real or pseudo science poured new verbiage into the street, every separate school or -ism did likewise, without shame or restraint. We can gauge the result from the disappearance of the Dictionary properly so called. Consult the most recent and in many ways the best of them, *Webster's New World Dictionary,* and what you find is a miniature encyclopedia filled with the explanation of initials, proper names, and entries like "macrosporangium" or "abhenry," which are not and never will be words of the English language.

Under the spate of awe-inspiring vocables, the layman naturally felt that he too must dignify his doings and not be left behind in the race for prestige. Common acts must suggest a technical process. Thus we get "contact" and "funnel" as workaday verbs — and "process" itself: "we'll process your application" — as if it were necessary to name the steps or choices of daily life with scientific generality. I know a young businessman who makes jottings of his business thoughts; when he has enough on one topic he *folderizes* them.

What is wrong with all this is not merely that it is new, heedless, vulgar, and unnecessary (all signs of harmful vice in a language) but that jargon swamps thought. The habit of talking through cant words destroys the power of seeing things plain. "I'll contact you to finalize the agreement." What does it mean? The drift is plain enough, but compare: "I'll call at your office to sign the contract." The former raises no clear image or expectation, the latter does. Moreover, the former smells of inflated ego, it fills the mouth in a silly bumptious way.

But who cares? Why fuss? — good questions both. Nobody cares much because — we all think — it's the deed (or the thing) that counts, not the words. This conviction, too, is a product of modern technology, and its effect is great though unremarked. The power of words over nature, which has played such a role in human history, is now an exploded belief, a dead emotion. Far from words controlling things, it is now things that dictate words. As soon as science was able to chop up the physical world and recombine it in new forms, language followed suit; and this not only among scientists making up new vocables, but among the supposed guardians of the language, the poets and men of letters. It is highly significant that around 1860 writers deliberately began to defy usage and turn syntax upside down. Lewis Carroll and Edward Lear made good fun with it; " obscure " poets such as Rimbaud * sought new depths of meaning. There was in this a strong impulse to destroy all convention, for Victorian moralism had made the idea of conventionality at once suspect and hateful. The revolt succeeded and its spirit is still alive; novelty-hunting is now a linguistic virtue, or to express it differently, a common influence is at work in Jabberwocky † and James Joyce, in the scientist's lingo and in the advertiser's " Dynaflow," " Hydramatic," or " Frigidaire " — which end by becoming household words. In short, modern man is feeling his oats as the manipulator of objects and he shows it in his manhandling of words.

This helps to explain why the predominant fault of the bad English encountered today is not the crude vulgarism of the untaught but the blithe irresponsibility of the taught. The language is no longer regarded as a common treasure to be hoarded and protected as far as possible. Rather, it is loot from the enemy to be played with, squandered, plastered on for one's adornment. Literary words imperfectly grasped, meanings assumed from bare inspection, monsters spawned for a trivial cause — these are but a few of the signs of squandering. To give examples: the hotel clerk giving me a good room feels bound to mention the well-known person whom " we last hospitalized in that room." Not to lag behind Joyce, the advertiser bids you " slip your feet into these easy-going *leisuals* and breathe a sigh of real comfort."

Undoubtedly these strange desires are often born of the need to ram an idea down unwilling throats. We all fear our neighbor's wan-

* Jean Nicolas Arthur Rimbaud (1854–1891), French poet, companion of Paul Verlaine (1844–1896).

† " Nonsense poem " by Charles L. Dodgson (1832–1898), whose pseudonym was Lewis Carroll.

dering attention and try to keep him awake by little shocks of singularity, or again by an overdose of meaning. Unfortunately, novelty-hunting proceeds from the known to the unknown by a leap of faith. "It was pleasant," writes the author of very workmanlike detective stories, "to watch her face and find his resentment *vitiate* as he made excuses for her."

III

THE notable fact is that all this occurs in printed books, written by writers, published (usually) by first-rate firms that employ editors. In speech, the same blunders and distortions come from educated people. It is all very well to say, as one expert has confidently done, that "what certain words really mean is moving toward what they seem to mean," the implication being that after a while everything will be in place. Actually, this leaves meaning nowhere, if only because we're not all moving in step. The *New Yorker* spotted a movie theater sign on which "adultery" was used to mean "adulthood." From an English periodical I learn that some new houses "*affront* the opposite side of the street." If Mrs. Malaprop is going to become the patron saint of English, what is going to prevent "contention" from meaning the same thing as "contentment" or the maker of woodcuts from being called a woodcutter?

There is no getting around it: meaning implies convention, and the discovery that meanings change does not alter the fact that when convention is broken misunderstanding and chaos are close at hand. Mr. Churchill has told how Allied leaders nearly came to blows because of the single word "table," a verb which to the Americans meant dismiss from the discussion, whereas to the English, on the contrary, it meant put on the agenda. This is an extraordinary instance, and the vagaries of those who pervert good words to careless misuse may be thought more often ludicrous than harmful. This would be true if language, like a great maw, could digest anything and dispose of it in time. But language is not a kind of ostrich. Language is alive only by a metaphor drawn from the life of its users. Hence every defect in the language is a defect in somebody.

For language is either the incarnation of our thoughts and feelings or a cloak for their absence. When the ordinary man who has prepared a report on sales up to June 30 rumbles on about "the frame of reference in which the co-ordination campaign was conceived," he is filling the air with noises, not thoughts.

For self-protection, no doubt, the contemporary mind is opposed to all this quibbling. It speaks with the backing of popular approval when it says: "Stop it! You understand perfectly well what all these people mean. Don't be a dirty purist looking under the surface and meddling with democratic self-expression." To haggle over language *is* quibbling, of course. All precision is quibbling, whether about decimals in mathematics or grains of drugs in prescriptions – fairly important quibbles. The question is whether in language the results justify the quibble. Well, the public is here the best judge, and it is evident that as a consumer of the written word, the public is always complaining that it cannot understand what it is asked to read: the government blanks, the instructions on the bottle or gadget, the gobbledygook of every trade, the highbrow jargon of the educators, psychiatrists, and social workers, and – one must also add – the prose of literary critics. The great cry today is for improved communication, mass communication, the arts of communication, and yet under the pretext of being free and easy and above quibbling, those who do the most talking and writing indulge themselves in the very obscurities and ambiguities that cause the outcry.

They are abetted, moreover, by another offspring of the scientific spirit, the professional student of language. In his modern embodiment, the linguist takes the view that whatever occurs in anybody's speech is a fact of language and must not be tampered with, but only caught in flight and pinned on a card. This is "scientific detachment," and it has gone so far that under its influence in many schools all the categories of grammar, syntax, and rhetoric have been discarded. The modern way to learn English or a foreign language is to absorb a phrase-by-phrase enumeration of all that might conceivably be said in ordinary talk – a directory instead of a grammar.

This brings us back to our first difficulty, how to teach the millions the use of their mother tongue *in composition*. We have made nearly everybody literate in the sense of able to read and write words. But that is not writing. Even those who profess disdain for the literary art and the literary quibbles respond automatically to good writing, which they find unexpectedly easy to read and retain, mysteriously "pleasant" as compared with their neighbors' matted prose. The linguists themselves pay lip service to "effective" speech, approving the end while forbidding discrimination among the means.

Now many thousands of people in the United States today exercise this discrimination; there is amid the garbage a steady supply of good writing, modestly done and published – in every newspaper and magazine, over TV and radio, in millions of ads and public notices, in railroad timetables, travel booklets, and printed instructions on objects of daily use. Good writing is good writing wherever it occurs, and some of the impugned comics which are supposed to defile the native well of English in our young are far better than acceptable.

It is therefore idle and erroneous to condemn "the newspapers" or "the radio" en masse. Here too one must discriminate, and the failure to do so is one cause of the trouble — the strange cultural trait whose origin I have sketched and which makes us at once indifferent to our language, full of complaints about it, and irresponsible about mangling it still more. In these conditions people who write well learn to do so by virtue of a strong desire, developed usually under necessity: their job requires lucidity, precision, brevity. If they write advertising copy they must not only make it fit the space but make the words yield the tone.

Tone — that is the starting point of any teaching in composition. What effect are you producing and at what cost of words? The fewer the words, and the more transparent they are, the easier they will be to understand. The closer the ideas they stand for and the more natural their linkage, the more easily will the meaning be retained. Simple in appearance, this formula is yet extremely difficult to apply, and even more arduous to teach. You cannot work on more than one pupil at a time and you must be willing to observe and enter into his mind. On his part, the discipline calls for a thorough immersion in the medium. He must form the habit of attending to words, constructions, accents, and etymologies in everything he reads or hears — just as the painter unceasingly notes line and color and the musician tones. The would-be writer has the harder task because words are entangled with the business of life and he must stand off from it to look at them, hearing at the same time their harmonies and discords. It is an endless duty, which finally becomes automatic. The ideal writer would mentally recast his own death sentence as he was reading it — if it was a bad sentence.

IV

NOW such a discipline cannot be imposed from without, and not everybody needs it in full. But its principle, which suffices for ordinary purposes, should be made clear to every beginner, child or adult. Unfortunately, the school system, even when progressive, makes writing an irrational chore approached in the mood of rebellion. The school does this in two ways: by requiring length and by concentrating on correctness. I know very well that correctness was supposedly given up long ago. The modern teacher does not mention it. But if the teacher marks spelling and grammatical errors and speaks of little else, what is a child to think? He gets a mark with the comment "imaginative" or "not imaginative enough" and most often: "too short," and he is left with no more idea of composition than a cow in a field has of landscape painting. How *does* one judge the right length and get it out of a reluctant brain? Nobody answers, except perhaps with the word "creative," which has brought unmerited gloom to many a cheerful child. Who can be creative on demand, by next Tuesday, and in the requisite amount? In all but a few chatterboxes, mental frostbite is the only result.

Meanwhile the things that are teachable, the ways of translating the flashes of thought into consecutive sentences, are neglected. They have been, most often, neglected in the teachers themselves. How do *they* write or speak, what do *they* read? If they read and write educational literature, as they often must for advancement, are they fit to teach composition? And what of the teachers of other subjects, whose professional jargon also infects their speech, what is their countervailing effect on a child to whom a good English teacher has just imparted a notion of the writer's craft? Suppose the teacher of a course on family life has just been reading *Social Casework* and his mind is irradiated with this: "Familial societality is already a settled question biologically, structured in our inherited bodies and physiology, but the answer to those other questions are not yet safely and irrevocably anatomized." Unless this is immediately thrown up like the nux vomica it is, it will contaminate everybody it touches from pupil to public – in fact the whole blooming familial societality.

The cure is harsh and likely to be unpopular, for it must start with self-denial. It can be initiated by the school but it must not stop there. As many of us as possible must work out of our system, first, all the vogue words that almost always mean nothing but temporary vacancy of mind – such words as "basic," "major," "over-all," "personal," "values," "exciting" (everything from a new handbag to a new baby); then all the wormy expressions indicative of bad conscience, false modesty, and genteelism, as in: "Frankly, I don't know too much about it" – a typical formula which tries through candor and whining to minimize ignorance while claiming a kind of merit for it; finally, all the tribal adornments which being cast off may disclose the plain man we would like to be: no frames of reference, field theories, or apperception protocols; no texture, prior to, or in terms of; and the least amount of co-ordination, dynamics, and concepts.

After the vocabulary has been cleansed, the patient is ready for what our Canadian friends at the Vancouver conference deplored the lack of in the modern undergraduate: analysis of thought. To show what is meant and let criticism begin at home, I choose an example from a New York City report of 1952 entitled "The English Language Arts." It begins: "Because language arts or English is so –" Stop right there! What are language arts? – A perfectly unnecessary phrase of the pseudo-scientific kind which tries to "cover." Besides, "language arts or English" is nonsense: ever hear of another language? Moreover, "language arts . . . is" doesn't sound like a happy opening for a report by and to English teachers. Let us go on: English is so what? Well, "language arts or English is so intimately connected with all knowledge and all living, it is the subject which most often bursts the dikes separating it from others." What do you mean, language is *connected* with living? And how does English connect with *all* knowledge and *all* living? Is the practical knowledge of the Russian engineer intimately connected with English? Do the amoebas speak English? And if this intimacy does exist, then what are these dikes that separate English from other subjects? Are these subjects no part of "all knowledge" with which English is connected – or rather, of which it too is a part?

Cruel work, but necessary if anything akin to thought is to arise from the written word. The Neanderthal glimmer from which the quoted sentence sprang is irrecoverable but its developed form should run something like this: "English, being a medium of communication, cannot be confined within set limits like other subjects; to the peoples whose speech it is, all theoretical knowledge, and indeed most of life, is inseparable from its use."

And this is so true that it justifies the operation just performed on the specimen of non-thought. For although it is possible to think without words and to communicate by signs, our civilization depends, as I said before, on the written word. Writing is embodied thought, and the thought is clear or muddy, graspable or fugitive, according to the purity of the medium. Communication means one thought held in common. What could be more practical than to try making that thought unmistakable?

As for the receiver, the reader, his pleasure or grief is in direct proportion to the pains taken by the writer; to which one can add that the taking of pains brings its special pleasure. I do not mean the satisfaction of vanity, for after a bout of careful writing one is too tired to care; I mean the new perceptions – sensuous or intellectual or comic – to be had all day long in one's encounters with language. Imagine the fun people miss who find nothing remarkable in the sentence (from Sax Rohmer*): "The woman's emotions were too tropical for analysis"; or who, trusting too far my disallowance of

* Pseudonym of Arthur S. Wade (1883–), English author of sensational fiction, including the Fu Manchu stories.

" contact " as a verb, miss the chance of using it at the hottest, stickiest time of year: " On a day like this, I wouldn't contact anybody for the world."

QUESTIONS

1. In Section I, with what beliefs about " bad writing " does Barzun disagree? What method does he employ to explain the *nature* of writing? What does he consider the chief " danger to the language "? Why are " drivelings," " bombard us with paper," and " infinite duplication of dufferism " effective in their connotation?

2. What is the principal topic of Section II, and what groups of people are related to it? What connection exists between the main idea of Paragraph 3 and that of the paragraph on page 69 beginning " But who cares? " How does jargon tend to defeat the purpose of written or oral expression?

3. What you say is more important than how you say it; so long as your meaning is clear, nothing else matters. Under what circumstances might these statements be considered valid? How does Barzun meet such arguments?

4. Does the author employ sufficient concrete material to support his generalizations? Select two or three examples (or groups of examples), such as those in Paragraph 3, Section II, or Paragraph 2, Section III, and try to explain why they are effective.

5. Frequently Barzun concludes a paragraph with a sentence which " clinches " the thought. Show how this result is achieved in the paragraph on page 69 beginning " But who cares? "; in Paragraph 2 and the last paragraph of Section III; and Paragraphs 2 and 6 of Section IV. Are these sentences *merely* clever?

6. How, according to Barzun in Section IV, do teachers contribute to the " English as she's not taught "? What two skills does Barzun emphasize in his " cure "?

ALICE HAMILTON, M. D., earned her medical degree at the University of Michigan at a time when women doctors were very uncommon. She did graduate work at German universities and at Johns Hopkins. Her entire professional life has been devoted to industrial medicine. She served under Jane Addams at Hull-House, directed occupational disease surveys, and was Special Investigator for the Department of Labor on Poisonous Trades. President Hoover appointed Dr. Hamilton to the Commission on Social Trends. She is the author of many books and reports on industrial toxicology, including *Industrial Poisoning in the United States* (1925), and has contributed many articles to medical journals and other magazines. The story of her pioneering research is told in her autobiography, *Exploring the Dangerous Trades* (1943). Dr. Hamilton now lives in retirement in Hadlyme, Connecticut.

WORDS LOST, STRAYED, OR STOLEN

by ALICE HAMILTON, M.D.

WORDS have always been of great interest to me, and their misuse gives me a sense of more than discomfort: of actual indignation, as if a friend were being mistreated. I cannot claim to be a writer, but then a music critic is not a musician, nor an art critic a painter. I am a reader, so I feel I have a right to criticize authors, journalists, editorial writers, who, to my mind, are doing violence to the English language by surrendering precious words to base uses or by substituting cheap words for valuable ones.

Take some of the lost words. It is hard to see why the useful and simple " because," " since," " owing to," should have been lost, but apparently they have been pushed out by the would-be elegant " due to." This is no longer an adjective and does not have to qualify a noun; it is a preposition on its own, and its queer new use increases all the time, invading even the highbrow weeklies and the " slick " magazines. " Due to the fact that " is bad enough – such a cumbrous substitute for a simple " because " or " owing to " – but what are we to say to such sentences as these, which I have been picking up for a long time? " There were no homeless children due to a local wave of adoption." " He lost time from work due to drinking." " No accident can happen due to glaring headlights." " The amount of undernourishment is not large due to past plenty." "The man died soon after help came due to the injuries." Somehow "because" and "since" are rejected as low-brow. The educated say "due to the fact that"; the uneducated, "on account."

Among the stolen words are some valuable ones, such as "advice" and "advise" – and that does seem a pity, when we have the perfectly good word "inform." We even have "tell," though I suppose no businessman's secretary could use words as simple as "tell" or "say." "Yours of the 14th instant received and contents duly noted. In reply would advise . . ." But what shall we use when "advise" is completely surrendered to the business world? "Counsel"? But how formal. Business is also stealing another good word which it does not need but which we do. To be "interested" now is to be induced to buy or subscribe to something.

"Middle" seems to have strayed away, and its place is being taken by its brother "midst," which for some mysterious reason seems to impress itself on writers as more elegant. Webster says that "midst" implies a number of enveloping objects, as, in the midst of a forest; while "middle" is the part of an object which surrounds the center. But we do not keep to this rule, and "midst" is more and more pushing into the places formerly held by "middle," so that now we continually come across queer things such as these: "in the midst of the session"; "in the midst of the controversy"; even "in the midst of his life." Shall we come finally to "the midst years"?

"Satisfied" is straying, is pushing into the place long filled properly by "convinced" or even the lowly "sure." The result is sometimes startling. For instance: "The man's family is satisfied that he was murdered." Of course that may be literally true, but the family did not mean to tell the world so. Apparently the reporter who wrote about Bernt Balchen's unsuccessful rescue mission did not realize how callous was his statement that "Balchen is satisfied that none of the missing men is still on the ice."

The journalists have stolen another useful word which they do not need at all. "Argument" has a definite meaning and a dignified one. Then why make it take the place of "quarrel," "dispute," or even a "drunken brawl"? "The murder followed an argument in the saloon." What are we to use, for instance – if "argument" is lost – when scientists disagree about the atom bomb, or economists about a depression?

More amusing is the increasing rejection of "believe" and "think" in favor of "feel." Notice how often statesmen, journalists, commentators, tell you what the "feeling" is in the State Department, the Foreign Office, the Pentagon. Both American and English public men seem now to depend on their "feelings" about the most controversial questions. Does it show that we accept the dictum of the newer psychology that all our decisions are based on emotion, not on thought?

It is to me especially irritating to see the word "sick" straying so far into limbo, though it is not yet irreparably lost. Here we are slavishly following the English in rejecting it for "ill." The English seem to be too modest to use such coarse words as "vomit" or even "throw up," and to be "sick" in England is to do just that. I came across an amazing sentence in an English medical article. "The man was plainly very ill, but had not yet been sick." And just the other day I found this in an English novel: "I think I'm going to be sick. It's not anything I ate. It's that I have a delicate nervous system. Excitement makes me feel ill. I get sick with it." — "I should go and get it over." — "Be sick, you mean?" — "Yes, it's a wonderful feeling."

The trouble with "ill" is that it has so many bad associations: ill will; an ill wind; ill luck; ill used; "ill fares the land" and Annie of Lochroyen's tragic cry, "Oh woe betide my ill mother. An ill death may she die!" Yet more and more our newspapers avoid the vulgar "sick" and substitute "ill." Do not we all shrink a little when we read "an ill baby," "an ill woman"? And even the English could hardly say "a love-ill swain."

The word "obscene" has a definite meaning and there is no other word to take its place, but it is being stolen and made to serve as a simple hate-word. It is used to describe extreme cruelty, such as that of Buchenwald and Auschwitz, or the destruction of the Warsaw ghetto, even the Ku Klux Klan, the deliberations of the Politburo, the Dies Committee. Edna St. Vincent Millay used it to describe the Sacco-Vanzetti case; Borgese, the Fascist salute; Waldo Frank, the members of the Reichstag; the *Nation,* the Horst Wessel song. Mencken wrote that the Scopes trial was "so farcical it was almost obscene." Now, however detestable all these may be, we have no right to call them obscene and thereby rob ourselves of a useful word when we have no other to take its place.

English-speaking people have long prided themselves on having the word "home" in their language, while the Latins have to use some weak substitute like *chez soi.** But now we are letting "home" stray into low company so far that we are in danger of losing it altogether. This is because of our inveterate belief that if we put a nice word in the place of one we dislike ("mortician," for instance, the man who takes charge when we "pass away") we thereby change the thing we

* Literally, at the home of oneself.

dislike to a likable thing. So we call an undertaker's establishment a "funeral home"; and all sorts of institutions for the sick, the insane, the delinquent, are called "homes" when there is and can be nothing homelike about them. When I lived at Hull-House, "home" was far from being a beloved word. A poor widow said to me, "I'll work my fingers to the bone before I'll let my children go to a home." The once beautiful word "asylum" is straying along the same down-path.

That brings us to the wickedest of steals, "disinterested." Think what a valuable word that is and how irreplaceable. The quality of disinterestedness is one of the finest of which human beings are capable, and there is no way to describe it in a single word except just that one. Yet out of sheer laziness we are letting it substitute for the perfectly adequate "uninterested," and this crime is being committed, not by the uneducated or the business world, but by "intellectuals" who know better. Editors ought to join a crusade against this unscrupulous steal and reject any manuscript that contains such outrages as: "The statement met with complete disinterest on the part of the assembly." "Unfortunately the man was disinterested and I came away depressed."

I will not go into the many forms of gobbledygook – legal, medical, business, sociological – that plague us. Bad as they are, they are read mostly by professionals only; they do not often invade literature. My own profession is pretty bad, but certainly less so than the legal. However, it is hard to understand why it has given up the good word "fever" and taken to using "temperature." You will hear not only a layman but a doctor ask, "Has he a temperature?" Well, if he has not he must have been dead a number of hours. And why should a patient be "ambulatory" instead of "up and about"? Why should we give up that convenient old word "bedfast"? Social workers have their own dialect and have rejected "poor." We may still use it provided it does not deal with physical poverty, but we must no longer speak of "the poor" except when we quote the Bible. We must say "underprivileged" instead – not "a poor child" but "an underprivileged preadolescent."

Changes in language that lead to greater clarity or conciseness or vividness – as some of our American slang does – are to be welcomed, but that is not true of any of the examples I have given. Maybe we need an "Académie américaine" to call a halt and rescue our lost, strayed, or stolen words.

QUESTIONS

1. What distinctions among " lost," " strayed," and " stolen " words are revealed by Dr. Hamilton's examples? Are these distinctions mutually exclusive? Are they *real* distinctions?

2. Dr. Hamilton apparently considers " due to " an adjective (second paragraph). But she writes (fourth paragraph from the end): " This is because of our inveterate belief. . . ." Would " due to " be preferable to " because of " in this sentence? Explain.

3. Dr. Hamilton is amused by the increased use of " feel " in place of " believe " and " think," and she wonders if this usage indicates decisions based on emotion instead of thought. In the first paragraph of the essay, she herself writes: " I am a reader, so I feel I have a right to criticize authors, journalists, editorial writers, who, to my mind, are doing violence to the English language. . . ." Is Dr. Hamilton's use of " feel " in this sentence deliberate? Are her decisions about words based on emotion or thought?

4. Show how the opening paragraph sets the mood and tone of the essay. Mood may be defined as the emotional attitude or feeling, such as admiration, anger, hate, reverence, wonder, etc., which the author has toward his subject and which he wants the reader to share. Tone may be defined as the author's attitude toward the reader. The author's tone may be one of reproach, warning, pity, condescension, etc., or it may be a matter-of-fact tone. Like mood, tone has a broad emotional range.

E. M. FORSTER's best known work is the highly praised novel, *A Passage to India* (1924). The well-deserved praise of this work should not obscure Forster's achievements as a short story writer and critic (both of literature and society). He is the author of *Where Angels Fear to Tread* (1905), *A Room with a View* (1908), *Howards End* (1910), *Aspects of the Novel* (1927), *Abinger Harvest* (1936), *Marianne Thornton: A Domestic Biography, 1797–1887* (1956), and the libretto for Benjamin Britten's opera *Billy Budd* (1951).

THE IVORY TOWER

by E. M. FORSTER

THE phrase "The Ivory Tower" was first used, in the literary sense, by Sainte-Beuve, when he was examining the work of his friend and contemporary Alfred de Vigny. De Vigny had led an active life, but he was aloof and fastidious, rather disdainful, prone to mysticism, and when he took to writing he tended to withdraw from the hurry, noisiness, muddle, and littleness of the world, and contemplate action from the heights like a god, or from within a fortress where he remained unscathed. To hit off this tendency, Sainte-Beuve borrowed from religion the phrase *la tour d'ivoire,* the tower where the poet retreats *avant midi,** before the heat and the weariness of the battle have developed. The phrase had been used for centuries as a symbol of the Virgin Mary, and it occurs in the Song of Solomon, but Sainte-Beuve first applied it to literature.

It has come in again lately in a derogatory sense as a synonym for "escapism." "Escapism," like most words ending in *-ism,* is abusive, and prejudges the issue it professes to define. There is much to be said for escaping from the world, when it is the world of 1938, so that, if we are to discuss the problem dispassionately, "The Ivory Tower" in Sainte-Beuve's sense seems the better title. It is noncommittal. Is there such a thing as an Ivory Tower? And if there is, shall we fortify it and make it stronger, or shall we try to pull it down? To put the problem in other words: Can books be an escape from life, and if they can be, ought they to be? Do writers (all or some) escape from life when they write? Do readers (all or some) escape when they read? And when we speak of "life" here, what meaning do we attach to that much be-

* Before noon.

labored word? The subject strays into philosophy and politics, but its main line is literary: the proper function of books.

Let us start with a generalization upon human nature.

Man is an animal, but a queer one. He possesses the herd instinct, so that he readily forms tribes, gangs, nations. But, unlike other gregarious animals, he has the instinct for solitude as well. Consequently he is always contradicting himself in his conduct and getting into muddles — one of which we are examining now. He wants to be alone even when he is feeling fit. That is one of the differences between a man and a chicken. A chicken wants to be alone only when it is feeling poorly. When a hen withdraws herself from her female companions and even from her gentleman friend and walks about in solitude with a glassy eye, making sad little noises, you know she is probably ill. The other hens think so too, and give her a peck in passing, to show how different they are feeling themselves.

But a man who goes about alone is probably not ill, but trying to enter his Ivory Tower. He needs the Ivory Tower just as much as he needs the human chicken-run, the city. Both are part of his heritage — solitude and multitude. He is the gregarious animal who wants to be alone even when he feels well, and his glassy eye and sad little noises are often symptoms of something important. He may be getting a clearer view of the world, or thinking out a social problem, or developing his spirit, or creating a poem. He may be bored with the life around him, which is regrettable, and, worse still, he may be afraid of it. But, whatever his motive, he has an incurable desire to be alone. The instinct may not be as old as his gregarious instinct, but it goes back to the beginning of civilization, and has a particular bearing on the development of literature, philosophy, and art. As far back as history stretches, we can see men trying to retire into their Ivory Towers and there to resist or to modify the instincts which they possess as members of the herd.

If we look back nearly two thousand years, at the country which was recently Czechoslovakia, we shall see there a general conducting military operations. The general is thoroughly competent, but when he has a spare moment he takes out his pen and begins to write philosophy. His name is Marcus Aurelius. He had, and knew he had, an Ivory Tower. It was to him the more important side of his heritage; the public side, when he worked with the herd and was regarded as their emperor, meant nothing to him.

If we look back four hundred years we can see a tough, unscrupulous politician, who loves bits of Italy, his country, and is merciless in his methods of serving them. He is also a practical farmer, who runs his own estate, so when the evening comes he is covered in mud in both senses of the word. Then he washes himself, puts on a nice suit of clothes, has candles of the best-quality wax lit in fine candlesticks of silver, and sits down to read about the heroes and the virtues of antiquity. His name is Machiavelli. Machiavelli too had an Ivory Tower, though it was to him the less important side of his heritage: he needed to retire into it after getting the better of his fellow men.

A third example. Sixty years ago there lived a great revolutionary, who did more than anyone else to put his fellow men against the existing structure of society. All his life was devoted to this – he worked for the herd and through the herd. And yet he could not stop himself from occasionally writing a poem, a lyric poem. He had no illusions about the merits of his poems, yet he says: "The best of them made me see what Poetry is – an unattainable fairy palace, at the sight of which my own creations fell to dust." The name of this yearning writer is Karl Marx. To Marx the Ivory Tower was not at all important, and he will be surprised at being assigned one. He would dismiss it as a regrettable bourgeois weakness, and his followers have developed some important arguments against it. But he illustrates my point – that it is part of the human heritage, that it pops up in the most unlikely landscapes, and that to deny its existence is false psychology.

A fourth example is Milton. Milton understands our problem, and his life illustrates it perfectly. He began in seclusion: he was a scholar and a Cambridge intellectual who knew himself to be a poet, and deliberately planned his æsthetic career. *Il Penseroso* is a manifesto of that early faith; it invokes the delightful sadness which exists in the globe of its own shade, and is untainted either by regrets or by fears, and it looks forward – at the age of twenty-five – to an old age which will attain "to something like prophetic strain." Wisdom is to come to the poet through seclusion, and in the Ivory Tower itself: –

> Or let my lamp, at midnight hour,
> Be seen in some high lonely tower,
> Where I may oft outwatch the Bear,
> With thrice great Hermes, or unsphere
> The spirit of Plato . . .

There young John is to be happy and wise, and his descents into human activity, when he makes them, are no more than visits to a country dance; the muddles and the cruelties of daily life never entangle him, nor its poverty, nor disease.

> These pleasures, Melancholy, give,
> And I with thee will choose to live.

That is the Milton of the first period, and then – while he is finishing off his education in Italy (a necessary step, for *Il Penseroso* is bad Italian) – the civil wars start, and his plans have to be scrapped. He is obliged to take sides, as intellectuals all over the world are doing today; he has to come down from his tower and take service under the Commonwealth, and "write with his left hand" for nearly twenty years. One would have expected that to be the end of him, but he has a third phase which makes him very valuable as a specimen: he returns to the Tower and writes *Paradise Lost* and *Samson* in it. His side has lost, but the seventeenth century, unlike the twentieth, did not kill intellectuals who fought on the losing side, and Milton is allowed to work out his poetic plan. We know how the plan was carried out, and how once more – aided this time by his blindness – he detached himself from the world. But Melancholy – what has become of her in the interval? She is no longer the bringer of pleasures, but one of the Furies, the sister of Fear and Remorse; she presides over the lazar house and the punishment of dissolute days: –

> . . . In fine,
> Just or unjust alike seem miserable,
> For oft alike both come to evil end.*

That is the "prophetic strain" which he promised himself when he was twenty-five, and it's a terrible sort of tower to be shut up in, brass for ivory; still it does recall the architecture of his youth, and so is significant for us. It suggests that there are some types who naturally prefer solitude to multitude, and revert to it if they can. In many cases the man is worn out by the business of daily life before he can get back, but the normal tendency is to get back.

II

THESE examples suggest that "escapism" is not new, not a bourgeois weakness or an economic by-product, but is to be deduced from the queer nature of man, who gathers together in groups like his cousins the monkeys, or his distant connections the chickens, but who also wants to build up a private life of his own. Both these tendencies contribute to civilization. They also distract it. We are troubled today, each of us, because we can lead neither the private nor the public life with any decency. I cannot shut myself up in a Palace of Art or a Philosophic Tower and ignore the madness and the misery of the world. Yet I cannot throw myself into movements just because they

* From John Milton's *Samson Agonistes*, ll. 702–704.

are uncompromising, or merge myself in my own class, my own country, or in anyone else's class or country, as if that were the unique good. We are in a muddle. We veer from one side of human nature to the other: now we feel that we are individuals, whose duty it is to create a private heaven; and now we feel we ought to sink our individuality in something larger than ourselves – something which we can only partially like and partially understand, just as Milton only partly liked or understood the cause of the Commonwealth.

Although this restlessness of man has always existed (he will never build Utopia because it would cease to be Utopia when built), it is specially obvious today because of his increased resources. Today politics are more insistent than ever before. We can't get away from Nationalism, Fascism, and Communism, – three isms, – nor from armaments, their result, nor from moral rearmament, their dreary and ineffective counterpoise. The world is frightening. It is also boring, because the tragic march of events seems to be accompanied by no tragic splendor. Public taste declines, the countryside is being destroyed, the towns vulgarized.

When I walk in the town I know best – London – and see the architectural changes in Regent Street or in St. James's Square, which were once so dignified, I realize that we have indeed no abiding city, even when that city is the capital of an Empire. And when I go into the country and find it gashed with arterial roads, spattered with advertisements and spiky with pylons and screeching with bombers, I say with the Psalmist, though in another sense, " If I go up into Heaven, thou art there; if I take the wings of the morning and dwell in the uttermost parts of the sea, I still cannot escape from politics, from commercialism, or from the science that has been harnessed in their service." Fifty years ago one could escape – by moving away. A hundred years ago Browning's Waring could give all civilization the slip and vanish from the midst of his friends into the unknown. They wonder where he has gone, explore one romantic possibility after another, and come to the quaint conclusion that he must be in Spain.

> Ay, most likely 't is in Spain
> That we and Waring meet again
> Now, while he turns down that cool narrow lane
> Into the blackness, out of grave Madrid.*

* From Robert Browning's " Waring," ll. 135–138; Waring has been identified with Alfred Domett, a young poet who disappeared from England and later achieved success in politics in New Zealand. In the poem, Browning analyzes the possible motives of such an act.

These lines bring out with brutal force the contrast between that old world, where a man could escape from men, and our world, where, in the physical sense, escape is impossible. Waring, today, couldn't slip off in his little boat. He would require a passport, duly visaed and endorsed, and if he got lost there would be a Police S O S for him in the nine o'clock news. The last person to attempt escape of this physical sort was the late Colonel Lawrence.* He failed, although he had influential friends who gave him their help and tried to hide his tracks. He went down to the depths of the Tank Corps and into the uttermost parts of the sea, but it couldn't be done, because this is the twentieth century and the clock says no.

Now, because it is impossible for the body to escape, a good many people – many of the best critics of the younger generation among them – have come to the conclusion that it's wrong for the mind to escape. They argue that the duty of everyone, be he an engineer or a statesman, a creative writer or a mere reader, is to the community, and to the community as a whole; they condemn the private life as selfish, and they would pull down all Ivory Towers, whatever their architecture. I think that they are mistaken, and that their mistake arises from their taking too simple a view of human development, but they have much that's interesting to say.

In England we don't theorize much, but the two most theoretical countries in Europe – Russia and Germany – are working out a faith which is in the interests of the herd, and against those of the individual. Russia calls the herd the proletariat, Germany calls it the nation or the people (*das Volk*), but from our point of view their conclusions are the same. Herr Hitler, in an interesting speech about Art which he delivered in 1937 when opening the House of German Art at Munich, says, "No doubt the Nation is not eternal, but so long as it exists it constitutes a stable pole in the whirling flight of time. The individual must rally to support that stability. If he is an artist, he must set up a monument to his people rather than to himself; if he is an ordinary citizen, he must not indulge in the luxury of a private universe. For the Nation is more real than any of the men and women who make it up."

Lenin, in one of his earlier manifestoes, says the same, though he does not mention nationality or race, and though his tone is non-mystic. "Literature," he says, "ought to be Party Literature. No individual ought to get rich on it, and it ought not to be an individual affair. Down with non-party writers. Down with the literary super-

* Thomas Edward Shaw, "Lawrence of Arabia" (1888–1935), British soldier, archaeologist, and writer.

man. No more hypocritical talk about individual freedom! If the proletariat is free, the individual will be free, but not otherwise."

Words are confusing, and Nazi and Communist use different words just as they make different shapes with their hands. But this must not mislead us from realizing that neither of them has any use for the Ivory Tower. They deny to the individual the right to escape from the community of which he forms part. He cannot, of course, withdraw from it in the body, and they try to communize his mind also; and since the mind is the source both of creative art and of personal religion, and often functions best in solitude, both Nazi and Communist encounter trouble. The fight extends much deeper than political slogans, into the double nature of man.

III

Now the issue gets confused at this point by a sloppy and misleading use of the word "life." Escapism, we are told, is a retreat from life, a denial of life, a spiritual suicide. I read the other day in a left-wing paper that "Art should be an expression of life in all its aspects, not a means of escape from life."

This sounded convincing. But when I considered it carefully I realized that, while the first half of the sentence meant something, the second half was meaningless. For how can a living being escape from life, whether he's an artist or anyone else? Death is the only escape from life, but once dead he produces no art. Of course we often say a poem's dead, a picture's dead, and there's no harm in using these phrases as long as we know they are metaphorical and do not muddle ourselves. But the human mind is easily muddled, and the slinging about of "life" and "death" in a semi-mystic sense, as was often done by D. H. Lawrence, lands us in infinite confusion.

Marcel Proust is said to have "escaped from life" when he shut himself up all day in a cork-lined room and would not let the sunshine in — sunshine being held, for some mystic reason, to be less unreal than cork; Racine to have escaped when he withdrew from the French court to Port Royal and wrote plays for schoolgirls, one of these plays being *Athalie*; Edward Fitzgerald when he retired into the country and became a valetudinarian. All that is meant is that these people changed one sort of life for another — a busy for an inactive or contemplative. So we must amend that left-wing diction into sense: "Art should be an expression of life in all its aspects, and so should include an escape from what officials call life and artists hold to be officialism."

The idea that escape is, *per se*, wrong, is a bureaucratic idea. It has no basis in either ethics or æsthetics, and it comes to the front only in an age like this, when the community is highly organized and tries to boss the individual at every turn, educating him, taking his finger-prints, paying him if he produces children, punishing him if he doesn't vote at its precious elections, refusing him a passport if he hasn't been a good boy or is not accompanied by a good girl, controlling him at birth, death, work, and play. Run on such lines as these, a community runs easily, but if in this bureaucrat's paradise an individual sidesteps, there's instantly a jam, the traffic's held up, and the Five-Year Plan, or whatever it is, is retarded, no one knows for how long. An escape from the machine causes so much inconvenience to the operator that it is condemned as an escape from life, and the offender is accused of committing some spiritual crime. The offender may be merely a wastrel, but he may be a great artist, like Milton or Proust, who works best in solitude, and he may be and often is a quiet ordinary person who has to withdraw into his little fortress and build up a small private universe before he can see where he stands.

Of course the bureaucrat is neither a villain nor a fool. His trouble is everyone's trouble — the twofold nature of man, that gregarious animal who sometimes wants to be alone and is not necessarily sick when he mopes. If man could be split into two halves, the bureaucrat's problem would be simple: one half would render unto Cæsar what is Cæsar's, and, as part of a herd, consent to be organized into a community. And the other half would render unto God what is God's, and retire into that sanctum where religion and contemplation and the creative force all have their home, and where the individual, according to his capacity, constructs his private universe. There would be no friction between the two halves then.

Christ, out of touch with the complexities of civilization, evidently thought such a division possible, but man does not seem to be made like that. He is not in two halves, he is twofold, and hitherto all attempts to harmonize the civilization produced by the convoluted creature have failed. There was a great attempt in the Middle Ages. The theory of the Mediæval World State was evolved, according to which the Emperor, as representing Cæsar, was to rule men's bodies, and the Pope, as representing God, their souls. The theory broke down, much to the bewilderment of Dante, and the Emperor and the Pope fought.

And we, in our trouble today, again look for a division which will render unto the community what is the community's, and to the self what is the self's. We have not found it, and the New Jerusalem cannot be built until we do. When the public and the private can be combined, and place can be found in the industrial and political landscapes for those symbols of personal retreat, Ivory Towers, the foundations of a New Humanity will have been laid.

IV

WE retreat from the terrors and the boredom of the world. Here are the two chief reasons for escapism. We may retire to our towers because we are afraid, or we may retire because we're bored and indignant.

Though it's never safe to generalize, fear seems wholly bad. One's in a bad state while it's on – stupid, wretched, unreasonable, undignified, and moaning, "Oh, oh, what will become of me!" Like other people, I am sometimes in a terror over the state of Europe. "Oh, oh, what will become of me if there is a war!" I think, and remain like that until I can switch off, like someone who has got stuck on to an electric current. While in that plight, I am of no use either to myself or to Europe, or to anyone or anything. Presently the current's switched off and I go rather sheepishly on with my job, feeling that I've wasted some strength and some time.

Certainly fear is worse than no use. For while we are under its power we behave so badly to other people. We become heartless and cruel. We strike lest the other fellow strike first. Most of the misery of mankind, both in their political and social relations, arises from fear – it has done more harm than even greed. It breeds not only cowards but bullies, and between them they drag down civilization.

If, then, fear is the motive for our retreat, there's little to be said for the Ivory Tower, and little peace to be found inside it. We shut ourselves up there, trembling, doing nothing, afraid to face danger, and waiting from moment to moment for the blow that'll shatter our fragile fortress. This is escapism in the bad sense and deserves all the hard things that can be said against it. There's no release through it, and no creation.

But there's another motive for retreat: boredom; disgust; indignation against the herd, the community, and the world; the conviction that sometimes comes to the solitary individual that his solitude will give him something finer and greater than he can get when he merges in the multitude. This is how Wordsworth puts it.

> The world is too much with us; late and soon,
> Getting and spending, we lay waste our powers;
> Little we see in Nature that is ours;
> We have given our hearts away. . . .*

* This quotation and the next are from Wordsworth's well-known sonnet, "The World Is Too Much with Us."

This is the sound argument for escape. Wordsworth retreats, in his case from the world of commercial competition, because it blinds him to the loveliness which he believes to exist in natural scenes, and because he has wasted on it something which it cannot value – namely, his heart. He retreats to the world of a vanished mythology, which is gone as a creed, but relives because he brings it passion.

> . . . Great God! I'd rather be
> A Pagan suckled in a creed outworn;
> So might I, standing on this pleasant lea,
> Have glimpses that would make me less forlorn;
> Have sight of Proteus rising from the sea;
> Or hear old Triton blow his wreathèd horn.

"So might he"? But so he does, and so do we. We do have sight of Proteus and Triton, thanks to Wordsworth's imagination. He finds them because he has retreated from vulgarity and boredom to his tower. If he had begun the sonnet "The world is terrifying," he would have weakened the emotion as well as impaired the poetry. A frightened Wordsworth would not have caught sight of the sea gods, but they may well reveal themselves to an indignant one. He and his readers have chosen the legitimate path of retreat.

The mystics are still more uncompromising. They believe that retreat is imperative and our sole duty. "Let us flee to the Beloved Fatherland," counsels Plotinus, defining the Fatherland as "There, whence we have come, and There is the Father," and we get there not by moving our feet from land to land, but by "refusing to see"; we withdraw into ourselves and strain our sight until we catch a glimpse of the inner vision, which is the human birthright. That is to say, Plotinus believes not only that the individual is more real than the community, but that it is absolute reality. The motive of his flight, however, is the same as Wordsworth's: indignation and disgust, not fear.

Granting that there is this good motive for escape, what uses can be made of the Ivory Tower in 1938?

Practical conduct can be learned only by contacts with our fellow men, but when it comes to mysticism, to abstract thought, and to the detailed contemplation of events, we certainly need solitude. Mysticism is out of favor for the moment, and abstract thought is not much approved either. But the detached contemplation of events is the aim of every public-minded person. We all want to know what civilization is doing, what it is developing into, whether the present economic system will hold, whether the discovery of flying will transform the world abruptly or gradually, and so on. But in daily life we are so involved in these things that we cannot focus them properly. We desire to withdraw and behave as if they don't concern us, and then we have a better chance of seeing what they are up to.

Then as to literature. I don't want to overstate a case. Some writers — like Milton, or Matthew Arnold, or Proust, or Henry James, or Siegfried Sassoon — convey the impression that they have had to escape from the world before they could describe it. They have shut themselves up in the spirit, and perhaps in the body too. So that one is tempted to say that until a writer escapes he cannot create. That is probably true of meditative and analytical writing. But there is some writing that reads as if it had been composed in the midst of the hum of affairs — Chaucer's *Canterbury Tales,* and a good deal of Shakespeare. Chaucer and Shakespeare throb with the power that comes not from contemplation but from moving freely among men. Fielding's *Tom Jones* is another example of this, and an interesting one, because Fielding tries both methods. Most of his novel has the hum of affairs about it, but at the beginning of each book he has a philosophic chapter where he retires into himself and attempts to meditate. These prefatory chapters make detestable reading — horrid little leathern receptacles that lead nowhere and keep us away from the gayety, bustle, and decent carnality which make up the rest of the novel. Who wants to read what Fielding thinks about Avarice or the Stage when he can hear how Molly Seagrim fought in the churchyard and sent all the other trollops flying over the tombstones? Here's where Fielding's good, and he can also give us the gentleness and the spirit of Sophia Western. But he can't reflect, because he has a non-reflective mind. His place is in a west-country pub, amongst tankards of ale and an occasional bloody nose, not in a tower, where he just becomes a bore.

V

THE more one reads, the less one can generalize on the creative impulse. It is obvious that Fielding and to a large extent Chaucer and Shakespeare were not escapists, and did not shut out the world when they composed, either consciously or unconsciously. And it is obvious that Marcus Aurelius, Wordsworth, Shelley, Proust, did shut it out. They dealt with contemporary problems, but they saw them through a veil of detachment. All one can do is to indicate two classes of writers, extroverts and introverts, and to say that the former seldom enter their towers, and write badly when they do, whereas the latter write best in their towers.

One cannot generalize over readers either, so I will just indicate my own experience. I find that when I'm reading for information I'm *not* in a tower: I keep in touch with the outside world and connect what I'm reading with what I know of it. If I read about China, I think of what I know of China. If, on the other hand, I'm reading creative literature, I *am* in a tower, shut up with the author, and only aware of him.

> In Xanadu did Kubla Khan
> A stately pleasure-dome decree.*

These words don't make me think about China. All that I'm conscious of is Coleridge's vision. I have escaped with him from the outside world. And if my experience is usual it follows that for the reader, as for the writer, literature is sometimes a retreat, sometimes not. Are you shut off from the world or not when you read? Can you hear the dinner bell? Can you hear the telephone? These questions are worth putting, for there are various degrees of absorption. The most extreme was that of Archimedes, who was so absorbed in a problem that he refused to answer the questions put to him by a Roman soldier, and got killed.

There is, by the way, one obvious criticism that must be answered, and it is "Oh, how selfish! The writer or reader who shuts himself up is a traitor to the community." To which the reply is: "Quite true. But it is equally true that the community is selfish, and, to further its own efficiency, is a traitor to the side of human nature which expresses itself in solitude. Considering all the harm the community does today, it is in no position to start a moral slanging match." And we can also reply that the individual can be selfish in two ways, and that if he is selfish in the good way he wins a little victory not only for himself but for other individuals all over the world. It is a bad selfishness to cry, "Oh dear, what will happen to me if there is war or if my investments go wrong!" It is a good selfishness to cry, "Great God! I'd rather be a Pagan suckled in a creed outworn," because the escape here is into poetry, and blazes a path which others can follow.

Let me recall, in conclusion, the career of Milton. Milton is anything but a perfect character. Prim and bitter, one would never choose him for a friend. But he did perform the great feat of coming out of his tower and going back into it again, and performed it with a fullness that makes him an example for our race. Milton wobbled; and it is in

* The opening lines of Samuel Taylor Coleridge's "Kubla Khan; or, A Vision in a Dream."

wobbling that the chief duty of man consists. We are here on earth not to save ourselves and not to save the community, but to try to save both.

QUESTIONS

1. In Paragraph 2, Section I, Forster asks a series of rhetorical questions. What specific answers does he give to each of these questions? What special purpose does Forster have, as an Englishman writing in the year 1938, for considering these questions?

2. In Paragraph 4, Section I, Forster says that man possesses both the " herd instinct " and the " instinct for solitude." How is the development of this generalization on human nature related to Paragraph 1, Section II?

3. In Section II, Forster cites Hitler and Lenin as working in the interests of the herd and being against those of the individual. What sort of appeal to the reader's sympathy for the author's point of view do these allusions provide? How do these allusions help Forster to achieve his objective?

4. What attitude toward the bureaucratically organized community is expressed in Paragraph 4, Section III? How does Forster arouse in the reader an unfavorable response to the " bureaucrat's paradise "?

5. How does Forster distinguish between the motives that lie behind man's desire to escape? What is the function of this distinction in Section IV?

6. How does Forster's recollection of the career of Milton in the final paragraph of the essay help him to achieve the principal purpose of the essay?

W. T. STACE has had two careers, one in the British Civil Service in Ceylon (1910–1932) and another as a professor in philosophy at Princeton University (retired in June, 1955). Professor Stace was born in London and was educated in England, Scotland, and Ireland. Among the many books on philosophical subjects which he has written, the titles mentioned here suggest the broad scope of his inquiring mind: *Critical History of Greek Philosophy* (1920), *Philosophy of Hegel* (1924), *Meaning of Beauty* (1929), *Theory of Knowledge and Existence* (1932), *The Destiny of Western Man* (1942), and *Time and Eternity* (1952).

THE SNOBBISHNESS OF THE LEARNED

by W. T. STACE

THERE is a story told of a very well known living writer who produced a popular book on a branch of modern science – one of the best books of its kind now in print. He is said to have submitted his manuscript for criticism to a fellow expert, who, having read it, tossed it back contemptuously, saying, "You understand thoroughly the subject on which you are writing, and I have no adverse criticisms to offer. But why do you waste your time writing stuff of this sort?"

The story is quite possibly apocryphal. But that such a story can be passed round, and gain credence, illustrates very forcibly the fact that there is among learned men a widespread tendency to look down upon popular writing as something not worthy of their serious consideration, as something to be despised and discouraged.

On the face of it, this would seem to be an extraordinary attitude. That the discoveries made by men of science and the world conceptions of philosophers should be made as widely known as possible would be, one might expect, their especial desire. And how else can this be done, if not by translating their thought from the technical jargon in which it is apt to be expressed into plain English which the world can understand? How else can it be done, in fact, if not by the labors of the popular writer? It would seem obvious that the widespread dissemination of knowledge already attained is of at least equal importance with the discovery of new knowledge. For what, in the end, is the value of knowledge? His acquisition of knowledge is, to the expert, often an end in itself. He may be uninterested in its subsequent influence on the world. And it is quite right, and even necessary, that there should be men who take this point of view. The advance of knowledge mostly depends upon such men. But the matter, after all, cannot end there. To many others, discovery is of value because of the practical benefits which it confers upon mankind, as when pure science is applied to the extermination of disease or the invention of useful implements. But I would suggest that the supreme value of knowledge lies, not in the thrill which its discovery gives to the small band of experts, nor even in its practical usefulness, but in the enlargement and ennoblement of the human mind in general of which it is the cause.

Of the human mind *in general.* That means the minds, not of a few experts, but of the multitudes of civilized humanity. This has certainly been the case with the greatest discoveries of science. They have revolutionized human conceptions of the universe, given men at large a vaster sweep of mind; and it is this which has constituted their chief importance. The greatness of the Copernican hypothesis lay neither in its purely theoretical value for the scientist nor in the better application of astronomy to navigation or other practical affairs to which it may have contributed, but in the fact that it gave to mankind some conception of the immensity of the universe in which we live, and that it destroyed forever the petty views, the insolence, the self-conceit inevitably connected with the belief that the whole creation exists for, and revolves around, man.

This is why the Copernican theory constituted a revolution in human thought. This is why it is so vastly more important than, shall we say, the discovery of a new variety of ant, or of a new theorem in mathematics. Exactly similar remarks might be made about the theory of evolution. That too obtains its importance neither from its theoretical nor from its immediately practical bearings, but from its influence upon man's general conceptions of the world.

Thus what makes the difference between an important and a trivial scientific or philosophical discovery is precisely the influence which it exerts upon mankind in general, not upon the minds of a few learned men. And that is why, in philosophy, however interesting such a subject as symbolic logic may be to a few experts, it sinks into triviality beside the world conceptions of a Plato or a Kant. It is in itself a mere intellectual plaything, nothing of real importance, though it may become of importance if it can be applied to the solution of the great problems of philosophy. And it will be noted that it is precisely this trivial kind of subject which *cannot* be popularized.

In truth it matters little what the doctors of science or the doctors of philosophy think, believe, or say among themselves in their cloisters. What humanity thinks and believes — that is what matters. And the true function of the cloistered few is precisely to be the intellectual leaders of humanity and to guide the thought of mankind to higher levels. This function can only be carried out if *someone,* either they themselves or others, will translate their thought from technical language into the language of the market place. The best and the ablest discoverers and thinkers often possess both the ability and the desire to do this themselves. (It is worth noting that Einstein is the author of a *popular* book on relativity.) Or if their talents are not of the kind required for successful popular writing, it can be done by men who make a special business of spreading broadcast the best knowledge of their age. This type of popularizer is the liaison officer between the world's thinkers and mankind at large. Thus it appears that the function of the popular writer is profoundly important and responsible.

It is related that the soul of a dead man was conducted by Saint Peter on a tour of inspection of the Heavenly City. After seeing all the marvelous glories of the Lord, and the millions of white-clad worshiping souls, he was shown by his guide a little curtained-off enclosure in which half a dozen people were praying, cut off from all the rest of the multitude. These, he was told, were the Plymouth Brethren, who believed themselves to be the only people in Heaven. Those experts who look down upon the popularization, and who would, if they could, make all knowledge the exclusive property of a little coterie of intellectuals, show a spirit identical with that of the poor souls in the story.

But, it will be said, much, if not most, of what learned men think and discover *cannot* be made intelligible to the masses. This is, on the whole, untrue. The big conceptions, the important results of science and philosophy, *can* be communicated to the layman. What cannot be communicated is, as a rule, the detailed processes of discovery and argumentation which have led to those results. Every educated person now understands the main conceptions involved in the Copernican and Darwinian hypotheses, although the proofs and details may be a sealed book to the majority.

In a tube of antityphoid serum there are so many millions of dead bacteria. The methods by which the number is counted or calculated may remain a mystery to the layman. But the fact that there *are* these many can be understood by a child. The same principle holds true even in those sciences which seem to most of us too hopelessly mathematical. The *results* reached can usually be disentangled from their mathematical formulation and set forth by themselves. This is not true, of course, of pure mathematics itself, but only of those physical sciences which use mathematics as a mere instrument to reach their conclusions. And this is, after all, what one would expect. For mathematics is not itself knowledge at all. It is an instrument for obtaining knowledge. The actuary makes use of higher mathematics which no one except the expert can follow. But the resulting knowledge which he obtains is intelligible to everyone. The astronomer uses mathematics to calculate an eclipse, but none is required to understand his final prediction. And it is not fundamentally different with relativity. To think otherwise is like supposing that one cannot appreciate the scenery of Niagara Falls without understanding the mechanism of the railway locomotive which conveys one there.

Mathematics, said a famous writer, is a science of which the meanest intellect is capable. The statement by no means reflects, as one might be inclined to think, the mere partisan prejudice of a one-sided and narrow intelligence. There is a real truth in it.

It is obviously false if it is understood to mean that a stupid man can be a good mathematician. For plainly it is only a very clever man indeed who can be first-class in this, as in any other, subject. But his intellect may nevertheless be, and indeed is, mean if he is incapable of doing anything with it except juggling with symbols — however cleverly he may do this. For mathematics, as I said before, is not knowledge, but only an instrument for obtaining knowledge. A Newton or an Einstein uses mathematics to help him to reach out to great and grand conceptions of the Universe. This employment of mathematics as an instrument of general culture is the work of noble, and not of mean, intellects. But in so far as it cares for nothing save its own internal affairs, is without effect upon general culture, is a mere manipulation of symbols for their own sakes, it certainly can be cultivated, and successfully cultivated, by mean minds — that is, by minds which know nothing of, and care nothing for, what is really great in human culture.

It is because mathematics is a *means,* and not an *end,* that a purely mathematical education is a bad education — or, rather, no education at all. For the true purpose of education is to teach men what things in life are genuinely valuable. That is, it is concerned with ends. Therefore education ought not to concentrate upon means. They are a secondary matter. The true order is to learn first what to aim at, and then only what are the instrumentalities by which we may attain our ends. Mathematics, accordingly, should be part of a subsequent technical training. Thus the now old-fashioned preference for a classical — which really meant a humanistic — over a mathematical education, although it may have degenerated into a prejudice or even a pig-headed obscurantism, was originally rooted in a true insight.

The impression that philosophical and scientific ideas cannot be explained in plain language to plain people is also in large measure due to the fact that philosophers and men of science have not, as a rule, the wit to do it. It is due, in plain terms, to the stupidity of the learned men, not to the stupidity of humanity. They lack the mental flexibility and adroitness which are required if they are to come out of their hiding places in the laboratory and the library and make themselves intelligible in the big world of men. They can speak only one language, the language of cast-iron technical formulas. Change the language, take away from them their technical terms and symbols, and they no longer know where they are. They are like those inferior boxers who can only box according to the rules and are nonplused by anyone who disregards them and fights as the light of nature teaches him. They lack too that human sympathy with simple people which is also essential if the teachings of science and philosophy are to be made available to the many. They cannot move with ease in the world of men. And these too are the reasons why erudite men, great figures in their own secluded world, are so often observed to behave like buffaloes in society.

II

THE contemptuous attitude toward popular writing so often affected by learned men is, then, nothing but an unwarranted prejudice. And it may not be uninteresting to inquire into its psychological motivation. May I be allowed to recommend to the reader that, whenever in this human world he finds a totally unreasonable opinion adopted by large bodies of people, he make a practice of looking, not for *reasons,* but for *motives.* He will thus save himself much time which might otherwise be wasted in searching for rationality where none exists.

Why, then, do so many workers in intellectual fields look askance at any attempt to make the results of their labors intelligible to the world at large? It is true that some apparently plausible reasons may be urged. Popular writers tend to develop certain characteristic faults. Cheap cleverness not infrequently mars their writings. And they are apt to slur over difficult and profound conceptions, and to substitute superficialities — because they have not the gift of being both simple and profound at the same time. Thus a writer on Aristotle, who wished to make easy for his readers that philosopher's teleological conception of the cause of motion, wrote that in Aristotle's view " 'tis love, 'tis love that makes the world go round." *

But a moment's thought should be sufficient to convince one that these facts afford no basis whatever for a general contempt of popular writing. Popular writers may often be cheap and shallow. But to entertain a prejudice against popular writing because some popular writers are bad is like condemning all books because of the existence of certain inferior authors.

The real ground for the disfavor in which popular writing is held among experts is to be found elsewhere. It is rooted in class prejudice. The learned think themselves superior to the common herd. They are a priestly caste imbued with the snobbishness that is characteristic of caste systems. Their learning is the mark of their superiority. It must be kept within the limits of their own class. And the means by which this is accomplished consists in a learned language of long words and technical terms. Anyone who translates knowledge from the technical into the popular language is disregarding the rules of caste, and is thus taboo. Technical terms, long words, learned-sounding phrases, are the means by which second-rate intellectuals "inflate their egos" and feed their sense of superiority to the multitude. If an idea can be expressed in two ways, one of which involves a barbarous technical jargon, while the other needs nothing but a few simple words of one syllable which everyone can understand, this kind of person definitely prefers the barbarous technical jargon. He wishes to be thought, and above all to think himself, a person who understands profound and difficult things which common folk cannot comprehend. He wishes to feel himself cleverer than other people. The long words and clumsy phrases with which he encumbers the simplest thought are the badges of his class superiority. And as this kind of person is always in a majority in any large assembly of intellectuals, a definite prejudice against popular writing is engendered.

The poorer a man's intellectual equipment, the more does he revel in technicalities. A man with a wealth of valuable ideas is anxious to communicate those ideas, and will naturally tend to choose for that purpose the simplest language he can find. But a man whose intel-

* Obviously, it is not possible to explain Aristotle's teleological conception of the cause of motion in a short footnote. It may help, however, to know that Aristotle believed that since every motion presupposes a motive principle, one must assume the existence of a first motive force which is itself unmoved. This first motive force he calls The First Cause, or *primum mobile,* which he equates with absolute reality, or God. Since God is the ultimate source of all motion, and since God is also the object of desire, " 'tis love that makes the world go round." The serious student will find a more satisfactory explanation in a good encyclopedia or in a history of philosophy.

lectuality is a sham, and who has in truth nothing to communicate, endeavors to conceal his emptiness by an outward show of learning. The more unintelligible his language, the more profound will he appear to himself and (he hopes) to others. He fails to see that the love of long words and technical terms is in fact nothing but a symptom of his mental infirmity. It is a kind of intellectual disease. And perhaps those who suffer from this disease would like to have a technical term for their own malady. I will therefore make them a present of a new long word. I will christen their disease *macronomatamania.*

III

IT IS true that a few really great men, such as Immanuel Kant, have seemed to revel unnecessarily in technicalities. But let not all the macronomatamaniacs of the world attempt to shelter themselves under Kant's umbrella. Kant was great in spite of his obscure language, not because of it. And one does not become great by aping the weaknesses of a great man.

It is true, too, that technical terms are a necessity. In many branches of knowledge one cannot do without them. This is especially true in science. And it is true (but in a much lesser degree) in philosophy. About their use in science I will say nothing at all. Even regarding their use in philosophy I will not attempt in this place to say *what* their legitimate functions are, nor legislate as to where they should be used and where avoided. For that would be itself a technical inquiry, not suitable to this paper. I will, however, set down what I regard as an elementary first principle of a good style in philosophical writing. It is this: *Never use a technical term when a simple nontechnical word or phrase will equally well express your meaning.* And I would add as a gloss: *Cultivate in yourself a dislike and suspicion of all learned-sounding words and technical terms, a habit of regarding them not as fine things, but at best as necessary evils.* This will come easily to anyone naturally endowed with a hatred of humbug, and also to anyone with an artistic sense of the beauty and value of words; and the result of it will be that, whenever a technical term springs to the writer's mind, he will instinctively cast about to see whether he cannot replace it by plain English. Sometimes it will happen that he cannot do so without prejudice to his meaning. But often it will happen that he can.

I think that these principles should be applied, not only to popular writing in the usual sense, but to *all* philosophical writing of whatever sort, even that which is written by experts for experts. For the use of a good style and of plain decent English will always facilitate the communication of meaning, to whomsoever it is addressed. And if anyone asks for an example of a good philosophical style, of the kind I have in mind, I would point to the writings of Mr. Bertrand Russell as showing the best philosophical style of the present day. Mr. Russell, of course, uses technical terms, plenty of them; but never, I think, where they could reasonably have been avoided.

A technical term as such is, anywhere and everywhere, a barbarism, an eyesore, an offense to the soul, a thing to be shuddered at and avoided. Macronomatamaniacs, therefore, are not only to be suspected of emptiness, but also to be accused of lack of taste. When a man uses a hideous jumble of technical terms where he could use plain English words, he writes himself down as a person without the sense of the beauty and dignity of language.

After all, the issue is a simple one. Do you wish to communicate thought? Or are you impelled by some other motive — to appear clever, to boost yourself up as a highbrow, to impress the simple-minded with your superiority, or what not? If you write an article or a book, your sole motive *ought* to be to communicate what you conceive to be truth to as many people as possible. If a writer is governed by this motive, it is inevitable that he will express himself in the simplest language which he can possibly find. And if, in addition to this sincerity, he has also some sense of the beauty of language, he will choose short, sharp, simple, expressive words in preference to long, uncouth, and clumsy ones. He will not, for example, write "ratiocination" when all he means is "reasoning," nor "dianoetic" when the word "intellectual" would do just as well.

Unfortunately, however, to communicate ideas is by no means the most usual motive for writing books. And if a man writes because he thinks himself a superior person, and wishes to impose this same delusion upon other people, he tends to make his style as obscure and difficult as possible. He hopes that his obscurity will be mistaken for profundity. He will write, if he can, in a learned language instead of a simple one. He will prefer big words to little ones, and a barbarous technical jargon to plain English. And the American custom of forcing university professors to "produce" (that is, to write books), and of practically making their promotion in their profession depend upon their doing so, is responsible for no little evil in this matter. Not only does it result in the publication of floods of inferior books, which the world would be much better without; not only does it compel men who have no taste for writing, and no gift for it, to waste their time writing bad books when, if left alone, they might have made admirable and even great teachers; but it also demoralizes style, and develops macronomatamaniacs. For the man who has nothing to say worthy of publication is encouraged, almost compelled, to conceal his lack under a smoke screen of technicalities and obscure verbiage. He has to convince his university superiors of his intellectuality; and since he cannot do this by the inner worth of his thought, he must do it by putting out a spurious and pretentious conglomeration of learned-sounding words.

How easily this succeeds, how easily the world (including the learned world) is gulled by long words, the following incident may serve to illustrate. Years ago, in a certain university, there flourished a "Philosophical Society," in which the tendency to read papers couched in obscure and unintelligible language became rampant. A brilliant Irishman, wishing to prick the bubble, read before the society a paper called "The Spirit of the Age." In this paper there was not a single paragraph, not a single sentence even, which possessed, or was intended by the author to possess, the faintest glimmer of meaning. It was full of long words, of loud-mouthed phrases, of swelling periods. It *sounded* magnificent; it *meant* nothing. The society listened to it in rapt attention. Not one of the members perceived that the society was being fooled; and a long and learned discussion followed, in which not one of the members admitted that he had not understood the paper.

A man may write whole books of what is either totally meaningless or palpably false, and may secure by doing so a wide reputation, provided only that he uses long enough words. For example, the thought that there is no such thing as thought is self-contradictory nonsense. But if a man wraps up this same nonsense in a learned-sounding hocus-pocus about reflex arcs and conditioned reflexes, if he talks enough about neurons and the neural processes, and if he interlards his whole discourse with the technical terms of physiology, he may become the founder of a school of psychology, and stands a good chance of earning an enormous salary.

IV

BUT to come back to popular writing and its place in the world of learning. I would contend for two positions. First, the works of the pure popularizer — the man who has nothing of his own to say, but who popularizes other people's thoughts — is of the utmost importance. So far from being despised, he ought to be regarded as performing an absolutely vital function in the intellectual progress of mankind. And it is perfectly possible for him to be popular without being either shallow or cheap. Secondly, I would urge that, in a sense, *all* writing, even of the most original, learned, and abstruse kinds, should aim at being popular *as far as possible.* That such writing can always be made entirely suitable for the general reader is not for a moment contended. But the writer can at least aim at using technical terms as sparingly as possible, at avoiding unnecessary jargon, at expressing himself as simply and clearly as he can – even as beautifully as the nature of his subject permits. He can surely avoid giving the reader the feeling that he positively likes ugly words, that he revels in unintelligibilities, that he dotes on gibberish. Most readers will be grateful to him if they feel that he is at least trying to make some meaning clear to them, and not merely to stun, intimidate, and befuddle them with his cleverness. His writing will be popular in the only sense – and in the best sense – in which this can be demanded of him.

Nearly all the great philosophers of the English tradition have been in this sense popular writers, though I am afraid that the same cannot be said of the Germans. The style of Locke is lucid, if pedestrian; of both Berkeley and Hume beautiful in the extreme; of Mill clear and simple, though undistinguished and marred by some affectations; of Spencer perfectly lucid in spite of the "hurdy-gurdy monotony of him." William James, the greatest of American philosophers, had an absolute genius for graphic, telling, and brilliant English phrases. And of living writers, as I have already said, Mr. Russell's style is the best, and is a standing example of the fact that philosophy, and original philosophy too, can be written in plain English with an absolute minimum of technical terms.

QUESTIONS

1. Identify the three distinct answers which Stace gives to his own question in the third paragraph of Section I, "For what, in the end, is the value of knowledge?" Why are these answers listed in the particular order in which they occur?

2. According to Stace, what constitutes the chief importance of great scientific discoveries? Why does he mention the Copernican theory?

3. What does the author say is the function of the popular writer? What can the popular writer do successfully? What can he not do successfully? Why does Stace emphasize the limitations of the popular writer's powers?

4. How does the extensive discussion of mathematics in Section I (the four paragraphs beginning on page 96 with "In a tube of antityphoid . . .") relate to the major design of the essay?

5. What motives does Stace attribute to the learned men who are contemptuous of popular writing? Clearly, Stace intends the reader to respond unsympathetically to these learned men. How does his use of language in Section II contribute to this intention?

6. What relationship between language and intellect does Stace stress in the last paragraph of Section II? What sort of response does he intend his use of the word *macronomatamania* (the last word in Section II) to arouse in the reader?

7. In referring to the elementary first principle of a good style in philosophical writing (Paragraph 2, Section III), Stace says, "This will come easily to anyone naturally endowed with a hatred of humbug, and also to anyone with an artistic sense of the beauty and value of words; and the result of it will be that, whenever a technical term springs to the writer's mind, he will instinctively cast about to see whether he cannot replace it by plain English." Study closely the words and phrases of this sentence and point out the effect which they are designed to have on the reader. Why does Stace strive to create such an effect?

8. Identify the author's two main contentions in the concluding section of the essay. Relate the purpose of each previous section to the contentions of the conclusion.

GEORGE F. WHICHER received his A.B. from Amherst College and his A.M. and Ph.D. from Columbia University. From 1915 until his death in 1954 he taught English and American literature at Amherst. He edited many texts, wrote numerous scholarly articles and reviews, and was the author of a life of Emily Dickinson, *This Was a Poet* (1938). He also wrote *Walden Revisited* (1945) and *The Goliard Poets* (1948). Robert Frost's long association with the Amherst faculty gave Professor Whicher the opportunity for a lifelong friendship with the poet. In the following essay he gives us his friendly interpretation of the American poet on the occasion of the publication of a new selection from his poems, *Come In, and Other Poems* (1943), edited by Louis Untermeyer.

OUT FOR STARS

A Meditation on Robert Frost

by GEORGE F. WHICHER

STREAMLINING is one of the most popular fallacies of our time. If you apply streamlining to poetry the argument runs about as follows: Since the chief aim of poetry is to bring about a formal ordering or integration of the feelings, communication cannot be its main purpose. Consequently poetry that eliminates communication is purer, and hence better, than poetry that admits a "message." The poem should not attempt to rival the scientific textbook; or as Archibald MacLeish has so incisively put it, "A poem should not mean but be."

With the modernist poet's fastidious avoidance of meaning (once he has stated his *ars poetica*), it is instructive to compare the practice of a great poet like Dante, who seems curiously unaware of how much he might have improved his *Commedia* if he had not sought to use it as an instrument of communication. Instead of reducing the element of meaning to the lowest possible terms, Dante appears almost avid to multiply meanings, to double and redouble the implications of his thought. Can it be that disdain of meaning is a symptom of the poverty of poetry in a time of failing convictions?

A renewed perception of the many levels of implication beneath the innocent-looking surfaces of Robert Frost's poems reminded me recently of the manifold harmonies of Dante's great poetic instrument.

Reading again in Mr. Untermeyer's expert selection, *Come In,* the lyric that so happily lends its title to the book, I became aware that the words of the poem were opening vistas in several directions, as from one spot in the forest the eye may fancy that it discerns colonnaded aisles leading off ahead, behind, and on either hand.

Particularly in the last two stanzas I thought I could detect an effect like "underpainting," layer upon layer, beneath the plain intent of the words: —

> Far in the pillared dark
> Thrush music went —
> Almost like a call to come in
> To the dark and lament.
>
> But no, I was out for stars:
> I would not come in.
> I meant not even if asked,
> And I hadn't been.

Here is a poem which, though it does not shirk the obligation of lucid statement, is not exhausted when its surface meaning has been communicated. Instead the simplicity and clearness of the incident recorded leave the reader unimpeded by verbal perplexities, not to turn away satisfied unless he is a singularly obtuse reader, but to look further into these limpid depths and perceive what he can, whether of cloudy reflections of his own mind or of ultimate intentions lurking in the poet's.

After the labor of assimilating to our being much poetry that aims not to mean but to be, the pleasure of encountering a poem that actually conveys a well-defined reading of experience is enormous.

Taken literally, the lines I have quoted record a very ordinary incident of a walk at twilight. A man with an eye for the first stars is distracted momentarily by the poignant beauty of the thrush's song, but he refuses to follow its lure into the darkening woods or to accept its mood of lamentation. The laconic last two lines confirm the New England setting of the poem.

Indeed the intonations are so characteristic that they can hardly fail to recall to the many persons who have listened to Robert Frost's remarkable readings from his poems the voice of the poet himself. Every other part of the poem is equally authentic. Much that Frost has written attests his intimate acquaintance with country things: he can be trusted to select the moment of the day when the wood-thrush's song sounds clearest. His reference to stars is no casual literary gesture, but a tribute to a lifelong passion for astronomy, amply confirmed in other poems.

Not only the person speaking, but the setting of the poem is utterly true to life. It might be any one of the New Hampshire or Vermont farms where Frost has lived, since he has seldom lodged far from the edge of the woods and the companionship of trees. I do not know where this poem was written, nor what landscape was present to the writer's mind, but to me it seems to fit perfectly the region of Ripton, Vermont, where he has latterly spent his summers.

The dark woods might be the half-mile stretch of state forest, largely pine, between his cottage on the Homer Noble place and "Iry" Dow's, the home-place of his current venture in farming. To get from one property to the other by road is a matter of several miles, and it is natural, therefore, to cut through the woods. But if one were going nowhere in particular it would be easy to refuse the walk beneath the trees for a climb to upland pastures, whence as from a shelf hung high on the slope of the Green Mountains one may look off westward across a narrow strip of Lake Champlain to tumbled Adirondack masses on the rim of the world and above them the evening star.

Ripton is typical "Frost country," though the bulk of his writing was done before he came to live in this neighborhood. It reached the height of its prosperity about the time of the Civil War. The mounting tide of human settlement then flowed up to the higher clearings; since then it has mostly receded, leaving behind a sparse population on "marginal" land and many cellar holes. Among the people are some whom Frost might name along with the best he has encountered anywhere in rural New England. Others are not to be clearly distinguished from the oddments on any beach at low tide.

There was "Iry" Dow, for example, now departed, who for upwards of forty years professed to make his living as a blacksmith, though prevented by a weak heart from making any strenuous exertions. Consequently a great deal of conversation flowed between blows on the anvil. "That Iry Dow," said one irritated customer, "is as much slower 'n stock-still 's stock-still is slower 'n greased lightnin'." The year before he died the village elected him to the legislature so that he might continue his endless talk without the bother of now and then pretending to beat on a horseshoe. Nothing that Frost found among these people would have suggested any need of revising what he had previously written of other little towns north of Boston.

The surrounding country, dominated by the ridge of the mountains, once partly settled, then unsettled again, is full of the wild things, both animals and plants, that the poet has so often observed and described. A great lover of woodlands and Morgan horses, the late Joseph Battell, once possessed much of Ripton, and his will is still reflected in the quantity of standing timber. So bold and numerous are the deer that vegetable gardens need the protection of an electrically charged wire. Overgrown roads follow the brooks and lead to abandoned mowings high on the ridges.

II

In one respect, however, Ripton is peculiar. It contains Bread Loaf, the summer school of English which Frost helped to found some twenty-five years ago and which he still benevolently frequents. Frost, in fact, would not be fully himself unless there were an educational project somewhere in the offing for him to cherish and humorously despair of, for he is a born teacher with a knack of charging dry subjects with intellectual excitement and a large patience for struggling learners.

Teaching to him is a natural extension of his unfeigned interest in people. I have seen him ask friendly, insistent questions about the little country town where a man was born and brought up, and have watched the man, at first answering with diffidence because for years he had been apologetic about his simple beginnings and anxious to live them down, gradually warm to his memories, discover a fresh respect for the sources of his being, and go out from the interview (as he said later) with a new dimension added to his personality. I doubt if Frost knew how much that conversation meant to the other man. He was just expressing an interest in the ways of little towns.

It is against the background of Ripton, then, that I picture Frost hearing thrush music, as it is there that I recall him in many other postures: a stocky figure but alert in motion, wearing an old suit and scuffed shoes, a freshly laundered soft shirt open at his throat, his white hair tousled in the wind, his seafarer's blue eyes twinkling. One would find him skirting a mowing field, crossing a stone wall to a pasture where blueberries grew, measuring the water in the spring, or playing softball with younger friends on a diamond wrung from the hayfield, where running for a fly was an adventure. Then would come hours of such converse as I never expect to repeat.

For me the poem I have quoted is inseparably bound up with these personal memories of the man and the region. But for anyone, even for anyone ages hence, it is marked with authentic traits of individuality, images to the ear and to the eye, that distinguish it from conventionalized writing just as readily as a portrait can be told from an idealized face when archaeologists study the sculptures found in the buried cities of Yucatan.

In the first instance, then, the poem is justified by its absolute integrity of substance. Whatever it speaks of is something that the poet has absorbed completely into himself, generally by seeing it, hearing it, living through it; less frequently by imaginative reading. But though the poem may appear simple and complete on the literal level, its texture may be dense with implied cross-references. In such poetry it is not inappropriate to look for undermeanings, at one's own risk, of course. The meanings may be all in the reader's eye, or again they may attain to a certain significance if they are confirmed by what the poet has elsewhere written.

III

FROST himself may be held responsible if readers persist in looking in his poems for more meaning than meets the casual eye. Though he denies a didactic intent, he is not unwilling to have his poetic records of experience flower in explicit apothegm. Only there is seldom or never any indication of his writing for the sake of the moral. In that respect he differs completely from makers of fables. La Fontaine, as Mr. Untermeyer claims, might conceivably have shaped the substance of Frost's "At Woodward's Gardens" into an apologue entitled "The Boy, the Monkeys, and the Burning-Glass," ending with the epigram: —

It's knowing what to do with things that counts.

But Frost's first instinct is to make sure of the reality of his material; nine-tenths of his poem is painstakingly devoted to picturing his monkeys, not as actors in a fable, but as actual monkeys. He calls our attention to their "purple little knuckles," and condenses all the confusion of the simian brain into one delicious line: —

They bit the glass and listened for the flavor.

Not until that has been fully done does he turn to the moral as a means of rounding the poem. To call such a piece of writing a fable, as at least two good critics have recently chosen to do, is to label it as something less than it actually is.

Except where Frost has completed his poem by attaching an abstract meaning to it — not necessarily a statement of the poem's whole meaning — he is entitled to insist that his intention has been to present, not the symbol of a thought, but an image of an experience. To this there is only one answer: that experience as Frost absorbs and interprets it often spreads out into so many ramifications that thoughts get tangled in it like stars seen through tree branches.

To consider now more searchingly the stanzas that I have quoted about the thrush, would it not be possible to read the episode as a literary parable? A poet of our time hears a birdlike voice from the dark wood (ancient symbol of error) singing of irremediable ills. The call to "come in to the dark and lament" awakens an impulse to become a modernist poet of the decadent school, to take the veil (or, as Frost once put it, "take the blanket") of calculated obscurity and imitate the fashionable lead of the French Symbolistes.* The summons, however sweetly conveyed, can be resisted by a poet who has long considered it inappropriate "to write the Russian novel in America," and who prefers to keep on in the way he was going.

To place this interpretation on the poem (and I do not imply that the poem demands it) is to emphasize Frost's remarkable independence of the contemporary note in letters. Though he has studied the experimental poetry of recent years with attention – and some amusement – he has never felt called to share in any experiments except his own, which have been more far-reaching in their metrical subtlety than many readers realize. Ever since as a young poet barely out of his teens Frost was advised by a New York editor to try to write like Sidney Lanier, he has been set in his determination to write like no one but Robert Frost.

His aloofness has been held against him. It has been asserted that any sensitive spirit of our time must be wounded by the spectacle of the world as it exists, and must respond by exhibiting his mutilations in public. Frost's obvious cultivation of soundness and balance, therefore, has been taken as indicative of a refusal to face the bitter realities that really matter, of his retreat to a protected backwater safe from the storm. This to a man who, unlike many of his critics, has worked in the factory and on the farm, who has known poverty as well as grief, and who has waited twenty years for recognition of his work to overtake him!

If Frost has not been willing to come in to the dark and lament, it has not been because he was unacquainted with the night, but because he had something to do that pleased him better. Perhaps he has felt that the business of putting love in order, of creating form out of

* Influenced by Charles Baudelaire (1821–1867), Arthur Rimbaud (1854–1891), and Paul Verlaine (1844–1896), the symbolist movement reached the height of its importance, in France, between 1870 and 1886. The symbolists attempted to suggest or symbolize basic ideas or emotions in clusters of images and metaphors. Stéphane Mallarmé (1842–1898) was the leading theorist and practitioner of the movement; others were Gustave Kahn (1859–1936), Henri de Régnier (1864–1936), and Jules Laforgue (1860–1887). Yeats, Eliot, and Joyce were strongly influenced by the French symbolist movement.

the formless, can be better done by a poet who declined to be warped by the pressures of modern living. At any rate he has been unwavering in his allegiance to an Emersonian conception of human wholeness.

His deep-seated instinct for centrality and balance brings us back to the poem of the thrush to discover its meaning as ethical symbol. We are not disappointed. What else does the poem portray but one of the familiar dilemmas of man's existence? His walk lies between the two extremes represented by the dark woods and the stars. To the heavenly extreme he can never attain, to the other he is unwilling to let himself descend, but he may be aware of both and may on occasion incline a little one way or the other. That is what our living is, discovering where the extremes lie and where we belong on a sort of scale drawn between them.

There are innumerable such scales in politics, in religion, in education. If we do not complete the scale, we risk falling into the illusion of progress — that is, of supposing that we are drifting inevitably toward a far-off divine event; or we are conscious only of what we have fallen from and invent the myth of original sin. Looking toward one extreme only, we commonly speak of savagery in contrast to civilization. Frost recently made us aware of the other end of the scale when he declared, "The opposite of civilization is Utopia." Thus the scale is completed, and man is put back between the poles — where he belongs.

One result of thinking of the normal human position as somewhere midway between two extremes is to awaken a fierce distrust of extremists and totalitarians, no matter how high-minded they may be. Once we are forced as far as we can go toward either extreme, we are committed, we lose our power to maneuver, we must adopt the party line. Only from a central position can we be said to have the ability to choose that makes life dramatic. Frost would not trade the freedom of his material in the world as he finds it for any number of freedoms in Utopia. What he holds precious is the privilege of meeting the exigencies of life by apt recalls from past experience, with only enough newness to freshen thought.

IV

BUT what if the world's crisis is so desperate as to justify a concerted movement to one extreme or the other in the attempt to alleviate it? Are we always to see life waste away into war, insanity, poverty, and crime and do nothing about it? Here indeed we touch on ultimate values. In an address to Amherst seniors a few years ago Frost declared that the thought of coming to condone the world's sorrow is terrible to contemplate. It is our darkest concern. Yet unless I misread the poem, Frost has indicated the inevitable response of a wise man in the poem we have been discussing. To be resolutely " out for stars " is not to be concerned overmuch with the still, sad music of humanity.

The poet must nerve himself to say with Housman: " Be still, my soul, and see injustice done." It is his function to realize the millennium, not in terms of social adjustments, but either

> right beside you book-like on the shelf,
> Or even better god-like in yourself.

Frost has spoken with deep compassion of the Shelleyan natures who insist on bearing their share, or more than their share, of the world's miseries, but he has not hesitated to proclaim that the call to struggle for society's betterment is " poetry's great antilure." He is not attracted by

> the tenderer-than-thou
> Political collectivistic love
> With which the modern world is being swept.

The poet, in so far as he is a poet, must not be too cognizant of mankind's wounds or his own. His business is not to make humanity whole, but to explore the uses of wholeness. It is naïve to hang the class struggle on his shoulders. In the American tradition one does not have to join the army to be a good citizen.

If anyone still should ask, Why is the function that the poet performs so important that he may seek exemption from duties incumbent on his fellows? the best answer is read once again the lovely stanzas of " Come In " or the new poem that stands as an afterword in the anthology of Frost's writings that Mr. Untermeyer has just compiled. Is it nothing to us that someone should be out for stars? Is it nothing in a universe where every star we can examine seems to be engaged in radiating incredible light and heat — is it nothing in our preoccupation with war and wages and prices, to be reminded of the sense in which a star by its mere existence can " ask a little of us here "?

> It asks of us a certain height,
> So when at times the mob is swayed
> To carry praise or blame too far,
> We may choose something like a star
> To stay our minds on and be staid.

QUESTIONS

1. What attitude toward " modernist poetry " does Whicher reveal in the first two paragraphs of the essay? What connotative differences are there between the words " modernist " and " modern "?

2. Why does Whicher devote the last four paragraphs of Section I and the first three paragraphs of Section II to a detailed description of the " Frost country " around Ripton, Vermont?

3. What, specifically, is Whicher referring to when he says the poem is marked with " authentic traits of individuality, images to the ear and to the eye, that distinguish it from conventionalized writing "?

4. What, according to Whicher, is the function of the poet in our society? Does the analysis of Frost's poem justify Whicher's view?

5. Does Whicher's interpretation of the poem grow exclusively out of the poem? Or has he read things into the poem which are not properly part of the poem itself?

ALFRED GERALD CAPLIN, better known as AL CAPP, displayed his talent as a cartoonist when at the age of eleven he drew and sold comic strips to the children near his home in Bridgeport, Connecticut. Later he studied at the Pennsylvania Academy of Fine Arts, the Philadelphia Museum of Fine Arts, Boston University, and Harvard University. Having served an apprenticeship as a "ghost artist" for other cartoonists, he began the production of *Li'l Abner* in 1934. Some fifteen years later, about five hundred newspapers were publishing the comic strip. A purveyor of ideas and humorous incidents rather than adventure, he has contributed articles to various magazines, has written *The Life and Times of the Schmoo* (1948), and is the author of the article on comic strips in the *Encyclopædia Britannica.*

THE COMEDY OF CHARLIE CHAPLIN

by AL CAPP

IT IS the ambition of every newspaper cartoonist to get published in something that won't be used to wrap fish in the next morning, and so, the other day, I was writing a book. It was a book about comedy. I came to the part about Charlie Chaplin, remembered some of his gags, and wrote about them. Then, when I read what I had written, I stopped, because I was afraid my memory had been playing tricks on me. Was he that good? I had to know. After some nagging, United Artists arranged a screening for me of the only Chaplin film then available in its New York office. It was *City Lights.* It hadn't been out of the can in years.

In the projection room were about a dozen people: United Artists publicity men and executives (whose idea of escape from the drabness of *their* lives is to not go to the movies), two girls, and a Wife. The girls were a couple of cute secretaries who wandered into the projection room to wait wearily, because they had dates with the executives, and the Wife had suddenly turned up, I rather think, because the excuse of her executive husband that he had to stay late at the office because some cartoonist with influence wanted to see a twenty-year-old movie sounded to her like the kind of lie he might whip up to cover up the fact that he had a date with one of the secretaries.

Nobody in that projection room really wanted to be there except me, and I was pretty uncertain myself. Here I was taking the chance that a second look, after all those years, might prove that Chaplin wasn't such a hell of an artist after all.

Then, at the opening shot, everybody began to laugh. And for an hour and a half we all roared and howled and bellowed with delight, until the final scene. This is when the blind girl, no longer blind, realizes that the miserable little tramp to whom she is giving a quarter is the dream knight of her blindness; and when the tramp realizes that the masquerade is over and that she knows him as the ludicrous, flea-bitten thing he is, and when his heart is both overflowing with joy that she can see, and breaking with sadness that she can see *him*.

So shattering was the tragedy of those last few minutes that, when the lights went on, none of us in that projection room dared look at the others. While we'd laughed, we had been delighted to laugh openly and in concert, but suddenly (although all through the masterpiece are forebodings of its final tragedy) our hearts had been touched, and we were embarrassed for our tears, and ashamed to look one another in the face. Because in each face was the thing that men are most ashamed for other men to see, and that is self-pity.

Terrible disasters had happened to Chaplin all through the film – and the more terrible they were, the harder we laughed. For we were laughing at him. And then, because he is the most understanding and exquisite of artists, Chaplin's final tragedy became somehow our tragedy. He entered into us. We felt then all he felt, and the pity in us was no longer pity for a thing apart, because that comes out laughter; it was pity for a thing that great art had made a part of ourselves, and we were all embarrassed – each for the others as well as himself – when the lights went on.

Well, I had taken a second look, and I'd found that I was right the first time, only not right enough.

All comedy is based on man's delight in man's inhumanity to man. I know that is so, because I have made forty million people laugh more or less every day for sixteen years, and this has been the basis of all the comedy I have created. I think it is the basis of all comedy.

But I had forgotten, until I saw Chaplin again, that comedy can become sublime when it makes men sorrow at man's inhumanity to man by making men pity themselves.

When the history of art in our time is written, and when the ideological passions of our time are laughable curios, the great artist that our time has produced will be recognized as Charlie Chaplin.

Just as Shakespeare's *Hamlet* was, at first, regarded as a good job done by a well-known entertainer who had done other good jobs; and was applauded, forgotten, and then looked at again by another generation (whose added respect this entertainer had earned by now being dead), and only then discovered to be a job so very good, indeed, that it was better than any other job ever done — so will Chaplin's *City Lights* take its place among those works of art that men cherish and revere and use as proof that they are not animals, but have in them a touch of divinity, since one of their kind created this.

City Lights was released in 1929. It was a great success, it made a lot of money, everyone saw it — and then it was forgotten. Because, after all, it was merely a movie, and we all know that a work of art can endure only if it is done on canvas or printed on a page, because those are the traditional, respectable materials of art, and a can of film is not.

II

FOR anyone whose profession is to be visual comedy, it is as necessary to study the work of Charlie Chaplin as it is for the engineer to study mathematics. It is a crime that our libraries and schools don't have permanent examples of his work, as they do of the work of Michelangelo and Mozart. They should be available to students not only of visual comedy but of fine arts, sociology, history, ballet, drama and composition, as are all masterworks.

In the Chaplin films you will find thousands of miraculously funny gags (and no matter how much they've been copied, his originals have still a pure, bright freshness). You will find scores of unique characters, each warmly funny because, no matter how wildly they're drawn, they're based on real, instantly recognizable types. You'll find a treasure-trove of hilarious and intricate comedy situations — you'll find everything that comedy is made of. But the most important thing you'll find is this: that for all his dazzling succession of gags, characters, and situations, Charlie Chaplin told again and again, with infinite variation, one story — the story of man's inhumanity to man. And that is a very funny story.

You say you remember the Chaplin pictures and they were all about pie-throwing, cop-being-chased-by, and the horribly efficient machines that fed miserable helpless factory workers automatically, so they wouldn't have to stop using their hands to work? Well, analyze any Chaplin picture, any Chaplin gag. For instance, an old classic called *The Pilgrim*.

The title itself is a comment on the cruel foolishness of a familiar kind of American thinking. With us that word "Pilgrim" has come to exude a certain rich, ripe, aristocratic air. To be descended from "the Pilgrims" means you are, somehow, a better, a realer, a little more than merely 100 per cent American. It means to some people (and you'll find 'em in Congress and on committees to "protect" and "preserve" their own idea of "real" Americanism) that they have a right to be stuffy and irritated about the coming to this country of the ragtag and refuse of Europe and Asia. Some Americans feel that, because they are descended from the Pilgrims, they are our aristocracy, and hence have a right to yammer and complain about other pilgrims.

So Chaplin, who told in his picture the story of a boatload of frightened, starving, sniveling, dirty, depressed D.P.'s of twenty years ago, called the most miserable of 'em all — the character he played — "The Pilgrim" to remind us gently that those who rant and rave against the coming to America of today's D.P.'s are the children of precisely the same kind of D.P.'s of another day. The title itself is a reminder to man that his inhumanity to his fellow man is one of the most ridiculous things about him.

One of the first scenes of this comedy classic is a delicious example of Chaplin's carrying of man's inhumanity to man to its ultimate absurdity — namely, the inhumanity of men *other* men have been inhuman *to*.

The refugees travel steerage of course. They are given one meal a day; one bowl of slops. But not quite one bowl, because at mealtime, while there are *two* rows of refugees seated, facing each other across the table, there is only *one* row of bowls. Which row of refugees gets a chance at the slops depends on which way the boat rolls, because, while the poor starving wretches must remain seated where they are, drooling and clutching their spoons, the slop bowls slither from one side to the other with the crazy rhythm of the boat.

And for twenty years, audiences have been laughing their heads off at this scene.

Why?

It is because we are eternally delighted at the inhumanity of man to man.

First, at the colossal evil of the shipowners who have devised such a simple and satanic scheme to degrade and cheat their most helpless guests. And second, at the crookedness of the helpless themselves, as they, in turn, devise little ways to cheat each other out of a morsel of slops here, a morsel there.

And the fact that countless audiences of normal, decent human beings have screamed with happy, carefree laughter at this almost unbearably heart-rending scene is a further and highly helpful example of real man's inhumanity to cinema man.

III

NEXT to Death, man's greatest fear is Hunger. Yet Chaplin has made us laugh at *his* hunger. In *The Tramp* we first see him a starving bum, looking hungrily into the window of a cheap restaurant, watching a fat man being served a huge steak. The starving, fascinated bum drools.

Now right here is where everybody in the audience begins to grin. Chaplin's starvation gives us a nice, warm feeling. We feel nice and warm because, unlike that poor soul, we know *we're* going to eat after the show. His misery emphasizes our security. And thinking of our security makes us feel good, so we grin. Not starving is a nice thing. And nice things make us grin.

On with the story. The fat man cuts the steak with a flourish and lifts a juicy morsel to his mouth. The fascinated bum unconsciously mimics every move. He's lost in a dream world of steak. The fat man tentatively munches the morsel, the bum munches his dream morsel; he is floating in ecstasy until he sees that the fat man has suddenly stopped munching and is looking indignant. The bum instantly stops munching too, and he looks indignant, although *he* doesn't know what the hell they're both so indignant about. The fat man roars to the waiter that his steak is too rare, and orders him to take it back. The fat man is the second most furious person in the scene. The first most furious is the bum. You see, he was having a wonderful time with that dream steak until the fat man ordered it taken away. The fat man will get his real steak back. The bum won't ever again get his dream steak. His dream has been shattered. And we sit there, watching this pitiful scene, and roar with laughter.

We didn't laugh because we were heartless wretches. We laughed because we are normal human beings, full of self-doubt, full of vague feelings of inferiority, full of a desperate need to be reassured. Somehow that whole scene made us feel superior. First, no matter how badly off any one of us was, we were all in better shape than that bum. The fact that we'd had enough spare cash to buy a ticket to that movie made us superior to him. That was the first thing that made us feel good. Next, we saw him starving. That wasn't going to happen to us — another reason for feeling superior, better off at least than one person.

As the scene continued, it gave us a feeling of emotional and intellectual superiority. That was when the bum, so immersed in the sight of the fat man cutting the steak, began to imagine that *he* had a steak. He had been happy munching his dream steak. He had become wildly, luxuriously lost in his dream. He didn't know that he was, inevitably, due for a terrible shock when he realized that the steak wasn't *real*. But we did. We were way ahead of him. We had the inside dope and we delightedly anticipated his hideous disappointment when he found out something *we'd* known all along. We laughed because we were smarter than he was. We laughed because we were pleased with this tiny reassurance of our own superiority.

A millionaire passes in a limousine. He looks at a silver dollar dubiously — he bites it. It bends slightly. He grimaces. It's a counterfeit. He throws it out into the gutter. The bum finds it. Delirious with joy, he rushes into the tough restaurant and, drunk with power, orders a plate of beans.

And the people laugh.

Why?

Because we're smarter than he is and that makes us feel good. We know plenty that he doesn't know. He thinks he's rich. We know he isn't. He thinks he's going to have a fine time. We know better.

The bum devours his first plate of beans and orders another. All the time, he lovingly fingers his silver dollar, he polishes it on his sleeve, he kisses it. He trusts that silver dollar — it gives him confidence, security, dignity; it gives him a place in the world. It even gives him the right to be nasty to the ape-waiter, whose fatness he had been admiring just a moment ago, before the silver dollar.

Now the ape-waiter pretends to admire *him!* The silver dollar has changed everything. The waiter hopes to get the change from it as a tip.

We laugh because we know the bum is going to get a beating from the waiter when he finds out, and although we're sorry for the bum, we're going to enjoy the beating.

Well, Chaplin finds out before the waiter does. While the ape is off to bring him his third plate of beans, he drops the silver dollar. It doesn't ring true. It makes a dull, lead-like thud. Sweating, he bites it. It bends, horribly. It's a phony. The world comes crashing down around the bum's head.

We laugh — we smell blood.

The waiter brings his third plate of beans and indicates that his working day is up. He'd like Chaplin to hurry through this, pay for it, tip him, and let him go home. Chaplin miserably giggles that of course he'll hurry. He wouldn't dream of keeping him waiting. He indicates that he too is a man of affairs, and can't afford to linger over a mere plate of beans. His assurances are elaborate and verbose, and take up a lot of time. That's what the poor wretch wants to do – take up a lot of time before the inescapable revelation comes and he is beaten to a pulp.

We laugh at Chaplin's pitiful, transparent lies. He hopes to avert the massacre, but we know he can't. Sitting there in the theater, we are all gods on Olympus, watching an inferior being trying to escape the destiny we, in our omniscience, know must be his. Gosh, we feel good, even the most miserable of us.

As the waiter cuts off Chaplin's long-winded explanation of how fast he'll eat the beans, and tells him to get on with it, the fat man (the one who likes his steak well done) is whizzed by the table, being beaten to a bloody pulp by a dozen ape-waiters. Chaplin's own ape-waiter explains this: "He was," he tells him, "a nickel short."

The audience screams with joy.

The poor bum knows now that, if he ever finishes that plate of beans, his fate will be a thousandfold bloodier. Studiously averting the waiter's impatient eye, he makes an elaborate and pitiful ceremony of each bean. First he carefully selects one, after much thought (a lovely bit, because no two things look more alike, or taste more alike, or have less individual personality, than beans from the same plate). Having thoughtfully selected from the thousand the one bean which at that moment seemed most to suit his mood, he doesn't eat it. He peels it. He slices it. He seasons each half of each bean. He tastes one half, puts it back, tastes the other. He thinks about the taste, as a gourmet would ponder over rare wines.

And we laugh because we know how futile it all is – we know how sick he feels inside, how terrified he is, how hopeless he is – and so, naturally, we feel great.

Chaplin, more than any other comic of our time, understood his fellow man's pitiful and cruel mixture of insecurity and inhumanity.

A few years ago, Chaplin was shown around a great automobile factory. Its owners were mighty proud of their new gadgets. They were proud because their new gadgets were time-saving. Chaplin was horrified because they were also man-killing.

The superiority of gadget to man, the slavery of man to gadget, was to him a hilarious perversion of the only sane reason *for* the gadget – namely, to make man's life easier.

So Chaplin made a picture called *Modern Times.* In it he played a harassed little worker in a gigantic factory. Because this worker had become part of the gadget he operated, he had become utterly dehumanized. He moved jerkily, in complete coordination with the time-saving gadget, instead of gracefully and inefficiently like one of those time-wasting human beings; he ate when the gadget fed him and not simply when he was hungry, like a sloppy and unreliable man; he didn't waste time thinking — the gadget worked perfectly, so *that* wasn't necessary. There was one thing, however, that the gadget couldn't do — it couldn't go to the toilet for him.

This was very humiliating to his boss, and it worried that good man considerably — but in the toilet he had another gadget. When Chaplin had been there long enough (according to scientific schedules, time-charts, and Gallup polls), a vast face of his boss appeared on a screen above the bowl and told him to stop fooling around and get the hell back to work.

Well, people howled at *Modern Times*, and industry howled *to* Chaplin. It was un-American, said they, to make people laugh at the inhumanity of gadget to man. Gadgets, they claimed, were a blessing to man. It had been okay for the comic to make people laugh at a vaguely inhuman Society that generally kicked 'em around, but it was unfair, and unsporting really, to make people laugh at a specific system of dignified industrial "efficiency" that robbed them of their dignity as human beings.

IV

IN practicing the art of love, men endure their most terrible confusions, miseries, and disasters. No matter how great and certain a man may have become in every other area of his life, in courtship (trying to convince a certain sweet someone that you are the sweetest someone ever produced by a certain other sex) all men are unsure, fumbling, and feel rotten most of the time.

No confused, despondent lover ever saw a Chaplin picture who didn't come away feeling considerably cheered up. Cheered up because, no matter how inept in his love-making he had been, he had seen someone even more inept; no matter that the fair object of his affections had been unresponsive, the girl Chaplin courted had been downright contemptuous. Chaplin understood that the surest way to delight a world of lovers who suffered because they weren't loved enough was to show them a lover who wasn't loved at all.

There was always a beautiful girl in the Chaplin pictures. And the only reason she had anything to do with Chaplin was that nobody else wanted her because of some terrible handicap — terrible to everyone except Chaplin, who was grateful for any attention from any girl, no matter what was wrong with her, just as long as she was recognizably a girl and recognizably alive. The instant, however, the girl was all right again, she would inevitably abandon Chaplin.

The utter defeat of Chaplin as a lover made our own unsatisfactory romances seem much less humiliating. Nothing that ever happened to any of us could possibly be as disappointing as what always happened to him.

At least, if we had been spurned by a Beloved, there was something left. Hope. Hope that another, less ambitiously selected or more wisely courted, Beloved would accept us. *We* had a chance. Not Chaplin. Nobody wanted him. Nobody ever would.

We laughed at Chaplin's romances because no matter how often we had been licked, we could get started again and it *might* come out good; and because, on the other hand (and a comforting thing it was for us to realize), no matter *how* often he started again, it couldn't come out anything but bad, because he was licked before he started.

We knew that once the lame girl who looked fondly up at him from her wheelchair could walk, she'd walk away from him. We knew that the starving dance-hall blowzer who had agreed to come to his little cabin for dinner would forget him and that date the minute anyone in the saloon offered to feed her there, because what she was interested in wasn't romance — it was fast chow. We knew that the blind girl was sweet to him only because she couldn't see him, and that the instant she could, she'd laugh her pretty head off at him.

We felt fine watching Chaplin's courtships because he gave us a couple of things that make men feel fine. Omniscience; *we* knew something the poor little bum didn't know — that he didn't have a chance. We knew something that would have crushed his hopeful heart if he were as wise as his art had made us; we knew his desperate, eager efforts were all in vain. We knew that no girl would ever want him, and that emphasized the fact that some girl would or did want us, and that gave us the other thing that makes men feel fine, security.

In my own work — this is a footnote — I have tried to make cheerier a world of disappointed lovers. No lover is ever anything but disappointed, since the greatest of all disappointments is the final triumphant possession of the love one has dreamt of having. It's never as wonderful as your dreams of it, because there are no limits to wonderfulness in dreaming. I try to make a disappointed lover feel better by having "Li'l Abner" never know what to do about a succession of eager, luscious girls who throw their juicy selves at him. "Li'l Abner" doesn't know what to do, and so he does nothing. And that makes every male who reads "Li'l Abner" feel fine. Because *he* would know what to do. No matter how fumbling or stupid he has been, compared with " Li'l Abner " he's Don Juan. It makes him feel fine to be Don Juan. So he feels fine about " Li'l Abner."

The more secure a man feels, the more ready he is to laugh. So Chaplin — the instant he appeared — gave us all a feeling of security. Certainly none of us, no matter how badly off we were, were as badly off as this bundle of rags.

Let's go back to the picture I began with, *City Lights*. In it Chaplin, homeless, penniless, nervous about cops, meets a very rich man. We know that he has millions, not because he wears a silk hat and white tie well, but because he wears them badly and sloppily. This guy is so rich that he is contemptuous of attire that would overawe a less rich man. Also he is very drunk. He is so drunk that he does not cringe from Chaplin in distaste. He embraces Chaplin. He tells the little bum that he loves him and is going to show him a good time. Chaplin is deliriously happy and so we laugh at him.

We know that the rich man, once he sobers up, will loathe the pitiful little bum. We know that Chaplin's security isn't going to last, and ours to a degree is. Chaplin is at the mercy of a rich drunk's whim. If things go badly — that is, if the drunk sobers up — Chaplin will have nothing. We are better off than somebody. We are such a hell of a lot better off than he is that he has made us feel secure and protected and we laugh.

Arm in arm, the slobbering millionaire and the little bum wander off in search of food and fun. After a night of wild, expensive revelry, arm in arm they lurch back to the millionaire's town house. The butler, a man of aristocratic impulses although a servant, wants to beat up the tramp and toss him back into the gutter. But the millionaire still loves him. The bum is his li'l pal. He is to be given everything in the house.

Chaplin takes on airs and graces. He orders the butler around. He snaps his fingers in his face. The butler grinds his teeth and waits. He knows that his master will be sober in the morning. He knows that in the morning his master will see the bum as clearly as he does. He knows that the bum will get his, and we know it, but the bum doesn't.

The millionaire wakes up. He is terribly sober. He sees the bum sleeping next to him. He calls the butler in and asks who it is. Brutally aroused, the bewildered bum pleads with the millionaire to remember their everlasting, to-the-death friendship of only a few short hours before. The millionaire looks at him coldly, uncomprehendingly, and with distaste. He orders the butler to throw him out.

Disillusioned and embittered, the little bum resumes his miserable existence. Months pass. One night a figure in top hat and tails lurches out of a gaudy café and throws his arms around him. It is the millionaire again. Again he is plastered, and again he loves the little bum, with a passion that knows no bounds. He weeps that their friendship is everlasting, that he will fight for him to the death, that everything he has is his, and he wants to give him a big party. At first the little bum is suspicious. He has been fooled before. But as the millionaire continues to slobber over him, that old look of love and trust comes back into the bum's eyes. And this is where we laugh loudest. The little bum is such a sucker. We would know enough, even the dumbest of us, never again to trust that man. But Chaplin isn't smart. He isn't even as smart as we are. We feel fine.

And that's what a comedian is for, isn't he? To make people feel fine?

QUESTIONS

1. The title indicates that the author will explain the nature of Chaplin's comedy. What additional emotive purpose or purposes are revealed in the essay? In what ways are human beings made to appear in a somewhat unfavorable light?

2. Capp's style and diction are informal, to say the least. Find examples of slang, colloquialisms, and picturesque description or narrative. How is the diction suited to the author's purposes?

3. Examine the length and structure of the sentences and paragraphs in any one section of the essay. Are the many short, simple sentences and " choppy " paragraphs appropriate for the material?

4. What variations on the theme of man's inhumanity to man are found in (a) the incident of the refugees in Section II, (b) the bum and the fat man in Section III, and (c) the bum and rich man in Section IV? Show how the device of irony is used in (b) and (c).

5. At what point in Section I does the controlling idea about the nature of comedy become apparent? Are the illustrations of this idea appropriate and convincing? Show that the structure of the essay helps to reinforce the unity achieved by the ruling idea. How is Section IV related to Section I?

6. What incidents from the Chaplin pictures illustrate the point that the dividing line between comedy and tragedy is very thin and sometimes difficult to determine?

EDWARD WEEKS has been Editor of *The Atlantic Monthly* since 1938, having earlier been Associate Editor of the magazine (1924–1928) and Editor of the Atlantic Monthly Press (1928–1937). Mr. Weeks, besides being a lecturer on literary subjects, is " The Peripatetic Reviewer " of *The Atlantic Monthly*, and in his sprightly columns he reviews books and surveys the literary scene. In addition to many essays, articles, and reviews in a wide variety of magazines, he has published the following books: *This Trade of Writing* (1935), *The Open Heart* (1955), and *Great Short Novels* (an anthology, 1941).

THE MEANING OF LITERARY PRIZES

by EDWARD WEEKS

TWO hundred years from now, when subjects for Ph.D. theses will be even further to seek than they are today, when there will hardly be a minor poet, an obscure essayist, or an obscene fiction writer whose past has escaped these academic detectives – in that dim future some bright boy will suddenly begin to wonder about the Literary Prizes of the Twentieth Century, and his degree will be assured. For prizes are a phenomenon of our time: their foundation coincides with the increasing popularity of reading; their revenues have helped to liberate authors from commercial competition, and their recognition is, in a generous sense, the equivalent of what the laurel wreath meant to the Greek and what royal or Medici patronage meant to the Renaissance artist or poet. Cash, it seems, is the most satisfying reward an industrial age can bestow; it is our most powerful stimulant for new enterprise. Four hundred thousand francs are held today in trust by the French Academy for the first person to establish communication with the planet Mars. We offer cash awards for the daring exploits in aviation, cash awards for those who most advance the cause of peace, cash awards for the winners of dance marathons. Our writers are stimulated by the same inducement.

Prizes played little part in the literature of the nineteenth century. Certain honors, it is true, were reserved for the mature few: in England a gentle pasture was apportioned to that elderly browser, the Poet Laureate; there was an occasional title conferred upon a writer at the Birthday Honours,* and in a pinch there were grants – Samuel Johnson long hoped for one a century earlier – bestowed by king or wealthy patron upon an author in need. But such endowments were very rare. And in the United States they took the more indirect form of sinecures. Nathaniel Hawthorne was made our Consul at Liverpool; Herman Melville sought a similar appointment to relieve his financial worries, and even as recently as 1904 you will find President Roosevelt placing Edwin Arlington Robinson in the Customs Office as a means of encouraging the poetry to come. But writers of the nineteenth century, writers whom we now classify under the tag of "Victorian," seldom secured such relief. They found hope in the fact that the reading public was steadily widening, they sighed with relief when in the 1880s the passage of copyright laws put an end to pirated editions, and they were thankful for the serialization of their work, indicating, as it did, a fresh source of earned income. But cash awards were left out of their reckoning.

The first literary prizes to appear in the twentieth century were without any stigma of commercialism: the Nobel Prizes in Sweden, the Prix Goncourt and the Prix Femina in France, the Hawthornden Prize in England, the Pulitzer Prizes in the United States, however they might qualify the age, nationality, or subject matter of the author, were, broadly speaking, rewards in recognition of literary excellence.

The Nobel Prizes † perpetuate the memory and wealth of Alfred Bernhard Nobel, a Swedish inventor whose fortune was made by his discovery of dynamite in 1865–1866. As if to counteract the danger of some of his inventions, his will provided as beneficent a series of gifts as could well be imagined. In 1850 Nobel visited the United States, where he served an apprenticeship under an elder Scandinavian inventor, John Ericsson, who was one day to design the *Monitor,* but whose livelihood at that time was very precarious. Perhaps it was the remembrance of those struggling years that first gave Nobel the idea of a fund to aid scientists in their experiments, and to support them during their terms of discouragement. As his fortune enlarged, so did the idea of his bequest. On his death he willed that the interest on his capital should each year be divided into five prizes, one to be awarded in the domain of Physics, one in Chemistry, one in Physiology or

* The birthday of the English monarch, celebrated in June, is the occasion for honoring British and Commonwealth men and women for outstanding achievement and service to the Crown or the state.

† For these details I am indebted to *The Nobel Prize Winners in Literature,* 1901–1931, by Annie Russell Marble. – AUTHOR

Medicine, one in the cause of Peace, and one in Literature. According to the will the latter is to be given annually to "the person who shall have produced in the field of literature the most distinguished work of an idealistic tendency." The choice is made by the Swedish Academy. The value of the award, which now fluctuates between forty and forty-eight thousand dollars,* ought to be sufficient to provide security for any intellect – save perhaps those in the U.S.S.R.

The Prix Goncourt, since its first award in 1903, has proved to be the most exciting, the most coveted plum in France. It goes almost invariably to a young writer and its influence is more marked than the citations which the French Academy bestows upon the mossbacks. The Prix Goncourt, as has been well said, is a "steppingstone, not a tombstone." One other award in France has had its repercussions abroad. In 1904 two French periodicals, *Femina* and *La Vie Heureuse,* joined forces in awarding a prize of five thousand francs to "the best work of imagination in the French language" – the best, that is to say, in the eyes of a committee of French women writers. In the amity of postwar feeling the Femina Committee created a like prize which, since 1919, they have conferred upon English authors. And in 1932 they created the Prix Femina Américain.

The most valuable literary awards in Great Britain are, first, the James Tait Black Memorial Prizes which, in the spring of the year, are adjudged to a biography and a novel of British origin, "the best" in this case being determined by the professor of English at Edinburgh; secondly, the Hawthornden Prize, which is designed for "the best work of imaginative literature" by an English writer under forty-one. The Pulitzer Prizes in Letters are similarly confined to American authors, and by the original deed of gift were somewhat restricted in subject matter as well.

That the latter restrictions might prove onerous was little suspected by the Committee when in May 1926 they awarded the novel prize to *Arrowsmith* by Sinclair Lewis. Mr. Lewis was a realist who occasionally saw life as through a glass darkly. He is also a redhead and it irked him to think that his work should be regarded as having conformed to any set formula. His rejection of the award followed swiftly on the heels of the original announcement; his action caught the front page, and the reasons for it were explained by Mr. Lewis in the following letter which was printed in the *Publishers' Weekly* of May 8: –

I wish [so wrote Mr. Lewis to the Pulitzer Prize Committee] to acknowledge your choice of my novel *Arrowsmith* for the Pulitzer Prize. That prize

* The value of the award now fluctuates around thirty thousand dollars.

I must refuse, and my refusal would be meaningless unless I explained the reason.

All prizes, like all titles, are dangerous. The seekers for prizes tend to labor not for inherent excellence but for alien rewards; they tend to write this, or timorously to avoid writing that, in order to tickle the prejudices of a haphazard committee. And the Pulitzer Prize for Novels is peculiarly objectionable because the terms of it have been constantly and grievously misrepresented.

Those terms are that the prize shall be given " for the American novel published during the year which shall best present the wholesome atmosphere of American manners and manhood." This phrase, if it means anything whatever, would appear to mean that the appraisal of the novels shall be made not according to their actual literary merit but in obedience to whatever code of Good Form may chance to be popular at the moment.

That there is such a limitation of the award is little understood. Because of the condensed manner in which the announcement is usually reported and because certain publishers have trumpeted that any novel which has received the Pulitzer Prize has thus been established without qualification as *the best* novel, the public has come to believe that the prize is the highest honor which an American novelist can receive.

The Pulitzer Prize for Novels signifies, already, much more than a convenient thousand dollars to be accepted even by such writers as smile secretly at the actual wording of the terms. It is tending to become a sanctified tradition. There is a general belief that the administrators of the prize are a pontifical body with the discernment and the power to grant the prize as the ultimate proof of merit. It is believed that they are always guided by a committee of responsible critics, though in the case both of this and other Pulitzer Prizes, the administrators can, and sometimes do, quite arbitrarily reject the recommendations of their supposed advisers.

If already the Pulitzer Prize is so important, it is not absurd to suggest that in another generation it may, with the actual terms of the award ignored, become the one thing for which any ambitious novelist will strive; and the administrators of the prize may become a supreme court, a college of cardinals, so rooted and so sacred that to challenge them will be to commit blasphemy. Such is the French Academy, and we have had the spectacle of even an Anatole France intriguing for election.

Only by regularly refusing the Pulitzer Prize can novelists keep such a power from being permanently set up over them.

Between the Pulitzer Prizes, the American Academy of Arts and Letters, and its training school, the National Institute of Arts and Letters, amateur boards of censorship, and the inquisition of earnest literary ladies, every compulsion is put upon writers to become safe, polite, obedient, and sterile. In protest, I declined election to the National Institute of Arts and Letters some years ago, and now I must decline the Pulitzer Prize.

I invite other writers to consider the fact that by accepting the prizes and approval of these vague institutions, we are admitting their authority, publicly confirming them as the final judge of literary excellence, and I inquire whether any prize is worth that subservience.*

Whatever the provocation, the wording which defined the Pulitzer Prize Novel was subsequently changed. That fiction award is now intended for " the best novel published during the year by an American author, preferably dealing with American life." It may be added that Mr. Lewis had no thought of declining the Nobel Prize when it came his way four years later.

II

THE Nobel Prize is unquestionably the greatest honor in the contemporary world of letters. It favors no nationality; it takes into account not one book but the entire range of a writer's work, and naturally enough it is awarded in most cases in the autumn of a career when maturity has had its say. It is, in short, recognition of achievement and an epitaph of the past. Obviously, I make an exception of the one American prize winner when I say this: Mr. Lewis, I hope, has many years of production ahead.†

The lesser prizes which I have specified are more partisan in their intent, more contemporary in their choice. In terms of hard cash not one of them amounts to much more than one fortieth of the Nobel Prize. But they possess a sterling virtue which as an editor I am quick to appreciate. They single out an author who might otherwise be neglected; they beat the drum for him, they remind you that here's a man whose book you can't afford to miss. Few bookmen in England had heard of Henry Williamson until the Hawthornden Prize helped to illuminate the value of his *Tarka the Otter*. When the judges of the Prix Goncourt in 1933 chose *Man's Fate* by André Malraux for their award they called your and my attention to one of the most vigorous of the younger talents in France. In the first eleven months of its publication, a first novel, *Now in November*, by Josephine Johnson, sold approximately 10,000 copies. During the forty-eight hours following its selection for the Pulitzer Prize the publishers received 9,000 reorders. In short, these lesser national prizes act as a stimulant not only to the writer but to the public.

No one not in the trade can have a fair idea of the battle of books.

* Writing on August 8, 1935, Mr. Lewis comments on his own letter: " I still think this is a reasonable comment on prizes in general, although I do think that the standard of freedom in the judging of novels for the Pulitzer Prize has vastly improved in the nine years since 1926, when I wrote the above. Certainly *Now in November* by Josephine Johnson was an admirable choice." — AUTHOR

† Sinclair Lewis died in 1951.

The competition between authors is more fierce, more unrelenting, today than ever I can think of. Democracy did not complete its education when it trained the crowd how to read. Once you begin to relish books you are tempted to write them. And there's the rub. Despite the lean years since 1930, despite the reduction in office force, despite the recognized and drastic decline in book buying, American publishers cannot bring themselves to issue less than approximately 5000 new and different titles every year.* If a college graduate consumes twenty-five books in a twelve-month he's doing better than average. Do those two figures balance?

There is evidently a crying need for emphasis and selection. The point is that literary prizes made their appearance at a time when more books were being written than the public could possibly enjoy, at a time when some selective, or, if you like, some exterminating process was urgently needed by the casual reader, and — for this is equally patent — at a time when the industry of writing had become so overpopulated that writers were unable to secure a decent recognition, much less a good butter-and-eggs livelihood. A substantial cash prize, you see, had the effect of making almost everybody happy; deserving new literature was set apart for immediate attention; the reader was given an incentive to buy and talk about a book such as he never experienced before; and the author was given not only a feather for his cap but a bank roll nearly sufficient to pay his debts.

A theatrical producer or an editor knows that not until the public begins to talk about his play or his book is success definitely in sight. "Word-of-mouth advertising," like sex appeal or an infectious laugh, is something money cannot buy. It goes without saying that people will talk about a prize winner: half of them will praise it to the skies, the other half will say that they can't for the life of them see why the judges picked it out. Not even the Nobel Prizes are exempt from this hypercriticism. The expostulation of certain old but rather well-known fogies concerning the nomination of Mr. Sinclair Lewis was enough to make one grin. There is a perversity in us that sets us to finding fault the moment we hear that someone or something is acknowledged as extraordinary. But, perverse or otherwise, tongues will always wag when honors are awarded. So reputations are made.

It did not take publishers long to recognize that the acclaim, the emphasis, given to a prize book was the best advertising possible. The Pulitzer Prize in fiction is said to prompt reorders of from thirty to sixty thousand copies. Well, thinks your ambitious editor, why not award a prize of our own: we'll consult some nonpartisan judges, we'll

* The number has more than doubled since this essay was written.

grade the candidates as fairly as possible, and we'll have at least one book on our list that the public will want to read. Thus by a logical step literary prizes passed into commerce. We have today prize contests for short stories, for first novels, for college humor, prize contests for mystery stories and for non-fiction, for manuscripts which are to be serialized, published, translated, dramatized, broadcast, and finally dumped into Hollywood.

III

IT IS, I think, rather amusing to conjecture what goes on behind the closed doors of the Swedish Academy when the Nobel Prizes are at stake, what passes through the mind of that solitary Scotch professor before he confers the James Tait Black awards, what ideals, what motives, and what apprehensions plague those carefully veiled committees which dispense the Pulitzer Prizes. The Swedes must take a bird's-eye view of all contemporary literature. What about that Argentine with the unpronounceable name — is he really first-rate and are Argentine reviewers to be trusted? And what about Herr Schnapps, who has been banished from the Fatherland and whose books have been burned by *Der Führer*? What about Signor Ravioli who has been banished from Italy and whose life works have been condemned by Mussolini? What about Ivan Caviar, that Russian exile novelist now being lionized in Paris? You can picture the international complications. And meanwhile in other countries responsible souls — the English professor at Edinburgh, the French ladies of the Prix Femina–Vie Heureuse, the frowning representatives of Mr. Pulitzer — are cogitating upon "the best" — *really* the best — novel, play, or biography of the year. Snooks has never had it — but his last book was such *vieux jeu*.* Why must Jones be so sensual — isn't he doing it to catch the public eye? That Brown woman writes very well, but she hasn't a thing worth saying! . . . "Ladies and gentlemen, we take pleasure in announcing . . ."

But it is no longer a matter of conjecture as to what happens when a publisher awards a prize. I have weathered eight book competitions, my duties being those of the presiding editor and one of the final judges. Eight spring freshets of manuscripts have periodically swept into our shop. When the men from the shipping room stop bringing them up by hand, when along the hall come the creaking wheels of the office truck loaded to the gunwales with those unmistakable brown packages, I know that the season of competition has arrived.

* Out of date, old-fashioned.

Long picnic tables (but this is no picnic) are laid out on wooden horses and upon them are stacked the candidates as fast as they can be opened and registered in our file. To catalogue a thousand manuscripts so that each may — if necessary — be returned to its rightful address with the provided insurance and postage is an exacting task. Manuscripts should not be lost in transit; no two of them should be allowed to inhabit the same cardboard box — though, like lovers, they will try to if you are not careful; care also must be taken that the readers' reports — blunt and outspoken as they can be — are not inadvertently sent home with the rejected. We want no hurt feelings. Meantime my desk has been deluged with envelopes of illustrations, letters containing last chapters which were inadvertently omitted from one or another of the candidates, affidavits intended to prove that an historical drama of Henry VIII in rhymed couplets is true, every word of it — these and half a hundred other complaints, inquiries, and protestations swamp my correspondence baskets.

When these details crowd in on me for attention I realize why Rip Van Winkle went away.

To meet the emergency a staff of first readers take their place in the office, tried and true critics who have responded to my call on previous occasions. And then we begin to fish our stream. To make our routine picturesque, think of us as salmon fishermen, casting the day long. The small fry — " I am sending you an 18,000-word painting of my Uncle William, a sea captain," or, " I hope you will want this 20,000-word book on God versus Science," manuscripts under the required length — are dropped back into the current as fast as they come. But it takes more time to separate the right fish from the kelts * (which have length, but little weight or brilliance). Manuscripts judged to be without hope are marked with the letter " D " — not for " damnation," but " decline " — and beneath this stigma is written a report, as short and telling as possible. The " D's " are stacked up on one special table and there they await my inspection. For as the presiding editor, the veteran angler, as it were, I must make sure that nothing good has been lost sight of. I shall never forget an incident that occurred early in my experience. In the midst of examining a pile of " D's " I came upon a substantial manuscript, carefully typed and bound, which for reasons unexpressed the first reader had ticketed as " on the whole a rather vulgar story." I had not read far in it myself before I realized that " vulgar " was not the word. That book was eventually awarded the prize. The first reader's license was not renewed.

* Salmon that have spawned.

The unmistakably bright fish are, of course, of different weights and sizes. They are played more slowly, and when a good one comes to the surface a shout goes up and the word spreads. They, too, are segregated on a special table from which they will be withdrawn for two, three, or half a dozen readings, depending upon the insistence of their claims. Each reader as he finishes sums up his own conclusions and adds them to the dossier. This judging of the bright fish goes on long after the last hopeless manuscript has been returned to its maker. The number narrows down from thirty to fifteen, and again to seven or eight. A typewritten digest of the opinions passed upon these finalists is then prepared for the five editorial judges, and at last, when the atmosphere has become decisive, a round-table meeting is held: the digests are discussed, a vote taken — and a telegram of congratulations dispatched. This business of selection occupies from eight to nine weeks. The effect upon the readers is exciting and wearing; the pace of the work tires the eyes and upsets the digestion. In a recent contest we judged 1400 manuscripts totaling approximately 98 million words.

I have said that every manuscript save those disqualified by being too short is read at least twice. This is true — though it is not to say that they are read from cover to cover. A precedent insists that a reader give the first fifty pages of every manuscript a fair hearing. Remembering how important are our first impressions throughout life, it would seem to me only natural that a writer should spend a good deal of time satisfying himself that his story gets off to a good start. Within the first fifty pages an impression is created of whether or not the author is at home with words, whether he is a stylist; within their scope the narrative has to be set in motion and the characters introduced to the reader and identified with enough magnetism to make one wish to know them better. Spotty typing, errors in spelling or punctuation, won't worry a trained reader. He is intent on something else: he has got to keep his ear tuned for the really distinctive style and his eye on the lookout for a manuscript which, however rough it may appear on the surface, has within it the makings of a good book. If the style is plainly unimpressive, the reader will begin to skip forward, reading for the story alone, watching the development of the plot and character and giving particular heed to the climax. When Mary shoots John, when the automobile goes over the cliff, when the sea captain sinks or swims, then you can tell whether the book will meet the test of credibility.

It can be a grind, this search for the hidden talent, but, like anything worth doing, it is relieved by touches of unsuspected humor along the way. Mixed metaphors, figures that have slipped out of hand, characterizations which tell more than they intend, have a way of rewarding the eyes when least expected.

Let us suppose that I turn into my tenth manuscript on a rainy April morning and find at the outset this introductory letter from the author: —

GENTLEMEN:

Am entering this novel for consideration in your Prize Contest. The work has been truly inspired. God gave it to me almost chapter by chapter with but a minimum of interference on my part from December 1st to March 25th. Trusting the results with God and you, I remain . . .

Suppose that several hours later I am laboring with another and quite different novel when suddenly I am rewarded by this happy characterization: —

Sarah Lovelock's face with its mass of bright bobbed hair was very intriguing. Her conversation, when surrounded by men, bubbled, not gushed, but she was capable of long discussion that had depth, too.

Or again, suppose that the end of the day is at hand. I reach for just one more candidate to complete my quota and find that not altogether unexpected phenomenon, a travel diary disguised as a tourist romance but based, as the young author tells us, upon "a good memory which is common to people who love profoundly." The work is illustrated with picture postcards. And in the spring of 1934 there is this sobering thought: —

March 30. Liverpool.

A terrible thing has happened. Mrs. Purvis was killed. Her neck was broken by being folded up in a folding bed. Evidently she and Mr. Purvis were unfamiliar with the contraption: when he got up he touched the wrong button or something slipped. Anyhow it folded up quick as a wink before he could do a thing. It was very sudden and very grave.

I sometimes think I know more about my acquaintances after they are gone.

Believe me, such accidents are not confined to the work of amateurs. They have been known to occur in the pages of the best-equipped writers. If I allude to them it is not to sneer, but rather to pay my respects to those touches of natural comedy which are so heaven-sent in relieving the tension of our day.

Sometime in the course of our judging a single bright manuscript will emerge — to use our fishing figure for the last time, call it a 36-

pound Restigouche * salmon — which is gradually recognized as having set a standard. As reader after reader examines this work the conviction grows that the other contenders will either have to surpass this competitor or be dismissed. Is this evidence of that conformity which Mr. Sinclair Lewis found so objectionable? I don't think so. For the truth is that we have no preconceived notion of what the standard-bearer is to be. Having judged a number of previous competitions, we are of course familiar with the points of excellence in the previous prize winners. But we recognize, and so I believe does Mr. Lewis, who has himself acted as a judge in the Harper contests, that neither among the judges nor among the more promising competitors is there any determination to repeat a success.

It not infrequently happens that two such standard-bearers appear, books which have no more resemblance than that between a dancing pump and a riding boot. Compared with these two the other finalists are clearly also-rans. Each of the two books, of course, has its supporters, and when the time comes to argue their respective merits the question is not, "Which will sell the best?" The question is simply, "Which is the more interesting, the more distinctive book?" Whatever the terms of the award may be and however the competition may be restricted, — whether for first novels, for proletarian novels, or for books of non-fiction, — the decision in the end and in the mind of every judge must be determined by this double-barreled query: "Is it interesting and is it distinctive?"

The initial distinction between literary awards and publishers' prizes is simple enough. The first is a recognition of achievement; the second, a stimulant to evoke the best work procurable. Literary awards in most cases are conferred upon writers of established reputation; publishers' prizes, on the other hand, are much more apt to single out new writers of promise. I think Mr. Lewis is right when he asserts that all prizes are "dangerous." In the case of literary awards there is always the danger that the honor may become too sanctified, the definition of the winner too rigid, the deliberations of the committee too pompous. In the case of the publishers' prizes there is the danger — an insistent one today — that too much may be expected of the prize-winning book. It is one thing to offer a prize for a book of whatever subject. But in my judgment it is much more difficult and much more fallacious to hold out a prize for a manuscript which will be at once a good book, a good magazine serial, a good plot for a play, and a good scenario for Hollywood. When prize offers are put to-

* A river in eastern Canada, in its lower course separating New Brunswick from Quebec.

gether representing those four industries, the chances are four to one that Hollywood will win. You may get an exciting yarn, but the chances are four to one that it won't be literature. Such dangers must be clear enough to any reflective reader. But to say that a thing is dangerous is not to say that it is essentially bad. Literary awards and publishers' prizes both, it seems to me, have proved their worth. In a time of overproduction they have provided us with a much-needed method of selection. More often rightly than wrongly, they have held up for the public's regard a book to be read; not infrequently they have been the means of discovering genuine talent. Prizes, I think, are the best form of patronage surviving in a democratic world of letters.

QUESTIONS

1. What effect is created in the opening paragraph of the essay by the author's use of the terms "academic detectives" and "bright boy"? What attitude toward literary prizes is established in the first two paragraphs of the essay?

2. What is the function of the letter by Sinclair Lewis, which Weeks quotes in Section I of the essay? What evidence in the author's presentation of Lewis's letter indicates that Weeks may not be so opposed to literary prizes as the two opening paragraphs of the essay suggest?

3. Identify the shift in emphasis which takes place in Section II. What evidence of apparent disparagement of literary prizes still remains in this section? What purpose is served by maintaining, deliberately, this ambiguous point of view?

4. In Paragraph 1 of Section III, what is the author's purpose (beyond mere amusement) in conjecturing "what goes on behind the closed doors of the Swedish Academy when the Nobel Prizes are at stake"? Why does he describe in so much detail the process by which the winners of publishers' prizes are selected?

5. Summarize the author's reasons for believing that prizes "are the best form of patronage surviving in a democratic world of letters." What is the author's strategic purpose in appearing to disparage literary prizes in the opening section of the essay and flatly praising them in the conclusion?

Personalities

BERTRAND RUSSELL

GAMALIEL BRADFORD

C. W. CERAM

JUDGE CHARLES E. WYZANSKI, JR.

ROLLO WALTER BROWN

BERTRAND RUSSELL (the third Earl Russell, Viscount Amberley), grandson of the Lord Russell who was Queen Victoria's prime minister, was born in Wales and was educated at Trinity College, Cambridge. Internationally known as a mathematician, sociologist, and philosopher, he has taught at Trinity College, the University of Peking, the University of Chicago, and the University of California at Los Angeles. Invariably an independent thinker, he served a brief term in prison for his pacifist activities in World War I, but supported the democracies in World War II. He is the author of over fifty volumes on mathematics, philosophy, sociology, and education. He has even tried his hand at creative writing in a group of five short stories with the arresting title *Satan in the Suburbs* (1953). Despite his wry comment that his intelligence has been steadily declining since he was twenty, he received the Nobel prize for literature in 1950 – at the age of seventy-eight.

MAHATMA GANDHI

by BERTRAND RUSSELL

MAHATMA GANDHI was unquestionably a great man, both in personal force and in political effect. He molded the character of the struggle for freedom in India, and impressed his own ideals upon the new governing class that came into power when the English went home. There is, at the present day, a general awakening throughout Asia, but the spirit and policy of India, thanks largely to Gandhi, remains very different from that of any other Asiatic country.

Gandhi, like some other great men, developed slowly. Quite extraordinary psychological acumen would have been necessary to discern his future in the shy youth who studied law, first in India and then in England. His autobiography contains a picture of him as he was in his early days in England, and there is nothing in it to suggest the future loincloth; on the contrary, his costume is faultlessly correct and would pass inspection by the "Tailor and Cutter" without any criticism.

Some of the characteristics that he displayed throughout his life were already in evidence at this time. He had a wide and unsectarian interest in religion, and listened to Christian teaching without hostility, though without acceptance. He had already that scrupulous honesty which later distinguished him. He had been married, as was the custom of this country, while still a schoolboy, but when he came to England he left his wife in India and was not generally known by his English friends to be married. He believed, rightly or wrongly, that a certain young lady was becoming interested in him, and he therefore wrote a long letter to her chaperone explaining his matrimonial position. He had been brought up to be a vegetarian on religious grounds, but his brother, who wanted to become "modern," induced him on a few occasions to taste meat. He found it made him ill, and he disliked the deceiving of his parents that was involved. He therefore reverted to strict vegetarianism before his journey to England. All through his life he attached an importance to questions of diet which it is a little difficult for most modern Europeans to understand. But although in England he observed as far as he could the customs in which he had been brought up, he did not become in any degree a rebel, and did not apparently encounter the kind of treatment by which rebels are created.

After a year or so in India, he went on professional legal business to South Africa, and it was there that events soon pushed him into the career which made him famous. He landed at Durban and had to travel to Pretoria. The incidents of this journey are treated vividly and precisely in his autobiography. He took a first-class ticket at Durban, and apparently the railway authorities had no objection to selling it to him. But after he had been in the train for some time, a railway official insisted that however much he might have a first-class ticket, he must travel in a third-class carriage. Gandhi refused to yield voluntarily, so he was pushed out of the train, which went on without him. He sat throughout the night in the station waiting room, shivering with cold, because his overcoat was in the luggage of which the railway company had taken charge, and he would not ask of them the favor of being allowed to get it out.

"I began to think of my duty," he writes in his autobiography. "Should I fight for my rights or go back to India; or should I go on to Pretoria without minding the insults, and return to India after finishing the case? It would be cowardice to run back to India without fulfilling my obligation. The hardship to which I was subjected was only superficial. It was only a symptom of the deep disease of colour prejudice. I should try, if possible, to root out the disease and suffer hardship in the process. Redress for wrongs I should seek only to the extent that would be necessary for the removal of the colour prejudice. So I decided to take the next available train to Pretoria."

A part of his journey had to be done by stagecoach, as there was at that time no railway from the Natal frontier to Johannesburg. He had a ticket for the journey by coach of which the validity was not questioned, but as he was a "colored man," the conductor of the coach considered that he could not be allowed to travel inside.

For a time he was allowed to sit next to the driver while the conductor sat inside, but presently the conductor decided that he wanted to smoke, and ordered Gandhi to sit on the floor of the roof. Gandhi describes the incident: "So he took a piece of dirty sackcloth from the driver, spread it on the footboard and, addressing me, said, 'Sammy, you sit on this, I want to sit near the driver.' The insult was more than I could bear. In fear and trembling, I said to him, 'It was you who seated me here, though I should have been accommodated inside. That insult I put up with. Now that you want to sit outside and smoke, you would have me sit at your feet. I refuse to do so, but I am prepared to sit inside.' As I was struggling through these sentences the man came for me and began heavily to box my ears. He seized me by the arm and tried to drag me down. I clung to the brass rails of the coach box and was determined to keep my hold even at the risk of breaking my wrist-bones. The passengers were witnessing the scene — the man swearing at me, dragging and belabouring me, and I remaining still. He was strong and I was weak."

It is difficult to guess how this scene would have ended but for the intervention of some of the passengers, who apparently had some inkling of humanity. Thanks to them, Gandhi was allowed to remain where he was, and a Hottentot, who had been sitting on the other side of the driver, was made to vacate his seat for the conductor. The feelings of Hottentots about this incident remain for a future page of history.

He had some further adventures on the journey, but of a less dramatic sort. No good hotel would give him lodging, and it was only with some difficulty that he procured a first-class ticket from Johannesburg to Pretoria. This he did by writing a long letter to the stationmaster, and then appearing at the station so faultlessly dressed that the stationmaster observed, "I see you are a gentleman." If he had met Gandhi in later life, clad in his loincloth, he would not have been able to say this.

At this time, as Gandhi's reflections show, although he was outraged by the color prejudice that he encountered, he had no conception of general human equality. He was aware of himself as an educated man, a man whose family in their own country had a certain social prominence. He was rendered indignant by the fact that all Hindus in South Africa were called "coolies," however little they might work with their hands. He had not yet thought of Negroes as having the same right to equality as he was claiming for himself, and at first he was not particularly interested in the wrongs of Indian indentured laborers. It was only step by step, through a number of years, that his outlook on human affairs developed to the point where the untouchables became his main preoccupation. I think, however, that the indignities which he suffered on this first journey in South Africa were what first awakened him to the intolerable humiliations to which classes and nations which are deemed "inferior" are subjected by the insolence of their "masters." I should therefore judge that it was this journey which was the turning point in Gandhi's life.

II

GANDHI returned to India in 1896, and while in India he gave large publicity to the bad treatment of Indians in South Africa. What he had to say on this subject was quoted in many Indian newspapers and brought him into contact with Indian leaders. This agitation had repercussions in South Africa, where the white population became filled with fury against Gandhi. His Indian friends in South Africa telegraphed to him to return to that country, which he did. All sorts of measures were adopted to prevent him from landing. First the ship on which he had come was kept in quarantine for a long time, without any medical justification. Then he was warned not to land with the other passengers, but to slip ashore surreptitiously after dark. He would not do this. His refusal nearly cost him his life. His own account in his autobiography is so vivid that it must be quoted: —

"The number of persons present about the wharf was not larger than what is to be usually seen there. As soon as we landed some young lads saw us. As I was the only Indian who wore a turban of a particular type, they at once recognized me, and began to shout, 'Here's Gandhi! Here's Gandhi! Thrash him! Surround him!' and they came up towards me. Some began to throw stones. Then a few older Europeans joined the boys, and gradually the party of rioters began to grow. Mr. Laughton thought that there was danger in our going on foot. He therefore beckoned for a rickshaw. Up to now I had never sat in a rickshaw, as it was thoroughly disgusting to me to sit in a vehicle pulled by human beings. But I then felt that it was my duty to use that vehicle. Five or six times in my life I have experienced that one whom God wished to save cannot fall even if he will. If I did not fall at that moment I cannot take any credit for it to myself. These rickshaws are pulled by Zulus. The older Europeans and the young lads threatened the rickshaw puller that if he allowed me to sit in his rickshaw they would beat him and smash his rickshaw to pieces. The rickshaw boy therefore said 'Kha' (No), and went away. I was thus spared the shame of a rickshaw ride.

"We had no alternative now but to proceed to our destination on foot. The mob followed us. With every step we advanced, it grew larger and larger. The gathering was enormous when we reached West Street. A man of powerful build caught hold of Mr. Laughton and tore him away from me. He was not therefore in a position to come up with me. The crowd began to abuse me and showered upon me stones and whatever else they could lay their hands on. They threw down my turban. Meanwhile a burly fellow came up to me, slapped me in the face and then kicked me. I was about to fall unconscious when I held on to the railings of a house near by. For a while I took breath, and when the fainting was over proceeded on my way. At that time I had almost given up any hope of reaching home alive. But I remember well that even then my heart did not arraign my assailants."

He was saved from further injury, perhaps even from death, by the wife of the Superintendent of Police, whose name was Mrs. Alexander. She had been a friend of his before, and insisted upon walking beside him so that the mob, even with the worst will in the world, could not injure him much without injuring her too, which they did not wish to do. Finally the police heard what was happening, and escorted him to the police station. From there he reached his destination without further injury.

It was not until many years later that Gandhi became in any general sense a rebel against authority. At the time of the Boer War he did war work for the British, and justified his doing so on the ground that Indians owed something to British protection. He argued at this time that "the authorities may not always be right, but so long as the subjects owe allegiance to a State, it is their clear duty generally to accommodate themselves, and to accord their support, to acts of the State." He did not think that arguments as to the injustice of the British case in the Boer War justified a British subject in disobedience, or even in an attitude of passivity. Many things are surprising in Gandhi's development, and this is certainly one of them.

III

GANDHI possessed every form of courage in the highest possible degree. We have already seen his courage in facing the Durban mob. He showed another sort when, shortly after the end of the Boer War, the pneumonic plague broke out. The pneumonic plague, as everyone knows, is even more deadly and even more infectious than the bubonic plague, but without a moment's hesitation Gandhi devoted himself to the care of the victims, and did everything in his power for them until the outbreak had been adequately coped with. He was not under any kind of official obligation to do this work. I think that few men would have behaved with the wholehearted and immediate devotion which he displayed on this occasion.

The Boer War and its aftermath give more occasion for cynical disillusionment than most events in British history. The war was brought on by the intrigues of moneygrubbing financiers, who spread a network of corruption that descended far down in the social scale. It was fought by the British, first with incompetence and then with inhumanity. It was in this war that concentration camps were invented. Boer women and children were taken to these camps, where they died in large numbers of enteric fever, brought on by the sanitary carelessness of the authorities.

Throughout the war two arguments had been used by the British Government to mitigate its imperialistic character. It was said that the Boers treated non-Europeans very much worse than the English colonists, and it was said that when the war was ended, British miners would find lucrative employment in the mines of South Africa. The British Government, however, decided that Chinese indentured labor would be cheaper than the labor of British miners. A great wave of popular indignation swept out of power the Government which had introduced Chinese labor. Those who had voted for the Liberals imagined that a victory had been won. The Chinese, it is true, were sent back to China, but their place was taken by Indian indentured labor. At the same time legislation was introduced to make the position of Indians in South Africa worse than it had been. At first the British Government refused to sanction this legislation, but very soon it granted self-government to the Transvaal, a measure which was universally hailed as a "noble gesture," and as allowing to the brave Boers the enjoyment of that liberty for which they had fought so well.

The brave Boers immediately saw to it that only they should enjoy the blessings of liberty. The oppressive measures which the British Government had refused to sanction were immediately carried, and the British Government no longer dared to use its legal power to veto. The country had been made safe for mineowners and slave drivers, and the vanquished had been generously granted permission to persist in their slave-driving. This was the situation with which Gandhi had to contend.

The Transvaal Government was faced with a dilemma which generally confronts governments in such a situation. On the one hand cheap colored labor was very convenient, while on the other hand there was a general hatred of Asians, and a desire, so far as possible, to have no non-Europeans except Negroes. With this end in view, acts were passed to compel a sifting of Indians, with a view to diminishing their numbers and to reducing those who remained to a much more subservient condition. Gandhi led the opposition, and it was in this campaign that he first developed the method of *Satyagraha.*

The essence of this method, which he gradually brought to greater and greater perfection, consisted in refusal to do things which the authorities wished to have done, while abstaining from any positive action of an aggressive sort. If the police could be provoked into brutalities, so much the better, but those who were brutally treated were to submit to the treatment with complete passivity. The method always had in Gandhi's mind a religious aspect. He came gradually to object more and more to violence, while at the same time preaching, with ever greater emphasis, the duty of not resisting violence with violence. As a rule this method depended upon moral force for its success. The authorities found it intensely repugnant to persist in ill-treating people who did nothing whatever in self-defense.

The method was, however, subject to two limitations. One of these, which led Gandhi to what he called a "Himalayan blunder," was the likelihood that excited crowds would be carried away and would forget to observe the limitations that Gandhi endeavored to impose. On some occasions in India Europeans and policemen were killed by the infuriated mob — occasions when the first impulse had come from Gandhi, but he was unable to restrain the subsequent fury. The other limitation to which the method is subject is one which did not arise either in South Africa or in India, but certainly would have arisen if the method had been employed against Nazis or Russian Communists. If the authorities are sufficiently brutal, they can exterminate nonviolent resisters without experiencing that moral repugnance from their acts which in the end paralyzed the British in India. During the Second World War, for example, disciples of Gandhi would lie down on the rails of railways and refuse to move. English drivers would not run over such men, and the result was that railway traffic was paralyzed. I cannot think that if the drivers had been Nazis and the men on the rails had been Jews, the result would have been the same. But in the circumstances with which Gandhi had to deal, his method was capable of bringing successes that probably no other method would have brought.

Take, for example, the "battle" which occurred during the campaign against the salt tax, which was described by an eyewitness, Webb Miller,* in an account of which the following is a summary: "The raid which Gandhi had planned on the salt-pans at Dharsana was now carried out by 2,500 volunteers, led by his second son, Manilal. Before they advanced, Mrs. Naidu † led them in prayer and appealed to them to be true to Gandhiji's ‡ inspiration and abstain from violence. 'You will be beaten, but you must not resist; you must not even raise a hand to ward off blows.' Round the depot a barrier of barbed wire had been erected and a ditch dug. As the first picked column of the volunteers went forward, police officers ordered them to disperse; they still advanced in silence. Suddenly scores of police fell upon them and rained blows on their heads. Not one man so much as raised his arm to fend off the blows. Soon the ground was carpeted with the prostrate bodies of men writhing in pain, with fractured skulls or broken shoulders, their white clothes stained with blood. Then a second column advanced, without wavering, knowing well what awaited it. There was no struggle; the volunteers simply marched forward until they, too, were struck down. Now the tactics were varied. Groups of twenty-five men advanced, sat down and waited. As they sat, the enraged police fell upon them, beat them on the head and kicked them in the abdomen or the testicles. Some were dragged along the ground and thrown into the ditches. Hour after hour this went on, while stretcher-bearers removed the inert, bleeding bodies. Over three hundred casualties were taken to hospital with fractured skulls and other serious injuries; two died. Mrs. Naidu and Manilal Gandhi were arrested."

This sort of thing filled every decent English person with a sense of intolerable shame, far greater than would have been felt if the Indian resistance had been of a military character.

There was, of course, also an opposite effect. The police and some of the British authorities in India were rendered furious as a reaction from their own shame, and became more brutal than they would have been against less passive opponents. But this was not the effect that was produced at a distance by those who read of what was being done. English people who were not familiar with India, and had no direct financial interest in maintaining the British raj, felt that something must be done to put an end to such atrocities. General Dwyer, who at Amritsar ordered soldiers to fire for ten minutes upon a

* United Press correspondent, killed in fall from a train in London in May, 1940, at the age of forty-seven.

† Wife of the Hindu poet and reformer Sarojini Naidu.

‡ The added syllable provides a Hindu term of endearment for Gandhi.

packed, peaceful mob, unable to escape, killing many and wounding many more, was recalled, and a Conservative Government even went so far as to deprive him of his pension. It is true that he had a number of admirers who presented him with a large sum of money and a Sword of Honor, but this did not represent average British feeling. People who were neither exceptionally rich nor exceptionally brutal began in the end to feel that if British rule could be preserved only by such methods, then it was not worth preserving.

But all this belongs to the later stages of Gandhi's career. To return now to South Africa, the next large campaign in which he was involved concerned the three-pound tax which was imposed upon indentured laborers when the period of their indenture terminated. Very few of them possessed three pounds, and if they were unable to pay the tax, it was remitted on condition of their serving a new period of indentured labor. This meant in practice for most of them that they had unintentionally and unwittingly incurred a life sentence. The conditions of indentured labor were semiservile, and by means of this tax it was transformed by a trick from being temporary to being probably permanent. The agitation which Gandhi conducted against the poll tax was spectacular, and had the political merit of bringing the indentured laborers into the campaign. Gandhi induced them to strike and to undertake a long march, in the course of which he himself was arrested. The movement was so successful as to produce a state of economic paralysis which compelled the Government to capitulate. After this, the South African authorities behaved with a modicum of decency and enlightenment until Gandhi was dead.

IV

GANDHI's successes throughout his career depended upon a combination of deep religious conviction and astute political insight. He was immovable when he was certain that one of his many moral principles was involved. He was flexible whenever there was negotiation within the limits of his principles. When his followers got out of hand and practiced violence that he could not countenance, he would punish himself by a fast. And as his devoted adherents imagined him becoming daily more emaciated and risking death on account of their misbehavior, they inevitably repented and, like naughty children, promised not to do it again. His motive in all this was religious, but the effect was to reveal his power upon the whole movement that he had created. Who could venture to disobey a revered and beloved leader who would inflict upon himself suffering, and perhaps death, in expiation of the sins of others? It was a perfect technique, but it was perfect because in his own mind it was not a technique, but obedience to the dictates of duty.

Gandhi's moral sense had various aspects that are strange to most modern Europeans. Matters of diet had an importance to him which is a little puzzling. In the midst of events of the most enormous importance, it would occur to him that he ought not to eat salt or pulse, and he would feel about this with the same earnestness that he felt about the fate of India. For example, he took a vow against milk, but once, when he was very ill, the doctor said he would die unless he took milk. His wife pointed out to him that the word he had used in his vow applied only to the milk of the cow or the buffalo, and did not include the milk of the goat. It was therefore permissible for him to drink goat's milk. He was aware that his death would be a loss to India, and on this ground he allowed himself to accept his wife's argument, although it appeared to him somewhat sophistical.

His own account of this matter is as follows: "The will to live proved stronger than the devotion to truth, and for once the votary of truth compromised his sacred ideals by his eagerness to take up the *Satyagraha* fight. The memory of this occasion even now rankles in my breast, and fills me with remorse, and I am constantly thinking how to give up goat's milk. But I cannot yet free myself from that subject of my temptations, the desire to serve which still holds me."

Many modern Europeans will have difficulty in understanding his motives for the vow of complete chastity in marriage which he made at a time when he was trying to help the Zulus who were being persecuted for what the Government chose to call a "rebellion." He felt, so he tells us, that he could not be wholehearted in his work, or have all the strength of endurance that it demanded, unless he gave up the joys of family life. This attitude was common in the early Church but now, to a European, feels somewhat strange. Probably for him the decision was a right one. He did and endured things which it is very difficult to do and endure. In spite of bad health, he continuously risked his life by fasts and other hardships. It may be that no less absolute devotion would have enabled him to achieve the great measure of success which he did finally achieve. As to this, no one except himself could be the judge. However that may be, it is impossible to understand him psychologically so long as we think of him in purely modern terms. To build him up psychologically from European ingredients we must make a combination of early Christian saints with medieval ecclesiastics, adding to both, however, something of the sweetness of St. Francis.

For India, which is not a modern country, his character and his religion were what was needed. A more modern-minded man, for example, could not have been nearly so successful in the campaign on behalf of the untouchables. But while his memory deserves to be revered, it would be a mistake to hope that India will continue to have the outlook that to him seemed best. India, like other nations, has to find her place in the modern world, not in the dreams of a bygone age. His work is done, and if India is to prosper, it must be along other roads than his.

QUESTIONS

1. Explain how the characteristics of Gandhi mentioned in Paragraph 3, Section I, are revealed in the incidents reported in the first three sections of the essay.

2. How is Gandhi's decision (Paragraph 5, Section I) related to the stagecoach incident which follows? For what reasons does Russell consider Gandhi's travels in South Africa (Section I) the " turning point " in Gandhi's life? What, in Russell's opinion, had formerly been lacking in Gandhi?

3. What do the lengthy quotations from Gandhi's autobiography and from the correspondent Webb Miller (Sections II and III) have in common? Why may the quotations be considered more effective than Russell's own paraphrase or summary?

4. What is the unifying idea of Section III? What purpose is served by the commentary on the Boer War and its aftermath, in Paragraphs 2–5, Section III? Is this a digression, or is it closely related to the main idea of the section? Explain.

5. How is the opening paragraph related to the closing paragraph of the essay? What do these paragraphs reveal about the author's attitude toward Gandhi? What is the significance in the evaluation of Gandhi's methods of the paragraph on page 145 beginning " The method was . . ."?

GAMALIEL BRADFORD is best known for his psychological treatment of historical and literary figures, the best example undoubtedly being *Damaged Souls* (1923). Bradford (1863–1932) wrote, among other books, *Confederate Portraits* (1914), *Portraits of Women* (1916), *American Portraits* (1922), and *Daughters of Eve* (1930). Also of interest are his autobiography, *Life and I* (1928), and his posthumously published *Journal* (1933).

MARK TWAIN

by GAMALIEL BRADFORD

WHEN I was a boy of fourteen, Mark Twain took hold of me as no other writer had then and as few have since. I lay on the rug before the fire in the long winter evenings, while my father read *The Innocents Abroad* and *Old Times on the Mississippi* and *Roughing It* and I laughed till I cried. Nor was it all laughter. The criticism of life, strong and personal, if crude, the frank, vivid comments on men and things, set me thinking as I had never thought, and for several years colored my maturing reflection in a way that struck deep and lasted long.

Such is my youthful memory of Mark. For forty years I read little of him. Now, leaping over that considerable gulf, reading and rereading old and new together, to distil the essence of his soul in this brief portrait, has been for me a wild revel, a riot of laughter and criticism and prejudice and anti-prejudice and revolt and rapture, from which it seems as if no sane and reasoned judgment could ensue. Perhaps none has, or ever does. But I have done what I could.

This much is clear, to start with: that Mark is not to be defined or judged by the ordinary standards of mere writers or literary men. He was something different – perhaps something bigger and deeper and more human; at any rate, something different. He did a vast amount of literary work and did it, if one may say so, in a literary manner. He was capable of long, steady toil at the desk. He wrote and rewrote, revised his writing again and again, with patience and industry. He had the writer's sense of living for the public, too, instinctively made copy of his deepest personal emotions and experiences. One of his most striking productions is the account of the death of his daughter Jean; yet no one but a born writer would have deliberately set down such experiences at such a moment, with publication in his thought. And he liked literary glory. To be sure, he sometimes denied this. In youth he wrote, "There is no satisfaction in the world's praise anyhow, and it has no worth to me save in the way of business." Again, he says in age, "indifferent to nearly everything but work. I like that; I enjoy it, and stick to it. I do it without purpose and without ambition; merely for the love of it." All the same, glory was sweet to him.

Yet one cannot think of him as a professional writer. Rather, there is something of the bard about him, of the old, epic, popular singer, who gathered up in himself, almost unconsciously, the life and spirit of a whole nation, and poured it forth more as a voice, an instrument, than as a deliberate artist. Think of the mass of folklore in his best, his native books! Is it not just such material as we find in the spontaneous, elementary productions of an earlier age?

Better still, perhaps, we should speak of him as a journalist; for a journalist he was, essentially and always, in his themes, in his gorgeous and unfailing rhetoric, even in his attitude toward life. The journalist, when inspired and touched with genius, is the nearest equivalent of the old epic singer, and most embodies the ideal of giving forth the life of his day and surroundings with as little intrusion as possible of his own personal, reflective consciousness.

And as Mark had the temperament to do this, so he had the training. No man ever sprang more thoroughly from the people or was better qualified to interpret the people. Consider the nomadic irrelevance of his early days, before his position was established, if it was ever established. Born in the Middle West toward the middle of the century, he came into a moving world, and he never ceased to be a moving creature and to move everybody about him.

He tried printing as a business; but any indoor business was too tame, even though diversified by his thousand comic inventions. Piloting on the vast meanders of the Mississippi was better. What contacts he had there, with good and evil, with joy and sorrow!

But even the Mississippi was not vast enough for his uneasy spirit. He roved the Far West, tramped, traveled, mined, and speculated, was rich one day and miserably poor the next; and all the time he cursed and jested alternately and filled others with laughter and amazement and affection, and passed into and out of their lives, like the shifting shadow of a dream. Surely the line of the old poet was made for him, —

> Now clothed in feathers he on steeples walks.

And thus it was that he met his friend's challenge to walk the city roofs, where they promenaded arm in arm, until a policeman threatened to shoot and was restrained only by the explanatory outcry, "Don't shoot! That's Mark Twain and Artemus Ward."

This was his outer youthful life, and within it was the same. For with some the feet wander while the soul sits still. It was not so with him. Though he always scolded himself for laziness, complained of his indolence or gloried in it, yet when he was interested in anything, his heart was one mad fury of energy. Hear his theory on the subject: "If I were a heathen, I would rear a statue to Energy, and fall down and worship it! I want a man to – I want *you* to – take up a line of action, and *follow* it out, in spite of the very devil." And practice for himself never fell short of theory for others.

To be sure, his energy was too often at the mercy of impulse. Where his fancies led him, there he followed, with every ounce of force he had at the moment. What might come afterwards he did not stop to think – until afterwards. Then there were sometimes bitter regrets, which did not prevent a repetition of the process. He touches off the whole matter with his unfailing humor: "I still do the thing commanded by Circumstance and Temperament, and reflect afterward. Always violently. When I am reflecting on these occasions, even deaf persons can hear me think."

Perhaps the most amusing of all these spiritual efforts and adventures of his youth were his dealings with money. He was no born lover of money, and he was certainly no miser; but he liked what money brings, and from his childhood he hated debt and would not tolerate it. Therefore he was early and always on the lookout for sources of gain, and was often shrewd in profiting by them. But what he loved most of all was to take a chance. His sage advice on the matter is: "There are two times in a man's life when he should not speculate: when he can't afford it and when he can." Apparently his own life escaped from these all-embracing conditions, for he speculated always. A gold mine or a patent, an old farm or a new printing machine – all were alike, to him, vast regions of splendid and unexplored possibility. And much as he reveled in the realities of life, possibility was his natural domain – gorgeous dreams and sunlit fancies, strange realms of the imagination, where his youthful spirit loved to wander and shape for itself cloud futures that could never come to pass, as he himself well knew, and knew that to their unrealizable remoteness they owed the whole of their charm.

But, you say, this was, after all, youthful. When years came upon him, when he had tasted the sedate soberness of life, dreams must have grown dim or been forgotten. Far from it. His lovely wife called him "Youth" till she died, and he deserved it. Though he was married and a great author, and had a dozen homes, he never settled down, neither his feet nor his soul. The spirit of his early ideal, "A life of don't-care-a-damn in a boarding house is what I have asked for in many a secret prayer," lingered with him always. You see, he had restless nerves, to which long quiet and solitary, sombre reflection were a horror. And then he had perfect, magnificent health, the kind that can endure boarding houses without ruin. "In no other human being have I ever seen such physical endurance," says his biographer. And Mark himself declared that he never knew what fatigue was. Who that was made like this would not be glad to wander forever? So Mark was most happy and most at home when he was wandering.

He saw and liked to see all things and all men and women. The touch of a human hand was pleasant to him, and the sound of a human voice, speaking no matter what lingo. He made friends of pilots and pirates and miners and peasants and emperors and clergymen – above all, clergymen, over whom he apparently exercised such witchery that oaths from him fell on their ears like prayers from other people. No man ever more abused the human heart or railed more at the hollowness of human affection, and no man ever had more friends or loved more. To be sure, he could hate, with humorous frenzy and, it would seem, with persistence. But love in the main prevailed; and, indeed, what anchored his wandering footsteps was not places but souls, was love and tenderness. He had plenty for the pilots and the pirates and clergymen. He had much more for those who were nearest him. His infinite devotion to his daughters, most of all to his wife, who was fully worthy of it, and who understood and brought out the best in him and tolerated what was not so good, is not the least among the things that make him lovable.

As he was a creature of contradictions, it is no surprise to find that, while he prayed for boarding houses, he loved comfort and even luxury. He would have eaten off a plank in a mining camp, and slept on one; but the softest beds and the richest tables were never unwelcome, and one attraction of wandering was to see how comfortable men can be, as well as how uncomfortable.

Now, in order to have luxury, you must have money. And Mark, in age as in youth, always wanted money, whether from mines in Nevada, or from huge books sold by huge subscription, or from strange and surprising inventions that were bound to revolutionize the world and bring in multi-millions. He always wanted money, though rivers of it ran in to him – and ran out again. He spent it, he gave it away, he never had it, he always wanted it.

And always, till death, his soul wandered more than his body did.

And his adventures with money were always matters of dream, even where the dreams were punctuated with sharp material bumps. Again and again some exciting speculation appealed to him, as much for its excitement as for its profit. He built great cloud castles, and wandered in them, and bade his friends admire them, and made colossal calculations of enormous success. Then the clouds collapsed and vanished, and the flaw in the calculations became evident — too late. Calculations were never a strong point with him, whether of assets or liabilities. He spent a white night working over the latter. "When I came down in the morning, a gray and aged wreck, and went over the figures again, I found that in some unaccountable way I had multiplied the totals by two. By God, I dropped seventy-five years on the floor where I stood!"

Even his loves had an element of dream in them, and surely dream made up a large portion of his hatred. Certain natures offended him, exasperated him, and he amused himself with furious assertion of how he would like to torment them. If he had seen one of them suffer, even in a finger's end, he would have done all in his power to relieve it. But in the abstract, how he did luxuriate in abuse of these imaginary enemies, what splendor of new-coined damnation he lavished on them, and all a matter of dreams.

Something of dream entered also into his widespread glory; for such wealth of praise and admiration has surely not often fallen upon walkers of the firm-set earth. During the first decade of the twentieth century he drifted in his white dream-garments — as Emily Dickinson did in solitude — through dream crowds, who applauded him and looked up to him and loved him. And he ridiculed it, turned it inside out to show the full dream lining, and enjoyed it, enjoyed his vast successes on the public platform, enjoyed the thronging tributes of epistolary admirers, enjoyed the many hands that touched his in loving and grateful tenderness.

And at the end, to make the dream complete, as if it were the conception of a poet, a full, rounded, perfect tragedy, misfortunes and disasters piled in upon the dream glory and thwarted and blighted it, even while their depth of gloom seemed to make its splendor more imposing. Money, which had all along seduced him, betrayed him, for a time, at any rate, and he wallowed in the distress of bankruptcy, till he made his own shoulders lift the burden entire. One of his daughters, who was very dear to him, died when he was far away from her. His wife died, and took happiness with her, and made all glory seem like sordid folly. His youngest daughter died suddenly, tragically. What was there left?

Nothing. Toys, trifles, snatched moments of oblivion, billiards, billiards till midnight, then a little troubled sleep, and more billiards, till the end.

In perhaps the most beautiful words he ever wrote he summed up the fading quality of it all under this very figure of a dream: —

"Old Age, white-headed, the temple empty, the idols broken, the worshipers in their graves, nothing but you, a remnant, a tradition, belated fag-end of a foolish dream, a dream that was so ingeniously dreamed that it seemed real all the time; nothing left but You, centre of a snowy desolation, perched on the ice summit, gazing out over the stages of that long *trek* and asking Yourself, 'Would you do it again if you had the chance?'"

II

MARK TWAIN is generally known to the world as a laugher. His seriousness, his pathos, his romance, his instinct for adventure are all acknowledged and enjoyed. Still, the mention of his name almost always brings a smile first. So did the sight of him.

There is no doubt that he found the universe laughable and made it so. The ultimate test of the laughing instinct is that a man should be always ready to laugh at himself. Mark was. The strange chances of his life, its ups and downs, its pitiful disasters, sometimes made him weep, often made him swear. But at a touch they could always make him laugh. "There were few things that did not amuse him," writes his biographer, "and certainly nothing amused him more, or oftener, than himself." One brief sentence sums up what he was never tired of repeating: "I have been an author for twenty years and an ass for fifty-five."

And he not only saw laughter when it came to him: he went to seek it. He was always fond of jests and fantastic tricks, made mirth out of solemn things and solemn people, stood ready, like the clown of the circus, to crack his whip and bid the world dance after him in quaint freaks of jollity, all the more diverting when staid souls and mirthless visages played a chief part in the furious revel.

On the strength of this constant sense and love of laughter many have maintained that Mark was one of the great world humorists, that he ranks with Cervantes and Sterne and the Shakespeare of *As You Like It* and *Twelfth Night,* as one who was an essential exponent of the comic spirit. With this view I cannot wholly agree. It is true that Mark could find the laughable element in everything; true also that he had that keen sense of melancholy which is inseparable from the richest comedy. Few have expressed this more intensely than he has. "Everything human is pathetic. The secret source of humor itself is not joy, but sorrow. There is no humor in heaven." Yet the very extravagance of expression here suggests my difficulty. Somehow in Mark the humor and the pathos are not perfectly blended. The laughter is wild and exuberant as heart can desire, but it does not really go to the bottom of things. Serious matters, so-called serious matters, are taken too seriously; and under the laughter there is a haunting basis of wrath and bitterness and despair.

To elucidate this, it is necessary to examine and follow the process and progress of Mark's thinking. In early years, as he himself admits, he thought little — that is, abstractly. His mind was active enough, busy enough, and, as we have seen, his fancy was always full of dreams. But he let the great problems alone, did not analyze, did not philosophize, content to extract immense joviality from the careless surface of life, and not to probe further. Even the analysis of laughter itself did not tempt him. In this he was probably wise, and he maintained the attitude always. "Humor is a subject which has never had much interest for me." Indeed, the analysis of humor may be safely left to those gray persons who do not know what it is. But much of the jesting of Mark's youthful days is so trivial that it distinctly implies the absence of steady thinking on any subject. Not that he was indifferent to practical seriousness. Wrong, injustice, cruelty could always set him on fire in a moment. There was no folly about his treatment of these. But at that stage his seriousness was busy with effects rather than with causes.

Then he acquired money and leisure and began to reason on the nature of things. This late dawning of his speculative turn must always be remembered in considering the quality of it. It accounts for the singular gaps in his information about simple matters, for the impression of terrific but not very well guided energy which comes from his intellectual effort. It accounts for the sense of surprise and novelty in his spiritual attitude, which Mr. Howells has so justly pointed out. He seems always like a man discovering things which are perfectly well known to trained thinkers, and this gives an extraordinary freshness and spirit to his pronouncements on all speculative topics.

When he grew aware of his reasoning powers, he delighted in them. His shrewd little daughter said of him, "He is as much of a philosopher as anything, I think." He was a philosopher by inclination, at any rate. He loved to worry the universe, as a kitten worries a ball of yarn. Perhaps this seemed to make up in a small way for the worries the universe had given him. He loved to argue and discuss and dispute and confute, and then to spread over all bitterness the charm of his inextinguishable laughter. His oaths and jests and epigrams convulsed his interlocutors, if they did not convince them.

As to his theoretical conclusions, it may be said that they were in the main nihilistic. But before considering them more particularly, it must be insisted and emphasized that they were wholly theoretical and did not affect his practical morals in the least. Few human beings ever lived who had a nicer conscience and a finer and more delicate fulfilment of duty. It is true that all his life he kept up a constant humorous depreciation of himself in this regard. If you listened to his own confessions, you would think him the greatest liar in existence, and conclude that his moral depravation was equaled only by his intellectual nullity. This method is often effective for hiding and excusing small defects and delinquencies. But Mark needed no such excuse. What failings there were in his moral character were those incident to humanity. As an individual, he stood with the best.

The most obvious instances of his rectitude are in regard to money. In spite of his dreams and speculative vagaries, he was punctiliously scrupulous in financial relations, his strictness culminating in the vast effort of patience and self-denial necessary to pay off the obligations of honor which fell upon him in his later years. But the niceness of his conscience was not limited to broad obligations of this kind. "Mine was a trained Presbyterian conscience," he says, "and knew but the one duty — to hunt and harry its slave upon all pretexts and all occasions." He might trifle, he might quibble, he might jest; but no one was more anxious to do what was fair and right, even to the point of overdoing it. "I don't wish even to seem to do anything which can invite suspicion," he said, as to a matter so trivial as taking advantage in a game.

And the moral sense was not confined to practical matters of conduct. Human tenderness and kindliness and sympathy have rarely been more highly developed than in this man who questioned their existence. The finest touch in all his writings is the cry of Huck Finn, when, after a passionate struggle between his duty to society and his duty to friendship, he tears the paper in which he proposed to surrender the nigger, Jim, and exclaims, "All right, then, I'll *go* to hell." And Mark himself would have been perfectly capable, not only of saying he would go, but of going.

As he loved men, so he trusted them. In the abstract, judging from himself, he declared they were monsters of selfishness, greedy, deceitful, treacherous, thoughtful in all things of their own profit and advantage. In the individual, again judging from himself, he accepted them at their face value, as kindly, self-sacrificing, ready to believe, ready to love, ready to help. Being himself an extreme example, both in skeptical analysis and in human instinct, he often fell into error and trusted where there was no foundation to build on.

In consequence, his actual experience went far to justify his skeptical theories, and he presents another example, like Swift, like Leopardi, of a man whose standard of life is so high, who expects so much of himself and of others, that the reality perpetually fails him, and excess of optimism drives him to excess of pessimism. For example, his interesting idealization or idolatry of Joan of Arc, his belief that she actually existed as a miracle of nature, makes it comprehensible that he should find ordinary men and women faulty and contemptible enough compared with such a type.

It is not the place here to analyze Mark's speculative conclusions in detail. They may be found theoretically elaborated in *What Is Man?* practically applied in *The Mysterious Stranger* and the *Maxims of Pudd'nhead Wilson,* and artistically illustrated in *The Man Who Corrupted Hadleyburg* and innumerable other stories. They may be summed up as a soulless and blasting development of crude evolutionary materialism, as best manifested in the teachings of Robert Ingersoll. Man's freedom disappears, his best morality becomes enlightened selfishness, his soul is dissipated into thin air, his future life grows so dubious as to be disregarded, and the thought of death is tolerable only because life is not. The deity, in any sense of value to humanity, is quite disposed of; or, if he is left lurking in an odd corner of the universe, it is with such entire discredit that one can only recall the sarcasm of the witty Frenchman: "The highest compliment we can pay God is not to believe in him."

In all this perpetually recurrent fierce dissection of the divine and human one is constantly impressed by the vigor and independence of the thinking. The man makes his views for himself; or since, as he repeatedly insists, no one does this, at least he makes them over, rethinks them, gives them a cast, a touch that stamps them Mark Twain's and no one else's, and, as such, significant for the study of his character, if for nothing more.

On the other hand, if the thinking is fresh and vigorous, one is also impressed and distressed by its narrowness and dogmatism. Here again the man's individuality shows in ample, humorous recognition of his own weakness, or excess of strength. No one has ever admitted with more delightful candor the encroaching passion of a preconceived theory. I have got a philosophy of life, he says, and the rest of my days will be spent in patching it up and "in looking the other way when an imploring argument or a damaging fact approaches." Nevertheless, the impression of dogmatism remains, or, let us say better, of limitation. The thinking is acute, but does not go to the bottom of things. The fundamental, dissolving influence of the idealistic philosophy, for instance, is not once suggested or comprehended. This shows nowhere more fully than in the discussion of Christian Science. Everything is shrewd, apt, brilliant, but wholly on the surface.

The effect of the bitter and withering character of Mark's thought on his own life was much emphasized by the lack of the great and sure spiritual resources that are an unfailing refuge to some of us. He could not transport himself into the past. When he attempted it, he carried all the battles and problems of today along with him, as in *A Connecticut Yankee in King Arthur's Court.* He had not the historical feeling in its richest sense. Art also, in all its deeper manifestations, was hidden from him. He could not acquire a love for classical painting or music, and revenged himself for his lack of such enjoyment by railing at those who had it. Even nature did not touch great depths in him, because they were not there. He felt her more theatrical aspects – sunsets, ice storms. Her energy stimulated a strange excitement in him, shown in Twitchell's account of his rapture over a mountain brook. I do not find that he felt the charm of lonely walks in country solitude.

It is on this lack of depth in thinking and feeling that I base my reluctance to class Mark with the greatest comic writers of the world. His thought was bitter because it was shallow; it did not strike deep enough to get the humble tolerance, the vast self-distrust, that should go with a dissolving vision of the foundations of the individual universe. His writing alternates from the violence of unmeaning laughter to the harshness of satire that has no laughter in it. In this he resembles Molière, whose Scapins are as far from thought as are his Tartuffes from gayety. And Mark's place is rather with the bitter satirists, Molière, Ben Jonson, Swift, than with the great, broad, sunshiny laughers, Lamb, Cervantes, and the golden comedy of Shakespeare.

Indeed, no one word indicates better the lack I mean in Mark than " sunshine." You may praise his work in many ways; but could anyone ever call it merry? He can give you at any time a riotous outburst of convulsive cachinnation. He cannot give you merriment, sunshine, pure and lasting joy. These are always the enduring elements of the highest comedy. They are not the essential characteristics of the work of Mark Twain.

III

BUT perhaps this is to consider too curiously. The total of Mark's work affords other elements of interest besides the analysis of speculative thought, or even of laughter. Above all, we Americans should appreciate how thoroughly American he is. To be sure, in the huge mixture of stocks and races that surrounds us, it seems absurd to pick out anything or anybody as typically American. Yet we do it. We all choose Franklin as the American of the eighteenth century and Lincoln as the American of the nineteenth. And most will agree that Mark was as American as either of these.

He was American in appearance. The thin, agile, mobile figure, with its undulating grace in superficial awkwardness, suggested worlds of humorous sensibility. The subtle, wrinkled face, under its rich shock of hair, first red, then snowy white, had endless possibilities of sympathetic response. It was a face that expressed, repressed, impressed every variety of emotion known to its owner.

He was American in all his defects and limitations. The large tolerance, cut short with a most definite end when it reached the bounds of its comprehension, was eminently American. The slight flavor of conceit, at least of self-complacent satisfaction, the pleasant and open desire to fill a place in the world, whether by mounting a platform at just the right moment or wearing staring white clothes in public places, we may call American with slight emphasis, as well as human.

But these weaknesses were intimately associated with a very American excellence, the supreme candor, the laughing frankness which recognized them always. Assuredly no human being ever more abounded in such candor than Mark Twain. He confessed at all times, with the amplitude of diction that was born with him, all his enjoyment, all his suffering, all his sin, all his hope, all his despair.

And he was American in another delightful thing, his quickness and readiness of sympathy, his singular gentleness and tenderness. He could lash out with his tongue and tear anything and anybody to pieces. He could not have done bodily harm to a fly, unless a larger pity called for it. He was supremely modest and simple in his demands upon others, supremely depreciative of the many things he did for them. "I wonder why they all go to so much trouble for me. I never go to any trouble for anybody." The quiet wistfulness of it, when you know him, brings tears.

Above all, he was American in his thorough democracy. He had a pitiful distrust of man; but his belief in men, all men, was as boundless as his love for them. Though he lived much with the rich and lofty, he was always perfectly at home with the simple and the poor, understood their thoughts, liked their ways, and made them feel that he had been simple and poor himself and might be so again.

He was not only democratic in feeling and spirit, he was democratic in authorship, both in theory and practice. Hundreds of authors have been obliged to write for the ignorant many, for the excellent reason that the cultivated few would not listen to them. Perhaps not one of these hundreds has so deliberately avowed his purpose of neglecting the few to address vast masses as Mark did. The long letter to Mr. Andrew Lang, in which he proclaims and explains this intention, is a curious document. Let others aim high, he says, let others exhaust themselves in restless and usually vain attempts to please fastidious critics. I write for the million, I want to please them, I know how to do it, I have done it. "I have never tried in even one single instance, to help cultivate the cultivated classes. . . . I never had any ambition in that direction, but always hunted for bigger game — the masses. I have seldom deliberately tried to instruct them, but have done my best to entertain them. To simply amuse them would have satisfied my dearest ambition at any time."

It is hardly necessary to dwell upon the weak points in this theory. Whatever Mark, or anyone else, professes, it cannot be questioned that he prefers the approbation of the cultured few, when he can get it. Moreover, it may easily be maintained that the many in most cases take their taste from the few; and if this does not hold with a writer's contemporaries, it is unfailing with posterity. If a writer is to please the generations that follow him, he can do it only by securing the praise of those who by taste and cultivation are qualified to judge. In other words, if Mark's works endure, it will be because he appealed to the few as well as to the many.

However this may be, there can be no question that Mark reached the great democratic public of his own day and held it. To be sure, it is doubtful whether even he attained the full glory of what he and Stevenson agreed to call "submerged authorship," the vast acceptance of those who are wept over at lone midnight by the shopgirl and the serving maid. But his best books — *Tom Sawyer, Huckleberry Finn, Life on the Mississippi, The Prince and the Pauper* — may justly be said to belong to the literature of American democracy; and the travel books and many others are not far behind these.

In view of this fixed intention to appeal to the masses and to affect the masses, it becomes an essential part of the study of Mark's career and character to consider what his influence upon the masses was. He talked to them all his life, from the platform and from the printed page, with his sympathetic, human voice, his insinuating smile. What did his talk mean to them, how did it affect them, for good or for evil?

In the first place, beyond a doubt, enormously for good. Laughter in itself is an immense blessing to the weary soul — not a disputable blessing, like too much teaching and preaching, but a positive benefit. "Amusement is a good preparation for study and a good healer of fatigue after it," says Mark himself. And amusement he provided, in vast abundance, muscle easing, spirit easing.

Also, he did more than make men laugh, he made them think, on practical moral questions. He used his terrible weapon of satire to demolish meanness, greed, pettiness, dishonesty. He may have believed, in the abstract, that selfishness was the root of human action, but he scourged it in concrete cases with whips of scorpions. He may have believed, in the abstract, that men were unfit to govern themselves, but he threw scorn biting as vitriol on those who attempted to tyrannize over others.

Finally, Mark's admirers insist, and insist with justice, that he was a splendid agent in the overthrow of shams. He loved truth, sincerity, the simple recognition of facts as they stand, no matter how homely, and with all his soul he detested cant of all kinds. "His truth and his honor, his love of truth, and his love of honor, overflow all boundaries," says Mr. Birrell. "He has made the world better by his presence." From this point of view the praise was fully deserved.

Yet it is just here that we come upon the weakness. And if Mark made the world better, he also made it worse — at any rate, many individuals in it: for, with the wholesale destruction of shams, went, as so often, the destruction of reverence, "that angel of the world," as Shakespeare calls it. The trouble was that, when Mark had fairly got through with the shams, there was nothing left. One of his enthusiastic admirers compares him to Voltaire. The comparison is interesting and suggestive. Voltaire, too, was an enormous power in his day. He wrote for the multitude, so far as it was then possible to do it. He wielded splendid weapons of sarcasm and satire. He was always a destroyer of shams, smashed superstition and danced upon the remains of it. But Voltaire was essentially an optimist and believed in and enjoyed many things. He enjoyed literature, he enjoyed glory, he enjoyed living; above all, he believed in and enjoyed Voltaire. When Mark had stripped from life all the illusions that remained even to Voltaire, there was nothing left but a naked, ugly, hideous corpse, amiable only in that it was a corpse, or finally would be.

Mark himself frequently recognizes this charge of being a demolisher of reverence, and tries to rebut it. I never assault real reverence, he says. To pretend to revere things because others revere them, or say they do, to cherish established superstitions of art, or of morals, or of religion, is to betray and to deceive and to corrupt. But I never mock those things that I really revere myself. All other reverence is humbug. And one is driven to ask, what does he really revere, himself? His instinctive reverence for humanity in individual cases is doubtless delicate and exquisite; but in theory he tears the veil from God and man alike.

To illustrate I need only quote two deliberate and well-weighed utterances of his riper years. How could you wither man more terribly than in the following?

"A myriad of men are born; they labor and sweat and struggle for bread; they squabble and scold and fight; they scramble for little mean advantages over each other; age creeps upon them; infirmities follow; shames and humiliations bring down their prides and their vanities; those they love are taken from them and the joy of life is turned to aching grief. The burden of pain, care, misery, grows heavier year by year; at length ambition is dead; pride is dead; vanity is dead; longing for release is in their place. It comes at last, — the only unpoisoned gift earth ever had for them, — and they vanish from a world where they were of no consequence, where they have achieved nothing, where they were a mistake and a failure and a foolishness; where they have left no sign that they have existed — a world which will lament them a day and forget them forever."

For those who thus envisaged man there used to be a refuge with God. Not so for Mark. Man deserves pity. God — at least, any God who might have been a refuge — deserves nothing but horror and contempt. The criticism is, to be sure, put into the mouth of Satan; but Satan would have been shocked at it: he was not so far advanced as Mark: —

"A God who could make good children as easily as bad, yet preferred to make bad ones; who could have made every one of them happy, yet never made a single happy one . . . who mouths justice and invented hell — mouths mercy and invented hell — mouths Golden Rules, and forgiveness multiplied by seventy times seven, and invented hell; who mouths morals to other people and has none himself; who frowns upon crimes, yet commits them all; who created man without invitation, then tries to shuffle the responsibility for man's acts upon man, instead of honorably placing it where it belongs, upon himself; and finally with altogether divine obtuseness, invites this poor, abused slave to worship him."

Can it be considered that doctrines such as this are likely to be beneficial to the average ignorant reader of democracy, or that the preacher of them made the world wholly better by his presence? It is true that they do not appear so openly in Mark's best-known books, true that the practical manliness and generosity of Tom and Huck largely eclipse them. Yet the fierce pessimism of Pudd'nhead Wilson stares at the reader from the popular story of that name and from the equally popular *Following the Equator,* and even in the history of Tom and Huck the hand that slashes reverence is never far away.

The charge of evil influence fretted Mark as much as that of irreverence. He defends himself by denying that there is such a thing as personal influence from doctrines. Our happiness and unhappiness, he says, come from our temperament, not from our belief, which does not affect them in the slightest. This is, of course, gross exaggeration, as the story of Mark's own life shows again and again. One can perhaps best speak for one's self. It took years to shake off the withering blight which Mark's satire cast for me over the whole art of Europe. For years he spoiled for me some of the greatest sources of relief and joy. How many never shake off that blight at all! Again, in going back to him to write this portrait, I found the same portentous, shadowing darkness stealing over me that he spread before. I lived for ten years with the soul of Robert E. Lee, and it really made a little better man of me. Six months of Mark Twain made me a worse. I even caught his haunting exaggeration of profanity. And I am fifty-six years old and not very susceptible to infection. What can he not do to boys and girls of sixteen?

It is precisely his irresistible personal charm that makes his influence overwhelming. You hate Voltaire; you love Mark. In later years a lady called upon him to express her enthusiasm. She wanted to kiss his hand. Imagine the humor of the situation — for Mark. But he accepted it with perfect dignity and perfect tender seriousness. "How God must love you!" said the lady. "I hope so," answered Mark gently. After she had gone, he observed as gently and without a smile, "I guess she hasn't heard of our strained relations."

How could you help being overcome by such a man and disbelieving all he disbelieved? When he clasps your hand and lays his arm over your shoulder and whispers that life is a wretched, pitiable thing, and effort useless, and hope worthless, how are you to resist him?

So my final, total impression of Mark is desolating. If his admirers rebel, declare this utterly false, and insist that the final impression is laughter, they should remember that it is they, and especially Mark himself, who are perpetually urging us to take him seriously. Taken seriously, he is desolating. I cannot escape the image of a person groping in the dark, with his hands blindly stretched before him, ignorant of whence he comes and whither he goes, yet with it all suddenly bursting out into peals of laughter, which, in such a situation, have the oddest and most disconcerting effect.

Yet, whatever view you take of him, if you live with him long, he possesses you and obsesses you; for he was a big man and he had a big heart.

QUESTIONS

1. According to the opening paragraph, in what ways did Twain affect Bradford? Explain how these reactions are used later in the essay. Is this method effective in aiding the reader?

2. What purpose is served by the second sentence in Paragraph 1, Section II? How is it related to Section I? Is the second sentence of Paragraph 1, Section III, related in the same way to Section II? Point out other examples of the same device.

3. Although Bradford says, "Mark Twain is generally known to the world as a laugher," he believes that Twain does not rank "with the greatest comic writers of the world." Point out the steps in Section II by which Bradford reaches this conclusion. What paradoxical qualities of Twain are mentioned in this part of the essay? What contrasted attitudes toward life are suggested?

4. In Paragraphs 1–6 in Section III, what traits does Bradford select as "typically American"? If Twain were as skeptical as Bradford suggests, what objections might he have made to this explanation of the term "American"?

5. How is the idea developed in ten paragraphs of Section III (starting with the paragraph beginning, "In view of this fixed . . ." on page 161) related to the purpose of the selection — to present a "portrait" of Twain?

6. Summarize the evidence in the essay that Bradford, although affected strongly by Twain, is critical in his estimate. In what ways has he allowed for differences of opinion about Twain?

C. W. CERAM is the pseudonym of Kurt W. Marek, a German critic, publisher, and archaeologist. Although since 1945 he has lived in Hamburg, serving as editor of a British-sponsored paper and as editor for a German publishing house, he is well known throughout the United States for his *Gods, Graves and Scholars,* a " best-seller " published in 1951. " The Man Who Found Troy " is a part of this book. *The Secret of the Hittites* (1956), described as a " scientific thriller," also has proved extremely popular.

THE MAN WHO FOUND TROY

by C. W. CERAM

THE life of Heinrich Schliemann is the story of the poor minister's son who at the age of seven dreamed of finding a city, and who thirty-nine years later found not only the city but treasure such as the world has seldom seen.

It began this way. A little boy stood at a grave in the cemetery of the little village where he was born, far up in the North German state of Mecklenburg. The grave was that of the monster Hennig.* He was said to have roasted a shepherd alive, then to have kicked the victim for good measure. For this cruelty, it was said, Hennig's left foot, covered with a silk stocking, each year grew out of the grave like some strange plant.

The boy waited by the grave but nothing happened. He went home and begged his father to dig up the grave and find out where the foot was that year.

The father told the boy fables, fairy tales, and legends. Himself a confirmed humanist, he told the boy about the battles fought by Homer's heroes, about Paris and Helen, Achilles and Hector, about mighty Troy, which was burned and leveled. For Christmas he gave his son Jerrer's *Illustrated History of the World.* The boy looked at the pictures of the massive walls and the great Scaean Gate.† " Is that how Troy looked? " he asked. The father nodded. " And it is all gone, and nobody knows where it stood? " " That is true," the father replied.

" But I don't believe that," said the boy, Heinrich Schliemann.

* Probably a medieval robber knight named Henning von Holstein.

† The western gate of ancient Troy. Ceram has succeeded admirably in making clear to the reader the location of ancient cities in Asia Minor. With no important exceptions, the proper names not found in the dictionary are clarified by the context.

"When I am big, I shall go to Greece and find Troy and the King's treasure."

The father laughed. But that prophecy of the seven-year-old became a reality. Years later in the preface to his book *Ithaca, the Peloponnesus, and Troy* Schliemann wrote: "When my father gave me a book on the main events of the Trojan War and the adventures of Odysseus and Agamemnon – it was my Christmas present for the year 1832 – little did I think that thirty-six years later I would offer the public a book on the same subject. And do this, moreover, after actually seeing with my own eyes the scene of the war and the fatherland of the heroes immortalized by Homer."

Schliemann's youth was filled with adventure. In 1841 he went to Hamburg and was signed as cabin boy on a vessel bound for Venezuela. After fourteen days at sea the ship ran into a wild storm and foundered off the Dutch island of Texel in the North Sea. He made shore but landed in a hospital, exhausted and in rags. A recommendation from a family friend enabled him to get employment as an office boy in Amsterdam.

In a miserable, unheated garret room he began his study of languages. Within two years, by an unusual method of self-teaching, he had mastered English, French, Dutch, Spanish, Portuguese, and Italian. After being promoted to correspondent and bookkeeper with another Amsterdam firm doing business with Russia, Schliemann began to learn Russian. Six hectic weeks later he was conversing fluently with Russian merchants come to Amsterdam to attend the indigo auction.

He was as successful in business as in languages. The shipwrecked cabin boy, the office worker – and master of eight languages – became first a small wholesaler, then, with dizzying speed, a royal merchant. Invariably he picked the shortest road to commercial success. When only twenty-four years old he went to St. Petersburg as agent for his firm. A year later he founded his own export-import business and rose to be Judge of the St. Petersburg Commercial Court and director of the Imperial State Bank in St. Petersburg.

He was wealthy before he was fifty. "My enterprises had been wonderfully blessed by Heaven," he says with unconcealed pride, "to such a degree that by the end of the year 1863 I was already in possession of means far beyond my most ambitious expectations." And to this he added, in a casual tone: "I [now] retired from business so that I could devote myself entirely to the studies that so completely fascinated me." In 1868 he made his first expedition to Ithaca, through the Peloponnesus and the Troad.

II

In Schliemann's day Homer was conceived to be a mere name, his Ilium an indeterminate, lost world. The great chronicle of the siege of Priam's citadel was deemed by some to be a tale containing a great deal of invention and a few grains of truth. And by others the *Iliad* was relegated entirely to the shadow realm of myth. But Schliemann read Homeric poetry as bare reality. He believed implicitly. This was as true when he was forty-six as it had been when, as a boy, he had been fascinated by the picture of the fleeing Aeneas. He was aware that all Greek antiquity, including the great historians Herodotus and Thucydides, had accepted the Trojan War as an actual event, and its famous names as historical personages.

The scholars of his time believed that the site of ancient Troy — if Troy had existed at all — was near a little village called Bunarbashi. At Bunarbashi were two springs, and some more daring archaeologists argued that ancient Troy might possibly be located thereabouts. For it is written in Homer, in the twenty-second song of the *Iliad* (verses 147–52): " And [they] came to the two fair-flowing springs, where two fountains rise that feed deep-eddying Skamandros. The one floweth with warm water, and smoke goeth up there from around us as it were from a blazing fire, while the other even in summer floweth forth like cold hail or snow or ice that water formeth."

For a fee of 45 piasters Schliemann hired a Greek guide and rode out bareback to have his first look at the land of his boyhood dreams. " I admit," he says, " that I could scarcely control my emotion when I saw the tremendous plain of Troy spread out before me, a scene that had haunted my earliest childhood dreams."

But this first impression was enough to convince him, believing literally in Homer as he did, that Bunarbashi was not the site of ancient Troy. For the locality was fully three hours away from the coast, and Homer describes his heroes as able to travel back and forth several times daily between their moored ships and the beleaguered city. Nor did it seem likely to Schliemann that a great palace of sixty-two rooms would ever have been built on such a small knoll. The setting was not right for cyclopean * walls, breached by a massive gate through which the crafty Greeks entered in a wooden horse.

Schliemann examined the springs of Bunarbashi and was surprised to find that in a space of 1650 feet he could count not merely two — the number mentioned by Homer — but thirty-four of them. He made

* Derived from the Cyclopes, a race of giants in Greek mythology; here used in the sense of " huge " or " massive."

a careful survey of the countryside in his *Iliad* and reread the verses telling how Achilles, the "brave runner," chased Hector three times around the fortress of Priam, "with all the gods looking on." Following Homeric directions as best he could, Schliemann traced out a likely course about the hill. At one point, however, he encountered a drop so steep that he had to crawl down it backwards on all fours. Since, in Schliemann's view, Homer's description of the landscape was as exact as a military map, surely the poet would have mentioned the incline had his heroes scrambled down it three times "in hasty flight."

With watch in one hand and Homer in the other, he paced out the road between what were purported to be the two hills securing Troy, this road winding through the foothills to the shore off which the Achaean ships were supposed to have been anchored. He also reenacted the movements of the first day of battle in the Trojan War, as portrayed in the second to the seventh songs of the *Iliad*. He found that if Troy had been located at Bunarbashi, the Achaeans would have had to cover at least 52 miles during the first nine hours of battle.

The complete absence of ruins clinched his doubts about the site. "Mycenae and Tiryns," Schliemann wrote in 1868, "were destroyed 2335 years ago, but their ruins are of such solid construction that they can last another 10,000 years." And Troy was destroyed only 722 years earlier. It seemed highly unlikely that the walls described by Homer would have disappeared without a trace. Yet in the environs of Bunarbashi there was not a sign of ancient masonry.

Ruins there were aplenty, however, in other not too distant places. Even the untrained eye could not miss them at New Ilium, now called Hissarlik, a town some two and a half hours northward from Bunarbashi and only one hour from the coast. Twice Schliemann examined the flat top of the mound at Hissarlik, a rectangular plateau about 769 feet long on each side. This preliminary survey pretty well satisfied his mind that he had located ancient Troy.

He began to cast about for proof and discovered that others shared his opinion, among them Frank Calvert, American vice-consul, but Englishman by birth. Calvert owned a part of the mound of Hissarlik and had a villa there.

For a short while Schliemann wavered when he found no springs at all at Hissarlik, in striking contrast to his discovery of thirty-four at Bunarbashi. But Calvert pointed out that in this volcanic region he had heard of several hot springs suddenly drying up, only to reappear after a short period. And so Schliemann casually cast aside everything that hitherto had seemed so important to the scholars. Moreover, the running fight between Hector and Achilles was plausible enough in the Hissarlik setting, where the hill sloped gently. To circle the city three times at Hissarlik they would have had to run 9 miles. This feat, Schliemann thought, was not beyond the power of such warriors.

Again Schliemann was more influenced in his thinking by the judgment of the ancients than by the scholarship of his day. He recalled how Herodotus had reported that Xerxes once visited New Ilium to look at the remains of "Priam's Pergamos," and there to sacrifice a thousand cattle to the Ilian Minerva. According to Xenophon, Mindares, the Lacedaemonian general, had done the same. Arrian * had written that Alexander the Great, after making an offering at New Ilium, took ancient weapons away with him and ordered his bodyguard to carry them in battle for luck. Beyond this, Caesar had done much for New Ilium, partly because he admired Alexander, partly because he believed himself to be a descendant of the Ilians.

Had they all been misled by a dream? By the bad reporting of their day?

And so a man possessed went to work. All the energy that had made him a millionaire Schliemann concentrated on realizing his dream.

In 1869 he married a Greek girl named Sophia Engastromenos, who was as beautiful as his image of Helen. Soon Sophia, too, was absorbed in the great task and was sharing his fatigues, hardships, and worries. He began to dig at Hissarlik in April, 1870. In 1871 he dug for two months, and another four and a half months in the two succeeding years. He had a hundred workers in his employ. Nothing could hold him down, neither deadly mosquito-borne fevers and bad water nor the recalcitrance of the laborers. He prodded dilatory authorities and he ignored the incomprehension of narrow-minded experts who mocked him as a fool.

The Temple of Athena had stood on the highest ground in the city, and Poseidon and Apollo had built the walls of Pergamos — so it was recorded in Homer. Therefore the temple should be located in the middle of the mound, Schliemann reasoned, and somewhere round about, on the original level ground, would be the walls constructed by the gods. He struck into the mound, boldly ripping down the walls that to him seemed unimportant. He found weapons and household furnishings, ornaments and vases, overwhelming evidence that a rich city had once occupied the spot. And he found something else as well: under the ruins of New Ilium he disclosed other ruins, under these still others. The hill was like a tremendous onion, which he proceeded to dismember layer by layer.

* Flavius Arrian, Greek historian who lived in the second century A.D.

Each day brought a new surprise. Schliemann had gone forth to find Homeric Troy, but as time went on he and his workers discovered no fewer than seven buried cities, then two more — nine glimpses, all told, of primitive ages that previously had not been known to exist.

The question now arose which of these nine cities was the Troy of Homer, of the heroes and the epic war. It was clear that the bottommost or first level had been a prehistoric city, much the oldest in the series, so old that the inhabitants had not known the use of metals. And the uppermost level had to be the most recent, and no doubt consisted of the remains of the New Ilium where Xerxes and Alexander had made sacrifice.

Schliemann dug and searched. In the second and third levels he found traces of fire, the remains of massive walls, and the ruins of a gigantic gate. He was sure that these walls had once enclosed the palace of Priam, and that he had found the famous Scaean Gate.

He unearthed things that were treasures from the scientific point of view. Part of this material he shipped home, part he gave over to experts for examination, material that yielded a detailed picture of the Trojan epoch, the portrait of a people.

It was Heinrich Schliemann's triumph, and the triumph, too, of Homer. He had succeeded, the enthusiastic amateur, in demonstrating the actual existence of what had always counted as mere saga and myth, a figment of the poetic fancy.

A wave of excitement coursed through the intellectual world. Schliemann, whose workers had moved more than 325,000 cubic yards of earth, had earned a breathing spell and he set June 15, 1873, as the date for the termination of the diggings. On the day before the last shovelful of earth was to be turned, he found a treasure that crowned his labors with a golden splendor.

III

It happened dramatically. Even today, reading about this amazing discovery takes one's breath away. The discovery was made during the early hours of a hot morning. Schliemann, accompanied by his wife, was supervising the excavation. The workmen were down 28 feet, at the lower level of the masonry that Schliemann identified with Priam's palace. Suddenly his gaze was held spellbound. He seized his wife by the arm. "Gold!" he whispered. She looked at him in amazement. "Quick," he said. "Send the men home at once." The lovely Greek stammered a protest. "No buts," he told her. "Tell them anything you want. Tell them today is my birthday, that I've just remembered, and that they can all have the rest of the day off. Hurry up, now, hurry! "

The workers left. " Get your red shawl! " Schliemann said to his wife as he jumped down into the hole. He went to work with his knife like a demon. Massive blocks of stone, the debris of millennia, hung perilously over his head, but he paid no attention to the danger. " With all possible speed I cut out the treasure with a large knife," he writes. " I did this by dint of strenuous effort, and in the most frightful danger of losing my life; for the heavy citadel wall, which I had to dig under, might have crashed down on me at any moment. But the sight of so many immeasurably priceless objects made me foolhardy and I did not think of the hazards."

There was the soft sheen of ivory, the jingle of gold. Schliemann's wife held open the shawl to be filled with Priam's treasure. It was the golden treasure of one of the mightiest kings of prehistory, gathered together in blood and tears, the ornaments of a godlike people, buried for three thousand years until dug from under the ruined walls of seven vanished kingdoms. Not for one moment did Schliemann doubt that he had found Priam's treasure-trove. And not until shortly before his death was it proved that Schliemann had been misled in the heat of enthusiasm. Troy lay neither on the second nor on the third level, but on the sixth. The treasure had belonged to a king who had antedated Priam by a thousand years.

What to do now with this golden hoard? Schliemann allowed news of the find to get out, but by various adventurous means, aided by his wife's relatives, was able to smuggle the treasure to Athens, thence out of the country. When Schliemann's house was searched and sealed on orders from the Turkish Ambassador, not a trace of gold was found.

Was he a thief? The law regulating the disposal of antiquities found in Turkish territory was loosely framed, and highly subject to interpretation according to the caprice of local officials. Having sacrificed his whole career to the fulfillment of a dream, Schliemann could hardly be expected to be excessively scrupulous at this point in the game. He was determined to preserve his hoard of golden rarities for the delectation of European scholarship.

IV

ONE of the darkest and most sinister chapters in the semilegendary history of ancient Greece is the impassioned story of the Pelopidae * of

* In Greek mythology, the descendants of Pelops, son of Tantalus. Ancient Peloponnesus (literally, isle of Pelops), the southern peninsula of Greece, takes its name from the founder of the Pelopid line.

Mycenae, especially that part of it dealing with Agamemnon's return and death. For ten years Agamemnon had been away, laying siege to Troy, and Aegisthus had made good use of his absence.

> We were yet
> Afar, enduring the hard toils of war,
> While he, securely couched in his retreat
> At Argos, famed for steeds, with flattering words
> Corrupted Agamemnon's queen.

Aegisthus ordered a lookout to be kept for the returning husband and then lay in wait with twenty men. He invited Agamemnon to a banquet – "thinking shameful knavery" – and "struck him down at the banquet, as one slaughters the ox at the crib. None of Agamemnon's friends escaped, all following him." Eight years passed before Orestes, the filial avenger, appeared to kill his adulterous mother, Clytemnestra, and Aegisthus, his father's assassin.

Tragic poets have often dramatized this famous theme, and the memory of the "king of men," ruler of the Peloponnesus, one of the mightiest and richest of historical characters, has remained forever green in posterity's mind.

Mycenae had golden as well as sanguinary connotations. According to Homer, Troy was rich, but Mycenae even richer, and the word *golden* was the adjective that he characteristically used in describing the city. Enchanted by his discovery of Priam's treasure, Schliemann was eager to find new riches. And – contrary to universal expectation – this he actually did.

There was no doubt whatever about the site of the city called Mycenae. The dust of thousands of years covered the ruins, and sheep were grazing where once kings had held sway. Still, the ruins were there to behold. The Lion Gate, main palace entrance, stood high and open in full view. Accessible, too, were the so-called "treasuries" (once thought to be bakers' ovens), the most famous of which was that of Atreus, first Pelopid and father of Agamemnon. This subterranean room is 50 feet high and shaped like a dome, the bold arch of which, made of huge unmortared blocks, is a self-supporting span.

Schliemann found that several ancient authors had located the graves of Agamemnon and his murdered friends at Mycenae. The citadel site was obvious enough, but the graves were another matter entirely. Schliemann had found Troy by depending on his Homer. In this instance he staked his claim on a certain passage in Pausanias which, he declared, previous archaeologists had incorrectly translated and misunderstood. Up to this time it had been assumed – and two of the greatest experts of the day, Dodwell, an Englishman, and Curtius, a German, supported the idea – that Pausanias had pictured the graves as outside the walls of the citadel of Mycenae, but Schliemann maintained that they must be inside the wall. He went ahead and dug, and his diggings shortly proved that again he was on the right track.

"I began the great work on August 7, 1876, with 63 workers. . . . Since August 19 I have carried on the excavating with 125 laborers and four carts, on the average, and have made good progress."

The first important find, after he had uncovered an enormous number of vases, was a curious circular structure, made of a double row of stone slabs set on edge. Schliemann believed immediately that the stone circle was a bench on which the elders of the Mycenaean citadel had sat in the agora while addressing assemblies, taking counsel, and dispensing justice. Here, he believed, Euripides' herald had stood – as recorded in *Electra* – while he called the people to the agora.

"Learned friends" confirmed his view. Presently he found the following sentence in Pausanias, relating, to be sure, to another agora: "Here they built the place of senatorial assembly, in such fashion that the heroes' graves would be in the midst of the meeting place." Thereafter he knew with the same certainty that had led him safely through six layered cities to the "treasure of Priam" that he was standing on Agamemnon's grave.

And when, in short order, he found nine stelae, four of them with well-preserved bas-reliefs, his last doubt vanished, and with it, too, all scholarly restraint. "Indeed, I do not hesitate for a moment," he wrote, "to announce that here I have found the graves that Pausanias, following tradition, ascribes to Atreus, to Agamemnon, king among men, to his charioteer, Eurymedon, and to Cassandra and her companions."

Meanwhile the work on the treasuries near the Lion Gate progressed slowly. Masses of stony rubble aggravated the difficulties of excavation. But here, too, Schliemann's mystical certainty would not be shaken. "I am convinced," he wrote, "of the absolute validity of the tradition which says that these mysterious structures were used as storage places for the treasure of primeval kings." The first find, taken from the debris that he had heaped to one side in an attempt to gain entrance, exceeded in delicacy of form, beauty of execution, and quality of material anything of a similar sort discovered in Troy. There were fragments of friezes, painted vases, terra-cotta idols of Hera, stone molds for casting ornamental articles ("these apparently of gold and silver"), as well as glazed clay objects, gems, and beads.

The amount of work involved in the project is suggested by Schliemann's following observations: "So far as the diggings have progressed to date, nowhere do I find debris piled deeper than 26 feet, and this extreme depth only near the big circular wall."

V

THE discovery of the first grave was noted in Schliemann's journal on December 6, 1876. The grave must have been opened with great care. For twenty-five days Sophia, the tireless helper, explored the earth with fingers and pocketknife. Eventually five graves were found, in them the skeletons of fifteen dead. On the strength of this revelation Schliemann sent a cable to the King of Greece: —

"It is with extraordinary pleasure that I announce to Your Majesty my discovery of the graves which, according to tradition, are those of Agamemnon, Cassandra, Eurymedon, and their comrades, all killed during the banquet by Clytemnestra and her lover, Aegisthus."

Schliemann did not entertain the least doubt about his discoveries. "The bodies were literally covered with gold and jewels," he wrote at the time. Would such valuables have been interred with the bodies of ordinary persons, he inquired. He found expensively fashioned weapons, seemingly placed in the grave so that the dead would be armed against any contingency in the shadow world. Schliemann pointed to the obviously hasty burning of the corpses. The burial crew, it appeared, had hardly taken time to let the fire do its work before piling gravel and earth on the scorched victims. This implied the haste of murderers frantic to hide their crime. True, the corpses had been furnished with funerary gifts and accouterments, but this concession could be explained by the force of custom. As for the graves as such, they were anything but pretentious — indeed, as unworthy, one might imagine, of the rank of the deceased as hatred could make them. Had it not been said that the murdered were "thrown like the carcasses of unclean animals into miserable holes"?

Schliemann sought to buttress his identification of the graves by recourse to his beloved authorities, the writers of antiquity. He quoted from the *Agamemnon* of Aeschylus, from Sophocles' *Electra,* from Euripides' *Orestes.* It simply did not occur to him to question the correctness of his notions. Today, however, we know that his theory was false. He had, it is true, found royal graves under the agora of Mycenae; they were not, however, the graves of Agamemnon and his followers, but of people who most likely had lived some four hundred years earlier.

This discrepancy did not really matter. The important thing was that Schliemann had taken a second great step into the lost world of prehistory. Again he had proved Homer's worth as historian. He had unearthed treasures which provided valuable insight into the matrix of our culture. " It is an entirely new and unsuspected world," Schliemann wrote, " that I am discovering for archaeology."

The golden relics found by Schliemann were of enormous value, and not exceeded in opulence until Carnarvon's and Carter's finds in Egypt. " All the museums of the world taken together," Schliemann said, " do not have one fifth as much."

In the first of the five graves he found on each of three skeletons five diadems of pure gold, laurel leaves, and crosses of gold. In another grave, containing the remains of three women, he collected no fewer than 701 thick golden leaves, together with wonderful ornaments in the shape of animals, flowers, butterflies, and cuttlefish. Besides these he found golden decorative pieces showing figured lions and other beasts, and warriors engaged in battle. There were precious pieces shaped like lions and griffons, and others showing deer at repose and women with doves. One of the skeletons wore a golden crown, on the fillet of which were fastened thirty-six golden leaves. The head wearing the crown had almost completely crumbled to dust. In another grave was a skeleton so near dissolution that only a fragment of the skull was still stuck to the elegant diadem at its head.

Most important of all, he found certain gold masks and breastplates, which, according to tradition, were used in outfitting dead kings to protect them against malign influence after death. Down on his knees, his wife hovering over him ready to lend a helping hand, Schliemann scraped away the layers of clay sheathing the five corpses in the fourth grave. After a few hours' exposure to the air the heads of the skeletons dissolved into dust. But the shimmering golden masks kept their shape, each mask representing completely individual features, " so utterly different from idealized types of god and hero that unquestionably each of the same is a facsimile of the dead person's actual appearance."

Evenings, when the day was done and the shadows of night were creeping over the acropolis of Mycenae, Schliemann had fires lit " for the first time in 2344 years." Watch fires – recalling those which once had warned Clytemnestra and her lover, Aegisthus, of the approach of Agamemnon, but this time serving to frighten thieves away from great treasures.

VI

SCHLIEMANN'S third series of excavations failed to reveal any more buried gold. Of vastly greater significance, however, they brought to light the dead city of Tiryns. Schliemann's discoveries at Tiryns, coupled with what he had already turned up at Mycenae, and with additional finds made a decade later on Crete by the English archaeologist Arthur Evans, made possible the world's first picture of the prehistoric Minoan culture that once dominated the Mediterranean littoral.

There is no doubt that in the interval between the time he attacked the mound of Hissarlik like a child smashing at a toy with a hammer and the time he excavated at Mycenae and Tiryns, Schliemann had grown immensely in archaeological stature. Both Dörpfeld and the great English investigator Evans attest this fact. Schliemann's scientific development cannot be minimized merely because of fallacies bred by an excess of enthusiasm and impetuosity.

In 1876, at the age of fifty-four, Schliemann first drove a spade into the ruins of Mycenae, and in 1878–79, with Virchow's assistance, he dug for the second time at Troy. In 1881, at Orchomenus, the third city characterized as "golden" by Homer, he uncovered the Treasury of Minyas. In 1882, with Dörpfeld, he dug for the third time in the Troad, and two years after this began his excavations in Tiryns.

Once more the familiar pattern unfolded. The archaeologists had previously contended that the walls were medieval remains. As usual, Schliemann paid no attention. Tiryns was supposedly the birthplace of Heracles, and among the ancients the walls of the citadel were thought of as one of the world's wonders. Pausanias compared them with the pyramids of Egypt.

Schliemann dug and brought to light the foundation walls of a palace exceeding in grandeur all found hitherto. Soon there appeared the outlines of a citadel crowning the limestone crag. In the outer bailey, which contained stores and stables, the wall was 7 to 8 yards thick, but in the inner *enceinte,* where the ruler lived, its thickness reached 11 yards. Here the spade brought to light the outlines of the Homeric palace, with pillared walls and chambers, the men's court with the altar, the stately megaron * with porch and antechamber, and even a bathroom where Homer's heroes had bathed and anointed themselves.

But there were still more interesting discoveries: the character of the pottery and the wall paintings. Schliemann immediately recognized the similarity of the pottery, the vases, and the jars to those he had found in Mycenae and to those unearthed by other archaeologists

* Archaeological term derived from the Greek *megas,* meaning "great." The central hall of the Mycenaean house; the hall was rectangular in shape and had a circular hearth in the center.

at Asine, Nauplia Eleusis, and the islands, most notably Crete. Here he found also vases displaying the so-called "geometric pattern," which had allegedly been brought by the Phoenicians to the court of Thotmes III as early as 1600 B.C. So he set out to establish in detail that he had discovered traces of a cultural complex of Asiatic or African origin — a culture, indeed, which had spread over the whole east coast of Greece, which embraced most of the islands, but which probably had a cultural focus in Crete. We now call this culture Minoan-Mycenaean. Schliemann had found the first traces of it.

Schliemann wanted to be home with his wife and children for Christmas of 1890. He was tortured by an ear ailment. Yet he was so preoccupied with his plans that he was satisfied with a superficial examination by hotel physicians in Italy. They reassured him. But on Christmas Day he collapsed in the Piazza della Santa Carità in Naples and lost his power of speech. Through the long night Heinrich Schliemann struggled for his life, never losing consciousness. Then he died.

When his body was brought to Athens, the King and the Crown Prince of Greece, the diplomatic representatives stationed in the Greek capital, the head of the Greek government, and the leaders of all the Greek scientific institutes came to pay their respects at the bier. Looking down on this ardent lover of all things Greek, on him who had enriched the knowledge of Hellenic antiquity by a thousand years, was the bust of Homer. Schliemann's wife and two children also stood by the coffin. These children were called Andromache and Agamemnon.

QUESTIONS

1. Why is the incident related in Paragraphs 2–5, Section I, an appropriate introductory device? What would be the effect of omitting the first two sentences and beginning with "A little boy stood. . . ."?

2. How did Schliemann differ, in his beliefs and his methods of arriving at conclusions, from the scholars of his time? Trace briefly his reasoning, in Section II, which led him to locate the ruins of ancient Troy. What was ironical about his discoveries?

3. Judging from Ceram's account, what motivated Schliemann in his archaeological expeditions? Desire for fame and treasure? Fulfillment of a vow made in childhood? Intellectual curiosity? Although Schliemann was a successful businessman, what did he have in common with the scholars?

4. What aid does Ceram give the reader in identifying the proper names with which he may not be wholly familiar? Would this method also be useful if the writer were explaining a process involving technical terms?

5. What was the principal value of Schliemann's findings as indicated in Section VI?

6. Upon what qualities does this biographical narrative depend for its appeal? What seems to be the attitude of the author toward Schliemann? Has he tried to glorify the character of Schliemann?

JUDGE CHARLES E. WYZANSKI, JR., was born in Boston and was educated at Phillips Exeter Academy and at Harvard University, where he received both the A.B. degree (1927) and the LL.B. degree (1930) with high honors. Carleton College, Tufts College, and Harvard University have granted him honorary degrees. His life has been devoted to various phases of the legal profession. He served as legal secretary to Judge Augustus Hand and Judge Learned Hand. During the 1930s he held several government posts, including that of Special Assistant to the Attorney General of the United States, and in 1941 he became a United States District Judge in Massachusetts. His interest in education is indicated by his having served as a lecturer on government at Harvard University and as a visiting professor at Massachusetts Institute of Technology. He was President of the Board of Overseers of Harvard University until 1957 and a trustee of the Ford Foundation. Probably no one is better qualified – by training, experience, and association – to evaluate the achievements of the late Justice Brandeis than is Judge Wyzanski.

BRANDEIS

by JUDGE CHARLES E. WYZANSKI, JR.

ON NOVEMBER 13, 1856, in Louisville, Kentucky, was born Louis Dembitz Brandeis, who can be fairly claimed to rank in influence upon American law second only to John Marshall. He was not the philosopher-poet that Holmes was; nor had he the range of scholarship or the purity of detachment which characterized Cardozo; and he was without the magisterial command that Hughes so magnificently embodied. Yet, even in company with those giants, Brandeis made the second long stride which gave American law a pace distinctive from, if responsive to, English jurisprudence.

John Marshall showed what judges could draw from a written constitution to support the ancient doctrines of government under law. L. D. Brandeis demonstrated, first at the bar and then on the bench, that legislative history and the legislators' avowed concern with economics, social policy, and statistical science could furnish not merely the inarticulate premises but the express grounds of judicial opinion.

From 1916 to 1939, when Brandeis served as a Justice of the Supreme Court of the United States, any visitor to the Court would have been struck by his presence. Much was attributable to his countenance, Lincolnian in its benevolent sympathy and austere beauty. Something was due to the electric shock of his white hair, unforgettably sculpted by Eleanor Platt.* And then, as Brandeis talked, the soft Southern voice, so persuasive in its appeal to reason, so simple in its choice of words, so moral in its undertones, moved the auditor even more perhaps than the majestic utterances of Chief Justice Hughes, the vigorous clarity of Justice Roberts, and the urbane gentility of Justice Sutherland.

On the bench in front of Justice Brandeis, but not before any other judge, was crooked a gooseneck lamp, obviously lacking the ornate resplendence of standard judicial equipment. Its immediate purpose was severely utilitarian — for none followed more closely and with less interruption the arguments and page references of counsel at the bar. But may it not also have been a symbol to notify the stranger that although the Court had been moved into a palace of justice over Brandeis's protest, L.D.B. had a distaste for ostentation?

Were you to see the Justice in his home, there you would find no display of wealth or elegance. He himself would probably be wearing the dark blue serge suit that annually he bought by mail from Filene's Boston store. If he were in his apartment at Florence Court, the furniture would be typified by a green sofa with a long stiff back which perhaps began its career in a shipment from a Victorian store to Otis Place in Boston. On the wall was a photographic reproduction of the statue of Venus de Milo. If you were allowed to go a floor above, to his crowded study, the surrounding books were law reports from the federal and Massachusetts courts, and a collection of albums filled with clippings reporting Brandeis's cases as an advocate and his championship as "the people's lawyer" of controversies before court, commission, and Congress in the first decade and a half of the twentieth century.

Perhaps, if your intimacy with the Justice reached back into those earlier days, and even more probably if you shared his concern with the aims of Zionism, you might be invited to the Justice's summer cottage at Chatham for an hour's visit strictly clocked by Mrs. Brandeis. If possible, there were even fewer signs of luxury there than on California Street in Washington. Some books were placed not on shelves but in packing cases. And on the wall were framed not famous etchings or impressionist paintings but something far more revealing: a legal instrument — a contract executed several decades before in which

* American sculptress, born in 1910, known for her likenesses of Brandeis, Einstein, Judge Learned Hand, Frederick Keppel, and other famous men.

Mr. Brandeis agreed to pay to each of his daughters an allowance of five cents each week and they in turn agreed to polish his shoes, all on the understanding that "there are no catchwords in this contract."

Whether you came to his home on the Cape or in the District of Columbia, you would meet (mixed with the famous – the Senators, the wife of the President, the heads of executive agencies) a number of both men and women who were engaged in tasks that, though they might not be newsworthy, had a critical importance in the civic and cultural life of the nation: the librarian of the Labor Department; a manufacturer of tags who, before the congressional social-security legislation, had tried an unemployment compensation system in his own plant; the associate editor of the Encyclopedia of Social Sciences; the chief economist of the Department of Agriculture; the most original mind on the staff of the Interstate Commerce Commission; a New York magazine writer who sought to interest a larger public in the intricacies of governmental bureaus; a young lawyer representing New England textile interests; a publisher of pocket books; an expositor of the growth of savings-bank life insurance; a member of a Jewish charitable association's board; an associate counsel of an international intergovernmental organization; the secretary of the chairman of the Senate Committee on Finance; the president of the Seaman's Union; a young professor from the Harvard Law School; a statistician from a Wisconsin public utility commission.

The Justice would take aside visitors, one or two at a time, and ask them on what they were working and what had struck them as interesting. From the judge would come a word of encouragement to pursue the investigation of the causes of an alleged evil, or to remain in the small office in a Southeastern community, or further to consider a particular administrative or legislative problem. Sometimes the judge would broach a topic in which he thought his guest would have interest, and then would find the response unexpectedly negative. Once, for example, he spoke to me of the development of small village community life in Palestine. It took no extensive plumbing to find me completely ignorant. The Justice said nothing. But some days later I found in my morning's mail a set of pamphlets on Palestine, all rolled in a slit plain envelope with no identification beyond the familiar strong, straight handwriting of L.D.B.

It was by hand that all his correspondence and his opinions were written after he went to Washington. He gave up all stenographic assistance and never used as substitutes dictating machines or even, to any extent, a typewriter. But he did have one curiously expensive habit. In preparing an opinion as a Justice of the Court he regularly sent many rough drafts to the Court printer, and then worked from galleys as other lawyers would work from typewritten drafts. Sometimes, as in his celebrated dissent in the O'Fallon case, he dispatched perhaps more than a score of versions of his opinion to the printer's shop on Twelfth Street before he was satisfied with the product. A reason for this extraordinary use of printed rather than typewritten copies may have been that only when a document appeared to him as he thought it would appear to a reader was he able to judge its quality. But whatever the reason, the result was as striking stylistically as it was substantively.

The process of constant revision, rearrangement of ideas, and reshuffling of paragraphs and sentences made the final opinion in each sense of the word highly "articulate." The text had an organic tightness that did not rely for its clear relationships merely on enumeration of separate sections of the text. Footnotes were arrayed with a compelling completeness of supporting authority. And the several points raised by counsel or by other judges were comprehensively answered. To a sensitive, strictly literary taste, the style might seem gaunt. But this criticism must be taken as praise, not blame, by anyone who regards as a test of prose its faithful reflection of the mental and moral standards of the author.

II

THUS Brandeis emphasized the special responsibility which falls upon a judge of our highest court to contribute in its deepest sense to the political growth of the American people. From the time of Chief Justice Marshall, the opinions of the Supreme Court have been a text unto the people. Read in the daily press, studied in the common school, knotted into the rope of enduring history, they may well be the largest single contribution to the philosophy of the American way of life. Conscious of this aspect of his office, Brandeis shaped his opinions not merely as judge but as teacher. No one who has digested his judicial opinions will be surprised at the tale told by one of his most distinguished law clerks, Professor Paul A. Freund of the Harvard Law School. Brandeis had been assigned a case to write for the Court. After he had analyzed the facts, derived the principles to guide the conclusion, and achieved his judgment, Brandeis was not yet content to utter the opinion. For he was still inquiring of his law clerk, "What can we do to make it more instructive?"

Unlike so many leaders in his profession, Brandeis almost never wrote memorial tributes or similar biographical essays which in form purport to sketch the character of other lawyers and judges, but which so often in substance become revelations of the aspirations and accomplishments of the author, rather than of the subject. Once, and in a manner unforgettable to anyone who has read this now difficult-to-procure record, Brandeis came close to painting the sort of double-mirror portrait of which I am speaking. I allude to the magisterial summary of the character of Louis R. Glavis which, as his counsel, Mr. Brandeis gave to the Congressional Joint Committee to Investigate the Interior Department and Forestry Service, conducting the so-called Ballinger investigation. Does Brandeis describe himself or Glavis when he tells us of the four cardinal virtues of a witness — power of observation, perfection of memory, clarity of expression, and ability to envisage the whole situation into which his testimony fits? And is there a more thoughtful defense of Brandeis's own professional career, or for that matter a more pertinent tract for the present times, than the argument offered Congress in support of the concept of loyalty exhibited by Glavis and by Ballinger's stenographer, Frederick M. Kerby?

One issue which perplexed the investigating Congressmen, the wider public, and not least Brandeis's fellow counsel in the case was whether there rested a moral duty of disclosure upon a subordinate in the Civil Service who had discovered what he thought were departures from principle by his superior officer. In Glavis's case the subordinate believed that his chief, Secretary Ballinger, was surrendering portions of the public domain to private rapacity. The stenographer Kerby knew from the letters he had transcribed that Secretary Ballinger, Attorney General Wickersham, and President Taft had misled the Congressional Committee as to the chronological order in which documents had been prepared, and thus had altered their import and value. What was the duty of Glavis and Kerby under these circumstances? How far, and to whom, were they warranted in becoming informers? Was there an overriding obligation to individuals with whom one had been confidentially associated? Could this conflict of attachments be resolved by a profounder understanding of the principle of loyalty?

Whether or not we accept it as valid, the answer Brandeis fashioned states with admirable clarity one viewpoint: —

> The danger in America is not of insubordination, but it is of too complacent obedience to the will of superiors. With this great Government building up, ever creating new functions . . . the one thing we need is men in subordinate places who will think for themselves and who will think and act in full recognition of their obligations as part of the governing body. . . . We want every man in the Service . . . to recognize that he is part of the

governing body, and that on him rests responsibility within the limits of his employment just as much as upon the man on top . . . they cannot be worthy of the respect and admiration of the people unless they add to the virtue of obedience some other virtues – the virtues of manliness, of truth, of courage, of willingness to risk positions, of the willingness to risk criticisms, of the willingness to risk the misunderstandings that so often come when people do the heroic thing.

These are so plainly the virtues which Mr. Brandeis himself possessed, and they are so excellent a definition of the independent man, that I shall devote the remainder of this paper first to a canvass of the leading themes with which his name is indelibly associated, and then to an appreciative critique of his personal way of life. It is not an exaggeration to say that like Franklin, Washington, Jefferson, Hamilton, Lincoln, and Holmes, Brandeis has become for many men much more than a hero in American narrative history. He has become a symbol of particular threads woven into the enduring pattern of American life. He has become the embodiment of the independent man, the inner-directed man of rational bent and moral integration.

III

THE overriding problem of the independent man living in Brandeis's age and ours is the reconciliation of his essential spiritual nature with the powerful forces of an expanding industrial society, a society proceeding at unprecedented speed to produce novel instrumentalities, to spread geographically, to reach new levels of population, to concentrate into fewer hands vast administrative power, and to standardize both information and criteria of judgment so that they may be digested by the mass of men possessing a minimum of bite and taste.

Concern over the relationship between the individual and the mass is, of course, a topic with a longer history than the twentieth century. And even the accentuated phases of this problem which are attributable to the accelerated technological advance since the Victorian era have a bibliography of inordinate length. So Brandeis would claim no patent for his discovery of the central illness of his time. Nor would he, I am sure, suggest he deserved credit for diagnosing as one of the chief causes " the curse of bigness."

The Brandeis program can be conveniently analyzed under his treatment of public power and private power. One advantage of this procedure is that it reveals that the Brandeis opposition to bigness, while always an important criterion, was never an exclusive one, at least where what was at stake was public or governmental power.

For more than a century and a half, or since the overthrow of the yoke of what was regarded as British tyranny, American political science had been keyed to the task of preventing oppressive government. According to the schoolbook version, the devices chiefly relied upon were the federal structure of our Union, the tripartite division of the government into executive, legislative, and judicial branches, judicial review of arbitrary official action, a bill of rights, and representative government.

Our federal structure was an historical consequence of a victorious Revolutionary War consolidating the foreign, commercial, and fiscal interests of diverse colonies accustomed to a large measure of self-determination. The pressures which produced our United States Constitution established a framework which promptly excited widespread admiration. It is unnecessary to recite the degree to which parts of the then British Empire copied our Constitution, or to repeat the panegyric which we received from the most celebrated historian of liberty, Lord Acton. For him the pluralistic structure of the United States, contrasted with the unitary administration of the French Republic, represented our distinctive contribution to the principle of political freedom.

As a judge, Mr. Justice Brandeis often had occasion to show his allegiance to the federal principle. In the cases where progressive legislation of local governments was assailed, he frequently resisted the attack by resorting to the principle that our Constitution protected the right of experimentation in the insulated chambers drawn by state boundary lines. Yet it would be naïve to assert that that principle, of which Mr. Justice Holmes was an even more ardent champion, remained with either of them as inflexible dogma, especially when the coin was reversed and Congress sought to legislate in areas theretofore local. Brandeis, despite occasional votes, as in *Schechter Corporation v. United States,* declaring unconstitutional the National Industrial Recovery Act, was almost always the upholder of, sometimes even the instigator of, that expansion of central governmental power whose growth seems to the critical eye to have made the present United States an increasingly unitary power. This admittedly strong statement I believe can be supported by noting the role of Brandeis in fostering the furthest reaches of congressional taxing and spending power, as well as in the interpretation he gave to the commerce power and the war power, and his refusal to find more than a precatory injunction in the Tenth Amendment.*

* The amendment which reserves to the states any powers not delegated to the Federal Government. As Judge Wyzanski indicates, Brandeis in his decisions usually favored a strong national government.

May I, as a dramatic example, state from personal knowledge his obscure though decisive role in the initiation of our federal-state unemployment compensation system? For now after two decades the tale has moved from the realm of gossip into the realm of history. It was in his apartment that his non-lawyer daughter, in his absence, made the highly legalistic suggestion of a new federal excise tax, modeled on the federal estate tax, with a credit to the taxpayer of amounts paid by the taxpayer to state unemployment compensation systems to be created under state law. Whatever may be said of the constitutionality of the plan – and on this point I am free from doubt, as was the majority of the Supreme Court in 1937 – and whatever may be said of the degree to which the plan preserved opportunities for local administration and for minor variations in local substantive policy, the plan effectuated a marked increase in the relative degree of national control in our federal system.

But the support which social security received was only symptomatic of what appears to me to be the unmistakable trend of other Brandeis decisions. He always regarded as virtually absolute, aside from issues of due process, the grants to Congress of power to tax, to spend, to regulate commerce, and to declare and carry on war. To be sure, he sometimes privately urged that these national powers should be used to supply money, information, or legal backing for state laws. But whether this advice was followed or not, the political result, achieved mainly during his time on the Supreme Court, was to aggrandize the central power.

Likewise, so far as concerns adherence to the hornbook principle of "separation of powers," the impact of the decisions during the Brandeis period was hardly in the spirit of the American founding fathers. As an advocate before the Interstate Commerce Commission, as a sponsor of a bill ultimately merged in the Clayton Act to establish the Federal Trade Commission, and as a judge interpreting regulatory New Deal legislation, Brandeis is properly regarded as one of the architects of our modern system of administrative agencies, which commonly combine some subsidiary executive, legislative, and judicial powers.

So that I may not be misunderstood, let me make explicit that I am not on this score attacking Brandeis. I happen to share his viewpoint. But I recognize, as I am sure he did, that he participated in a most significant increase in public power in the direction of bigness and contrary to individual initiative. He acquiesced in the conversion of government from a largely negative role in combating force and fraud into an affirmative instrument, moving in novel ways, to establish for private persons, corporations, and industries approved patterns of minimum conduct, sometimes appealingly called "fair" conduct.

IV

HOWEVER, if the swelling of the Washington bureaucracy owes something to a favorable wind blown from Brandeis's quarter, he was at the same time most active among those who reduced the pretensions of the Supreme Court to be a super-legislature. His strict avoidance (with one conspicuous exception in *Erie Railroad Co. v. Tompkins*) of unnecessary constitutional issues has become legendary. He had an admirable judicial tolerance toward legislation which in his private capacity he disliked. Witness the ironical fact that one of the dissents with which his name will always be associated was in *New State Ice Co. v. Liebmann,* where he voted to uphold a legislative grant of an ice monopoly of which he might not have approved as a voter.

Even in the field of civil liberties — where the celebrated letter of March 15, 1789, from Ambassador Thomas Jefferson to Congressman James Madison suggests that the Supreme Court of the United States was intended to have a more liberal veto than it had exerted over economic, commercial, or like legislation — Justice Brandeis exercised his judicial negative with restraint. Examined closely, the Brandeis opinions in this field are more often directed at improvement of judicial procedure, at the establishment of safeguards against the reception of tainted evidence, at scrutiny of the precise facts of record, and at cautious interpretation of the legislative command, than they are at invalidation of deliberate legislative choices as to repressive measures.

This was thoroughly consistent with the Justice's deep belief in responsible, representative government. He had no illusion as to his personal omniscience. His tendency was to adopt those courses which gave opportunity for legislators, or administrators, or lower courts to speak more clearly. What he strove to do was to make others examine difficult problems as carefully as he did, so that before final action they would inform the judgments for which they justly bore responsibility. Indeed this is why time and again he will be found supporting investigatory powers, disclosure statutes, and even private group action aiming at a wider dissemination of basic statistical material.

If, as I have suggested, the program in which Justice Brandeis at least acquiesced strengthened during his lifetime the forces of public power and of bigness in government, the record is quite the reverse in the field of private power.

Monopoly, and even bigness which fell short of monopoly, he consistently opposed for practical considerations which he believed experience had taught. He thought men were so inherently limited that they could not intelligently command large enterprises with mastery of detail and economy of operation. He was skeptical of vast concentration of power not because it was inevitably wicked but because he thought it tended to be slothful, unimaginative, and unresponsive to the needs of the market, the problems of the worker, and the claims of the investor. More than the likelihood of corruption, the certainty of capriciousness in large enterprise was what Brandeis feared.

With this outlook, there are many who agree – not least Mr. Justice Douglas, who, to the expressed delight of Mr. Justice Brandeis, became his successor on the Supreme Court of the United States. But it is doubtful whether on the extreme limits (as distinguished from the main trend) of this issue Brandeis can ever get on his side more than a sharply divided vote.

To a large extent, bigness in the modern world seems inevitable unless we are prepared to emulate Switzerland or a Scandinavian country. Our high standards of consumption at relatively low cost are in large part the result of mass production, as we are every day reminded by the automobile and the household gadgets which lighten the housewife's toil. Our military security at the moment rests chiefly on the products of nuclear fission coming from enterprises on a scale so mammoth that only one or two nations can undertake similar establishments.

Those who disagree with Brandeis argue that the evils he discerned are not peculiar to bigness, and are not curable by a planned program of dispersal of power. What the opponents assert is that there are two sounder methods of dealing with the dangers of which Brandeis spoke.

The first is the less important and, to the uncommitted mind, the less warranted by the evidence of experience. It is the promotion of countervailing forces operating exclusively in the economic realm. They are composed, first, of the rival giants in the same area of business; and second, of the giants in those fields of supply, labor, and consumption directly tangent to the first area.

If there can be achieved such a desired resolution of forces operating in the economic realm, then one fortunate by-product of bigness in private enterprise will be the balance which vast establishments of private power are able to exert on the even more vast domain of public power. Our generation has learned what history never before taught so clearly: that public power, even when nominally executing programs for the common man and the social interest, is not always to be trusted with total authority. Absoluteness always becomes arbitrariness. If we are to have a government constantly promoting the general welfare and not the selfish interest of a dictator or of an administrative class of civil servants, it is not sufficient to rely on verbal constitutional limitations, nor on automatic checks internal to our mighty Leviathan. Only if private forces are also of considerable moment and have the courage that comes from independent power can we avoid the capriciousness inevitable in unmitigated totalitarianism.

The second method for dealing with bigness which is advanced by those who dissent from Brandeis's view has an element of paradox, but is nonetheless, I believe, persuasive. The dissenters say, "Justice Brandeis, we agree with you that power and bigness are heavily freighted with risk. Grave dangers there are of abuse, arbitrariness, selfishness, corruption, inefficiency, loss of nerve, staleness, and dull inertia. But, sir, these are not dangers peculiar to bigness, and are not cured solely by competition. You, sir, when you planned the library at Louisville, the savings-bank insurance system in Massachusetts, the yardstick method of calculating gas rates in Boston, were convinced that the mechanism you had provided, so admirably adapted to your theories, would prove your case for small units. If you were to come back now, and again scrutinize your favored institutions, would you not agree with us that what made those enterprises so successful was not their scale but the quality of the gifted man that conceived them and for a time guided their operations? When he left they lost some of their unique quality. In all life proof abounds that he who is a good and faithful servant over a few things can usually be set over many things."

For, as Lord Radcliffe's * Reith Lectures and his apt citation of the experience in India of British civil servants showed, the "problem of power" is less a question of the magnitude than of the morality of responsibility. Power and bigness are no more inherently good or bad than are water and land. All turns on the use made of them. And men in large and small undertakings alike may be trained to self-discipline. In this they may be aided by codes of professional behavior. They are even more helped to become better stewards and better men by the habitual vision of greatness in others.

* Cyril John (Baron) Radcliffe (1899–), prominent English lawyer. The lectures were given for the British Broadcasting Corporation in 1951.

V

THUS it is primarily because of his example of personal greatness, not because of his program and doctrine, that we stand so in debt to Brandeis. His practice was even sounder than his precept. If we reject as thoroughly impractical his notion that jobs should be cut down to man-size, and instead reluctantly conclude that to achieve peace, to reduce illness, poverty, and ignorance, and to promote the efficient use of human and natural resources, large-scale organizations with oversize jobs are inevitable in our times, Brandeis illustrated for us perhaps better than anyone else how to fill such posts.

First is his method of work. He sought out the detail and pondered it while he savored its significance. When Brandeis understood all that there was to know about the facts, he himself (at least until his last years) prepared his own statement of his findings and conclusions. I well remember a remark the Justice made to me when I first entered the public service: "The reason the public thinks so much of the Justices of the Supreme Court is that they are almost the only people in Washington who do their own work."

There are those, I am sure, who will say that this practice is well enough for a judge, removed from most of the harassments of ordinary office life, considering problems neatly packaged in bound records with defined issues, and not under strong inducement to solve forthwith urgent practical problems, but that this is a ridiculous model for the crowded executive or other man absorbed in active struggle. I suggest that the rejection of the Brandeis model often comes too fast. It is extraordinary how much even the man charged with vast administrative responsibilities can gain in discriminating judgment, in overall appraisal, in effectiveness of communication, and in that respect of his fellow workers which breeds authority, when he speaks from personal knowledge of detail. What initially may appear a sacrifice of time comes back manyfold in the form of durable increased reputation.

More than his method of work, Brandeis's *moral character* deserves prolonged contemplation. You may suppose that those emphasized words are a conventional tribute of the type customarily paid to all but the most venal men who have ever held high office. But I mean no such naïve standard compliment. Brandeis's morality, though it was the undoubted foundation of a life of unusual consistency and, in that sense, integrity, presents shortcomings as well as extraordinary depths that repay extended consideration.

One shortcoming has struck most commentators who have assayed the claim that Brandeis was in the Renaissance sense "a complete man." Of the three cardinal values, Brandeis prized highly only two – truth and goodness. Beauty received scant attention. Absence of a vibrant interest in art and poetry is perhaps not always meaningful. But here it is, I suspect, of importance, for it underlines how severely rational was the ethics to which he adhered. His moral order is economic, not poetic, in its foundations. Far from the mark are the comparison of Brandeis to the Biblical prophets and the appellation of Isaiah which he won from President Franklin D. Roosevelt. Mysticism, poetry, the prophetic vision that passeth understanding, never governed Brandeis's utterances. Indeed Brandeis was not like the Old Testament type of moralist the Jewish people has produced – for his ultimates are hardly tinged with emotion. Certainly he was not, like Spinoza, "God-intoxicated." Nor was he suffused with an indiscriminate love of all mankind. And just as he was not overwhelmed by an awareness of fraternal love or of its magic key to the solitariness that lies at the core of all men, so he was not troubled by irrational evil in the world, nor by man's innate perversity which some orthodox theologians ascribe to original sin, and which others of us regard as being waywardness as mysterious as our sudden impulses for good.

But the most intriguing and optimistic aspect of Brandeis's moral life, the one that I believe especially repays study, is what seems to me its progressive improvement beginning in middle life. Some there are who prefer to worship heroes who sprang full armed at birth from the head of Zeus. And for those used to rites appropriate for such primitives, Brandeis is a quite unsatisfactory model. As was the case with Abraham Lincoln, whom Brandeis so much resembled in physical appearance, certain episodes in Brandeis's youth and early maturity are so contrary to the idealism proclaimed in later life that some hostile critics have doubted his sincerity.

There are others who suppose that there was at some stage in Brandeis's life a dramatic forking of the road. Some have suggested it came with marriage to a strong wife with a deep social conscience, reared in a family consecrated by a high sense of duty. Others offer a rationale in terms of an inner response to specific outside stimulus: horror at the Homestead strike,* contact with the garment workers in New York, gradual withdrawal by the Boston Brahmins of the hospitality early extended to Brandeis, a determination to become a factor in politics, the acquisition from legal practice of an "independent fortune" which made it easier for him to be an "independent man."

* In Homestead, Pa., 1892, strike of Iron and Steel Workers against the Carnegie Steel Company, which lasted over four months and resulted in so much violence that the militia was called out to restore order.

All of these analyses strike me as naïve substitutes for a far more common, but nonetheless wonderful and encouraging, explanation. Brandeis himself was the exemplar *par excellence* of his own doctrine that "responsibility is the great developer of man." L.D.B. was a man of constant inward growth. And let us not take from him the glory that he won, by our pretending either that he was always noble or that he became so by external pressure. He grew by trial and error. We are reminded of the dilemma presented to Senator Albert J. Beveridge while he was collecting material for his four-volume biography of Lincoln. As he proceeded with his investigation of original sources, Beveridge became so alarmed at what he regarded as discreditable episodes in Lincoln's early life that he contemplated burning his papers and abandoning the project. Then Beveridge determined that to the reflective student Lincoln was the greater man because it was by conquering himself that he had won the world.

The life of Brandeis had no such depths as the Illinois politician's from which to rise, nor did it ascend quite to Lincolnian heights of pity and love; yet it is a great, perhaps the greatest American, saga of the independent man of our times, the man who believes that ultimate questions must be referred not primarily to some official power or legal proclamation, but to an inward authority — an authority that may be religious, or humanistic, or humanitarian; an authority for which the ethical and creative aspects of the individual man are paramount considerations; an authority that promotes the unflagging search for those arrangements of life, of work, and of leisure which enlarge the capacity of man to discover truth, to achieve beauty, and to foster a fraternal fellowship.

QUESTIONS

1. In Section I, what topics are developed to make clear the personality of Brandeis? What qualities of the Justice receive special emphasis?

2. Note the first sentence of Paragraph 2, Section II. Has Wyzanski in this essay followed the *general* practice of Brandeis? Justify your answer.

3. Section III and Section IV are closely related. What specific problem is the basis of this relationship? In each section, point out the details of Brandeis's contribution.

4. In Section IV, explain how the last three paragraphs may affect the reader's judgment of Brandeis's attitude toward "bigness."

5. How is the transition from Section IV to Section V effected? Explain the meaning of the second sentence in Paragraph 1, Section V.

6. Considering especially Section V, how would you describe Wyzanski's attitude toward Brandeis? Is it subservient? coldly analytical? adversely critical? openly worshipful? How does the material in Paragraph 5 and in the last two paragraphs of the section affect your answer?

Rollo Walter Brown went to Harvard for a second master's degree after receiving his bachelor's and master's degrees from Ohio Northern University. He has had a long and active career as a college teacher (at Wabash, Carleton, Harvard) and writer of biographies, novels, and essays. One of his early books, *How the French Boy Learns to Write* (1915), grew out of his interest in Franco-American relations and teaching methods in French schools. He has lectured widely on literary topics and contributed articles and essays to many magazines. He has been especially drawn to the writing of biography, and his biographies have been called "at once a character analysis and a narrative." Mr. Brown is the author of many books, of which the following list is only a sample: *Dean Briggs* (1926), *Lonely Americans* (1929), *Next Door to a Poet* (1937), and his autobiography, *The Hills Are Strong* (1953). This portrait of Professor George Lyman Kittredge is based on Brown's own recollections as a student in "Kitty's" classes and was later incorporated into a book, *Harvard Yard in the Golden Age* (1948).

"KITTY" OF HARVARD

by ROLLO WALTER BROWN

There could be no doubt about the matter: George Lyman Kittredge consisted of more than one man. Just how many men were required to constitute him, nobody seemed able to say. But that he was not less than two, everybody who knew him was ready to admit.

The first of these two – the one he was most widely thought of as being – was the "Kitty" of Harvard Hall. Undergraduates with vivid imaginations made sketches of the old building on the point of blowing up, with zigzag electric fragments of Shakespeare – "Kitty" spelled it "Shakspere" – shooting from windows and roof, whenever "Kitty" held forth. To many of them for a lifetime the total meaning of Harvard Hall was "Kitty."

The sight of him as he came to the ten o'clock class was in itself something that had to be recognized as dramatic. In the pleasant autumn or spring, men stood high on the steps or out on the turf in front and watched in the direction of Christ Church to see who could catch the first glimpse of him.

"There he comes!" somebody called, and then everybody who was in a position to see watched him as he hurried breezily along – a graceful tallish man in very light gray suit and gray fedora hat, with a full square beard at least as white as his suit, who moved with energy, and smoked passionately at a big cigar. Students used to say that he smoked an entire cigar while he walked the short distance along the iron fence of the old burying-ground and across the street to Johnston Gate. But as he came through the gate he tossed the remnant of his cigar into the shrubbery with a bit of a flourish, and the students still outside hurried in and scrambled up the long stairway in order to be in their places – as he liked – before he himself entered. If any of them were still on the stairway when he came in at the outer door like a gust, they gave way and he pushed up past them, and into the good-sized room and down the aisle to the front, threw his hat on the table in the corner, mounted the two steps to the platform, looked about with a commanding eye, and there was sudden silence and unrestrained expectancy.

"Any questions?" he asked – meaning questions about matters considered at the last meeting of the course. After five minutes of these questions he was ready to begin.

The play under consideration was *Macbeth* – let us say; and he was ready to take up Act III. Always his method was a careful examination of every line, every significant word, with a running commentary on problems of drama and theatre. At the end of the year we were supposed to know five plays – sometimes a sixth – so thoroughly that in the final examination we could spot any line or piece of line that he quoted (usually about sixty), tell what came just before and after, who said the words and to whom, and be able to comment on whatever was significant in the passage. Then there were somewhat more than six hundred lines of memory passages. And there were books of assigned reading. Even the least wise in the course filled margins of their copies of the text, and pages of gummed interleaving paper, with notes against an oncoming evil day.

"Now," he said, after he had read and commented upon Banquo's opening speech, and had reminded us once more that *Macbeth* is a swift-moving play, "there are three very important questions on this next page. They are neatly imbedded, yet for the purposes of the play, they stand out in red ink. What are they?" – and he glanced up and down the class list – "Mr. Howard."

Mr. Howard – it might have been Cabot or Flynn or Jones – did not seem to be present.

"Mr. Howard?" "Kitty" repeated, with the slightest trace of irritation in his voice.

When there was still no response he suddenly exploded. "The college office had two ghost men on my list for two or three weeks before I could get them off! Is this Mr. Howard another?"

There was no response.

"Is there anybody in this room who knows anything about this spook Mr. Howard?"

There was not a murmur, seemingly not even a breath, among the hundred and more students.

He slapped the book down on his desk so sharply that some of the men in the front row jumped. "By heavens, this is not to be endured! I asked a perfectly decent question, and I am going to have an answer if I have to take a poll of the entire class!"

A man back in the middle of the room hesitantly lifted a hand. "I am Mr. Howard."

"Then why didn't you answer?"

"I was not prepared."

"Kitty" flew into so vast a rage that even the top of his head was ruddy. "Well, couldn't you at least have identified yourself? Stand up, Mr. Howard" – and he made a movement as if to step down off the platform – "so that this class can see who you are. And" – after Mr. Howard had very promptly stood up – "you are to come over to Sever 3 at twelve o'clock and expostulate with me – in the Elizabethan sense."

He picked up the book and in a twinkling went on, quite as if nothing unusual had happened, to point out that the three questions down the page were the ones that Macbeth asked Banquo: –

"Ride you this afternoon?"
"Is't far you ride?"
"Goes Fleance with you?"

And then in an engaging smoothness of temper and in flowing brilliance he commented on one passage after another, made compact explanation of linguistic details, reminded us that it was not the words that had become obsolete that made the most trouble for us in understanding Shakespeare, but the words that had not become obsolete, and otherwise rounded out the whole of the scene until we felt as if we must be knowing the play somewhat as the audience knew it when it was originally produced.

He came to a very brief stage direction. "Note that Shakespeare is usually brief. If Mr. George Bernard Shaw had been writing that stage direction, he would have filled a page, at least."

There was a flutter of mirthfulness. It was the style then to laugh at any mention of this new playwright, as though of course he could not be much.

"Incidentally," he said, as he paced the platform, "there are other differences between William Shakespeare and Mr. Shaw."

There was greater mirthfulness still; and time flowed on harmoniously.

Some professor of economics had great charts and maps on rollers all over the front of the room, and there were two or three long gracefully sloping pointers at hand. "Kitty" picked up one of these and used it as a staff-like cane as he paced back and forth and commented. He was magnificent. He was an Anglo-Saxon king speaking to his people.

Once in his march as he socked the royal staff down, it came in two where there was a knot in the wood, and he made a somewhat unkingly lurch. A few students snickered very cautiously.

He glowered upon them. "You have a fine sense of humor!" Then without taking his eyes off the humbled faces, he drew his arm back as if he were hurling a javelin, and drove the long remnant of the pointer into the corner of the room. "Now laugh!" he dared them.

It was always a double experience. "Kitty" might suddenly step out of the Elizabethan world and pounce upon some man and scare him until he was unable to define the diaphragm – it once happened – and require him to come to the next meeting "prepared to discuss the diaphragm" as a preliminary to an hour of *King Lear*. No man might feel altogether sure that he would escape.

Once "Kitty" read with such a poetic impression of reality that a man who was later to be widely known as a magazine editor sat lost in rapturous enjoyment. Suddenly "Kitty" stopped. "Now what is the commanding word in that passage" – and he picked up the printed class list and let his eye run down over the names – "Mr. . . . Smith?" "Mr. Smith" had been so rapturously lost that he did not even know where the passage was. A neighbor whispered the number of the line to him and he answered correctly, "Why – 'God.'" "Don't you 'Why – God' me!" "Kitty" stormed back at him; and then gave him such a dressing down for using the unnecessary word as he had never known, so that he always had that to carry along with his memory of the perfect reading.

On another occasion "Kitty" picked up the class list, started on the *R*'s, became interested in one man's brilliant answers to his rapid-fire cross-examination, and left the rest of the *R*'s dangling in suspense throughout the three remaining months of the year.

Men knew that he was a miracle man, and thought it worth accepting all hazards in order to possess some part of his basic richness of life. They completed the year, grumbled a little about the mark he gave them – there were few *A's* – and very probably came back the next year to study the alternating group of plays. In that case they had the thorough knowledge of ten or eleven plays, instead of five or six; they knew eleven or twelve hundred lines of good passages by heart; they had vast information about drama and theatre and sources and language and Elizabethan life; and they had interesting fragments of such a store of miscellaneous knowledge and wisdom as they had not supposed until last year could be the possession of any one human being.

II

THAT was one of the men in the total George Lyman Kittredge. That part of him could not be brushed aside as if it were not an essential part. It was. But it was the more external part. Many of the men in the course in Shakespeare knew this well enough. They saw that it was their irresponsibility, or laziness, or grotesque ignorance, that touched him off into his tantrums. His disgust and amazement and scorn were release for a sensitive mind – usually in need of sleep – whose everyday high level made it impossible for him not to suffer in the presence of unlimited imperfections. And his graduate students who had never taken the course in Shakespeare found it difficult to believe the wild stories about him. For to them he was a courteous gentleman who begged them to smoke some of his good cigars, and know that they were potential scholars about to be admitted to the most honorable company of men on earth.

His courtesy did not prevent him from exercising the dominant mind. When a student explained somewhat fearfully that he had noticed in the dictionary that a certain word was accented on the second syllable, " Kitty " said, as he put the word down on the back of an envelope, " That's wrong; I'll see that that is changed." Through generations of Shakespeare students – and his place on the board of editors of one dictionary – he caused a shift in preference to the pronunciation of " Elizabethan " with an accented long *e* in the middle. But he could never establish " Shakspere " as a preferred spelling.

Sometimes, too, his overpositiveness came back upon him in ironic ways. He insisted on withholding a degree from a man for insufficient acquaintance with the drama who later became a national figure in playwriting. He once prevented a man from receiving honors in English with whom ten years later he marched down the aisle at a university commencement where both received honorary degrees — the young author and the white-haired professor.

Men who were chiefly concerned with the literature of the eighteenth and nineteenth centuries very justly felt that he placed heavy emphasis on the early centuries. But he insisted that the early centuries were of the utmost importance, and that they were full of interest. The age of Chaucer, he contended, was closer to us than the age of Pope. Always there were students who had looked upon Chaucer as some vague accident back there on the edge of the pure night of the Dark Ages, and for a time they sat skeptical, although they assumed that Chaucer was somebody about whom they should know a little.

But when they listened to Professor Kittredge — or " Mr. Kittredge " — they saw the age of Chaucer coming to such vividness of view that they had to admit that it outshone the nearer centuries in brightness. He invited them to see that " the spirit of radicalism was abroad in the land. To describe as an era of dumb submissiveness the age of Wyclif, and John Huss, and the Great Schism,* of the Jacquerie in France and Tyler and Ball in England, is to read both literature and history with one's eyes shut. . . . It was a scambling † and unquiet time when nobody was at rest but the dead. In a word, it was a good age to live in, and so Chaucer found it."

And so they found it — and the heroic world of Beowulf, and the world of English and Scottish popular ballads, and all the other less familiar worlds to which he introduced them. Something of his own vividness had gone into his original exploring, and now something of it went into the revelation of what he had discovered.

But whatever the area in which he for the moment was occupied, he was engaged in perhaps the most difficult — and most desperately needed — of all educational endeavors in the United States; that is, in having pure scholarship recognized as a source of life for all men. Scholarship is the final high honesty. Men worked with Professor Kittredge — always the least bit awesomely — and came to feel how great was the disgrace of a human mind that let itself be content with anything short of the completest disinterested understanding.

From his fortunate position he all the while was sending out great numbers of men to important college and university posts. They were such men as John M. Manly, of the University of Chicago, one of his earliest students; Walter Morris Hart, of the University of California;

* The period of divided spiritual allegiance in Western Christendom caused by a disputed election to the Papacy (1378–1417).

† Contentious, rambling, irregular, confusedly struggling.

John Samuel Kenyon, of Hiram College; Karl Young, of Yale; Carleton Brown, chiefly of Bryn Mawr; John A. Lomax, of the field of American ballads and folk songs; John Livingston Lowes, who came back from Washington University to teach in the Yard for the rest of his active life — and write *The Road to Xanadu.*

At times the objection made its way back to Cambridge that some of his disciples were not important men of this kind, but only "little Kittredges." And sometimes the reports were true. If men are basically small they are sure to adopt the accessible mannerisms of anyone whose superior qualities are out of reach. But Professor Kittredge's distinguished former students constituted a great company. In Texas, in Iowa, in Pennsylvania, in California, men accustomed to the axe-to-grind sort of thinking, in what they called the practical world, looked upon these honest scholars as an ultimate standard of excellence to be applied in matters of every perplexing sort.

And in Professor Kittredge it was more than honesty; it was high faith in honesty. His former students often traveled a thousand miles — sometimes farther — to have his counsel when they were in doubt. A young professor in a Midwestern college had confided in an older man in one of the chief universities of America about an original project that he had in mind for the next year, and then found that the older man had immediately hurried off a young colleague to work at the idea and be first in the field. Sleepless, the young professor went to consult someone who was wise.

Professor Kittredge sat erect and smoked at a great fragrant cigar and listened in silence until the man was through. Then he said without a moment's hesitation: "Don't let the matter trouble you for one minute. And don't modify your plans — not by as much as a hair. Scurvy business of that kind doesn't work out — in the end. It is not the other man's idea; he is working at it because his chief suggested it to him. He will make little of it. The idea is yours, from the inside of you, and consequently you will be aware of all sorts of possibilities in it that the other man, whoever he is, will never see." And when it turned out precisely so, Professor Kittredge said with a trace of a smile round his eyes and down into his white beard, "We have to count on its being like that."

III

HE GAVE his complete self to the world of the teacher. He required nothing else. In it he had labor and recreation and profound joy — without end. For forty-eight years (1888–1936) he taught at Harvard. He never took a sabbatical year of leave, nor a half-year. He did not like to have breaks in his work. He did not like to go off to other universities to lecture in term-time. He made a number of trips to Europe, but with one exception he made them in the summer vacation period. England was his great fascination east of the Atlantic. When he was made an honorary fellow of Jesus College, Cambridge, he was delighted and proud. When Oxford wished to confer on him an honorary degree he felt highly honored, of course. But the great joy of work was at home.

In this world of the teacher to which he was devoted, he carried on endless research. When he was confronted by the teacher's much discussed choice between teaching and research, he said, "Thank you, I'll take both."

In his own explorations the range that he covered was so wide that some persons actually believed that there were at least two persons named G. L. Kittredge writing at the time. He was interested in such matters as Increase Mather's views on smallpox, the ballads of Kentucky, the vocabulary of the Australasians, the history of witchcraft, the history of words for popular reading, cowboy songs, the early Teutonic notions of immortality, the toad in folklore, Chaucer on marriage, the history of religion, and scores of subjects thought of as more strictly within the field of language and literature. And his books ranged from *Chaucer and His Poetry* to *The Old Farmer and His Almanack* – and manuals of grammar and composition for high schools.

It was at Barnstable, down on the Cape, that he was able to do much of his own work. For there he had long summer weeks that were little interrupted. If one chanced to be at the house on Hilliard Street in Cambridge just when he was about to go away for the summer, one might well decide that he was leaving for all time, so completely did he seem to be transferring his scholarly effects. Eventually he built a study a little away from the house in Barnstable so that he might work in entire seclusion, with only the cheerful voices of his children and their friends on the tennis court to remind him pleasantly – if he heard them at all – that he was not completely isolated in time and space.

On the Cape, too, he could be elementally refreshed. On the Cape, he was happy to say, he – or his son – had come upon the perfect pessimist, a native who grew chickens. When it was suggested that a few chicks just outside a coop were sturdy youngsters, the native replied, "Yes, but the trouble is, the old hen hatched out six, and by God all of them have died on me but five."

The Cape was heaven for work; yet back in Cambridge in the autumn he carried his own work right along with his teaching – and thereby constantly gave his teaching enrichment. He moved briskly from his classroom to Gore Hall, and very quickly disappeared. Then one came upon him somewhere deep in the stacks, lost to the immediate world over a puzzling text or fat galleys of proofs. The library was nothing musty and dead for him. It was man recorded. When the great new Widener Memorial Library was spoken of as an elephant among the other buildings in the Yard, he asked, "What if it is? You could destroy all the other Harvard buildings to the northward, and with Widener left standing, still have a university."

If days were not long enough, always there were nights. Like Charles Péguy,* he considered night as the part of existence that holds everything together, that is sacred to man "wherein he accomplishes his being." But for Professor Kittredge this was not to be done through sleep; it was to be done through work.

For many years one of his intimate friends walked from Boston to Cambridge on Sunday afternoon, had supper with the Kittredges, and then the two read Greek together till eleven o'clock -- as relaxation. But that still left the body of the night ahead. So, too, was it when his "ballad course" met at his house in the evening, and some of the most enthusiastic lingered a little in the big study. It was when his own house had become quiet, and the lights in houses everywhere were beginning to disappear, and the roar of the city had lost its nearness, and the world was otherwise losing the last signs of its daytime confusion, that he knew freedom. In the enveloping quiet he could give himself to work without fear of distraction. If he felt the need of diversion, he could read one more detective story.

When Mrs. Kittredge chanced to know at two or two-thirty or three in the morning that he was still at work, she would slip down and remind him that it was time for him to be getting some sleep. Very obediently he would go off to bed for the rest of the night. In the course of years, Mrs. Kittredge wearied a little of making the trip downstairs and had an electric bell installed with a button by her bed. But he did not like it. In the perfect quiet of night it made him jump. Sometimes nobody reminded him that he ought to be in bed, and he did not think of the matter himself; and when Thomas the chore man slipped into the study at six in the morning to build a new fire, there sat Professor Kittredge peacefully asleep in his comfortable chair before the empty fireplace, with one hand clutching a book on the arm of the chair as firmly as if he were awake. On such a night he did not get to bed at all.

* Charles Péguy (1873–1914) was a French poet who wrote long, mystical epic poems in free verse, such as *The Mystery of the Charity of Joan of Arc.*

IV

WHEN a vivid man does a sufficient number of things that are unfailingly characteristic, legend begins to attach itself to his name. And when he lives on and on through one college generation after another until men who were in his classes almost a half-century before come back to visit their grandsons in the freshman class and find him still teaching with the same old fire, the contributions of legendary instance mount till they constitute a kind of running supplemental biography.

Men argued over the original color of his hair and beard, for he was gray — or white — so early that nobody could quite remember him when he was not gray or white. They liked to speak, too, of the fact that "Kitty" never bothered with any degree except an A.B. They laughed over the gushing woman who asked in disappointment why he had never taken a Ph.D., and his supposed reply: "Who would have examined me?" Or they repeated the story of the famous woman college president who wished a Harvard man as an instructor in English, but said she could not consider anyone who lacked a Ph.D., and of Charles Townsend Copeland's * stentorian reply to her: "Thank God, then we'll not lose Kittredge!"

Legend was helped, too, by the fact that in his highly charged life there was always unpredictable heartening for the less positive, the less courageous. When a frightened young candidate for honors in English had to say in reply to a question, "I'm afraid I can't answer; I have not read all of Wordsworth," Professor Kittredge brought him quickly to life and confidence by replying: "Neither have I! I couldn't be hired to!" When the efficiency experts were rising up everywhere in institutions, and one of them asked Professor Kittredge just how many hours and minutes it took him to prepare one of his "lectures" on Shakespeare, he replied: "I refuse to answer. It's one of my trade secrets." Then he relented and said, "Just a lifetime — can't you see that?" When graduate students in the field of English made their way to Professor K. G. T. Webster's † house at Gerry's Landing for a relaxing great dinner and then a joyous session on the third floor in a room that some of the guests thought of as an Anglo-Saxon mead-hall, Professor Kittredge was always so full of wit and generosity of spirit that the guests were stirred to believe they could face anything.

So there he was, about to be seventy-five, full of fiery power, and

* Charles Townsend Copeland (1860–1952) was on the Harvard English faculty from 1892 to 1928. "Copey" was especially noted for his courses in writing.
† K. G. T. Webster (1871–1942) taught English for many years at Harvard and was a specialist in medieval English poetry.

seemingly without a thought that he had already taught ten years past the usual retiring age. He walked energetically through the traffic of Harvard Square and the policeman said bravely but so that Professor Kittredge would be sure not to hear: " Be a little careful there, Santa Claus! " In the Yard the general assumption seemed to be that nobody quite dared to tell him that he must retire.

On his seventy-fifth birthday when he went to his class at Radcliffe, the girls had put seventy-five magnificent crimson roses on his desk.

What was this they had done? Often enough he had scolded them. Sometimes he had walked out on them when they did not come up to his expectations in brilliance. And now they had remembered him in this fashion. They had almost taken an unfair advantage of him – so startling was it all. He told them – and suddenly he was deeply touched – that he found it difficult to express his great appreciation. " If it would help, I'd declare a holiday. And I do hereby declare a holiday." Then quite as suddenly he recovered his usual manner, looked up, and said with a self-defiant kind of smile: " Now if only some of you will tell me how to get them home without looking like a bridegroom! "

At home he admitted modestly to his wife that not every man received that many roses from his girl students on his seventy-fifth birthday. In the afternoon when one of his former students and his wife dropped in to offer best wishes, he was in the happiest of moods. He told them how near he had come to being born on the twenty-ninth of February. He admitted in great joviality that undergraduates had at times led him to make " characteristic remarks " and do " characteristic things," and he drew out of the past a few instances himself. Yes, he supposed he would be giving up teaching sooner or later, for he had in mind finishing that annotated edition of such plays of Shakespeare as had interested him most, and that would keep him busy for a number of years ahead.

And so it did.

QUESTIONS

1. Brown says that Kittredge was at least two men. On what basis does Brown distinguish the two Kittredges?

2. From the information of Section I, reconstruct the nature of Kittredge's course in Shakespeare. What value does Brown place on this type of instruction and learning?

3. What is the significance of the episode in the last two paragraphs of Section II?

4. State briefly the theme of Section I and also of Section II.

5. What are the chief techniques by which Brown reveals the character and personality of Kittredge? How do these techniques contribute to the mood and tone of the essay? (See p. 80, Question 4 for definitions of mood and tone.)

6. What is the special appropriateness of the episode about the seventy-five roses (at the end of the essay)?

A Touch of Humor

RICHARD GORDON

ROBERT LYND

PHILIP WYLIE

RICHARD GORDON practiced medicine from 1945 until 1952 as an anesthetist and served for a time as a ship's doctor. In 1952, he gave up medical practice to devote his full time to writing. Out of his medical experience came his first two books: *Doctor in the House* (1952) and *Doctor at Sea* (1953); both were enormously successful and both were made into films. He is also the author of a novel, *The Captain's Table* (1954), and *Doctor at Large* (1955). Before he began writing for larger audiences, Dr. Gordon had written scientific papers and textbooks on anesthesia. In *Who's Who* he now lists medicine as his recreation.

THE COMMON COLD

by RICHARD GORDON

THE common cold is really a highly popular complaint throughout the temperate regions of the world where it is endemic. It has all the attractions of an illness and none of the disadvantages, for it never kills anyone and always gets better within a fortnight. Meanwhile it acts as a magnet for sympathy in midwinter, when sympathy is needed the most; it grants a week's leave from the office at a time when holidays are miserably balanced between recollection and anticipation; and as it makes no difference to the prognosis whether treatment is given or not, each cold offers its victims a delightful exercise in self-doctoring.

The English, who take their ailments less sadly than some of their other pleasures, have now passed more than six years of the free National Health Service with their enthusiasm for treating their own colds wholly undiminished. These home cures generally follow one of three distinct courses, and as each reflects the psychology of the sufferer let us examine them in detail. They are: 1) the Fresh-Air Treatment; 2) the Scientific Attack; 3) the Coddle.

The Fresh-Air treatment is practiced only by those large red-faced men in check suits who look you in the eye, slap their chests, and declare they've never owned an overcoat or been to a doctor in their lives, as if claiming freedom from original sin. They have a simple attitude to illness: it's all "psychological," from smallpox to fractured femurs. But they are only human, and in time claimed by both death and colds. The first sneeze affects them like a starter's pistol: they tear off their ties and waistcoats, stamp around the house throwing open the windows, jump into a cold bath, and upset their wives by doing breathing exercises all night in bed. The discomfort in which they wallow for a fortnight makes no difference to the course of the disease, but by rendering their surroundings unfit for human habitation they rarely manage to infect anyone else.

The Scientific sufferer takes a much calmer view of his cold. He is generally a precise, clerkish man, who files the medical articles from the *Reader's Digest* and reads the patent-medicine advertisements like a girl looking into a bride-shop window. During the winter he gargles for five minutes with antiseptic night and morning, wears wool next to the skin, and eats sufficient calcium to keep a schoolroom in chalks. As soon as his nose starts to run he calls at the druggist's and arrives home with his brief case clinking gently with small bottles. He announces to his wife: "Think I'm getting a touch of a cold, m'dear," as though he were having a baby. He makes for the bathroom and unpacks his bag, which is filled with cough mixtures, fever pills, throat lozenges, nose drops, eye lotions, gargles, and liniments. He sets the bottles carefully on the shelf and works his way through them thoughtfully and solemnly, like a sailor trying out the drinks in a strange port.

This type of invalid follows the directions on the label with scientific precision: if it orders "An eggcupful four-hourly," he fetches an eggcup; if it says "Rub on the chest till it stings," he scrapes away until his skin begins to peel. He then has a mustard bath, soaks his feet in salt water, puts on two pairs of flannel pajamas, and goes to bed with *The Household Doctor.* No physician ever watched the recovery of a wealthy patient more sadly than he notices his own returning health. For, once he has caught his cold, he does not lightly let it go. From October to May he richly justifies the famous mistranslation of *voici l'anglais avec son sang-froid habituel* – here comes the Englishman with his usual bloody cold.

The Coddler is usually a woman, with a far more fuzzy idea of her internal organs than the Scientific sufferer. Since girlhood she has been told that she must Take Care of a Cold or it will turn into Something Else; her life passes in a terror of Germs, which she imagines as small green animals, with red eyes and long teeth, that hide under the dustbin. Before she has blown her nose twice, the Coddler has phoned her husband's office and all her friends to explain that she has a cold, in the tone of someone announcing that smallpox has just broken out. She then pours herself a large Scotch, lights a fire in her bedroom, piles extra eiderdowns on the bed, shuts the windows, rubs herself all over with camphorated oil, phones out for grapes, calf's-foot jelly, chicken essence, barley water, Eau de Cologne, and the other prerogatives of illness, shifts the television upstairs, collects all the magazines in the house, and goes to bed. She stays there for a fortnight, her family fetching her egg-and-milk, lightly sprinkled with nutmeg, every other hour.

The interest shown by the English in their colds probably explains why the world's largest research unit for the disease is to be found at Salisbury, in southern England. This unit works in the Harvard Hospital, which was hopefully set up on the edge of Salisbury Plain by Harvard University at the beginning of the war to study the epidemics expected to sweep across England during the bombing. Although the bombs arrived, the epidemics fortunately did not, and for a long time the chief function of the Harvard Hospital was to entertain visiting British doctors with American rations. It was later taken over by the United States forces, and was presented to the British Medical Research Council and Ministry of Health in 1946.

The hospital has gained much publicity since the common cold investigations began, mainly because the experiments are conducted on human volunteers. The reason for this is simple. It has been known for forty years that a cold can be produced by dropping into the healthy nose bacteria-free filtrates of nose-washings containing virus from people suffering from the disease. Unfortunately, man and the chimpanzee are the only animals known to be susceptible to the infection, and chimpanzees are difficult to come by, expensive to feed, and awkward to keep alive in captivity. It is therefore much simpler and cheaper to use men.

About thirty-six volunteers are taken at the hopsital, and kept there for ten days at a time. The only qualifications for entrants are that they must be between 18 and 45, and free from serious illness or conditions like hay fever, asthma, and sinusitis. When the experiments were begun in 1946, the doctors had doubts that sufficient volunteers would step forward year after year to keep the investigations going, but this has been the simplest problem that the unit has had to face. In summer, you now have to book your room at the Harvard Hospital far ahead.

I don't think the volunteers step through the hospital gate in the spirit of John Hunter * or Paul Ehrlich,† resigned to suffer disease for the common good: to most of them the research unit offers an

* John Hunter (1728–1793), British anatomist and surgeon.
† Paul Ehrlich (1854–1915), German physician, bacteriologist, and chemist.

unusual chance to exchange a fortnight's comfortable free board and lodging for the risk of catching a cold. Many of the volunteers are students — particularly medical students — for whom the Harvard Hospital solves vacation problems: it gives them somewhere to live; it provides quiet and solitude for concentration; it keeps them away from cricket grounds, golf courses, pubs, cinemas, girls, and other traditional distractions to academic study; it is the only possible way for an undergraduate to save money, in order to enjoy these distractions more richly in the coming term; they receive three shillings a day wages and free beer.

The hospital itself is one of the untidy nests of badly painted wooden huts that were familiar enough in the English countryside during the war. Each of the huts has been turned into a house large enough to hold a family. It contains a couple of bedrooms, a sitting room, bathroom, and pantry, but it is occupied only by two volunteers — no one can complain of claustrophobia. The food is cooked in a central kitchen, brought in vacuum containers, and left on the doorstep in the traditional style for feeding plague victims. The visitors are provided with a radio and an internal telephone line which supports the social life of the hospital, telephonic chess being the favorite local sport.

Most of the volunteers arrive prepared to stick out ten days playing the prisoner in the Tower, but personal restrictions at Salisbury are slight. They are allowed to wander round the grounds, walk in the surrounding countryside, and use the putting green. The only standing regulation is that volunteers must never approach within thirty feet of anyone else. The printed instructions emphasize this rule to the point of explaining that should some emergency strike a hut during the night, the occupants must ring the alarm bell outside the resident doctor's quarters and then stand back thirty feet before yelling at him "Fire!" "Thieves!" "Murder!" or whatever is appropriate.

The volunteers are also provided with a large library. The books must be chosen on arrival and cannot be changed because of the risk of cross-infection — which occasionally leads to misfortunes of the type that overtook a shy young student of English who snatched an armful of volumes entitled, as he thought, *The Art of Making Fine Poetry,* only to find himself locked in for ten days with exhaustive information on the manufacture of high-grade chinaware.

The reason for the volunteer's being at Salisbury is recalled each morning by a short visit from the doctor and matron. They arrive in sterile masks and gowns, and for the first two days do no more than ask politely after the health of their guests. This period is reserved for the appearance of any colds picked up en route. On the third day, the doctor drops into the volunteer's nose a solution made up in the laboratory, which may contain active cold virus or may be an inert control fluid. To make cheating more difficult all round, neither the volunteer nor the doctor knows which solution is which. The volunteer is then given a record sheet similar to a score card, containing a list of symptoms like watering of the eyes, sore throat, nasal obstruction, cough, and headache, and sits back and waits. Usually nothing happens. Even if he has been given the active solution, only about 30 to 50 per cent of these inoculations develop into colds.

Eight years' work at Salisbury has produced no startling discovery about the common cold, but it has accomplished much creditable steady research. It has also disproved most of the facts about colds that we learned in the nursery, with other scraps of distasteful and inaccurate information like "rice puddings are good for you" and "spinach is full of iron." Do you remember Mother's horrified voice when you came in from playing pirates in the pond – "Take those sopping wet socks and shoes off *at once!* Do you want to catch your death?" – or the beating you got for jumping out of a hot bath and chasing the cat in the garden? And the number of things you were warned that caused colds, from removing your long-sleeved underwear before May 31 to sleeping with the windows open (or shut)? All these complications of childhood have luckily been shown at the Harvard Hospital to be groundless. The common cold is an infective disease like diphtheria or influenza, and you catch it from somebody else on the bus.

The research unit laboratory has now succeeded in growing the cold virus on cultures of human embryonic lung, and shortly it will be possible to study it more conveniently in the laboratory and disband the sturdy army of volunteers. Meanwhile, the common cold continues. The Harvard Hospital still has no suggestions for a cure better than my favorite remedy of a bottle of whisky and a hat, which is both simple and effective. This is how it works: On the first sign of a cold, go to bed with a bottle of whisky and a hat. Place hat on left-hand bedpost. Take a drink of whisky and move hat to right-hand post. Take another drink and shift it back again. Continue until you drink the whisky but fail to move the hat. By then the cold is probably cured.

QUESTIONS

1. This little essay offers particularly good opportunities for studying the ingredients of humor. What attitudes and responses does Gordon attempt to arouse in the reader? What devices does he use to achieve these attitudes and responses?

2. What is the relationship between the first six paragraphs of the essay (considered as a unit) and the rest of the essay?

3. What are the specific sources of humor in the three paragraphs beginning on page 211 with the words " The hospital has gained . . ."?

4. What is Gordon's expressed attitude toward the Salisbury experiment? Does he imply more than he expresses?

5. What is the author's principal intention in the essay? Has he sought *merely* to amuse the reader?

ROBERT LYND, for many years, under the pseudonym of "Y.Y.," contributed a weekly column to *The New Statesman and Nation*. Lynd (1879–1949) was a prolific writer on a wide variety of subjects. He also served as literary editor of the *London News Chronicle*. The scope of his interests is indicated in such books as *Home Life in Ireland* (1909), *The Pleasure of Ignorance* (1921), *Solomon in All His Glory* (1922), *Dr. Johnson and Company* (1928), *I Tremble to Think* (1936), *Life's Little Oddities* (1941), and *Things One Hears* (1945).

OBJECTIONS TO LAUGHTER

by ROBERT LYND

"LAUGHTER" is a word, we are told by the philologists, that is a distant cousin of the Greek κλώσσειν, "to cluck like a hen," and also of κράζειν, "to croak." But we need not go any further than our everyday speech to have it brought home to us that when we laugh we do something that puts us on a level with the lower animals. Half the words we ordinarily use to describe anybody laughing are words borrowed from a vocabulary descriptive of the various inarticulate sounds that must have made the chief music of life in Noah's ark. We say of a laughing human being that he "bellows" or "roars" or "cackles" or "crows" or "whinnies." Some people even speak of "barks of laughter" and of "hoots of joy." We say of one man that he "laughs like a hyena" and of another that he has a "horse laugh." And, even if a man is guilty of nothing worse than that noiseless form of laughter known as a smile, we often describe him as "grinning like an ape" or "like a Cheshire cat." It is true that, in describing weeping, we also occasionally use words that suggest a comparison with the lower animals. A child, like a dog, is said to "whine," and its sobs as well as its laughter are often spoken of as "bellowing," "roaring," and "howling." Still, the vocabulary of the forest and the farmyard seems to be much more freely applied to our expression of mirth than to our expression of woe.

We have often been told that the ability to laugh is one of the chief things that distinguish man from the other animals. The report that "the little dog laughed to see such sport" when the cow jumped over the moon is generally discredited as a legend. I am confident, however, that the people who say that animals never laugh are wrong. Animals undoubtedly make slightly different sounds from ourselves in their expressions of pleasure, and possibly they are pleased with different things, but when they are pleased they have a way, like ourselves, of making inarticulate sounds, and I see no reason to doubt that pigs, geese, starlings, dogs, parrots, and green woodpeckers at times make these sounds in a mood of what we call hilarity.

Certainly there seems nothing in the ordinary dictionary definition of the word "laugh" to suggest that laughter is something of which other animals than man are incapable. The first dictionary I consulted on the matter defined "laugh" as an intransitive verb meaning "to express mirth or joy by an explosive inarticulate sound of the voice and peculiar facial distortion." A dog undoubtedly is capable of that. The next dictionary said: "Laugh . . . to express feeling by a series of inarticulate explosive sounds due to the characteristic vibrations into which the vocal cords are thrown by the jerky, spasmodic character of the expirations." That is no better a description of a human laugh than of a donkey's bray. I doubt, indeed, whether anyone has ever succeeded in defining or describing laughter in terms inapplicable to the facial contortions and explosive sounds made by animals. All the descriptions of the act of laughter that I have met with have seemed to me equally applicable to the snarling of wild beasts and to the merriment of human beings at a dinner party.

Take, for instance, Professor Sully * in that excellent book, *An Essay on Laughter.* Near the beginning of the book, he has a description of a smile — which, as he tells us, viewed as a psychological event, is rightly regarded as a laugh, though as an incomplete laugh. "Smiling," he declares, "involves a complex group of facial movements. It may suffice to remind the reader of such characteristic changes as the drawing back and slight lifting of the corners of the mouth, the raising of the upper lip, which partially uncovers the teeth, and the curving of the furrows betwixt the corners of the mouth and the nostrils (the nasolabial furrows) which these movements involve. To these must be added the formation of wrinkles under the eyes — the most characteristic part of the expression — which is a further result of the first movements. The increased brightness of the eyes is probably the effect of their tenseness, due to the contraction of the adjacent muscles and the pressure of the raised cheek, though an acceleration of the circulation within the eyeball may have something to do with it."

I confess that I do not find a smile, so dissected, particularly human.

* James Sully (1842–1923), Professor in University College, London, author of many books on psychology.

To read of it is to conjure up a picture of the expression on the face of Red Riding Hood's wolf rather than the expression on the face of La Gioconda. And, when we pass from the smile to the laugh proper, Professor Sully's description is equally humbling to those who have taken pride in the thought that when they laugh they give convincing evidence of their difference from, and their superiority to, the other animals. Laughing, says Professor Sully, " is an interruption of the natural rhythm of the respiratory process, in which inspiration and expiration follow one another at regular intervals. The obvious feature of its interruption . . . is the series of short, spasmodic expiratory movements by which the sounds are produced. These are, however, preceded by a less noticed inspiration of exceptional energy and depth. These interruptions of the ordinary respiratory movements involve also an unusually energetic action of the large muscles by which the chest is expanded, *viz.*, those which secure the contraction and so the descent of the dome-shaped diaphragm and those by the action of which the ribs are elevated. The production of the sounds by the spasmodic expiratory movements shows that the passage from the trachea into the pharynx, *viz.*, the glottis or chink between the vocal cords, is partially closed. The quality of the sounds is explained by the particular arrangements, at the moment of the cachinnation, of the vocal apparatus, and more particularly the shape of the resonance chamber of the mouth."

Let those who are given to boasting of their sense of humor as though it were one of the highest achievements of which humanity is capable look on this " slow-motion " picture of a laugh and realize that all their sense of humor can do for them is to enable them, like any other animal, to make spasmodic expiratory movements through a partially closed passage from the trachea to the pharynx.

II

PERHAPS it was their realization of the essentially animal nature of laughter that led so many philosophers, saints, and authorities on behavior to condemn it. Plato, in the *Republic*, censures Homer for having degraded the gods by making them laugh in the sentence: " Inextinguishable laughter arose among the blessed gods, when they saw Hephaestus bustling about the mansion." And he expresses his dislike of laughter still more strongly in the same book when he makes Socrates declare that the guardians of the State ought not to be given to laughter, and that persons of worth must never be represented as being overcome by laughter. Pythagoras, again, is a philosopher of whom we are told that " he would avoid laughter and all pandering to tastes such as insulting jests and vulgar tales."

It is true that there have been philosophers of a less unbending disposition, such as Spinoza, of whom it is said that " after protracted studies " he " would mix with the family party where he lodged, and join in the most trivial conversations, or unbend his mind by setting spiders to fight each other; he observed their combats with so much interest that he was often seized with immoderate fits of laughter." But it is a significant fact that among philosophers there is only one who is known as the Laughing Philosopher, and the learned assure us that Democritus was not really a laughing philosopher at all.

I do not know whether we are any longer permitted to believe the story that Democritus used to walk down to the harbor of Abdera in his lighter moments and " laugh heartily at such variety of ridiculous objects, which there he saw." Even Burton, who repeats the story, describes Democritus as " a little wearish old man, very melancholy by nature," and an older authority declares that he used to train himself " by a variety of means to test his sense-impressions by going at times into solitude and frequenting tombs." Yet this man is apparently the nearest thing to a laughing philosopher that the world has seen.

As for the saints, though many of them have been cheerful men, few of them have been conspicuous for their hilarity. Some of them have even thought it was a sin to laugh. Saint John the dwarf, for example, on seeing a monk laughing uncontrollably at dinner one day was " so horrified that he at once began to cry," and Saint Basil wrote against the wickedness of laughing, declaring that it was the one bodily affection that the Founder of the Christian religion " does not seem to have known."

I fancy the saints of all the religions and all the churches have been the same in this respect. One does not imagine John Knox as a patron saint of laughter, and I am sure that the Presbyterian elder who rebuked someone for whistling on Sunday in the sentence, " Mon, this is no day for whustlin'," would have equally rebuked anyone whom he had heard laughing on the sacred day.

And when we leave the saints and come to more worldly authorities on behavior we find the same thing. The greatest English gentleman who ever left detailed instructions as to how to behave like a gentleman was Lord Chesterfield, and in his *Letters to His Son* he declares emphatically in more than one passage that a man who wishes to be regarded as a gentleman must avoid laughter above all things. Everyone knows the passage in which he warns his son: " Loud laughter is the mirth of the mob, who are only pleased with silly things; for true wit or good sense never excited a laugh, since the creation of the world. A man of parts and fashion is, therefore, only seen to smile, but never heard to laugh."

In a further letter, Lord Chesterfield returns to and reiterates his warning. He writes: –

> Having mentioned laughing, I must particularly warn you against it: and I could heartily wish that you may often be seen to smile, but never heard to laugh while you live. Frequent and loud laughter is the characteristic of folly and ill manners; it is the manner in which the mob express their silly joy at silly things; and they call it being merry. In my mind, there is nothing so illiberal, and so ill bred, as audible laughter. True wit, or sense, never yet made any body laugh; they are above it. They please the mind, and give a cheerfulness to the countenance. But it is low buffoonery, or silly accidents, that always excite laughter; and that is what people of sense and breeding should show themselves above. A man's going to sit down, in the supposition that he has a chair behind him, and falling down upon his breech for want of one, sets a whole company a laughing, when all the wit in the world would not do it; a plain proof, in my mind, how low and unbecoming a thing laughing is. *Not to mention the disagreeable noise that it makes, and the shocking distortion of the face that it occasions.* Laughter is easily restrained, by a very little reflection; but as it is generally connected with the idea of gaiety, people do not enough attend to its absurdity. I am neither of a melancholy nor a cynical disposition; and am as willing and as apt to be pleased as any body; but I am sure that, since I have had the full use of my reason, nobody has ever heard me laugh.

Chesterfield then goes on to denounce the "very disagreeable and silly trick of laughing," and to speak contemptuously of "a man of very good parts, Mr. Waller, who cannot say the commonest thing without laughing; which makes those who do not know him take him at first for a natural fool." And indeed Lord Chesterfield, in his assertion that nobody had ever heard him laughing, had noble predecessors through the ages. Johnson declares that nobody had ever heard either Swift or Pope laughing. And was it not said of the grandfather of the great Croesus that "he never laughed but once in his life, and that was at an ass eating thistles"? One feels that he might have chosen a more exciting occasion.

But it is not only the philosophers, the saints, and the authorities on manners who have belittled laughter. One of the most fastidious spirits of modern times, the poetess Alice Meynell, devoted a carefully reasoned essay to an appeal to her fellow countrymen to laugh a little less loudly and a little less frequently than they do. The English, she observed, though they speak less loudly than the Continental nations, are given to laughing more loudly in the theatres, and, disliking noise, she held up to them for imitation "the Oriental estimation of laughter as a thing fitter for women, fittest for children, and unfitted for a beard." Mrs. Meynell was mistaken, it seems to me, if she thought that in her objection to laughter she was singular. The ordinary man may occasionally laugh, but he does not think much of laughter. He has as poor an opinion of it, indeed, as Plato or Mrs. Meynell herself. That the ordinary man cares little for laughter can, I think, be easily proved.

Consider, for one thing, what has been the most widely read literature of the past two generations. Is it not a conspicuous fact that among the most popular novels four or five are by writers who never try to make us laugh, or, at least, who never succeed? Twenty years ago the "best-selling" English novelists were Miss Marie Corelli and Mr. (now Sir) Hall Caine. Today three out of four of our best sellers are writers who depend for their effect scarcely at all upon humor of situation or character. I do not forget that Dickens, the permanent best seller of English literature, was a humorist as well as a tragic sentimentalist. But, taking a general view of popular literature, we shall be safe in affirming that it is easier to become a best seller with a book that does not contain a single laugh than with a book that, in the language of the reviewers, contains a "laugh on every page." A novelist may leave out the laughter of life, indeed, and appeal to the public, not only for his own time, but for all time, as Defoe does in *Robinson Crusoe* and Richardson does in *Clarissa,* but no novelist has ever succeeded in becoming immortal through laughter alone. Sterne has his sentimental interludes. As regards Cervantes, again, we are constantly reproached by some of his most enthusiastic admirers if we do not share his sorrows with Don Quixote, instead of laughing at his misfortunes. It is the same with nearly all the masterpieces of comedy. They are most ardently appreciated, not for comic, but for serious reasons. If you take up a book on Aristophanes or Rabelais or Molière, you will almost certainly find that it sets out to explain his serious purpose rather than to echo his hilarity.

III

ALL this — the consensus of saints, philosophers, men of fashion, and ordinary human beings — seems to constitute a very strong case against laughter. And, indeed, laughter is open to the objection that it is not only offensive to others, but tiresome in itself. It is one of the abnormal, rather than one of the normal, activities of a human being. I notice that, even by a famous physiologist, it is included in a list of "certain abnormal forms of respiration," along with coughing, sneezing, clearing the throat, snoring, crying, sighing, yawning, and hiccoughing. All these things are good in their way, but none of them would be good all the time as a constant and normal part of our lives. Sneezing is a cure recommended by many modern doctors, for instance, for certain forms of catarrh. Useful as sneezing may be, however, no doctor has yet proposed it to us as an ideal that we should sneeze twenty-four – or even twelve – hours a day.

And the same thing is obviously true of laughter. The ordinary human being, if he went on laughing continuously for even three hours, would become totally exhausted. If you could imagine a farce so funny that every sentence sent the audience into fits of uncontrollable laughter, many people would be unable to sit out more than the first act; others would retire at the end of the second act; and the few who had enough staying power to last till the fall of the curtain would not have strength left to call the actors before it for a final round of applause. You will often notice at a farce that, however much laughter there is in the course of the performance, there is far less applause at the end of it than at the end of a tragedy or a melodrama. Even the comedies of Mr. Shaw, which have many other qualities besides laughableness, used to have an exhausting effect of this kind on the dramatic critics. Mr. Shaw once declared bitterly that during the performance of one of his plays he could see the critics rocking in their seats with laughter and that in the next morning's papers they would all solemnly denounce his play as tedious and boring. The explanation is simple. He had worn them down physically with laughter, just as he would have worn them down if he had made them sneeze or cough violently for three hours on end.

Laughter, like sneezing and coughing, is, as I have said, abnormal, and Rabelais himself would not be tolerable if it were not that he discreetly intermingles with his comedy long passages of boredom. A comic writer must be either tragic in parts or sentimental in parts – he must be a critic of society or have the saving grace of dullness – in order to take his place among the world's great writers.

Thus we arrive at the theory that laughter, being something abnormal like an accident or an electric shock, can play only a very small part in an ordinary man's life. Its very essence is surprise and a break in the monotonous continuity of our thoughts or our experience. It is a physical appreciation of the surprising things of life, such as – to take some elementary instances – the spectacle of a man falling suddenly on ice, or sitting down on the floor instead of on a chair, or being shot in the leg by someone who was aiming at a pheasant.

Such things make us laugh, of course, — as we read about them in *Pickwick Papers*, for example, — only if the results are not too serious. If a man died as the result of any of these accidents, nobody but a savage would think it funny, however surprised he might be. What makes us laugh is a mixture of the shock at an accident that looks as if it might be serious and the realization that it is not after all a hundredth part as serious as it might have been. The shock is obviously one of the things that make us laugh in such cases, but among civilized people the surprise of finding that the shock was superfluous is equally necessary.

You will see an excellent example of this in motoring accidents. At present, motoring accidents are not as a rule funny, because we are apprehensive that the results may be fatal. Recently, however, someone has invented a kind of cowcatcher for motor cars which tosses the astonished pedestrian into the air and deposits him safely in a net; and it is certain that if this comes into general use motor accidents in the future will become more generally funny. As you walk down Piccadilly on a spring afternoon, you will see whole clutches of messenger boys, policemen, clubmen in top hats, and all sorts of people, tossed by motor cars as by bulls and left sprawling, alive and kicking, in a tangle of network — a scene that, I am sure, will make most people laugh even more heartily than Democritus laughed at the sights he saw in the harbor of Abdera. Saints, philosophers, and perfect gentlemen may not laugh; but ordinary human beings will, and in this, I think, they will show their humanity. For to laugh at an accident that ends happily proves not so much that one enjoyed the accident as that one enjoyed the happy ending. We should find the accidents that happen to Don Quixote intolerable if any of them ended fatally. We enjoy them only on the understanding that the Don is a cork who sinks under the sea for a few moments to rise again and bob as buoyantly as ever on the surface. We laugh at the accident, indeed, on the assumption that the victim will speedily recover from it. The escape as well as the disaster contributes to our mirth. It is cruelty suddenly merging into kindness. Hence we find that, at its best, it is the characteristic of humane men — of Shakespeare and Cervantes, of Fielding and Dickens.

Even so we can see why, on this assumption, saints and Utopian philosophers are on the whole hostile or indifferent to laughter. The saint and the Utopian philosopher have a vision of a perfect world in which accidents do not happen. The saint realizes that, if Adam and Eve had never sinned, we should all have been as the angels, and angels never have their hats blown off or slip on the ice or sit down on the floor instead of a chair or get chased in their dressing gowns through the streets, like Mr. Winkle,* by needlessly suspicious husbands. Laughter is a confession of the sins and silliness of the world, but it is also a kind of genial acquiescence in these sins and sillinesses. To the saint, the stumblings of man are tragic, proving that he is not yet an angel. To men and women with a sense of humor, the stumblings of man — even on his way to perfection — are largely comic, proving that he is only a human being after all. We may deplore, if we like, the saint's lack of humor, but in this I think we may be wrong. He has a vision that we have not. Our sense of humor is only a compensation for our lack of his vision. We should never have possessed it if we had remained in Eden. It is the grace of our disgrace — a consolation prize given to a race excluded from Paradise.

IV

HENCE it is natural enough that laughter should play a comparatively small part in the great literature and records of the human race. No doubt the characters named in the Old Testament often laughed, but there is not a single laugh described in all its pages that infects us with mirth as we read of it today. The tears of David over the dead Absalom still touch the heart, but the merriment of the days before the Flood no longer moves us to sympathetic mirth. The laughter referred to in the Bible is for the most part the laughter of scorn. The more cheerful kind of laughter — the laughter of the fool, as it is called — is even compared to its detriment by the Wise Man to "the crackling of thorns under a pot." Homer, again, though he made the gods themselves laugh, has given us no supreme comic scene as a companion picture to that supreme tragic scene in which Hector parts from Andromache. There may have been Greek writers who were as comic as Mr. P. G. Wodehouse, but their fun died with them, and even Aristophanes, the greatest comic writer of antiquity, and some say of all time, is not, I am sure, as funny as he used to be.

Tragedy can live as long as a mummy — as long, one might almost say, as one of the immortal gods. It affects us as profoundly three thousand years afterward as it affected men in the year in which it was born. Laughter, on the other hand, is as a rule as volatile as eau de Cologne sprinkled on a handkerchief. A few great writers have

* Nathaniel Winkle, an amusing character in Dickens' *Pickwick Papers,* frequently the victim of hilarious but embarrassing mishaps.

been able to imprison this essence and give it, if not immortality, at least a life thirty times as long as that of the oldest brandy. A jest unfortunately does not improve with age as brandy does, and many even of Shakespeare's jokes have to be explained to modern readers in footnotes. At the same time, if we may change the metaphor, a small handful of men of genius have been able to make the best of their jokes permanently explosive, like Mr. Wells's radioactive bomb. This is, undoubtedly, one of the most difficult miracles in literature.

As to what the nature of the first laugh was after man had descended from the trees, the authorities on the subject differ. Father Ronald Knox * has lately put himself on the side of those who hold that satire preceded humor in the history of our race, and that therefore man laughed first out of derision at the pain and humiliation of his fellow creatures. For this view there is something to be said, for primitive savages who would see nothing amusing in *Pride and Prejudice* † are said to roar with laughter at the spectacle of a man getting a bad fall or writhing in pain with fever. On the other hand, the baby is the most primitive type of human being that we know, and the baby in the cradle begins to laugh long before it knows that there are such things as pain and humiliation in the world, or can appreciate the humor of an accident. You will see a baby lying on its back in a perambulator and, as it looks up at the leaves of a tree dancing and twinkling on a windy, sunny day, laughing with an exuberance equal to that of any grown-up man or woman at a disaster to a fellow creature. You can make it laugh by peeping out at it from behind a handkerchief. You can make it laugh by tickling it. It is in tickling, perhaps, that we find the best evidence of the non-satirical origin of laughter. The psychologists in their works on laughter have written a great deal about tickling, and some of them have even experimented on their children to discover which, in their right order, are the most ticklish parts of the body. The order given by one writer is: "The sole of the foot, the armpit, the neck and part under the chin, the ribs." Darwin even experimented in tickling anthropoid apes, and discovered that they gave out "a reiterated sound, corresponding with our laughter, when they are tickled, especially under the armpits." Several authorities maintain that when dogs are tickled they respond with what is described as "an incipient smile." Others declare that pigs like being tickled, but the author in whose works I have seen a reference to this

* The Right Reverend Monsignor Ronald Arbuthnott Knox (1888–), teacher, churchman, author, and translator of the Scriptures.

† One of the masterpieces of English fiction, written c. 1796–1797 by Jane Austen (1775–1817).

subject observes: "Never having been on tickling terms with pigs, I have nothing to say about them."

Certainly the pleasure of being tickled is one of the earliest pleasures known to a human being. One of the commonest metaphors used in describing laughter, indeed, is that which speaks of a person's being "tickled to death." This suggests – and I think it is Professor Sully's view – that laughter originated in play rather than in derision. In the baby it is an expression of happiness without a breath of malice in it. And, apart from the evidence of tickling, if laughter be some subtle form of malice, how can we explain the smile with which friends greet each other when they meet and which most people wear when they are being introduced to a stranger? When you are introduced to a man, you smile, not because you have noticed something wrong with his clothes or in his personal appearance, but because you are pleased to meet him, as the saying is, or pretend to be. This may seem to conflict with the theory that angels never laugh, for angels must often experience pleasure. The laughter of human beings, however, seems to me to express an animal rather than a spiritual pleasure. Meredith traced English laughter to its sources in the gastric juices. The laugh has undoubtedly evolved since the days when Pharaoh's daughter tickled the infant Moses, till now we are able to laugh at the wit of Anatole France and the humor of Chekhov. But it is still, at its best, play, even when salted with derision or bitterness.

As with play of all sorts, one of its chief functions is to release us from the hardening formulas of our daily lives. We cannot help attempting to imprison ourselves and all our opinions and experiences in formulas. We see our neighbors as formulas walking. We are turned into formulas ourselves by our habits. Thus we make a too rigid pattern of life, and deceive ourselves into believing that the world is a mechanical, settled, and law-abiding place in which nearly everybody will behave according to pattern. For instance, the ordinary English child has a formula in accordance with which he thinks that everybody ought to speak more or less like himself. When he hears a foreigner speaking, he is inclined to laugh. He will laugh at what he regards as the mispronunciations of a Scotsman or an Irishman. His laugh is partly derision – derision in defense of the pattern. But I think it is also a playful delight in novelty. Englishmen do not go to hear Sir Harry Lauder in his Scottish songs merely to deride the language of the "braw, bricht, moonlicht nicht." Similarly when they laugh at the mention of a "haggis," – as Englishmen, being queer creatures, do, – the laughter is not in derision of the Scottish diet so much as a playful escape from the pattern of the English menu.

Laughter at the antics of a drunken man is also due in part to the fact that in not too fatal a way he breaks the expected pattern of life. If an ordinary sober man lets a coin fall on the pavement, his swift stooping down and picking it up does not make us laugh, for this is what we expect him to do. See a drunken man trying to pick up a fallen coin, however. His attempts to preserve his balance at each new bend of the body, his misjudgment of the distance at which the coin lies from his hand, his quite disproportionate air of determination and sobriety, are all a contradiction of common life. He no longer acts with the mechanical regularity which we expect in the behavior of human beings. He has dissolved the human pattern, and we on our part are dissolved in laughter. There are some people who deny that laughter can take drunkenness as one of its themes, but this is because they see drunkenness entirely in terms of its tragedies. They see drunkenness, not as an accident, but as a doom, and, like the saints, are distressed because it is a negation of the perfect world. Ordinary men laugh at a thing, however, not because it is a negation of the perfect world, but because it is a contradiction of everyday life. If everybody were drunk all the time, nobody would see anything to laugh at in Sir Toby Belch.*

V

COMEDY gives us, indeed, a new and surprising pattern of life – a pattern that is a lampoon on the pattern to which we are accustomed. Mrs. Malaprop breaks the pattern of the ordinary English pronunciation and use of words, and as a result her "allegory on the banks of the Nile" still sets the theatre in a roar. Lear in his nonsense verses breaks the pattern of intelligible speech, and we love his nonsense bcause he enables us to escape for the moment from the iron rule of sense. People do not laugh when a cock crows, but I have heard the gallery laughing uproariously when a man in the audience imitated a cock crowing. This is because, when a cock crows, he is acting in accord with the accepted farmyard pattern, but when a man crows he is breaking the pattern of human behavior. The amusement many people get from talking and performing animals may be explained in the same way. The parrot that uses blasphemous language is not behaving according to the monotonous rules of bird life. The dog that rises on its hind legs and fox-trots across the stage defies the laws

* Rollicking, roistering knight, companion of Sir Andrew Aguecheek in Shakespeare's *Twelfth Night*, among whose lines appears the penetrating question: "Dost thou think, because thou art virtuous, there shall be no more cakes and ale?"

laid down by Nature for the behavior of dogs. Lord George Sanger *
amused thousands of people some years ago by introducing into his
circus an oyster that smoked a pipe. This would not have been amusing but for the fact that oysters do not, as a rule, smoke. Nobody would pay a penny to see a human being smoking a pipe. The oyster did not smoke a pipe either, but Lord Sanger was able to make people pretend to themselves that it did, and for one glorious moment the pattern of conventional oysterdom was smashed to pieces.

All the comic writers from Aristophanes to Shakespeare, from Swift to Lewis Carroll, have broken the pattern for us in a comparable way. They have taken us when we were tired of looking at life as though it were a series of demonstrable theories in Euclid, and have torn all those impressive triangles and circles into small pieces, and have dipped them in color and put them into a kaleidoscope, and have invited us to look at the result, in which all the legalism of Euclid has been turned into a chaos of ludicrous and distorted figures. Comedy has no respect even for the hypotenuse of a right-angled triangle. It does not care whether or not two parallel lines ever meet. It does not care whether the radii of a circle are equal. On the whole it prefers to suppose that they are not.

Laughter, then, springs largely from the lawless part of our nature. Hilarity is a kind of heresy — a cheerful defiance of all the laws, including the law of gravity. The planets are not amusing, since they obey fixed laws. Human beings are amusing because they do not. The saint or philosopher who believes that life should be lived according to law may therefore easily be tempted to regard laughter with suspicion. In this, however, I think he would be wrong. We must judge laughter, like other things, by its results. And a reasonable defense of laughter may be founded on the fact that it is not men with a comic sense who are the greatest lawbreakers. Murderers and thieves are not noted as a rule for their hilarity. They are for the most part serious men, who might have remained law-abiding citizens if only they had had a greater capacity for laughing.

It would be going too far to claim that all the laughers are virtuous men and all the non-laughers criminals. At the same time it is probably true that the laughing man, if he is virtuous, will as a result of his laughter be less offensively virtuous, and if he is vicious he will be less offensively vicious. Laughter gives a holiday both to the virtues and to the vices, and takes the imagination on its travels into a country

* Nineteenth-century Englishman, proprietor of a circus and author of *Seventy Years a Showman,* said to have called himself "Lord" because the American Buffalo Bill referred to himself as the "Honorable" William F. Cody.

in which the only principle is the principle of comic incongruity. Here man can resign himself to the enjoyment of life as a topsy-turvy wonderland as strange as any that Alice ever visited, and can see his dullest neighbors as a gallery of caricatures. It is a land of happy accidents, of large noses and blown-off hats, where words are misspelt and mispronounced, where men wear spats on their wrists instead of cuffs, the land of paradoxes and bulls and the things that could not happen. Whether it is worth visiting nobody will ever know for certain till the Day of Judgment.

The worst thing that can be said against laughter is that, by putting us in a good humor, it enables us to tolerate ourselves. The best thing that can be said for it is that for the same reason it enables us to tolerate each other.

QUESTIONS

1. Note the word " objections " in the title. How much of the essay is devoted to stating, supporting, and answering objections? To what other topics do the objections lead? Does the selection therefore lack unity? Justify your answer by citing evidence from the essay.

2. Section I is devoted largely to formal definitions of " laughter," " laugh," and " smile," to semi-technical analysis of the processes involved, and to the citation of authority. These methods (and others) are used by the serious research worker. How do the author's diction, ideas, and personal opinions modify the effect of the devices mentioned?

3. In Section II, how do the objections of saints and philosophers differ from those of " worldly people," like Lord Chesterfield? What point is demonstrated in the brief discussion of literature in the last two paragraphs? Why cannot a writer be *merely* comic?

4. The first sentence in Section III summarizes briefly the material in Sections I and II. What is added in Paragraphs 1–3, Section III? Point out the sources of laughter discussed in Paragraphs 4–6. What is the topic of the last paragraph in Section III? Note the " balanced " structure in the sentences of this latter paragraph. Why is this device appropriate here?

5. In Paragraph 3, Section IV, what conflicting theories about the origin of laughter are presented? What methods does Lynd use in Paragraphs 3–6 to support his own conclusion?

6. Read carefully the final paragraph of the essay. Considering what the author has said previously, try to explain the meaning of the two sentences. Show in what sense the statements are true and whether or not they form an appropriate ending for the selection.

PHILIP WYLIE is humorous, skeptical, somewhat pessimistic, and invariably stimulating. Originally he intended to be a doctor, and he is still interested in science, psychology, and psychiatry. His numerous hobbies include abstract mathematics, playing a piano-accordion, oil painting, fishing, and carpentry. He is the author of over twenty books, the most controversial of which are *A Generation of Vipers* (1942) and *An Essay on Morals* (1947). His *Crunch and Des: Stories of Florida Fishing* (1948) is the basis of a popular television series.

SCIENCE HAS SPOILED MY SUPPER

by PHILIP WYLIE

I AM a fan for Science. My education is scientific and I have, in one field, contributed a monograph to a scientific journal. Science, to my mind, is applied honesty, the one reliable means we have to find out truth. That is why, when error is committed in the name of Science, I feel the way a man would if his favorite uncle had taken to drink.

Over the years, I have come to feel that way about what science has done to food. I agree that America can set as good a table as any nation in the world. I agree that our food is nutritious and that the diet of most of us is well-balanced. What America eats is handsomely packaged; it is usually clean and pure; it is excellently preserved. The only trouble with it is this: year by year it grows less good to eat. It appeals increasingly to the eye. But who eats with his eyes? Almost everything used to taste better when I was a kid. For quite a long time I thought that observation was merely another index of advancing age. But some years ago I married a girl whose mother is an expert cook of the kind called "old-fashioned." This gifted woman's daughter (my wife) was taught her mother's venerable skills. The mother lives in the country and still plants an old-fashioned garden. She still buys dairy products from the neighbors and, in so far as possible, she uses the same materials her mother and grandmother did – to prepare meals that are superior. They are just as good, in this Year of Grace, as I recall them from my courtship. After eating for a while at the table of my mother-in-law, it is sad to go back to eating with my friends – even the alleged "good cooks" among them. And it is a gruesome experience to have meals at the best big-city restaurants.

Take cheese, for instance. Here and there, in big cities, small stores and delicatessens specialize in cheese. At such places, one can buy at least some of the first-rate cheeses that we used to eat – such as those we had with pie and in macaroni. The latter were sharp but not too sharp. They were a little crumbly. We called them American cheeses, or even rat cheese; actually, they were Cheddars. Long ago, this cheese began to be supplanted by a material called "cheese foods." Some cheese foods and "processed" cheese are fairly edible; but not one comes within miles of the old kinds – for flavor.

A grocer used to be very fussy about his cheese. Cheddar was made and sold by hundreds of little factories. Representatives of the factories had particular customers, and cheese was prepared by hand to suit the grocers, who knew precisely what their patrons wanted in rat cheese, pie cheese, American and other cheeses. Some liked them sharper; some liked them yellower; some liked anise seeds in cheese, or caraway.

What happened? Science – or what is called science – stepped in. The old-fashioned cheeses didn't ship well enough. They crumbled, became moldy, dried out. "Scientific" tests disclosed that a great majority of the people will buy a less-good-tasting cheese if that's all they can get. "Scientific marketing" then took effect. Its motto is "Give the people the least quality they'll stand for." In food, as in many other things, the "scientific marketers" regard quality as secondary so long as they can sell most persons anyhow; what they are after is "durability" or "shippability."

It is not possible to make the very best cheese in vast quantities at a low average cost. "Scientific sampling" got in its statistically nasty work. It was found that the largest number of people will buy something that is bland and rather tasteless. Those who prefer a product of a pronounced and individualistic flavor have a variety of preferences. Nobody is altogether pleased by bland foodstuff, in other words; but nobody is very violently put off. The result is that a "reason" has been found for turning out zillions of packages of something that will "do" for nearly all and isn't even imagined to be superlatively good by a single soul!

Economics entered. It is possible to turn out in quantity a bland, impersonal, practically imperishable substance more or less resembling, say, cheese – at lower cost than cheese. Chain groceries shut out the independent stores and "standardization" became a principal means of cutting costs.

Imitations also came into the cheese business. There are American duplications of most of the celebrated European cheeses, mass-produced and cheaper by far than the imports. They would cause European food-lovers to gag or guffaw – but generally the imitations are all that's available in the supermarkets. People buy them and eat them.

Perhaps you don't like cheese – so the fact that decent cheese is hardly ever served in America any more, or used in cooking, doesn't matter to you. Well, take bread. There has been (and still is) something of a hullabaloo about bread. In fact, in the last few years, a few big bakeries have taken to making a fairly good imitation of real bread. It costs much more than what is nowadays called bread, but it is edible. Most persons, however, now eat as "bread" a substance so full of chemicals and so barren of cereals that it approaches a synthetic.

Most bakers are interested mainly in how a loaf of bread looks. They are concerned with how little stuff they can put in it – to get how much money. They are deeply interested in using chemicals that will keep bread from molding, make it seem "fresh" for the longest possible time, and so render it marketable and shippable. They have been at this monkeyshine for a generation. Today a loaf of "bread" looks deceptively real; but it is made from heaven knows what and it resembles, as food, a solidified bubble bath. Some months ago I bought a loaf of the stuff and, experimentally, began pressing it together, like an accordion. With a little effort, I squeezed the whole loaf to a length of about one inch!

Yesterday, at the home of my mother-in-law, I ate with country-churned butter and home-canned wild strawberry jam several slices of actual bread, the same thing we used to have every day at home. People who have eaten actual bread will know what I mean. They will know that the material commonly called bread is not even related to real bread, except in name.

II

FOR years, I couldn't figure out what had happened to vegetables. I knew, of course, that most vegetables, to be enjoyed in their full deliciousness, must be picked fresh and cooked at once. I knew that vegetables cannot be overcooked and remain even edible, in the best sense. They cannot stand on the stove. That set of facts makes it impossible, of course, for any American restaurant – or, indeed, any city-dweller separated from supply by more than a few hours – to have decent fresh vegetables. The Parisians managed by getting their vegetables picked at dawn and rushed in farmers' carts to market, where no middleman or marketman delays produce on its way to the pot.

Our vegetables, however, come to us through a long chain of command. There are merchants of several sorts — wholesalers before the retailers, commission men, and so on — with the result that what were once edible products become, in transit, mere wilted leaves and withered tubers.

Homes and restaurants do what they can with this stuff — which my mother-in-law would discard on the spot. I have long thought that the famed blindfold test for cigarettes should be applied to city vegetables. For I am sure that if you puréed them and ate them blindfolded, you couldn't tell the beans from the peas, the turnips from the squash, the Brussels sprouts from the broccoli.

It is only lately that I have found how much science has had to do with this reduction of noble victuals to pottage. Here the science of genetics is involved. Agronomists and the like have taken to breeding all sorts of vegetables and fruits — changing their original nature. This sounds wonderful and often is insane. For the scientists have not as a rule taken any interest whatsoever in the taste of the things they've tampered with!

What they've done is to develop "improved" strains of things for every purpose but eating. They work out, say, peas that will ripen all at once. The farmer can then harvest his peas and thresh them and be done with them. It is extremely profitable because it is efficient. What matter if such peas taste like boiled paper wads?

Geneticists have gone crazy over such "opportunities." They've developed string beans that are straight instead of curved, and all one length. This makes them easier to pack in cans, even if, when eating them, you can't tell them from tender string. Ripening time and identity of size and shape are, nowadays, more important in carrots than the fact that they taste like carrots. Personally, I don't care if they hybridize onions till they are big as your head and come up through the snow; but, in doing so, they are producing onions that only vaguely and feebly remind you of onions. We are getting some varieties, in fact, that have less flavor than the water off last week's leeks. Yet, if people don't eat onions because they taste like onions, what in the name of Luther Burbank do they eat them for?

The women's magazines are about one third dedicated to clothes, one third to mild comment on sex, and the other third to recipes and pictures of handsome salads, desserts, and main courses. "Institutes" exist to experiment and tell housewives how to cook attractive meals and how to turn leftovers into works of art. The food thus pictured looks like famous paintings of still life. The only trouble is it's tasteless. It leaves appetite unquenched and merely serves to stave off famine.

I wonder if this blandness of our diet doesn't explain why so many of us are overweight and even dangerously so. When things had flavor, we knew what we were eating all the while — and it satisfied us. A teaspoonful of my mother-in-law's wild strawberry jam will not just provide a gastronome's ecstasy: it will entirely satisfy your jam desire. But, of the average tinned or glass-packed strawberry jam, you need half a cupful to get the idea of what you're eating. A slice of my mother-in-law's apple pie will satiate you far better than a whole bakery pie.

That thought is worthy of investigation — of genuine scientific investigation. It is merely a hypothesis, so far, and my own. But people — and their ancestors — have been eating according to flavor for upwards of a billion years. The need to satisfy the sense of taste may be innate and important. When food is merely a pretty cascade of viands, with the texture of boiled cardboard and the flavor of library paste, it may be the instinct of *genus homo* to go on eating in the unconscious hope of finally satisfying the ageless craving of the frustrated taste buds. In the days when good-tasting food was the rule in the American home, obesity wasn't such a national curse.

How can you feel you've eaten if you haven't tasted, and fully enjoyed tasting? Why (since science is ever so ready to answer the beck and call of mankind) don't people who want to reduce merely give up eating and get the nourishment they must have in measured doses shot into their arms at hospitals? One ready answer to that question suggests that my theory of overeating is sound: people like to taste! In eating, they try to satisfy that like.

The scientific war against deliciousness has been stepped up enormously in the last decade. Some infernal genius found a way to make biscuit batter keep. Housewives began to buy this premixed stuff. It saved work, of course. But any normally intelligent person can learn, in a short period, how to prepare superb baking powder biscuits. I can make better biscuits, myself, than can be made from patent batters. Yet soon after this fiasco became an American staple, it was discovered that a half-baked substitute for all sorts of breads, pastries, rolls, and the like could be mass-manufactured, frozen — and sold for polishing off in the home oven. None of these two-stage creations is as good as even a fair sample of the thing it imitates. A man of taste, who had eaten one of my wife's cinnamon buns, might use the premixed sort to throw at starlings – but not to eat! Cake mixes, too, come ready-prepared – like cement and not much better-tasting compared with true cake.

It is, however, "deep-freezing" that has really rung down the curtain on American cookery. Nothing is improved by the process. I have yet to taste a deep-frozen victual that measures up, in flavor, to the fresh, unfrosted original. And most foods, cooked or uncooked, are destroyed in the deep freeze for all people of sense and sensibility. Vegetables with crisp and crackling texture emerge as mush, slippery and stringy as hair nets simmered in Vaseline. The essential oils that make peas peas – and cabbage cabbage – must undergo fission and fusion in freezers. Anyhow, they vanish. Some meats turn to leather. Others to wood pulp. Everything, pretty much, tastes like the mosses of tundra, dug up in midwinter. Even the appearance changes, oftentimes. Handsome comestibles you put down in the summer come out looking very much like the corpses of woolly mammoths recovered from the last Ice Age.

Of course, all this scientific "food handling" tends to save money. It certainly preserves food longer. It reduces work at home. But these facts, and especially the last, imply that the first purpose of living is to avoid work – at home, anyhow.

Without thinking, we are making an important confession about ourselves as a nation. We are abandoning quality – even, to some extent, the quality of people. The "best" is becoming too good for us. We are suckling ourselves on machine-made mediocrity. It is bad for our souls, our minds, and our digestion. It is the way our wiser and calmer forebears fed, not people, but hogs: as much as possible and as fast as possible, with no standard of quality.

The Germans say, "*Mann ist was er isst* – Man is what he eats." If this be true, the people of the U.S.A. are well on their way to becoming a faceless mob of mediocrities, of robots. And if we apply to other attributes the criteria we apply these days to appetite, that is what would happen! We would not want bright children any more; we'd merely want them to look bright – and get through school fast. We wouldn't be interested in beautiful women – just a good paint job. And we'd be opposed to the most precious quality of man: his individuality, his differentness from the mob.

There are some people – sociologists and psychologists among them – who say that is exactly what we Americans are doing, are becoming. Mass man, they say, is on the increase. Conformity, standardization, similarity – all on a cheap and vulgar level – are replacing the great American ideas of colorful liberty and dignified individualism. If this is so, the process may well begin, like most human behavior, in the home — in those homes where a good meal has been replaced by something-to-eat-in-a-hurry. By something not very good to eat, prepared by a mother without very much to do, for a family that doesn't feel it amounts to much anyhow.

I call, here, for rebellion.

QUESTIONS

1. The title suggests an attack upon science. Why does it also have the effect of whimsical humor? Is it important that one man's supper has been spoiled?

2. Why is it inadequate to say of Paragraph 1, Section I, that here Wylie praises science and shows that he is qualified to discuss it? What do " I am a fan for Science " and ". . . I feel the way a man would if his favorite uncle had taken to drink " reveal about the mood and tone of the essay?

3. If science seeks in an objective fashion to discover truth, is science alone responsible for the food that is " less good to eat "? How is the term " science " or " scientific " qualified in Paragraph 5, Section I? How is this modification extended through the next three paragraphs?

4. Again and again Wylie asserts that food doesn't *taste* good. What devices has he used to avoid the effect of monotonous repetition? He says, for example, that peas " taste like boiled paper wads." Find other examples, and try to explain why they are effective. Has he avoided trite expressions?

5. What humorous application of the scientific method is made in Section II, in the paragraph on page 233 beginning " That thought . . ." and in the following paragraph?

6. How does the author reveal that his article is not *merely* an amusing complaint about his supper? In what way is the thought extended in the last four paragraphs of Section II? How do these paragraphs modify the purpose established earlier in the essay?

Social Patterns and Problems

RALPH BARTON PERRY

DAVID L. COHN

JAMES HOWARD MEANS, M.D.

JUDGE ELIJAH ADLOW

ALBERT JAY NOCK

RALPH BARTON PERRY, for many years an outstanding teacher, author, and lecturer, was at the time of his death (1957) professor emeritus of philosophy at Harvard University. He lectured widely in foreign universities, especially in Scotland and France, was enrolled in the Chevalier Legion of Honor (1936), and received honorary degrees from several major universities. An authority on William James, Perry received the Pulitzer Prize for *The Thought and Character of William James* (1935). His more recent books are *One World in the Making* (1945), *Characteristically American* (1949), *The Citizen Decides* (1951), *Realms of Value* (1954), and *The Humanity of Man* (1956).

DOMESTIC SUPERSTITIONS

by RALPH BARTON PERRY

SUPERSTITIONS are perpetuated mainly in the church and the home, because whatever is said out loud in either place is intended to edify those who hear it. Parents and other adult members of the family belong to the priestly caste. It is their business to preach the doctrine and to be ostentatiously on their good behavior. Like their colleagues of the church, they feel the strain and find it necessary to enjoy stolen hours of unfrocked relaxation, which they spend with others of the profession who are pledged not to betray them. There are so many whom circumstance has placed in this position, but who feel unequal to its duties, that there is a widespread tendency to centralize the work of edification in the boarding school, where it can be done by paid experts. As yet, however, this relief is too expensive to be generally enjoyed, and it still falls to the common lot of the adult to work, to pay taxes, and to officiate in the home.

Edification breeds superstition simply because fictions having sentimental value have to be preferred to facts. In the home this begins with the myths of Santa Claus and fairyland, and ends with the myth of the Perfect Gentleman and the Perfect Lady. In the home, as in the church, there are ecclesiastical as well as doctrinal superstitions — that is, superstitions having the function of protecting the prestige of the authorities. In the case of the home these superstitions have to do particularly with the pure benevolence, exemplary rectitude, and perfect manners of the parents. This idealized, fictitious parent may vary to any degree from the real parent. His activities off the stage, the friends with whom he associates there, and even his past history, are constructed and recast to fit the role of paragon which he assumes in the domestic drama.

Despite the weakness of his position otherwise, the adult member of the home enjoys this great advantage, that he fixes its superstitions in the form which they finally assume. He utilizes the experiences, deeds, and shrewd comments of the children, but puts his own interpretation on them. It is the adult who tells the story – sometimes, from motives of pride or retaliation, to other adults of rival domestic establishments; sometimes, for purposes of edification, to one of the children. In either case the moral that adorns the tale becomes its dominant feature, and it is the adult saga-maker who points the moral. He enjoys this advantage at his peril, however. For he is the most defenseless victim of his own eloquence. His rivals do not believe him because they possess prior domestic superstitions of their own. The children are protected by their inattention, levity, and worldly wisdom. But he himself hears himself so often, and takes himself so seriously, that he is like to become the only thoroughly orthodox adherent of his own teaching. It is in the hope of opening the eyes of the domestic adult, and enabling him to resist this insidious process of auto-suggestion, that these words are written.

There is, for example, a widespread belief that the mother, or wife, or resident aunt, or other domestic adult female, is the lover and champion of the home. Man is supposed to be a natural vagrant, only with great difficulty prevented from spending his idle time wandering from club to club, or from hole to hole on the golf links. Woman, on the other hand, is supposed to be by nature the nostic * or homing animal. Domestic dynamics, in short, are commonly explained as a resultant of the centrifugal force of the male and the centripetal force of the female. This is doubtless the more edifying view of the matter, because it idealizes what circumstance has decreed to be necessary. Since livelihood falls to the lot of the male and homekeeping to the lot of the female, it is prettier to suppose that the deepest passion of the one is the love of outdoors, and of the other the love of indoors; just as it would be prettier to suppose that a man compelled to earn his living as a night watchman was by nature a nocturnal animal.

The facts, however, do not agree with this edifying view of the matter. The greatest day in the history of a privileged woman is the day of her Coming Out. From that day forth she wages a more or less ineffectual struggle to stay out. On the other hand, the greatest hour in

* Derived from the Greek word *nostos*, meaning literally "a return home."

a man's day is the hour when he sets his face toward home. Every day, through hours of work, he is sustained by the same bright vision, which he derives from romantic fiction, or from his own creative imagination. He sees himself joyfully greeted by a household, no member of which has anything else to do, or any other wish, save to make him comfortable. They have all indulged themselves to their hearts' content earlier in the day, and now it is his turn to be indulged. It is understood that he, and *he alone,* is tired. Any attentions or amiability on his part are gratefully appreciated, but they are not demanded, or even expected, of him. After dinner, there is a certain comfortable chair waiting for him in an accustomed spot near a reading lamp. The contour of the upholstery is his perfect complement. He fits himself to the chair, reaches for the evening paper, and then experiences the purest rapture of domestic bliss. It consists in a sense of being "let alone," of snugness, relaxation, and a hovering protection. But, like all ecstasies, it is essentially indescribable.

This is man's sustaining vision. It is only a vision, but, like all visions, it shows where the heart lies.

Now, why is it only a vision? Because it leaves out approximately seventy-five per cent of the facts. All the other members of the household are tired, also, and are as conscious of having acquired merit and earned indulgence as is the male wage earner. Each, like the adult male, forms his own conception of the end of a perfect day by the simple method of opposition. The children, having spent most of the day in a restrained posture on a school bench, incline to riot. The woman, having spent the day indoors, desires to go out; and having seen no one during the day except the postman, the milkman, and the iceman, desires to associate more extensively with her kind. She, too, has been sustained during the day by a vision — children tucked in bed, her husband fired with social zeal, best clothes, a taxicab, a meal *prepared by somebody else,* and then a dance or the theatre, friends, gayety, and late to bed! Hence, while for the man the symbol of home is the armchair, for the woman it is the dressing-table. When the inward-bound man and the outward-bound woman meet on the threshold at the end of the day, then indeed is the ligature of matrimony strained!

What might or will be the case under a different social organization it is impossible to predict. The present domestic motivation is doubtless a more or less artificial pressure-effect of circumstance. Men work all day in order to be able to go home; women, in order to be able to leave home. Men are standing outside, looking in; women, inside, looking out. In both cases the force of inclination is equal and opposite to the force of circumstance. Thus the day of the man and the day of the woman and the day of the children culminate discordantly; and at the only hour when the family is united in the flesh it is divided in spirit. Somebody must spend the "free" evening virtuously and patiently doing something that *he* does not want, or else everybody must spend it in a joint debate that nobody wants. Possibly, in some future time, men and women will both work at home and go out to play; or will both go out to work and spend the evening in adjoining armchairs. Even then one does not see one's way clear about the children.

As it stands, then, man is the lover and champion of the home. To him it is a haven, a place of refuge, and an opportunity of leisure. Woman is the custodian and curator of the home. It is her place of business. "Woman's place is in the home" is not a description of female human nature, but a theory regarding the division of labor, or a precept, coined and circulated by men who want homes and need women to create them.

This corrected view of the home-sentiments throws a new light on certain habits of life which might be supposed at first to contradict it. There is, for example, man's well-known addiction to clubs. It is popularly supposed that he resorts to these places in order to get away from home. Quite the contrary. He goes to his club because his club is the nearest approximation to his ideal of home that is available. It is more homelike than home. A man's club does not exist for the promotion of social life, but for the purpose of avoiding it. It is essentially a place where the upholstery is deep, where one can read newspapers and eat, and where one is safe from intrusion. In other words, a man goes out to his club only from fear of having to go farther out.

Or, consider the popular view that women are more religious than men. The real point seems to be that women are more inclined than men to *go to church;* which is a very different thing. Sunday is related to the week as the evening to the day. For a man, therefore, it is a day at home; and for a woman, a day out. A man's idea of Sunday is to surround his house with barbed wire, lock and barricade the doors and windows, disconnect the telephone, put on his slippers and an old suit, and then devote the day to reading the paper and "puttering." A woman's idea of Sunday is to have everything cleaned and polished up, including the children; everybody in best clothes; and then have half of her friends in in the afternoon, and visit the other half in the evening. Now it is not difficult to see which program and mood most easily accommodates itself to public worship. If you are all dressed up and socially inclined, what can be more natural and agreeable than going to church? And if you are down cellar, in old clothes, building bookshelves out of a packing box, what can be more impossible?

According to the orthodox superstition, woman, as inwardly bent on religion and the home, is the natural conservative. She is regarded as the instinctive exponent of established things — of convention, authority, and the moral code. As a matter of fact, being more or less rigidly subjected to these things, her heart is set against them. Only men are really shocked; women pretend to be, because men would be still more shocked if they didn't. Men, who have had the making of laws, have a real respect for them; women publicly observe them, but secretly regard them as little better than a nuisance. It is the same opposite play of inclination and circumstance that has been observed in the narrower sphere of the home. Men, being placed by circumstance in positions of hazard and exposure, long for security; women, being accustomed to security, long for freedom and adventure.

II

BUT to return to our domestic superstitions. The most distinctive and highly developed domestic art is scolding. The orthodox belief is that scolding is a sort of judicial censure administered from motives of the purest benevolence. If there is a tone of anger in it, that is supposed to be righteous indignation, or the voice of offended justice, the scolder being for the moment the mouthpiece of the categorical imperative. Scolding is conceived to be a duty peculiar to the home because of the relation of guardianship in which one member of the family stands to another. Thus one is one's child's keeper, or one's wife's, or one's husband's, but not one's neighbor's.

Now, what are the facts? Among animals, where motives are more unashamed, scolding is a mode of threat or attack. It is a manifestation of enmity. There is no reason for supposing it otherwise in the case of the domestic life of man. Statistics would undoubtedly reveal an almost perfect correlation between the frequency and intensity of scolding and the parent's threshold of irritability — the latter depending on conditions of age, digestion, fatigue, temperamental irascibility, and personal idiosyncrasy.

Why should scolding be peculiar to the home? Not because the home is dedicated to benevolent admonition, but because the family circle provides perpetual, inescapable, intimate, and unseasonable human contacts. Individuals of the same species are brought together in every permutation and combination of conflicting interests and incompatible moods. There is no other grouping of human beings which provides so many stimuli for the combative instinct. When this instinct is aroused among the children, it is called quarrelsomeness, and is greatly deprecated by adults. When it is aroused in the adult himself, it assumes the more or less sublimated form of scolding. It flourishes in the home because it is both aroused and protected there. Scolding provides a reputable method of venting spleen when other outlets are stopped by law and convention. In the home, scolding can be indulged in with impunity so long as it does not arouse the neighbors. Its victims are defenseless; and the corporate pride of the family seals the mouths of its members, so that a decent repute may be preserved before the world. It is this conspiracy of silence and regard for appearances that has created the fiction of the happy fireside choir, where all voices carol in perpetual unison.

There would be no merit in this exposure, did it not serve to bring to light the real disciplinary value of home life, which consists, not in the eloquence and light of admonition, but rather in the aggravation of social experience. An individual who learns how to live cheerfully, or even how to live at all, in a home, finds little difficulty in living with his fellows anywhere else. The scolding of children teaches them not so much the error of their ways, as a practised skill in getting on with irritable adults, many of whom they will meet in real life later on. Perhaps the most superb manifestation of domestic life is the magnanimity of children – their swift forgetfulness of injury and their indulgence even of those human weaknesses of which they are themselves the victims. Both children and adults, consorting with one another in every combination of age and sex, in every condition of health, at every hour of the day, and in a great variety of moods and temperaments, exhaust the whole repertory of human relations and *learn how to live together.* The best name for this is patience. It is the lack of this which distinguishes the bachelor, the maid, the orphan, and in some degree the only child.

In the family, as elsewhere, example is said to be better than precept. The idea is that the child, carefully noting the heroic or saintly qualities of the father, mother, or resident aunt, – those qualities particularly celebrated in domestic song and story, – models his action closely thereon, and so of his own accord grows in wisdom and in favor at the same time that he grows in stature. But the observed results are so unlike this as to justify suspicion that here, too, we have to do with a superstition. And such is, indeed, unhappily the case. While it is doubtless true that the exemplar is better than the preceptor, in the family, at least, there is no ground for believing that example *works* any better than precept. What the child gives particular attention to in the domestic adult is the genial weakness, the human errancy, the comic relief, the discomfiture of dignity. He carefully notes that his father smokes and swears, and puts his feet on the table; and that his mother or resident aunt eats candy, uses slang, and puts her elbows on the table. He thereupon does these things himself, not because he is imitating a model, but because, having an inclination to do them anyway, he takes advantage of the fact that his monitor is for the moment disarmed.

It is not that the child is indifferent to example, but that he finds his examples elsewhere. The domestic adult is not in his line at all. He would as soon think of imitating him as the domestic adult himself would think of imitating the Emperor of Japan or the Grand Llama of Thibet. He has his own pantheon * and hierarchy of heroes in the real world outside. These are sometimes adults, more often the elders of his own tribe. In any case they are free from that odor of sanctity and strained posture of edification which disqualify the domestic adult. It should be added that this discontinuity, though it may prevent emulation, does not hinder, but rather promotes, a certain shrewd, critical observation; so that a child may find himself presently cultivating the complementary opposite of certain types of character that have been peculiarly familiar to him in his domestic environment.

III

MANY minor superstitions arise from domestic myopia. The intensity and the close propinquity of the domestic drama exaggerates all its values, both positive and negative. The normal genius of childhood is mistaken for individual distinction; and its normal limitations for individual delinquency. Within the family all children are remarkable; generic traits disappear from view altogether. The parent who will laugh heartily at a cartoon depicting the characteristic greediness, cruelty, truancy, disobedience, noisiness, irresponsibility, and general barbarism of a fictitious boy or girl, will at once stiffen into apprehensive sobriety when his own child betrays the least of these weaknesses. Viewing human life as a whole, he observes that children grow and outgrow, and that mischievous children have been known to spend their adult years outside the penitentiary; he may even recollect that he had a fault or two himself in early years; but as regards his own children, every offense is a crime, every evil a calamity, and every incident a crisis. His only salvation lies in frequent, unannounced visits to other families.

* From the Greek words *pan* and *theos*, meaning literally "all the gods." Perry thus suggests that the child is likely to find his objects of adoration outside the domestic scene.

IV

WE have finally to examine a fundamental superstition relating to the seat of domestic authority. In so far as the feudal principle, or the theocratic principle, or the autocratic principle, or the plutocratic principle, survives here and there, owing to the conservatism of the home, the father does manage to retain some semblance of authority. But patriarchy is on its last legs. There is little to it now but outward form and old court ritual. The father still gives his name to the family, sits at the head of the table, and – oh, yes, pays the bills! But there is more service than authority in the second and third of these prerogatives, since someone has to carve, and it is the making rather than the paying of bills that really counts. Of course, he can still tyrannize over the family by making himself so disagreeable that he has to be bought off; but in a family anybody can do that. It is not a power that attaches to the male parent as such. As father, he is still the titular monarch, and that is about all. If he were formally to abdicate, it would not alter the actual balance of domestic forces in the least.

Meanwhile, it is to be feared that he to some extent exploits the pathos of his fallen greatness, and wrings from the feelings of his wife, children, or sister-in-law various minor concessions affecting his comfort. Nothing can exceed the scrupulousness with which appearances are preserved in public. He still takes the curb when the family uses the sidewalk, and is the last to enter and the first to leave a public or private conveyance. But to one who knows life as it is, the irony and bathos of the modern age are summed up in two spectacles: Kaiser Wilhelm chopping wood at Amerongen, and the paterfamilias washing dishes in the pantry.

If the father has fallen from authority, who has superseded him? The mother? Not at all. The popular impression to that effect has no basis except the fact that the power of the mother has increased *relatively* to that of the father. But this is due to the fall of the father rather than to any notable rise of the mother. No, the new domestic polity is neither the patriarchy nor the matriarchy, but the *pediarchy.*

That the children should encroach upon, and eventually seize, the authority of the parents is not so strange as might at first appear. After all, it is only the domestic manifestation of the most characteristic social and political movement of modern times, the rise, namely, of the proletarian masses. Within the family the children constitute the majority, the unpropertied, the unskilled, and the unprivileged. They are intensely class-conscious, and have come to a clearer and clearer recognition of the conflict of interest that divides them from the owners and managers. Their methods have been similar to those employed in the industrial revolution – the strike, passive resistance, malingering, restriction of output, and, occasionally, direct action.

Within the family, as in the modern democracy, the control is by public opinion. It is government of the children, by the children, and for the children. But this juvenile sovereignty is exercised indirectly rather than directly. The officeholders are adults, whose power is proportional to their juvenile support. The real (though largely unseen and unacknowledged) principle of domestic politics is the struggle for prestige among the adults. Some employ the methods of decadent Rome, the *panem et circenses* *; others, the arts of the military hero or of the popular orator. But all acknowledge the need of conciliating the juvenile masses.

The power of juvenile opinion is due, not merely to its mass, and to the boldness and unscrupulousness with which it is asserted, but to its reinforcement from outside. It is more than a domestic movement: it is an interdomestic movement. The opinion of the children is thus less provincial than that of domestic adults. It has, furthermore, a force which it derives from its more intimate contact with the main currents of history. The domestic adult is in a sort of backwash. He is looking toward the past, while the children are thinking the thoughts and speaking the language of tomorrow. They are in closer touch with reality, and cannot fail, however indulgent, to feel that their parents and resident aunt are antiquated. The children's end of the family is its budding, forward-looking end; the adults' end is, at best, its root. There is a profound law of life by which buds and roots grow in opposite directions.

The domestic conflict is in many of its notable features parallel to the industrial conflict; and they may be of common origin. It is natural that similar remedies should be proposed. The Taylor † system and other efficiency systems have already broken down in both cases. Conservatives will propose to meet the domestic problem by higher allowances and shorter school hours, with perhaps time and a half for overtime and a bit of profit sharing. Liberals will propose boards of conciliation with child representation, attempts to link study and chores with the "creative" impulses, and experiments in divided management. Radicals and domestic revolutionists will regard all such halfway measures as utterly ineffectual, because they preserve the parental system in its essentials. They will aim to consummate the

* Literally, bread and circuses. The phrase is found in the Tenth Satire of the Roman satirist Juvenal (c. 60–140).

† Frederick Winslow Taylor (1856–1915), American engineer and inventor.

revolution as soon as possible by violence, and then to bring a new order into being through a dictatorship of a sectarian minority.

This new order would be an almost exact inversion of the parental order. Whereas, under the present system, the parents are supposed to control the home for the benefit of the children, providing them with the necessities of life, and giving them work and advice for their own good, under the new system, the children would control the home for the benefit of the parents and other adults, assuming full responsibility for their living, and employing their expert services only as might be required. However difficult it may be to put such a change into effect, there is, from the adults' point of view, much to be said for it.

QUESTIONS

1. Before reading this essay, look up the word " superstition " in the dictionary. In what sense does Perry seem to be using the word? Just what superstitions are considered in the essay? Define also " edification," frequently used, and " prettier," in Paragraph 4, Section I. How is the derivation of " pretty " related to Perry's meaning?

2. What general idea is the basis of development from Paragraph 4 to the end of Section I? Show how each of these paragraphs is related to the general idea. Do the last two paragraphs in Section I represent a digression? Why or why not?

3. Section II is devoted to (1) scolding and (2) example as opposed to precept. How are these two topics related? Although the author condemns or derides the supposed values of these activities, what special virtues does he find in them? Does Perry's conclusion seem to be that the child develops properly *because of* home influences, or *in spite of* them?

4. In the last three paragraphs of Section IV, the author suggests that remedies for the " domestic conflict " may be offered by conservatives, liberals, and radicals. To which of these three remedies does he refer in the concluding paragraph? What is the effect of the last sentence?

5. Satire may be defined as an effort to make something or somebody look ridiculous. The tone may vary from the gentle and chiding to the bitter and caustic. How would you describe the tone of this essay? (See page 80, Question 4 for a definition of tone.)

6. Irony may be defined as implied contrast between what is said and what is meant, or between the result expected and the result achieved, or between what appears to be true and what is actually true. Find evidence in the essay that the author has made use of this device.

DAVID L. COHN is an indefatigable observer and outspoken critic of American manners and morals. A widely traveled social historian, he was born in Greenville, Mississippi, and was educated at the University of Virginia and at Yale. He has published many articles in *The Atlantic Monthly* and other magazines on a wide variety of subjects dealing with the American scene. His books include a study of tariff policy, *Picking America's Pockets* (1936); a review of American manners and morals as seen through Sears, Roebuck catalogues, *The Good Old Days* (1940); an analysis of marriage, *Love in America* (1943); a war diary, *This Is the Story* (1947); a study of race relations in the South, *Where I Was Born and Raised* (1948); and a political history, *The Fabulous Democrats* (1956). His most recent book is *The Life and Times of King Cotton* (1957).

DO AMERICAN MEN LIKE WOMEN?

by DAVID L. COHN

IN MANY a bull session with our junior officers and GI's during the war, in camps and billets around half of the world, I put this question: Do American men like women?

The men were invariably startled by my query. It seemed silly to them in view of the American soldiers' universal reputation – one that does not do us too much good – as perhaps the most tireless skirt chasers of all time and all peoples. It was necessary to explain.

The question, I assured them, has nothing to do with psychologically abnormal males; nor with a man's liking or loving one or more women in the course of a lifetime. It does not bear upon the professional amorist, for he usually subconsciously hates women. It does not contemplate the sweet-talking Southerner, the cowboy-gallant Westerner, or the generality of our men who automatically snatch their hats from their heads when ladies come into the elevator. The question is deeper and broader.

Do our men like women as people? Are they really interested in the ideas, the points of view, the conversation of women? Are they responsive to women when the physical connotations inseparable from any relationship of the sexes are weak, as when one lunches with a woman beyond her physical prime but attractive because she is mellow, mature, stimulating? Do our men admit women to a rounded intimacy with them and treat them as equals, or do they keep them in a mink-lined purdah beyond which they are not permitted to go?

This explanation of my question seemed as startling to my companions as the question itself. They took it for granted — being men — that they liked women. Hadn't they wives or sweethearts at home, lights-o'-love throughout the world, and millions of pin-up girls on the walls of their billets? Hadn't they seen a great deal of girls in high schools and coed universities, danced with them, swum with them, picnicked with them, daydreamed about them? Weren't American men notoriously indulgent toward their women, making living as easy as possible for them, and smoothing their way at every step? Didn't all this prove that they really liked women?

Yet when the question had been tossed about, when it had been examined from a hitherto novel point of view, the great majority of the men said they did not like women in the terms of the question. It is scarcely necessary to add, however, that I do not state this as the conclusion of twelve million servicemen on the subject, but only of the limited group with whom I talked.

Illuminating my thesis by examples of everyday American life, I cited the urban dinner party. Here the so-called wise host usually serves an abundance of cocktails before dinner so that the men are glowing and talkative at table, each generous of talk with the lady to the right and the lady to the left of him; but as time passes and the dinner wines are not sufficiently potent to take up where the cocktails have left off, the men and the talk often slow down. Most of them, however, manage to stagger through the remainder of the meal with some grace, buoyed up by the knowledge that after the ice the company will separate for a time. Over coffee and brandy the men will have a dearly beloved stag party.

Released then from the heavy burden of women's society, they can be themselves as they discuss business, politics, and other things that really concern them, and revel in the warm male camaraderie of the golf club locker room. It does not occur to them, as they linger inordinately, that the ladies may be bored talking with one another. It does not matter to them that no woman goes to her hairdresser in the morning to look her best at dinner in the evening for the sake of spending much of the time with other women who have done the same thing. But all this does concern the haggard hostess, who often has to drag the men — including her husband — out of their trance to rejoin the ladies in the living room.

A similar process is operative in the informal circles of small towns. There, after dinner, the men huddle together like quail in cold rain.

They tell jokes, talk crops, baseball, business; rejoice in the solidarity of their male world which had been temporarily threatened during dinner. The women sit in their corner discussing items out of their exclusively feminine world: children, servants, gardens, gossip. Every little while the pattern is disrupted as a man darts into the kitchen to mix a drink, or a woman half-heartedly taps out a tune on the piano. Soon it is time to go home, and once more we have had a demonstration of the fact that, despite our gregariousness and slaphappy manners, we are perhaps the loneliest and most bored of peoples.

II

IN THIS country, where marriage, two times in five, is a stylized detour to arrive at a divorce (statisticians estimate that by 1965 more than one half of all marriages will end in divorce), the relationship between millions of couples is not a man-woman relationship. Shortly after Herbert and Azadia have married, he comes to regard her not as a woman but as the Little Woman, while she looks upon him not as a man but as a Boy. To her he is a dear, sweet boy, helpless and in need of mothering; the poor thing can never find his brief case and forgets his galoshes on rainy days. And if he cannot call her Mama instead of Azadia two years after marrying, he is likely to look upon the whole thing as a failure.

The maternal love of Azadia for Herbert may be all to the good so far as he is concerned. It permits him to remain spiritually in a state of suspended animation. He is the chrysalis which never becomes a butterfly, but sleeps always warm and secure within the cocoon without facing the dangers, or enjoying the sunshine delights, of living. A man-woman relationship would consume more of his time and energy than he is willing to devote to it. It might reduce some of the emotional content he pours into his work as assistant display manager for northwestern Minnesota for the International Tweezers Corporation. His full duty toward his wife – and proof of the fact in his mind that he is essentially a decent man – is discharged by regarding his wife as a lady in the sense that he regards his mother as a lady. In this way he continues to remember Mama without ever discovering Azadia, and the fact that she may secretly feel he is overdoing the lady business never enters his mind.

The Boys of this country are simply retarded adolescents whose ideal of femininity remains a girl in a bathing suit, and who are incapable of developing a mature feminine ideal through a synthesis of spiritual and physical values. Men of this kind are neither adult nor adequate in their relations with women. They are the oafs who make "propositions" to every woman in sight and then fly in panic to Mama's protecting skirts when they fear the proposition is about to be accepted. They are the brave lads who spoil the evening slippers of ladies by playing footsie with them under the dinner table; who think it manly ("sophisticated") to get drunk at the Country Club on Saturday nights and tell off-color stories to uninterested women, on the theory that this is virile and the stories are fatally aphrodisiac. They care nothing for an interchange of ideas with women, or for any wit more subtle than the barnyard joke. And the country is filled with them. Yet, mice tailored to look like men, they want to be mothered by their wives – a process that freezes their already arrested development and renders impossible any relationship on a mature man-woman basis.

Every day, therefore, is Mother's Day in the lives of many women and without benefit even of a potted begonia. But these women weary of men whose emotional content is no greater than that of a Popsicle; who oscillate between the tepid and the torpid. As women they want, not unnaturally, to be loved by men. They long for that experience which is so often denied them and, longing for it, divorce one Boy only to find themselves presently married to another.

Men who like women have an intimate relationship with them; but marriage, among us, is frequently an intimate relationship without intimacy. Consequently the land is awash with charlatans who earn a fat living in the name of psychiatry by telling Mama "Your husband does not understand you." At the same moment, perhaps, Papa, taking the stock approach of the philandering husband, is telling some other woman whose husband does not understand her that his wife does not understand him.

Understanding is of course inseparable from intimacy, and this does not mean merely physical relations, for they are not necessarily any more a part of intimacy than, in the maxim of the Pullman washroom, they are an introduction which one must acknowledge on the street. Intimacy arises only when two persons move to one music. It involves an integrating and meshing of personalities; a deep interest in the flora, fauna, hills, valleys, and streams of the other person's mind; in all that has lived there, has died, or is coming to birth. It implies a mutual respect for dignity; a time to speak, to be silent, to act, to refrain from acting. It can arise only when a man likes a woman as a woman; a concept transcending that of wife, mistress, or sweetheart.

Yet many of our marriages – two dimensional studies in frustration – are often lacking in intimacy of this kind, so that divorce, when it comes, is the putting apart of something that had never been joined. The results of lack of intimacy are disastrous. The woman who is not permitted to play a woman's role in her husband's life does not develop mentally and spiritually. She is simply in a marriage of which she is not a part. She remains a lonely woman and, failing to mature, seems to justify her husband's retrospective opinion that she had always been incapable of maturing.

Nearly forty years ago, the dilemma of such women was admirably stated by Edith Wharton in *The Custom of the Country.* Let us note one scene. The marriage between Ralph Marvell, an attractive but weak member of the old school of fashionable gentlemen, and Undine Spragg, a social climber, is not going well. Laura Fairford, Marvell's sister, is talking to Charles Bowen, a family friend: –

"Now that Ralph has had to go into business . . . it's cruel of her to drag him out every night. . . . Undine doesn't seem to notice how hard he works."

Bowen gazed meditatively at the crumbling fire.

"No – why should she?"

"Why *should* she? Really, Charles –!"

"Why should she, when she knows nothing about it?"

"She may know nothing about his business; but she must know it's her extravagance that's forced him into it . . . You talk as if you were on her side!"

"Are there sides already? If so, I want to look down on them impartially from the heights of pure speculation. I want to get a general view of the whole problem of American marriages."

Mrs. Fairford dropped into her arm-chair with a sigh. "If that's what you want you must make haste! Most of them don't last long enough to be classified."

"I grant you it takes an active mind. But the weak point is so frequently the same that after a time one knows where to look for it."

"What do you call the weak point?"

He paused. "*The fact that the average American looks down on his wife.*" [My italics.]

Mrs. Fairford was up with a spring. "If that's where paradox lands you!"

Bowen mildly stood his ground. "Well – doesn't he prove it? How much does he let her share in the real business of life? How much does he rely on her judgment and help in the conduct of serious affairs? Take Ralph, for instance – you say his wife's extravagance forces him to work too hard; but that's not what's wrong. It's normal for a man to work hard for a woman – what's abnormal is his not caring to tell her anything about it."

"To tell Undine? She'd be bored to death if he did!"

"Just so; she'd even feel aggrieved. But why? *Because it's against the custom of the country.* [My italics.] And whose fault is that? The man's again — I don't mean Ralph, I mean the genus he belongs to: homo sapiens, Americanus. Why haven't we taught our women to take an interest in our work? Simply because we don't take enough interest in *them*. . . . To slave for women is part of the old American tradition; lots of people give their lives for dogmas they've ceased to believe in. . . ."

If these should be regarded as the imaginings of a novelist, we may turn to that superb study of a typical American town, *Middletown*, by Robert and Helen Lynd.* There the Lynds found husbands speaking of their wives as purer creatures than men, emotional, unstable, easily hurt, and " largely incapable of facing facts or doing hard thinking." Middletown wives, on the other hand, said, " Men are nothing but big little boys who have grown up and must be treated as such." These couples apparently did not regard a high degree of companionship as essential for marriage; aside from sharing its primary functions and the mutual concerns of family, they had little in common.

" The men and women frequently either gravitate apart to talk men's talk and women's talk, or the men do most of the talking . . . ! " Yet since some form of community social life must be maintained, since there must be some mutual interests between married couples, and since they are not interested in group talk, the dilemma is solved by playing cards. Consequently one of the commonest joint pursuits of Middletown couples is card playing.

There comes a moment, however, when couples must face it alone in Middletown as elsewhere. A few of them read aloud together, but only a few, because " literature and art have tended to disappear as male interests. . . . More usual is the situation described by one prominent woman. ' He (my husband) is busy all day and when he gets home at night he just settles down with the paper and his cigar and radio and just rests.' "

Thus novelist and sociologist are one in their findings about this phase of American life. But in this land where men do not like women, where love is regarded as a secret infirmity, and where divorce, as we practice it, is the right of any husband (or wife) to leave his mate in the sleeping car and continue the journey with the girl (or man) he has just met in the diner, men put women on a pedestal. This treatment is often taken to be proof positive of the profound esteem in which we hold women; the pedestal being an American invention as distinctive as the cheeseburger. It is, to my mind, proof that men do not like women.

* Robert S. Lynd (1892–), Professor of Sociology, Columbia University, and his wife, Helen Merrell Lynd, published their exhaustive sociological study of Muncie, Indiana, in 1929; the full title is *Middletown — a Study in Contemporary American Culture.*

III

IT IS commonly assumed that American men began to put women on a pedestal in early pioneer days, when their scarcity gave them a high rarity value; and it is true that many a frail lady who went West to tend bar was soon snapped up in marriage and frequently became a good wife, good mother, and the matriarch of what are now first families. But it is also clear from the records that pioneer women were often treated pretty roughly; that their lives were hard and short, alternating painfully between repeated childbearing and strenuous physical labor. May it be that women were put on a pedestal for other reasons?

It seems to me that when pioneer times had passed, when men were no longer dependent upon their wives' or their children's labor, and above all, when they made the staggering discovery that there is more gold aboveground than underground, they placed woman on a pedestal because they did not know what else to do with her. She was not wanted at a man's side. She was not desired as a companion in intimacy. She could be taken down and put back without disturbing the essential pattern of man's life, and, at the same time, standing there on a pedestal she gives the satisfying appearance of a household goddess. One might pay homage to her at stated intervals and lay at her feet the fruits of the chase — cars, emeralds, country houses, old masters.

What are the reasons for our real attitudes toward women as opposed to our rather nauseating pretensions? One is, as R. H. Tawney puts it, that "industry has risen to such a position of exclusive prominence among human interests," that the world is "like a hypochondriac . . . absorbed in the processes of his own digestion." * Among us the business of living is so often business that historians call our civilization a business civilization. Men, in an environment where competition is fierce but money-prestige rewards are high, have little time to give to anything but business.

Business is exciting. It is all-absorbing, filled with heady scents of power more alluring than any perfume, more demanding than any petulant mistress. It may be that men so absorbed are good providers and the backbone of the country. And it may also be that if they had time for women, if business were not more enchanting to them than women, they might one day discover them and, with a delicious shock of surprise, find they liked them.

* The quotation is from Tawney's well-known book, *The Acquisitive Society* (1920), p. 183.

Many men dislike women because they were dominated by them throughout childhood and early youth. In no other country is the development of boys molded by women, in home and school, to so great a degree as in the United States. Nowhere else is their early training so little distinct from that of girls, for nowhere else are women teachers and coeducation so common, while long ago in the home father gave way to mother as the head of the house. But at the same time their environment requires of them, more than elsewhere, that they behave like "red-blooded boys." (One sees the outcroppings of this attitude in some of our novelists, who drag four-letter words into their texts as proof of their virility; in the language of young soldiers who mistake profanity for virility.) Hence in a violent reaction they exaggerate their maleness by rejecting all values that they regard as feminine: flowers, music, art.

One result of the system is that our men are as taboo-ridden as Andaman Islanders. In our culture, it is "manly" to drink whiskey but not wine; to take coffee but not tea; to collect daggers but not Persian silks. It is suspect to read verse; and to write it is almost certain to bring one's sexual normality into question. The consequence of women's guiding of boys' instruction is that many of them go into manhood and marriage outwardly docile beneath the yoke of domesticity, but inwardly resentful of women.

This theme is elaborated upon by Henry Elkin, an Army veteran, in a recent issue of the *American Journal of Sociology.** He explains the constant use of profanity in the Army — "hardly a sentence was spoken, and no exclamation was uttered, without at least one profane term" — as a method by which "the GI symbolically throws off the shackles of the matriarchy in which he grew up."

His conclusion — sound, as I see it, and capable of easy proof in terms of everyday life — is this: "It may be inferred from typical forms of Army speech and behavior that a very large proportion of American men have never developed beyond childhood stages of emotional experience and display strong anxieties and excessive reactions when they are expected to live by psychologically mature standards." Such men, obviously, do not like women in the sense of this paper and, given their upbringing, it is unreasonable perhaps to expect that they should.

A large group of American men vaguely feel that they ought to be adventurers as were their ancestors who roamed this continent. They suspect that they have been domesticated by women as poultrymen

* Elkin's views are in an article, "Aggressive and Erotic Tendencies in Army Life," *The American Journal of Sociology,* LI (March, 1946), 408–413.

have domesticated the wild jungle fowl and made a barnyard biddy out of a free bird. They have become proprietors of grocery stores. They are traveling salesmen who leave home at morning and return at night to pitch in after supper and help do the dishes. Instead of being adventurers on the Oregon Trail or voyagers to China in the fur trade, they are minions of business, slaves of a standard of living, robots of routine; and for this they often subconsciously blame women without a thought of how much their plight may be of their own making.

Finally, the American male is resentful of women because, just as they first took away and then took over the saloon, he feels they have pre-empted many of his former prerogatives. He would like to dream of women as the blue-eyed Helen – remote, inaccessible, and therefore maddeningly desirable. But actually she is the woman seated on the next chair at the cocktail bar, matching him drink for drink; the woman ahead of him on the golf course shooting in the low seventies; the woman telling *him* the off-color story; the woman doing a job as well as he can and doing it for half his salary.

The attitudes of American males – inside and outside marriage – toward women remain primitive. Yet the American husband, generous, hard-working, sentimental, but essentially indifferent to his wife as he was to the girls he knew before marriage, tends to be what is called "a good man." His kind is celebrated in a poem by D. H. Lawrence bearing the illuminating title "Good Husbands Make Unhappy Wives."

There is nothing in the teaching the average man receives at home as a youth, nothing in the hit-and-run amorous or sentimental relationships he has had outside the home, nothing in the literature of his country or in the philosophy of his elders or companions, to show him the profound satisfactions that may flow from cultivating a woman as a beloved garden is cultivated. It is for this reason that the United States is filled with neurotic wives, who, well kept but badly cared for, are potential material for the divorce mills, or who degenerate into that rather loathsome creature known as the spoiled woman.

QUESTIONS

1. What effect is created by Cohn's opening statement that he put the question, Do American men like women? to junior officers and GI's? What would have been the difference in effect had he included, say, senior officers or WAC's?

2. What evidence is there that the essay is not so much a report of the conclusions held by American soldiers as it is a report of the conclusions held by the author himself? How does this evidence affect a statement of the principal purpose of the essay?

3. What connotations are suggested by these phrases in Paragraph 3, Section I: "professional amorist," "sweet-talking Southerner," "cowboy-gallant Westerner," and "men who automatically snatch their hats from their heads"? Why does Cohn wish to arouse the particular responses which these phrases stimulate?

4. Section I concludes with the generalization that "despite our gregariousness and slaphappy manners, we are perhaps the loneliest and most bored of peoples." Do the details and particulars of this section justify the validity of Cohn's generalization?

5. Why does the author support his conclusions in Section II with evidence from a novel and a sociological study?

6. What, according to Cohn, are the reasons for what he calls our "real attitudes toward women"? What, according to him, are "our rather nauseating pretensions"?

7. What reforms does Cohn imply are necessary in order to improve the situation he has described? What differences of effect would the author have created, had he indicated the necessary reforms by direct statement instead of by implication?

JAMES HOWARD MEANS, M.D., is a native of Massachusetts. He received his higher education at Massachusetts Institute of Technology and at Harvard University (M.D., 1911). He has had a lengthy and illustrious career as physician and teacher. Since 1924 he has been Professor of Clinical Medicine at Harvard University and Chief of Medical Services at Massachusetts General Hospital. An avid student of the prevention and cure of disease as a national problem, Dr. Means has visited England to study the British National Health Service (*The Atlantic Monthly*, March, 1950), is concerned over the responsibilities of the American Medical Association (*The Atlantic Monthly*, October, 1950), and – as the following essay indicates – has very definite opinions on how to improve the health of our citizens.

GOVERNMENT IN MEDICINE

by JAMES HOWARD MEANS, M.D.

THE Federal government of the United States in the year 1952 offered varying degrees of medical care to some 25 million people, about one sixth of the nation. It spent for all its medical and health activities close to a billion dollars. Included in this huge sum are charges for research, educational, and public health activities as well as for the medical care of patients.

I lately derived an interesting figure from data contained in a report of the Committee on Labor and Public Welfare of the U.S. Senate, entitled " Health Insurance Plans in the United States," dated May 17, 1951. This report estimates that the total expenditure for medical care of every sort in the whole United States was about 10 billion dollars for the year 1949. If we divide this figure by 150 millions, the population of the United States in 1950, we get $66 per person per year expended for medical care. About 20 per cent of this was spent by government – Federal, state, and local. In 1929 this figure was only 10 per cent. The role of government in medicine thus appears decidedly on the increase.

Government in the United States has assumed medical responsibilities of one sort or another at all three of its levels – Federal, state, and local. On Federal medicine there is a wealth of source material from which we may obtain impressions. Probably the most comprehensive analysis of the situation is that of the " Task Force on Federal

Medical Services" of the Hoover Commission which was published in November, 1948. This report stressed first the magnitude of Federal medicine and its lack of an over-all or central plan. An enormous commitment has been entered into, and is being conducted "without even any clear decision as to certain of the large classes of the beneficiaries to be covered, with no estimate of the ultimate cost or of the effect upon other health measures of the nation."

According to the Hoover Commission study, there are three large and more than thirty smaller Federal medical systems which are operated independently of one another, going their own ways, making their own plans, building, staffing, and running hospitals and clinics with "little knowledge of and no regard for the operation of the others."

The three large systems are, of course, those of the Department of Defense, of the Public Health Service, and of the Veterans' Administration. We may confine our attention to the group of large Federal medical systems, which on the basis of either total number of patients served or cost amount to 90 per cent or more of the total. In the order of magnitude of the systems, the Veterans' Administration tops the list, then the armed forces, and finally the Public Health Service. But the Public Health Service stands first of all Federal agencies in the field of medical research and education.

The Hoover Commission's chief criticism of the medical services provided by the Federal government was not so much that the individual systems are poorly operated, as that they operate without regard to one another, really in competition with one another. Each seeks to build its own empire regardless of the others. The Veterans' Administration, for example, unquestionably offers well-integrated and high-quality medical care to veterans, but as the Task Force pointed out, the Veterans' Administration's hospital construction program conflicts directly "with the government's policy under the Hill-Burton Act of aiding non-federal hospitals for the purpose of establishing a sound hospital system for the country as a whole."

The Veterans' Administration's medical establishment is by far the most important of the medical care activities of the Federal government. A report to the Senate by the Committee on Labor and Public Welfare dated August 2, 1951, called the medical care program of the Veterans' Administration "one of the largest in the world. Potentially affecting some 21 million veterans, it operates on a budget calling for an expenditure of over 650 million dollars a year." Significantly larger figures for this have been given subsequently.

The Veterans' Administration hospitals and out-patient departments admit free all veterans for service-connected illness; and when beds are available, they will admit veterans to hospitals for nonservice-connected illness provided they state they cannot pay for the service. The growth potential of the Veterans' Administration's hospital system is thus unlimited. If the hospitals are not filled with service-connected cases, they fill up with nonservice-connected cases. Then, since the available beds are full, more beds are needed, and therefore more hospitals are constructed; and so on.

The professional service given has been of good quality, because under the policy inaugurated by General Bradley, selection of staff for the Veterans' Administration's hospitals has been through committees of medical deans. The inclusion of nonservice-connected cases, which goes back to 1924, has increased the professional interest of the service because of the more general nature of such cases. More able doctors are thus attracted, and the quality of medical care is improved for all.

As veterans become ever more numerous, however, there is the danger that the private and voluntary system of medicine, as we have known it in this country, may become completely encircled by the free (tax-supported) medicine of the Veterans' Administration. This is a far greater threat to the medical status quo and its voluntary institutions than is compulsory health insurance; but so obsessed is the American Medical Association leadership with the desire to kill the latter, that it has largely ignored the former. Indeed some of the doctors who are fighting what they call "socialized medicine" are serving in the Veterans' hospitals with the greatest equanimity. Yet if we have anything that approaches socialized medicine in the United States, the medical empire of the Veterans' Administration is it.

Government medicine in the United States, other than Federal, is to a greater degree public health work, medical education, and hospital service than it is medical care, that is to say, the services of physicians. Dr. R. C. Page, Chairman of the National Doctors' Committee for Improved Federal Medical Services, gives the following figures for the distribution of all hospital beds in the country: Federal hospitals, 194,000; state, county, and municipal hospitals, 843,000; nongovernmental hospitals, 414,000. Thus it appears that 71 per cent of the nation's hospitalization function is borne by one of the three levels of government – 13 per cent Federal and 58 per cent state and local. Except in the case of psychiatric, tuberculosis, or other hospitals for chronic disease, however, state and local hospitals are staffed primarily by physicians and surgeons in private practice who give their services or who serve for rather nominal fees.

The state governments are also making a great contribution to medical education in that they own and operate 31 of the total of 72 four-year medical schools of the country.

In the field of directly providing medical care, the state governments are steadily getting in deeper and deeper. They are entering new fields such as cancer, arthritis, and heart disease in ever expanding programs. As more and more doctors work for the Federal government, so too will more and more work for the state and local governments.

II

THE major recommendation of the Hoover Task Force was that all medical activities of the Federal government, except the military, should be unified under a single national health agency headed by a career director-general and including three main divisions – namely, medical care, public health, and research and training. Furthermore, the Hoover Report recommended that in the continental United States there should also be transferred to this national health agency all general and most station hospitals of the armed forces. For military reasons only it was recommended to leave within the Department of Defense those medical establishments directly serving the armed forces. "The medical service of an armed force," it was said, "is a necessary and an integral part of that force. To separate it from the force is wholly or largely to destroy its usefulness." This also seems good sense.

How the integration of Federal medicine should fit in with the executive branch of the government in its entirety is a controversial issue. One school of thought is that it should all be organized in a department of the government – a department of health headed by a minister of health of full cabinet rank. Another is that a new department of the government should embrace not only health but education and public welfare also. Which of these two solutions has the more merit, I will not presume to say. Either would provide for planning and integration, now quite lacking, and would constitute, therefore, an advance over what we have at the present time.

Such a unification also would make possible effective co-operation between governmental medicine and private medicine. If we need some sort of national health program, a necessary step in achieving it is to put the house of Federal medicine thoroughly in order. It doesn't, as it now stands, offer anything from which a national health program can be constructed. Only in the event that the continuous, unchecked growth of the Veterans' Administration's medical establishment engulfed all else could the emergence of a national health program from present-day Federal medicine be envisaged. Should that state of affairs ever eventuate, then we should be in much the same situation as Britain is today, only we should have got there by default instead of purposefully, as has Britain.

The most promising effort on the part of the Federal government to co-operate with private and local medicine to obtain better medical care for the people on a nation-wide basis is the hospital construction program being carried out under the Hill-Burton Act. In a country of increasing and gradually aging population, continuous construction of new hospital and public health facilities is imperative. Interruption in civilian hospital construction during the last war left the country with an estimated 900,000 shortage in total hospital beds. It was in an effort to correct this situation that the Hill-Burton bill was enacted. Under its provisions the Federal government can give in aid from a minimum of one third of the cost to a maximum of two thirds of the cost for the construction of hospital or health facilities by state, local, or private agencies. Federal funds are allocated to the states in accordance with population, need, and the relative per capita income of the states.

The states are required to assess their own needs in order to obtain Federal aid. Special emphasis is placed on promoting adequate hospitalization in areas of greatest need, originally in rural sections. Thus far 91,000 beds have been provided under the Hill-Burton program, and 1900 projects are being aided. Because well-trained young doctors dislike working without proper facilities, rural hospital construction under the Hill-Burton Act has helped induce them to settle in rural areas. A military objective is also being met, because the locations of hospital construction follow the evacuation channels from the large target cities out into the safer rural districts.

The hospital construction program of the Hill-Burton Act gives an excellent demonstration of how government can co-operate with voluntary effort to achieve a nation-wide program within the field of health. But since it has nothing directly to do with the distribution of doctors, it is incomplete, and it is for this very reason that it has not been opposed by organized medicine. It is very good so far as it goes, but it does not go far enough. Better distribution of medical personnel, for one thing, and co-ordination with the hospital building program of the Veterans' Administration are also needed.

I saw an editorial not long ago in a county medical journal in which the Hoover Report's account of the irresponsible building of hospitals by competing Federal agencies was cited. The point was made, however, that voluntary hospitals at times are guilty of this sin also. They too compete with one another. An example was given in which one voluntary hospital put up a new and large obstetric wing coincidentally with the closing of such service for lack of patients in several other hospitals in the same community. There should be planning, so this editorial writer claimed, in order that the total hospital beds in an area should efficiently meet community needs. Some community agency such as Red Feather or Hospital Council should exercise control of the distribution of hospital facilities in its area.

I entirely agree, in principle, with this sentiment, but I would say to this editor, let's go a little farther and do some planning for the distribution of doctors as well and organize them for the purpose of best meeting the people's needs. There I am sure he would part company with me, for when it comes to the affairs of doctors, his journal has always been very conservative. Let Uncle Sam plan his hospital building efficiently; let voluntary hospitals so plan theirs; but when it comes to doctors, economic freedom of the professional individual must be preserved. Only the law of supply and demand may be allowed to operate upon the doctors. Let it determine their distribution. When it comes to medical care, however, the law of supply and demand does not meet human needs. This was one of the reasons why Britain adopted its National Health Service.

III

ANOTHER area in which government has co-operated successfully with voluntary effort is research. This is a field which affects medical practice only to the extent of giving it new knowledge, better methods of diagnosis and treatment, better professional armamentaria.* The politicians, who in response to popular demand like to do something toward meeting the health needs of the people, are disposed to make liberal appropriations to further the investigation of the nature and causes of disease, because in this area there is no likelihood of stirring up political hornets' nests.

Various agencies of the government have medical research establishments of their own — the armed forces, for example, and the U.S. Public Health Service. At Bethesda, Maryland, an array of imposing buildings suggesting a large university on a beautiful campus is in fact the National Institutes of Health of the U.S. Public Health Service, a group of research institutes for the study of great problems such as

* The plural form of a Latin word meaning "arsenal." Here used to mean the equipment — instruments, apparatus, medicines, methods — of a physician.

cancer, heart disease, arthritis, and other enemies of man. Arising in the midst of the Institutes is a huge new edifice, the Clinical Center, actually a hospital of 500 beds where patients with diseases which it is desired to investigate can be cared for while their cases are under scientific study. This unit is to be opened for use early this spring. The Clinical Center is analogous to the well-known hospital of the Rockefeller Institute in New York, but on a very much larger scale.

In addition to operating their own research establishments, the armed forces and the Public Health Service also expend large appropriations in support of medical research by making grants-in-aid to university and other research institutions throughout the country. These have been of great importance in accelerating the tempo and, we hope, improving the quality of medical investigation. Not only are going projects reinforced, but new research foci are discovered and nurtured. I know of no finer contribution of the Federal government to medical progress than the research grants program of the Public Health Service. There is no coercion or regimentation of investigators, and no political influence whatever enters into the distribution of the aid. Applications for aid originate with the investigators, who are free agents, and aid is granted entirely on the basis of the scientific merit of the projects submitted as judged by groups of neutral experts. It is a fine example of co-operation between government and independent agencies to improve the health of the people.

The practice of medicine is in the nature of a public utility, such as transportation or communication, served largely in our country by private enterprise. Because such private enterprises tend to be monopolistic, while at the same time their services are needed by everybody, some governmental control of them is necessary.

The type of medical establishment in any country — how much of it governmental, how much private or voluntary — will depend upon the political philosophy of the country which it serves. In totalitarian Russia there is totalitarian medicine; in socialized Britain socialized medicine; and in the United States, which still believes in private enterprise, one finds a large private enterprise component in medical practice and in medical education and research. At the present time, however, our government and private medicine combined are not giving all our people the best medicine in the world, which they might have if our total medical effort were better planned and integrated.

The G.O.P. is on record as being opposed to Federal compulsory health insurance. It also insists that the health of the people as well as their proper medical care cannot be maintained if subject to Federal bureaucratic dictation. In the second of his ten pledges published on November 2, General Eisenhower, however, pledged that the "social gains achieved by the people, whether enacted by a Republican or Democratic administration, are not only here to stay, but are to be improved and extended." Inasmuch as Eisenhower had previously said that he is against socialized medicine, and even that he regards Federal aid to medical education as the first step toward the socialization of medicine, it is heartening to find him later pledging that social gains are to be extended. In the field of health legislation it will be interesting to see what form this extension will take.

In planning its constructive action the new regime will have the advantage of the excellent report made in December, 1952, by the President's Commission on the Health Needs of the Nation, a body appointed a year ago by Mr. Truman, Dr. Paul B. Magnuson chairman. It is greatly to be hoped that both Congress and the new administration will give the Commission's report very earnest consideration. Its recommendations cannot be regarded by any fair-minded person as in any sense radical. It does not recommend national compulsory health insurance, but instead suggests supplementing private prepayment plans by government in areas where the former prove inadequate. To me it looks like a good middle road program.

IV

ONE of the very pressing matters emphasized in this report is the support of medical education. Federal aid to medical education to overcome the growing shortages of doctors, nurses, and other trained health personnel has repeatedly been advocated. No informed person can dispute the necessity for a sufficient supply of such personnel. Of those who have been opposing Federal aid, it should be asked, where do they expect to get the necessary support? At present no adequate source other than government has been discovered.

In my opinion the most needed items for extension of health legislation are Federal aid to medical education, integration of the Federal medical services, and a program for co-operation between the Federal medical establishment and local or regional health plans, whether voluntary or governmental. Two of the major recommendations of the President's Commission on the Health Needs of the Nation were: first, the strengthening of centers of public health activities; and second, the offering of Federal aid to the medical care of patients through grants-in-aid to the states, in a manner analogous to Hill-Burton aid to hospital care.

It is very significant that Eisenhower in his speech on October 9 at

New Orleans admitted the inadequacy of private health insurance and said that the usefulness of Federal loans or other aid to local health plans should be explored.

One great advantage which we in the United States have over Britain, which has gone the whole way in the nationalization of its medical establishment, is that, being still largely a free enterprise country, we have freedom to try experiments in the provision of medical care and in the co-operation between government and voluntary effort.

The Canadians, who have in the main a medical situation that more closely resembles ours than Britain's, have shown more willingness than we to try experiments. A poll by the Canadian Institute of Public Opinion in 1949 showed 80 per cent of the people in favor of a national health insurance plan under the auspices of the Federal government, which would include both hospital and medical care. All three political parties have endorsed such a scheme in principle, and the Canadian Medical Association favors national health insurance of some sort, but preferably not administered by a government agency. Two Canadian provinces, Saskatchewan and British Columbia, have set up complete compulsory hospital plans, and Alberta and Newfoundland have partial health insurance services. In other parts of Canada a variety of health plans are in operation — some entirely doctor-run, some consumers' co-operatives, some sponsored by private insurance companies.

In 1948 the Dominion government inaugurated a five-year national health grants program to strengthen and improve, in co-operation with the provincial governments, the health and hospital facilities available to the people of Canada. In a speech made before both houses of Parliament on November 20, 1952, the Governor General said that his government proposes to ask that Parliament give consideration to the extension of this program of co-operation between Dominion and provincial governments. Thus it appears that nation-wide searching for better ways to bring health to all the people, particularly with reference to the role of government therein, is far more in evidence in Canada than it is in our own country. Planning at all levels — national, state, and local — is absolutely necessary, and it is to be hoped that the medical profession in the United States will see fit to co-operate with government along some such line as that which the Canadians are following at the present time.

QUESTIONS

1. How is Section I unified? Point out the main idea and the supporting ideas. In the opinion of Dr. Means, how is the attitude of the American Medical Association inconsistent?

2. Explain what use the author makes of (a) the Hoover Report and (b) the Burton-Hill Act in Section II.

3. By what methods has government co-operated with private enterprise in medical research, as indicated in Section III?

4. How does the method of governmental support urged in Section IV differ from the methods previously considered? Of what special importance is the opening sentence of Paragraph 2, Section IV?

5. What purpose is served by the reference to Canada, in the last two paragraphs of the essay?

6. Is the appeal of the author mainly intellectual, or emotional? Justify your answer. Why may not the essay be considered merely a piece of propaganda for socialized medicine?

ELIJAH ADLOW has had nearly thirty years of experience on the bench. It has given Judge Adlow a voice of authority in discussions of law and lawlessness. A native Bostonian educated in the public schools and at Harvard College and Law School, Judge Adlow is now Chief Justice of the Municipal Court of Boston. In an earlier essay in *The Atlantic Monthly*, "Our Something-For-Nothing Age" (May, 1953), Judge Adlow sharply criticized contemporary American standards of morality as reflected in attitudes toward legal claims.

TEEN-AGE CRIMINALS

by JUDGE ELIJAH ADLOW

AN ATTEMPT to protect juveniles from the contaminating influences of adolescents and adults has resulted in the establishment in many places of separate and independent courts for juvenile offenders. My court has no jurisdiction over juveniles, which means that all offenders under seventeen years of age are handled by the judges of a specially constituted Juvenile Court. This does not mean that the juvenile is a stranger to my court. In fact, one of the alarming conditions that contribute to the contemporary moral crisis derives from the number of crimes which are committed, in whole or in part, by juveniles. For the purposes of this article I shall not limit my observations to those under seventeen years of age, but shall consider all adolescents.

Not long ago two girls, aged nine and eleven, appeared in my court and by their testimony involved fifteen men in charges of most serious sex offenses. It was evident from the testimony given by these girls that in certain instances the girls solicited the men to commit the acts with which they are now charged. This is not the first time that unusually young girls have become involved with men. Since the beginning of World War II the abandonment of domestic responsibilities by many mothers in exchange for jobs in industry has left countless children in America to rear themselves. It was inevitable that some of these children would speedily show evidences of neglect. The direct result of this absenteeism from the home was noticeable during the war, when many cases involving indecent assaults on children and similar offenses were brought into the courts. The judges expected that with the return to normalcy, and the return of mothers to their homes, the conditions would abate. Unfortunately, a good many mothers who left home for a job are still working, and their families are expected to bring themselves up the best way they can.

What makes the revolt of modern youth serious is that it bears little resemblance to what was once viewed as juvenile delinquency. There was a time when the difference between a bad boy and a playful boy was merely one of degree. Today the crimes of violence in which the young indulge can never be mistaken for boyish pranks. The many cases of malicious destruction of property that have entailed great loss to the public are not the cumulative consequence of youthful exuberance but the product of calculated and planned mischief. The many assaults with dangerous weapons, some of which have had fatal consequence, are the acts of irresponsible desperadoes which differ little from the planned attacks on society by adult outlaws.

More alarming are the thefts and holdups. The petty pilferings that once represented a boy's transgressions were largely restricted to doormats, ash barrels, and milk bottles. But in the past few years I have had an eighteen-year-old boy in my court who, while employed by a wholesale electric supply house, loaded $10,000 worth of electric equipment on a freight elevator, lowered the elevator to the ground floor, and then secured a truckman to cart away the loot. Three boys, all seventeen years of age, were before me charged with breaking and entering and larceny. After getting an automobile, these boys broke into a Surplus War Goods Store and carted away $3500 worth of merchandise. Two others in the same age group looted the warehouse of a jewelry novelty wholesaler and carried away $6000 worth of merchandise. After making their getaway they stored the loot in a safe place and canvassed the community until they found an operator of a jewelry store who would buy the goods from them. There is nothing "juvenile" about this kind of delinquency.

Recently four boys, all under twenty-one, brazenly attempted to secure the release of a sixteen-year-old girl who was in the custody of the Massachusetts Youth Service Board at the Lancaster School for Girls. This is not the first time that young desperadoes have attempted to force the release of inmates in correctional institutions. The bold daring revealed in these escapades merely reflects the cold-blooded indifference of modern youths to the penal consequences of their acts. Nothing is done halfheartedly. So far as youth is concerned, its war against society is total war.

No juvenile groups have yet duplicated the adventures of Murder,

Inc. Yet there is ample evidence of their imitation of the extortion and blackmail gangs that have enjoyed nation-wide notoriety. Several months ago five boys between fifteen and seventeen were tried before a Suffolk County jury for extorting money from young boys by threatening them with bodily harm. Despite the conviction of two of these defendants by the jury, the disposition of the cases by probation of the offenders revealed a reluctance on the part of the court to take the entire matter very seriously. In this the court was displaying an attitude consistent with that of courts the country over, of indulging in wishful thinking wherever juvenile delinquency is concerned. If there is a serious juvenile delinquency condition in America today, the courts must share a part of the responsibility for it, but that share is insignificant when compared with the major factors which underlie the condition.

II

WE MUST remember the setting in which the modern youth plays his role. He reacts to environment as grownups do. It would be absurd to expect that at a time when adult America is indulging in an orgy of lawlessness, youth should reveal moderation and restraint. We cannot deny that the standards of communal morality have been lowered by this generation. An age that has witnessed more drinking, more gambling, and a more widespread indulgence in luxuries and comforts than ever before is bound to witness a gradual disappearance of those primitive virtues which sterner and more sober generations nourished and applauded.

The authority of parents has been weakened. And for the impairment of this most important element in character building the parents themselves are to blame. In many homes parents have viewed their responsibilities in a detached and indifferent manner, and their children could really be said to have been left to bring themselves up. I have had frequent occasion in recent years to interview young people who intended to marry and who applied to me for a waiver of the five-day law. I always inquire of these young people whether they have consulted their parents. I have been particularly careful to bring home to servicemen who are away from their parents the propriety of confiding in them before taking such a serious step as matrimony. While some have assured me that they already had obtained their parents' approval, I have been shocked at the number who reply, "Whatever I do is all right with my folks."

A generous application of liberal principles, so called, has resulted in parents' overindulging children and allowing them to do as they please. That they should gratify every whim, express themselves freely, do just as their " little hearts " desire, and have everything they want has been not only tolerated but encouraged. Instead of inhibiting violent tendencies and molding character by strict supervision and guidance, parents have deliberately refrained from stifling the impulses of youth lest some latent talent be frustrated. As a result, bedlam reigns where once was " Home, Sweet Home."

A generation that has been encouraged to express itself freely will little hesitate to join in those " pranks " which amount to vandalism and the malicious destruction of property. The monuments which have been disfigured, the public buildings that have been damaged, and the streetcars that have been wrecked combine to discredit a theory of child guidance which frowns upon restraint. Children can hardly be expected to respect the property of strangers when their destructive tendencies have known no curb in the home.

Frequently these youngsters come from good homes; their parents are excellent people, and no effort or cost has been spared to fit the children properly for their place in society. Consider the hoodlumism revealed by the raids on girls' dormitories by college boys in recent years, and it will readily appear that delinquency is not merely a problem of the slums. If children from the so-called better homes can share in this epidemic of disorder, what can we expect from those who have been denied the care of good and considerate parents? Children who are brought up in an atmosphere of drunkenness and brawling, who witness parents committing assaults upon each other, and who daily see the laws of God and man violated in their homes would have to be more than human if the atmosphere in which they were brought up did not leave its stamp upon them. Such homes are nothing less than breeding places for crime, and the records of our courts go to prove it.

A substantial portion of the young offenders brought into court come either from broken homes where the parents are living apart, from homes rendered destitute by the chronic alcoholism of one or both parents, or from homes presided over by parents with long criminal records. The stories disclosed by the police about conditions in these homes are unfit to print. Some are beyond belief. If the conditions which exist in some were ever brought to light, the public would wonder why the delinquency problem is not worse. It can be said with truth that some of these children never had a chance.

III

MODERN youth has a great deal of time on its hands. Actually, a shortsighted legislative policy has forbidden young people to engage in many pursuits which once afforded opportunities for wholesome employment. I have seen prosecutions under the Child Labor Law which did more harm than good. I have in mind particularly the owner of a cleansing and dyeing shop whose fifteen-year-old brother helped him after school and who was brought into my court for violating the Child Labor Law. If a young man is not as anxious to work as he might be, let us remember that laws like that have helped estrange him from habits of industry.

There can be no question that the improvement in the condition of the average man, with its increase in earnings, has contributed radically to the change in attitude of parents. Most of them overlook the part which strict discipline, scanty allowances, and hard work played in their moral and physical upbringing. Instead they are determined to give to their children what was denied to them. They buy them better clothes, provide them with larger allowances, enable them to participate in sports, to attend movies, to enjoy summer vacations, and to do all those things calculated to make life agreeable. They not only relieve them of the little tasks or chores which once were a part of a boy's life, but they even frown on the performance of any manual labor, particularly for hire. The industry that was once encouraged in youth as a virtue is now regarded as an interference with the right to enjoy life.

This generosity on the part of parents has had an evil effect on the generation upon which it has been lavished. The little gifts which once provided the great incentive to youth for obedience and industry are now without effect. What was once awaited as an act of kindness and generosity is now demanded as a right. And the kindness of parents which makes occasional work unnecessary has resulted in building up in young America a pronounced aversion for manual labor and toil. Fifty years ago the popular hero of fiction for our youth was Horatio Alger; today it is Superman. Instead of having its feet on the ground and being conscious of the stern realities of life, our younger generation has its head in the clouds and looks down on its parents as old-fashioned and out-of-date. The parents wanted a generation of "gentlemen" and they got them. They forget that it is important that they be "men" first. On behalf of our youth, it can be said that the parents wanted it that way.

Equally devastating to youth is the noticeable weakening of the moral viewpoint wherever we turn. The nineteenth century may have been hypocritical in its severity, but it extolled virtue and denounced vice and sin. There are serious differences of opinion as to the long-range implications of nineteenth-century austerity and severity, but for youth it meant a high moral standard which served to inhibit lust, to promote modesty and respect, and to encourage obedience to law.

This moral viewpoint has been weakened today by an amazing combination of social, economic, and political factors. One hundred years ago gambling was considered the pastime of the wicked; today it has the sanction of authority in the form of legalized pari-mutuel betting. One hundred years ago the moral forces in America waged a relentless war against alcoholism and managed to keep the evil under a fair measure of control; today we are paying an exorbitant price for the experiment of Prohibition in the form of an unlimited distribution of alcoholic beverages. What is called the licensing system is nothing more than a token regulation. As a consequence teen-age drinking has become a major aspect of the problem of juvenile delinquency.

Equally marked are the changes in concepts of decency and honor. We read in the daily paper that a judge has ruled in the Federal Court that even though a man had been convicted on several occasions of violating liquor and gambling laws, he is still worthy of becoming an American citizen. On another occasion we read of a judge stopping deportation proceedings against a criminal who had twice been convicted of manufacturing slugs which could be used in slot machines. This judge's pronouncement to the effect that such a crime did not involve the element of moral turpitude should suffice to alert us to the depreciated moral viewpoint of today.

Let us examine the headlines a bit further. A judge before whom an embezzler stands, makes the injudicious remark, in condoning the offense, "His pay was too low." What effect has such comment on the moral viewpoint of youth? Or let us consider the extreme in official bungling, when a deputy warden in a state prison publicly applauded the conduct of a group of prisoners who had mutinied against prison discipline. When public officials condone lawlessness, is it any wonder that young people become indifferent to high standards?

How has the class war in America affected youth's moral viewpoint? Whether one believes in labor's right to strike or not, it must be apparent to everyone that the chronic condition of unrest on the labor front, punctuated by occasional outbreaks of violence and lawlessness, has had sinister implications for the cause of law and order.

Its impact on young people has been noticeable, as is evident from their readiness to join in any mass demonstration promoting any cause.

Several years ago 3000 New York City high school children picketed the mayor's office for four days shouting, "We want more pay for our teachers." On the fifth day there was no demonstration; it was Saturday and there was no school.

In glancing through the newspapers of the last few years, we can find ample evidence of the activities of boys and girls as agitators. They picket City Hall to protest against closing a fire station or abandoning a school site. They join a strike called in protest against a change in the high school curriculum or the transfer of an athletic coach. Possibly these children have serious notions regarding the objectives which such practices promote; but, at the same time, the whole thing coincides with what their juvenile minds regard as "good fun." That the ultimate consequences of these demonstrations are to exalt insubordination and to weaken the arm of constituted authority hardly occurs to them. They have become pawns in the hands of those who thrive on agitation and unrest.

Not only our youths but our grownups have wilted under the spectacle of a viciously waged class war. In no small measure has the indifference of authority to the violence and lawlessness of the labor struggle resulted in a disrespect for law. On the political front the condition is equally disruptive. In recent years there has been an intensification of the struggle for political power in the United States. And the condition is evident at all levels of the political hierarchy. It derives principally from the fact that party government has been supplanted by gang government, and the officeholder wields power by virtue of his personal ascendancy. As a consequence he is campaigning for office 365 days in the year. Those who seek to replace him are equally active and vigorous. This war is being waged with the weapons of the forum; with crimination and recrimination; with sly innuendo and downright bombast. Young people are spectators in this war, and they gaze at the spectacle somewhat bewildered. They emerge from the experience with a feeling that a great many people are being entrusted with the powers of government without regard to their merit or personal integrity. If youth is waging a revolt against authority today, it is because conditions on the home front have done much to discredit authority.

Recently in Redwood City, California, a schoolteacher took his pupils to a nearby courthouse in order to show them "how justice works." In court the judge helped the show along by asking to see the teacher's driving license. When the judge discovered that the teacher's license had already expired, he immediately issued a summons to the teacher to appear before him on the charge of driving without a license. Such a judge is a menace. Instead of exalting the teacher in the eyes of his pupils, he discredited him and thereby undermined his authority in the classroom. In every sense he was contributing to the delinquency of a group of minor children. Every day in the year, and all over the United States, people who should know better are doing equally stupid things with no other objective than to appear smart.

IV

TO WHAT extent has the cultural setting in which modern youth lives been responsible for the moral breakdown? No one can deny that the world of today is a much more interesting place for boys and girls than that of the nineteenth century. They have movies, radio, television, and the modern newspaper. Millions of dollars are being spent each day to provide programs that will arouse their interest and entertain them. Some of these items are educational as well as entertaining. Doubtless many of them serve to improve the moral viewpoint of those reached by them. Others have questionable value as educational items, and there are some which are a distinct menace to the morals of the community.

We must never underestimate the role played by suggestion in influencing the behavior of youth. Thirty years ago, in the city of Boston, a boy who had escaped from a correctional institution sent out word that he intended to steal a car and race it through certain streets of Charlestown which were known as " The Loop." No such insane stunt had ever been attempted before. True to his word he appeared on the designated night and entertained thousands who had gathered to watch him, while the police, racing after him on motorcycles, made desperate but futile attempts to apprehend him. Since that night, over thirty years ago, hundreds of boys have imitated his escapade. They have stolen cars; they have killed and injured many innocent citizens. This one insane venture sufficed to set in motion a crime wave which has made the " loop speeder " a chronic problem to authority in Massachusetts.

Let us analyze a few more items which reveal youth's readiness to imitate. Several years ago a slightly deranged veteran stepped out onto the parapet at the ninth floor level of the Hotel Touraine in Boston. For hours he held a crowd spellbound on the street below while he refused to return to a place of safety. It was unfortunate that the episode was publicized. Within a few days similar exhibitionist stunts were staged in different cities in the United States. Need I remind you that every example of unusual behavior reported in the press or portrayed on television is usually followed by a multitude of similar stunts all over the United States? Consider the outbreaks on college campuses. Not even Harvard, Yale, and Massachusetts Institute of Technology could avoid the epidemic of exhibitionism which transformed sections of their student bodies into rioting mobs.

V

IF SOCIETY is bewildered by this spectacle of youth in revolt, its peace of mind has not been improved by the variety of suggestions which have been advanced to meet the situation. These all savor of the new liberalism. They ignore the part which the weakening of parental control over youth has played in precipitating the present crisis. Expanding the probation system, providing more public playgrounds, and raising the age limit for school attendance are but a few of the palliatives recommended. But no sober analysis of the problem can ignore their futility.

Human behavior is linked with character, and the process of character building commences at infancy and acquires its basic strength and quality in the home. No public agency can supply the training and instruction which a well-managed and properly supervised household affords. No one can replace parents in the training of children, and the sooner the new liberalism discovers this the sooner will it be on the right road to a solution. If society wishes to strike at the root of the evil, it must wage its campaign against those parents who refuse to discharge their responsibilities faithfully. The desire of women to retain their place in industry since the war is not without sinister implication. If the condition becomes fixed, we must expect an aggravated delinquency situation. While woman legally has a right to participate in industry, there is no moral sanction for abandoning a much more sacred responsibility. And the great decision which the modern woman must make is whether she prefers the career of motherhood to that of a worker. She cannot undertake both and succeed.

Few people see the long-range implications of juvenile delinquency. Few people realize that a majority of the men in the prisons in America today commenced their criminal careers between the ages of eight and thirteen. Some of these unfortunates had a predisposition to crime; others became criminal through their associations. As for the congenital delinquent, nothing we could have done would have spared him his fate. But the child who might have grown into an honorable career had it not been for the undesirable associations which brought him to his sad estate has a just grievance against a society that did not insulate him from these vicious influences. Policies which deny this protection to the coming generation are policies which will assure a bumper crop of criminals for the future.

I have already mentioned the calamitous consequences to the entire Boston community of the exhibitionism of the automobile-stealing, loop-speeding Jimmy Sheehan. His little crime wave turned into a major outbreak of juvenile delinquency. And the same imitation that multiplied the Jimmy Sheehans and the parapet jumpers is being discovered in the duplication of the crimes portrayed in the movies, on the radio, and on television. Left to his own resources the modern delinquent would still be indulging in the petty pilfering that once satisfied his criminal urge. In an atmosphere filled with suggestion, his criminal aspirations cease to be juvenile. It is because he is so much more dangerous today that he can no longer be treated as a child.

Within a year a seventeen-year-old boy with a record of previous arrests for larceny was apprehended in the act of stealing in a department store. As the store detective put his hand on him, the boy drew a razor and slashed the detective across the face. In my opinion this boy is a confirmed and dangerous criminal. I sentenced him to the Concord Reformatory. He appealed and I learned later that in the Superior Court his sentence was modified to one year in the House of Correction. Whether this judge's leniency was justified, only time will tell.

Whether the generation which has disquieted our era can be set right is a great question. Some have faith that various expedients of correction and reform provide a ray of hope. In the opinion of realists, however, who have seen society struggling in vain with the problem of crime, a large portion of the delinquent group must be charged off as lost. They are the casualties of the new liberalism. The only hope for the future lies in the resurgence of the home as the basic institution of the modern world. We must recapture the spirit of the home which our parents and grandparents knew, and young people must be brought up and not left to bring themselves up. The position of the parent must be restored to its former place of authority, and the power to govern the household must be asserted with kindness when possible and severity when necessary. Then, and only then, will character thrive and the foundation be laid for a law-abiding society.

QUESTIONS

1. In the last sentence of Paragraph 1, Section I, Adlow says, " For the purposes of this article I shall not limit my observations to those under seventeen years of age, but shall consider all adolescents." Why does the author not limit his observations to those under seventeen years of age?

2. What important distinction does Adlow make in Paragraph 3 of Section I? Why is the distinction which he makes in this paragraph especially important in understanding the author's intention in the essay as a whole?

3. How does Adlow secure a smooth transition from the first to the second section of the essay? What is the special aim of Section II? Determine whether or not the particular details are sufficient to support the generalizations of the author in this section of the essay.

4. What evidence does the author present to support his contention, in Paragraph 2, Section III, that most parents " overlook the part which strict discipline, scanty allowances, and hard work played in their moral and physical upbringing "?

5. In Paragraph 5, Section III, Adlow says, " This moral viewpoint has been weakened today by an amazing combination of social, economic, and political factors." Summarize the social, economic, and political factors which the author discusses.

6. What does Adlow mean, in Section V, by " the new liberalism "? Where else in the essay does he attack " liberal " views?

7. Why, in the last paragraph of Section V, does Adlow distinguish between those who " have faith that various expedients of correction and reform provide a ray of hope " and " realists " who believe that " a large portion of the delinquent group must be charged off as lost "?

ALBERT JAY NOCK was unusually secretive about his personal life but very frank in his criticism of the American scene. For over thirty years Nock (1873–1945) served as an irritant to smugness and complacency about existing institutions, especially affairs of state. He was an author, editor, clergyman, and teacher. In the 1930s he contributed to the *American Mercury* an anti-New Deal column called "The State of the Nation." The titles of his principal books are significant: *How Diplomats Make War* (1915), *The Myth of a Guilty Nation* (1922), *Our Enemy, the State* (1935), *Memoirs of a Superfluous Man* (1943). The last of these, especially, compelled interest and admiration on the part of reviewers even when they did not share the author's opinions.

UTOPIA IN PENNSYLVANIA

The Amish

by ALBERT JAY NOCK

A LONG time ago, "when I was still a prince in Arcadia," I became interested in the language and literature of the Pennsylvania Germans. I had been rather astonished – I don't know why – at discovering accidentally that they had not only a literature of their own, but a good one, and that a thriving organization called the Pennsylvania German Society was busy fostering and preserving it. This was a pleasant surprise; and at odd times during two or three years I dipped at random into this literature, thus finally getting a fair-to-middling acquaintance with it, especially with its religious and pastoral poetry, the side by which it is seen in perhaps its most amiable and attractive aspect.

By origin, the Pennsylvania Germans spoke the dialect of the Pfalz *; but in the course of a couple of centuries a good many English words have crept into their vocabulary to make everlasting sorrow and vexation for the outsider. A macaronic speech is easy enough to read when printed, but hardest of all (for me, at least) to understand when spoken. The Italian which one hears down Greenwich Village way in New York, for instance, is very difficult on this account, even when it is otherwise pretty good Italian. The Pfälzer

* The Palatinate, a state of the old German empire, along the Rhine.

dialect is not troublesome if you take it straight, but by the time you have shifted gears to accommodate two or three English words in the course of a long sentence, your interlocutor is away out of sight down the homestretch, leaving you in an exhausted and ignorant state; especially since the English words come out so heavily coated with a foreign inflection that it takes a minute or so to penetrate their disguise and recognize them. In dealing with the printed word, however, one escapes these tribulations. Here, for example, is the first stanza of a poem from Harbaugh's *Harfe.** Read it aloud at ordinary conversational speed to someone who knows German well, and see what he makes of it; then let him look at it as printed, and see what he makes of that: —

Heit is 's 'xäctly zwansig Johr,
Dass ich bin owwe naus;
Nau bin ich widder lewig z'rick
Un schteh am Schulhaus an d'r Krick,
Juscht neekscht an's Dady's Haus.†

The second verse is still more distressing. Here you have a colloquial English verb — slang, to the purist — handsomely tailored up with a good German prefix; and you have also an exact German rendering of an English idiomatic expression. These are heartbreakers; to the ear they carry nothing but grief and woe, yet see how familiar and domestic is their look in print: —

Ich bin in hunnert Heiser g'west,
Vun Märbelstee' un Brick,
Un alles was sie hen, die Leit,
Dhet ich verschwappe eenig Zeit
For's Schulhaus an der Krick.‡

But I must stop rambling around in this peculiar philology, and get on with my story. Some years later, when the first bloom of my interest in the Pennsylvania Germans had been rubbed off under pressure

* Henry Harbaugh (1817–1867), American preacher and poet who wrote *Harfe* (The Harp) in the Pennsylvania-German dialect.

† It is just twenty years,
That I have been out there;
Now I am back
And am standing by the schoolhouse on the creek,
Just next to my father's house.

‡ I have been in a hundred houses,
Of marble and brick,
And all that the people have,
That would I swap any time
For the schoolhouse on the creek.

of more immediate concerns, I noticed that they were being visited with the curse of publicity. Fictioneers, mostly of the female persuasion, *Gott soll hüten,*[*] were exploiting them in popular magazinedom. Reporters played them up by the side of their prowess in eating and their alleged prowess in witchcraft, the two accomplishments most likely to strike fire with the great American public. One or two cookbooks of dubious authenticity appeared. Then when lately the inhabitants of a certain district were had up in court for refusing to send their children to a State central school, I perceived that the Pennsylvania Germans were really in the news.

I did not read any of the fiction, nor did I care about the *Hexerei,*[†] but the two items about food and schools attracted me. The mention of food set up a nagging persistent hankering for a certain native country-made product which I had sampled many years before. I am not naming it because it seems to be scarce as hens' teeth, and having at last found it I am happily on the inside track and propose to stay there; so any inquiry about it will merely waste postage.

Thus my interest in the Pennsylvania Germans livened up again. My hankering for the food product would not subside, so I began to take measures. I wrote to the publisher of a book dealing largely with the region's cookery, asking him to sound out the young woman who wrote it; which he did, with no result. I wrote the chambers of commerce in the principal towns; the executive secretaries gave me names of some producers, to whom in turn I wrote without result. I then bethought me of my old friend Jeff Jones, who maintains a sales force in those parts; so I wrote him, suggesting that he turn his hellhounds loose to harry the whole countryside without respite, which I don't doubt he did, but they brought down no prey. At last I perceived that the matter required my personal attention. I determined to set forth in person and explore the counties of Lebanon and Lancaster with two objects in view. First, I would see what account of themselves the Pennsylvania Germans were actually giving. Second, I would find that food product if it existed, whether in the heavens above those two counties, or on the earth beneath, or in the waters under the earth. The opportunity presenting itself, I went and was successful. I found the food product, as I have already said, and bore it away in a burst of glory. I also found that the Pennsylvania Germans have a vast deal to say for themselves. One group especially excited my interest, and it is of them that I propose now to speak.

[*] God forbid.
[†] Witchcraft.

II

THEY are known as the Old Amish or House Amish. They are a split-off from the Mennonites, a religious body formed at Zurich early in the sixteenth century. In number, the Old Amish run to something between 8500 and 9000, and of these some 1500 are settled in the county of Lancaster, mostly on a stretch of rich farmland bordered by the Conestoga. They have been there since 1720, and their small rural communities grew up under odd names like Smoketown, Bird-in-hand, Blue Ball. I could get no reliable account of the origin of these names.

The Old Amish are reputed to be the best farmers in America, and a glance at their territory sets up a strong conviction that this is so. The Amishman is actually a farmer, not a manufacturer, like our large-scale single-crop producers. Nor is he a political farmer, of the kind whose perennial sorrows lie so close to the heart of Mr. Wallace. He cares nothing whatever for Mr. Wallace, and asks no political favors from anybody. His produce goes first to feed his family and his live-stock. If any be left over, he takes it to the public markets at Lancaster; and by the way, if you want to see something which you could really call a public market, go to Lancaster. I never in my life saw so much superexcellent superelegant produce of all kinds clustered together as I saw there, and practically all of it was Amish produce. But speaking commercially, the Amishman's market trade is on the side; what he gets out of it is loose change – lagniappe. He is not a truck-gardener. After the needs of his family are provided for, after he has put down great store and abundance of beef products, pork products, dairy products, vegetable and cereal products, all of his own raising – then if he can pick up an odd dollar or two in the markets, well and good; but not before.

Judged by current standards, the Amishman has an unorthodox view of his mission in life. His one cash crop is tobacco. If he were a right-minded man, he would put down all the land he could get hold of in tobacco, and let his family eat out of tin cans. But in the first place, he does not want any more land than he and his family can work properly under their own steam. He is not keen on hired help, and sees nothing in share-cropping. Then further, he has only very vague and uncertain notions about tin cans; I suspect you might have to go quite a way to find a can opener in an Amish household, or to find anybody who has ever seen one. For the Amishman, the idea of paying out good money for canned foodstuffs far inferior to what one can raise for oneself is one of those things that simply will not bear thinking about. Hence he limits his cash crop rigorously; it is strictly a side line, like his other market trade. It yields him plenty of money to go on with, for he needs hardly any, and he lets it go at that.

By sticking to this general policy for a couple of centuries, the Amish have worked themselves into an economic position that is pretty nearly impregnable. They have the real thing in "social security." Ten years ago, one of my town-dwelling friends wrote to a correspondent asking how Lancaster was doing under the depression. The correspondent telegraphed back, "What depression? There is no depression here." The Amish, putting it mildly, are exceeding well-to-do; or as the sinful would phrase it, they are rich as soap grease. I have heard say that Lancaster County is the richest agricultural region in the world, and I believe it; richest, that is, in good hard available cash money that can be dug up on demand at any moment, out of the Amishman's pants pocket.

The Amish beat the New Deal's whole program of social security, hands down. They have the best form of old-age pension that can be devised; when you grow old you simply take things easy, and live *wie Gott in Frankreich* * while your family carries on. No need for some officious nincompoop to come down from Washington and tell you how to do that. So also with "relief." No Amishman's name was ever yet on the relief roll of Lancaster County, and none ever will be. The Amishman does not waste a single bawbee on insurance, for he already has the best kind of insurance, on which he pays no premiums and his policy never expires. If lightning strikes his barn, his coreligionists in that district build him a new one; if he is ill, they help out with his work; if he dies untimely, they make arrangements to have things go on. No insurance company can compete with that.

He takes no oaths and signs no contracts or any form of written agreement, nor will he serve on juries or have anything to do with litigation; his religion forbids him all such. He lets his yea be yea and his nay nay, as the Bible commands, and he always keeps his given word. He is not a speculator or a borrower, and he does not hold public office. He is punctilious about taxes, paying the State's blackmail in full, and asking nothing in return but to be let alone – poor soul, as if that were not the very last thing the State would ever consent to do for anybody! The State lately foisted a grant of some $56,000 on the Old Amish for a PWA project in one of their townships, and they not only refused to accept it but appealed to the courts to have the noisome proposal nullified. It is no wonder that when this incredible miracle was reported at Washington the effect on the PWA personnel

* Like God in France.

was devastating; fifteen fainted away, eleven went into convulsions, and three of them died. I have this on good authority.

III

THE visitor does not have to look too closely to see what principle, what general theory of life, is at work here to bring this exemplary state of things about. It is religion. The Old Amish have the record of sticking longer and more faithfully to the original tenets, customs, and practices of their religion than any other Christian body in America; and it is this fidelity which has brought them where they are. This obviously says something for the Old Amish themselves, individually and collectively; but it also says something rather handsome for their religion. In the matter of getting results — and this is what all variants of religion presumably aim at — the Old Amish variant seems valid enough to stand up under the fire of criticism's most heftiest *Blitzkrieg*. Like the provisions of the Levitical law, its tenets, apparently arbitrary as many of them are, turn out to have a surprising deal of sound science and sound common sense behind them. In this they furnish material for advantageous comparison with the tenets and practices of other religious bodies. They will not, and should not, suggest to these bodies a wholesale taking over and substitution of Old Amish tenets and practices to displace their own. They do suggest, however, that if the other bodies want results comparable with those the Old Amish get under their conditions, they should make whatever modifications and displacements are appropriate to bringing them about under their own conditions.

The Old Amish believe that the agrarian life is the one most in accord with the Scriptures. This is their fundamental tenet; it merely puts a religious sanction on the agrarian doctrine * held by Turgot, Benjamin Franklin, and above all by Mr. Jefferson. The Amishman's logic of it is that man is a land-animal; God made him so. He derives his sustenance wholly from the land, and every kind and form of wealth that exists or can exist is producible only by the application of labor and capital to land; God made this arrangement. Therefore the more direct the mode of this application, the better and simpler becomes the fulfillment of God's will.

Now, whatever one may think of the theological side of this reasoning, the economic side of it is sound to the core. It is the basic posi-

* Belief that a rural, agricultural society is more sound economically and otherwise than an urban, industrial society. The Amish added the force of religious conviction to the ideas of Jefferson and others.

tion of fundamental economics, and there is no sophistry by which one can squirm away from it. But for the Amish the theological side is also sound, and they are strong on it; it sums up pretty much all the dogmatic theology the Amish have. They are probably a little weak on economic theory, but they are strong on the theological rationale of their agrarianism. It is the controlling principle of their lives. The result is that under this control their practice of sound agrarian economics has made them a solvent, stable, self-respecting people, as prosperous as any in the land and certainly the most independent; and it has also confirmed in them the sterling character and sterling moral qualities to which I have alluded.

Perhaps — I put it tentatively — perhaps this is about all that should be expected from this combination of forces. It is a highly respectable showing, to say the very least of it. I am told there is complaint against organized Christianity as being " out of touch with practical life " and therefore so dissatisfying that the churches are losing ground — well, here is one variant of organized Christianity, at any rate, which surely does not come under that censure.

Artemus Ward said the trouble with Napoleon was that he tried to do too much, and did it. Something like this may be the trouble with organized Christianity at large. The expectations it puts upon human nature may be a little excessive. The ultimate secular aim it proposes for the individual may not be quite simple and definite enough, and its confessional constructions may involve more metaphysics than the average mind can comfortably take in. I feel free to suggest this because I myself am far too simple-minded to get the drift of such apologetic literature, even of the most modern type, as has come my way. When I ask myself just what it is driving at, and what it proposes for me to drive at, I am wholly at a loss for an answer.

In these respects the Old Amish variant is exceptional. On its confessional side it has next to nothing, no formal creed, no metaphysical formulas, no elaborate theology. On its secular side, its aim for the individual is simple, clear, and moderate. Its counsels and assistances are all directed towards the twofold end of making him an upright man and a first-class farmer. Beyond this they seem not to go. Judging by results, one would think that the rest of organized Christianity might profit by analogous — not the same, or similar, but analogous — simplifications, both of confessional content and practical intention.

All the prescriptions, customs, and practices which the Old Amish variant enforces tend towards the same end, even those which, as I have said, seem petty and arbitrary. They have actually the character and sanction of religious ritual, and there is no trouble about understanding their full and exact import. With the best will in the world, one can hardly say so much for such other variants of organized Christianity as I am acquainted with. For instance, in the November *Atlantic* Dr. Bell * cites "one of the world's most harassed statesmen" as saying, "I could not live, I think . . . if I could not go to Mass. I assist several times a week." This devotion is all very well and highly commendable, but when this harassed statesman goes on to account for his devotion to this ritual practice in terms of what accrues from it (*mea culpa,* maybe *maxima culpa; prava et turpissima culpa,*† if you like – however, there it is) I don't understand one single word of what he is talking about.

On the other hand, I get the bearing of the Amishman's ritual prescriptions instantly and with no trouble at all. They all aim, as I have said, at making him an upright man and a good farmer; and anybody knows sufficiently well what a good farmer is and what an upright man is, and what qualities go into their making. Moreover, one can hardly fail to see that if conduct be three-fourths of life, and if religion be supposed to bear at all on conduct, the very simplicity, clearness, and directness of the Amishman's prescriptions, their strict avoidance of trying to do too much, are decidedly advantageous in respect of conduct, by comparison with the more indeterminate and apparently unrelated prescriptions laid down by other variants of organized Christianity. For instance, while Dr. Bell's harassed statesman may be an exception, I never knew or heard of a modern statesman, harassed or otherwise, who would boggle for an instant at lying like a hundred devils, if some political exigency required it of him; nor one who would not on like occasion break his word at a moment's notice, connive at any form of violence and crime, or act the part of an arrant swindler. The Amishman will do none of these things under any circumstances. Thus while religion's higher satisfactions such as the harassed statesman speaks of, whatever those are, may be inaccessible to the Amishman, he plods his way throughout the whole broad area of conduct with the firm step of a pretty tolerably well accredited citizen; and this, I repeat, no modern statesman that I know or ever heard of seems either able to do or even notably desirous of doing. The Amishman quite literally "lives by his religion," and his religion seems to be a workable one to live by. At any rate, he does not turn to it, or return to it, from motives of weakness, disillusionment, or fear. In this respect he appears to have a decided advantage over the reclaimed brethren Dr. Bell cites in his admirable article.

* Bernard Iddings Bell (1886–   ), American author, educator, and clergyman.
† My fault, maybe my greatest fault; wicked and most shameful fault.

Coming now to less recondite matters, the Old Amish get a little "edge" even on the Quakers, in not having any churches. They meet for worship in their houses, taking them in turn throughout the district. They have no stated ministry. Each district chooses its minister by lot from among its own number, to serve for a year. He has no special training; every Amishman is presumed to be qualified for a job of such simplicity, and no doubt is. He is not paid one single picayune. These economical arrangements keep down the overhead, thereby wholly doing away with the need for ministerial salesmanship, advertising, canvassing for new members, and all other money-raising devices — a need which appears most seriously, often exclusively, to preoccupy other Christian communities.

There is a sound idea here. If you want to "purify politics," whether Church politics or secular politics, begin by taking the money out of it. You won't have to do much else; human nature will do the rest. It is exactly Lincoln Steffens's idea of fixing the responsibility for the Fall of Man. Some blame Adam, while others put the blame on Eve; Steffens put it on the apple. If the apple had not been there everything would have gone smoothly. Obviously, then, the thing to do in like circumstances is to take away the apple. If you do this you can't have any trouble, and this is what the Old Amish have done, thereby giving evidence of a great brain and a level head.

By this device they have closed up every loophole against professionalism. Rapid rotation in unpaid office, combined with absence of all special training, is death on the development of a priestly class. Sacerdotalism does not stand a dog's chance with the Old Amish; and the elaborate metaphysical *Aberglaube* * of its associated sacramentalism stands no better chance. All this seems to suggest an opportunity for further simplification on the part of other Christian bodies. It is surely a fair question whether a competent practice of religion calls for quite as much apparatus, metaphysical and physical, as the main body of organized Christianity has constructed and is trying, none too successfully, to keep in running order. There need be, and should be, no thought of taking over the Old Amish pattern as it stands; yet no well-ordered mind should be above looking it over, on the chance of finding food for profitable thought.

Like orthodox Jews and Roman Catholics, the Old Amish send their children to schools of their own, to avoid contaminating contacts. They do not educate their children beyond the eighth grade, in the belief that this comprises all the book learning that a good farmer needs. There is much to be said for this view, and everything to be said for

* Superstition.

Mr. Jefferson's further view that this is as much as any but the very rarely exceptional child can use to any good purpose. America is now paying enormous amounts of margin on its cat-and-dog investments in a type of citizen " whose education is far too much for his abilities," as the Duke of Wellington said. Amish children may not enter the professions or the white-collar vocations, and this without prejudice to either; if, for instance, the Amishman has occasion to employ a physician, he gets the best one he can find and ungrudgingly pays him top prices. The only point is that in pursuance of the will of God those children are to stay on the land, and should be learning how to work the paternal acreage with love and reverence as well as skill. An Amish boy who wants to go to college and then take up a profession may of course do so, but not by easy gravitation. He must break with his religion, tradition, and family; and if his call is loud enough, and if he has grit enough to scrabble over this three-barred obstruction, the chances are that he is the sort to succeed. One cannot be sure but that this is as it should be, for we are discovering that the way to a desirable thing can be made altogether too easy. I am told, however, that the Amish children very seldom break over the traces, and one can easily see good reason why this should be so. They are already booked at birth for inheritance in about the soundest going concern in the United States, so why leave a bone for a shadow? They will always eat, and eat mighty well, always be well-clad, well-housed. They will never lose their jobs, never worry about their wives and children wanting bread, never punch a clock, truckle to a gang-boss, or scuffle for a living against cutthroat competition. They will always be able to look the world in the face and think and say exactly what they dam' well please about anything and anybody. Isn't that pretty much the old-time American ideal?

The Old Amish house themselves well, and keep their houses with the most painstaking neatness, but they have no central heating, their furniture is sparse and simple, and they have no ornaments. They use no electricity, thus escaping the distractions of the telephone, radio, telegraph, and motion picture. They do not use automobiles, but are finished experts with the horse and buggy; many, probably most of them, have never been farther away from home than the county town. They wear always the same cut of clothes, as distinctive as a uniform, with no adornment of any kind, not even buttons; their coats are fastened with hooks and eyes. If someone appears in their midst wearing buttoned garments, he is known at once as a " stylisher," and is given more or less of a wide berth. All these are religious observances. As can be easily seen, their aim is to encourage thrift and a wholesome simplicity of living, to promote domestic and communal solidarity, and to hit the golden mean between too much ease and comfort and too little. However rigorous and niggling such regulations may appear to us, it is a mistake to regard them as bearing heavily on their votaries, or to regard the Amish as a " stubborn, fierce and isolated people," as Matthew Arnold describes the Jews of early days. On the contrary, they have excellent humor, are fond of fun, and are extremely sociable and jolly among themselves; not, however, with strangers. They amuse themselves, as they do all things, simply and heartily; the lighter side of their life seems to be about what it was with their progenitors living in the Pfalz; or indeed, pretty much what it was with our own progenitors living in America not so many years ago.

IV

IN studying any order of fauna one gets some impressions less agreeable than others. I got a few from the Amish that I thought were hardly worth carrying away with me, so I was glad to forget them. What did me a great and lasting good was to see what I had come to think existed nowhere in America, a people with clear strong sense of the *ne quid nimis,** and a resolute determination to live by that sense. I was among them for only a short time, and saw their life only from outside; they are not partial to strangers. But even so, it was a cheering and hope-inspiring experience to touch the fringes of a well-to-do, prosperous, hard-working society which does not believe in too much money, too much land, too much impedimenta, too much ease, comfort, schooling, mechanization, aimless movement, idle curiosity; which does not believe in too many labor-saving devices, gadgets, gimcracks; and which has the force of character — fed and sustained by a type of religion which seems really designed to get results — the force of sterling character, I say, to keep itself well on the safe lee side of all such excesses.

* Literally, not anything too much, or moderation.

QUESTIONS

1. Section I explains why Nock wrote the essay. Point out the interests and incidents which form the basis of this section. How does the last paragraph of Section I limit the subject?

2. The obvious purpose of Section II is to show that the Amish are among the best farmers in America. What additional but unstated purpose is revealed in the references to Mr. Wallace, the New Deal, and the WPA project? What is the effect (emotional or intellectual) of such phrases as "officious nincompoop," and "paying the State's blackmail"?

3. What is the function of the first sentence in Section III? What is the controlling idea or theme of this section? Point out the main supporting or particularizing ideas. What comparisons and contrasts are employed in developing the thought of this section?

4. In Section IV, what significant limitation on the author's understanding of the Amish is indicated? What reservations might be made in accepting his conclusions as the final truth?

5. Exactly what does "Utopia" mean? In what ways, according to Nock, is the life of the Amish a Utopian one? What virtues and what defects, if any, do the Amish possess as *citizens* in a democracy?

As the Scientist Sees It

GEORGE R. HARRISON

VANNEVAR BUSH

HARLOW SHAPLEY

STANLEY CASSON

George R. Harrison was born in California and received his higher education at Stanford University. For more than thirty-five years he has been engaged in college teaching, research, and administrative work. As a teacher he has served at Stanford University, Harvard University, and Massachusetts Institute of Technology, and since 1942 he has been Dean of Science at M.I.T. A distinguished physicist, Harrison is known especially for his research in the field of optics. His clarity, breadth of vision, and seriousness of purpose are revealed in "Faith and the Scientist," the Stearns Lecture delivered at Phillips Academy, Andover, Massachusetts, in 1953.

FAITH AND THE SCIENTIST

by GEORGE R. HARRISON

This is the day of the ascendancy of science, for in the past fifty years scientific knowledge and methods have changed our manner of living more than any form of human endeavor has ever changed it in the past. In each decade now we get more new understanding of the processes of nature, and more ability to control them, than became available in any previous century. Science is coming to determine how much men can eat, how comfortable they are, how hard they must work, and even how long they will live. Many people view this dependence on what seems a materialistic and perhaps directionless effort with grave distrust, and feel that scientists should be curbed in their endeavors to set loose little-understood forces which immerse society in problems which they fear may prove insoluble.

Much misunderstanding arises because most of us, through our newspapers and magazines, make contact mainly with the slums of science, the half-world of such things as flying saucers and water dowsing. Some of us may worry about technological unemployment, for where will the workman find a job when all the factories are operated by machines under the surveillance of foremen servo-mechanisms? Or we may feel, with some poets and mystics, that science is making living not only less enjoyable, but more dangerous, in giving man new powers without at the same time helping him to choose between good and evil.

Such fears arise, I think, from a limited understanding of what science is and what it can accomplish. Our concern must be, not only with whether it adds to our comfort and safety, our health, security, and enjoyment of life, but also with whether it adds to our dignity and stature as individuals. We must take, as the ultimate measure of scientific progress, its influence on such spiritual values as freedom, integrity, and justice.

I mean here to discuss, not the machines that science provides which enable us to travel faster, to amuse ourselves more distractedly, and generally to increase the speed and anxiety of living, but the effect of science on the whole man. First let us consider man broadly as a physical being who receives sense impressions from the external world; then his mind; then, further, his emotional nature; and finally his spiritual nature — all as affected by science.

The demonstration by science of the unity of all Nature profoundly affects us all. When a spectroscope is used to analyze light from any distant star, it reveals there the same kinds of atoms we find on earth. In this confirmation of a *universe,* as contrasted with a billion unrelated stars, the scientist shares with the mystic awareness of that Oneness from which springs our most fundamental feeling of security.

To appreciate the implications of this unity, one should understand how even the most complex and diverse things in our world are built up as different manifestations of the same simple, basic elements. Physicists have found only three forces in the universe: electric, magnetic, and gravitational forces; and every push or pull we know is a combination of these. They hope, with unified field theories, to prove that these three kinds of force are really only manifestations of one elementary force, of which matter is another manifestation. In any case, we know that matter is interconvertible with energy, as demonstrated frequently these days in Nevada, and that matter is itself composed of three basic particles: protons, neutrons, and electrons.

Now imagine a universe filled with particles of these three kinds flying hither and yon, exerting on each other the three basic forces, without direction or interrelation. This indeed would be chaos. Of what use is such a universe? Where now are freedom, justice, and integrity?

To build the universe as we know it, a directive force is needed. This may come from without, or may even be built into the nature of the particles themselves. We now see pairing of electrons and protons, so that hydrogen atoms are formed. These in turn join in pairs to produce hydrogen molecules, which collect as clouds of hydrogen in space, forming great nebulae. Other protons join with neutrons in more complex groupings to form the nuclei of new varieties of atoms, which soon attract to their orbits their respective quotas of electrons. Eventually we see built up atoms of nearly a hundred sorts, and we have the basic elements of chemistry. The completeness of balancing of the forces in the various groupings of particles differs, so that some atoms, still unsatisfied, tend to join together as molecules, while others move about in space alone. Different residual forces, again, extend from the various molecules. Some types hold firmly together at the temperatures of earth and form solid matter like steel. Others cling loosely and form liquids like water. Still others attract each other so little that they bounce apart when they collide, and make up gases like helium and oxygen. Thus from the three fundamental particles have been formed nearly a hundred kinds of atoms, by an innate tendency to order which we may call " co-operation." These atoms in turn combine into several hundred thousand kinds of molecules, which further associate to form the millions of objects we can see.

Thus on the unity of our first picture is superposed the concept of order. The universe now is no longer chaotic; each particle moves not alone, but under the combined and ordered influence of its fellows. From only three kinds of particles with limited individual capacities have been produced millions of new entities forming a physical world. About all that a million electrons can do if left to their own devices is to exert a repulsive force on each other, and so in varying degrees with protons and neutrons. But let these three arrange themselves properly in atoms, and these atoms in molecules, and mold and combine these molecules to form substances, and you can make a spark plug that will help carry a plane across the Atlantic. By arranging selected molecules in still more complex ways nature can produce a bee, and then even a swarm of bees. These bees find that if they will co-operate in a hive, instead of living each to himself, they can keep warmer in winter, and so can gather nectar and spread pollen in spring several weeks before a hermit insect dare show his face.

So we find diversity arising from unity, and complexity from simplicity, through the exercise of a co-operative directing force. Men call this force by different names, but this need not concern us here, for now we are discussing only phenomena which science has revealed.

Physicists have discovered a great rule of nature which they call the Second Law of Thermodynamics. This seems to tell us how to measure our flight from chaos. Boiled down, it says that if you want to do anything especially remarkable in a physical system, you must supply some direction. Molecules left to themselves become chaotic in their motions. A house or a turnip or a man left without orderly control tends to decay; to produce any one of these objects requires directed effort. Every thing we call alive seems to contain such a directing force. A dead seed rots, but a single living seed contains enough directive power to populate — given a few hundred million years — a whole planet, not only with carrots but with men.

This all sounds pretty theoretical, and it is tempting to believe that scientists have really been able to accomplish little in understanding what life is and how to produce and control living things. But the door is being opened, and each day brings new insight. For example, in recent years various molecules have been found, plant hormones and auxins, with which we can cause leaves to drop off plants or to grow larger. Other molecules will make fruit cling more tightly to the branch; still others will start, speed up, or slow down flowering, make stems longer or shorter, induce the growth of roots, or kill one type of plant and not another. These chemical foremen, like servomechanisms in a factory, regulate the interactions of the various parts of the plant, so that it can function as a co-operative cherry tree instead of a rotting pool of independent molecules.

A living plant is a factory for storing the energy of sunlight in the fabrication of such complex molecules as starch, cellulose, and sugar from simple molecules of water and carbon dioxide. Eventually we should be able to regulate such factories as handily as we now control a factory for making tractors. Some of the auxins, superintendent molecules which direct the activities of many foremen molecules in a growing plant, are found to act as they do because they hitch on to other molecules through two coupling links instead of one, and act as keys which fit only certain molecular locks. Such a mysterious molecular key as indole-acetic acid, for example, turns out to be merely a special arrangement of carbon, oxygen, and other atoms.

Though chemists have identified in nature only about 100,000 different kinds of molecules, they have already fabricated nearly twice as many new kinds, from the same hundred original atoms. Many of these new molecules are found to have special powers, and it seems probable that eventually we shall find useful new jobs for almost every one, from freon through nylon and far beyond sulfathiazole.

II

NOW, what is a man? His body, "in form and moving" so "express and admirable," is made of protons, neutrons, and electrons; and he thinks with a brain composed of these and operating with the three fundamental forces of the physical world. To say this is not materialism, for if "God works in most mysterious ways His wonders to perform," not the least of His works, as we can see, involve protons, neutrons, and electrons. The study of their combinations helps us to understand our five senses, five paths of awareness to the brain, five "windows of the soul," by which we have our only contact with the external world.

Calling our senses five is an oversimplification, for we have more than five senses; we have at least three types of touch sensation: heat, pressure, and pain; and four types of taste, so that every flavor is a combination of sweet, salty, sour, and bitter. (The child who doesn't mind cod-liver oil and hates spinach is not being ornery; his taste buds merely respond differently from those of his mother.) We also have four types of vision, which all happen to involve the same pairs of eyes. The first type, night-vision, records no color, but paints its images in black and white on the retina; it operates best in faint light and is nearly 500 times as sensitive as the other three types of vision. These combine to give us more than 100,000 different sensations of color.

So sensitive are our retinas to green light – that is, to light whose waves are about one 50 thousandth of an inch long – that they can pick up as little as one 500 thousandth of a millionth of a millionth of a watt of power, and we can see a candle many miles away.

How was this sensitive detecting device developed, which is more elegant than any television camera? It contains a sharply focusing lens, surrounded by light-sensitive molecules which adjust it automatically to give the clearest image; self-regulating diaphragm, the pupil, and a shutter, the eyelid; and uses two projectors with which it introduced 3-D into vision some millions of years before the movies got around to this in 1953.

The marvelous twin cameras which send sensations to our brain from every object illuminated by even a millionth of the brightness of full sunlight sort out light rays so carefully that we get the fullest impact of reality through seeing. If necessary we can in addition verify the existence of an object by touching it, hearing it, smelling it, or tasting it. Beyond this, nature does not take us in contacting physical reality. And she has developed many forms of energy, such as cosmic rays and magnetic fields, which we cannot sense at all, yet which are no less real than those we sense directly.

So our senses are by no means perfect, and after exclaiming about the wonders of the eye, we must now examine its limitations. First, it is blind to more wave lengths of light than it can see. While insects can see somewhat with short-wave ultra-violet rays, humans cannot. (These insects, incidentally, have eyes consisting of multiple cones especially fixed for judging the direction of the sun for navigational purposes, and sometimes have polarizing filters to help steer by scattered light when the sky is overcast.) Also the sharpness of our vision is limited, and our lenses tend to deform and become cloudy. But now that nature has developed in man the brain needed to think scientifically, he can use this to extend his senses much beyond what nature has done.

Scientists have learned to supplement the sense of sight in numerous ways. In the front of the tiny pupil of the eye they put, on Mount Palomar, a great monocle 200 inches in diameter, and with it see 2000 times farther into the depths of space. Or they look through a small pair of lenses arranged as a microscope into a drop of water or blood, and magnify by as much as 2000 diameters the living creatures there, many of which are among man's most dangerous enemies. Or, if we want to see distant happenings on earth, they use some of the previously wasted electromagnetic waves to carry television images which they re-create as light by whipping tiny crystals on a screen with electrons in a vacuum. Or they can bring happenings of long ago and far away as colored motion pictures, by arranging silver atoms and color-absorbing molecules to force light waves into the patterns of the original reality. Or if we want to see into the center of a steel casting or the chest of an injured child, they send the information on a beam of penetrating short-wave X rays, and then convert it back into images we can see on a screen or photograph. Thus almost every type of electromagnetic radiation yet discovered has been used to extend our sense of sight in some way.

The evolution of the other senses is as interesting as that of vision, which nature has developed to nearly the maximum sensitivity permitted by the structure of light itself. Our ability to hear the commonest sound waves has reached its maximum possible sensitivity also. Some persons even are bothered by noises which arise from the random motions of molecules in the nerve endings of their ears. The threshold of sound awareness is said to be about the same in a human being, a catfish, or a bird, and the long-vaunted greater sensitivity of hearings of dogs and other animals probably arises from their ability to hear higher tones than we, and because they have less to distract them.

In many directions of evolution nature is stopped by limitations in her own materials. There are some things that just take too long to work out with protons and electrons by repeated trial and error, as, for example, to develop a wheel on a living creature. But often man can get around such blocks by taking thought. We fasten wheels to ourselves with automobiles, and our sense of hearing has been extended on radio waves so that we can hear the sound of a dropped pin around the world.

Thus, though we sense directly only a few of the energy manifestations in the external world, science has taught us how to transform many others so as not only to bring them into our ken, but to bend them to our service. And science reveals man's physical body as a fascinating assemblage of the same protons, electrons, and neutrons that constitute a stone, functioning in an even more remarkable co-operative effort. But not yet is this the whole of Man.

III

LET us now consider the mind. Man has developed the ability to set up a series of images within the brain which produce a reaction as effective as if they were sensations direct from the external world. Thus we learn to supplement sensation with thought, and can gain from many experiences which need occur only within our minds. Again something new is evolved in nature from the profitable co-operation of lesser elements.

All of our feelings and our thoughts appear to be end products of switching patterns in nerve circuits. To visualize this, consider mathematical computation. From counting on his fingers man has progressed through the stage of counting with stones to sliding beads on wires in the abacus; then to counting on the teeth of rotating gears in mechanical calculating machines; and now to the use of electron tubes with which thousands of sums can be carried out in a single second. Such devices are bulky, to be sure, for modern high-speed calculators, such as Whirlwind II at M.I.T., occupy many cubic feet of space and use thousands of tubes.

The best computing machines do not operate in powers of 10, which we first learned to like because of our ten fingers, but in powers of 2. This is because a simple electrical switch can easily express only two numbers, 0 and 1, or two reactions, " no " and " yes," by being closed to current flow, or open. As few as fifty switches can express 2^{50} numbers or reactions, which is more than a million billion, in terms of various patterns of being open and closed. An electron tube serves as a rapid and reliable switch, for which we need to find a less clumsy substitute. Nature, however, has already succeeded in developing electrochemical switches called synapses to connect nerve endings, which are so small that many billions of them can be squeezed into one human head. Apparently all our thoughts are in terms of remembered sensations and images of the external world, and all we feel or think or dream comes to us as combinations of these electrochemical yeses and noes. It is difficult to think of a colored mental picture as being only groups of stops and starts, until we remember that Technicolor or television images are nothing more than controlled chemical or electrical patterns, and that seeing red is merely a state of mind.

In addition to vast numbers of switches, a good high-speed computing machine must have a means of storing switching patterns and numbers, and this our brains have in countless cells which can be charged or discharged. Thus we have memory. By substituting for immediate sensation mental images of things we have previously sensed, we can perform all sorts of interesting internal mental experiments. Thus Newton, his optic nerve stimulated by an apple, thought not merely of apples but of planets, and had no need of a space ship to work out his law of universal gravitation.

The process we call learning consists of setting up mental switching patterns over and over, to train certain circuits and groups of switchboards to function together. The circuits of the mind improve vastly with use and exercise. Of course, if need arises nature can add billions of cells to the brain, though this requires a few thousand years. For us this is now unnecessary, however, because most of us are like the Vermont farmer who objected to coming to the lecture sponsored by the Board of Agriculture, on the ground that he already knew how to farm twice as well as was his custom. We have many more switchboards and trunk lines in our heads than we ever use, and spend much of our lives determining how many central exchanges we want to bother to set into operation, and how many we will relegate to the back room.

Cowling and Davidson * have listed seven essential qualities which it is the function of a true education to develop. The first is ability to concentrate, which merely means learning to keep stray sensations from messing up the circuits among our mental switchboards. Then comes accuracy of observation, which means learning to connect the nerve endings bringing in sensations with the proper mental circuits. Then comes retentiveness of memory, which involves exercising of the brain's condensers and storage mechanisms so that their charges won't leak out prematurely, keeping their contacts bright so that they will give sharp impulse patterns after many years, and bringing circuits into association. Then comes logical reasoning, which is the exercising of switching patterns in great groups so that currents

* Donald J. Cowling (1880–), President of Carleton College, Northfield, Minnesota, from 1909 to 1945, and Carter Davidson (1905–), President of Union College, Schenectady, New York, since 1946, are co-authors of *Colleges for Freedom* (1947).

emerge which will coincide with what the external world reveals. Then improvement in judgment is listed, an even higher faculty that depends on predicting in advance, as a result of experience, which circuits will best lead to a correct set of images. Then we have sensitivity of association, which involves developing the faculty of interconnecting vast swarms of switchboards without confusion, so that each on demand can be made sensitive to useful currents flowing in any others. Last of all, and most important, comes creative imagination. One of our highest faculties, this involves putting into operation vast new assemblages of switchboards and central stations in the untapped stockrooms of our minds, so that new circuits can learn to conduct merely as a result of the experience of other circuits.

Besides revealing the structure of our brains, science furnishes one of the most effective disciplines for improving our minds. It trains us in conserving the flow of mental current and in discriminating between emotional and intellectual processes. One of the great defects of modern education, especially of progressive education, is its diffuseness. It lacks insistence that the student learn to focus his attention in trains of thought which produce sharp, clear patterns in the brain, instead of a chaotic opening and closing of mental switches at random, governed by the feelings of the moment. Much of this fault comes from our methods of teacher training; the poorest education for an educator, it seems, is the study of education. He should first have interest in a specific discipline with which he can deeply engrave his own mental circuits.

IV

LONG before man learned to think, animals had developed emotions like fright and anger, tones of feeling which pervade the organism and produce responses in it. Higher emotions, like response to beauty, appeared later, and new ones are still appearing. Science is making progress in revealing the origins and structure of our emotions, which, affected by sensation and by thought, like them are embodied in electrochemical reactions, and can be profoundly affected by molecules which we call drugs and hormones.

Hazlitt wrote: “Man is the only animal that laughs and weeps, for he is the only animal that is struck by the difference between what things are and what they ought to be.” Science is the greatest agency yet discovered for changing things to what they ought to be. Even more important, science can help us decide what they ought to be, for we learn from experience, and science is the systematic production and analysis of experience.

This applies even to such concepts as beauty. The poet, painter, and musician have no monopoly on beauty, for the ardor of the creative artist also fills the scientist when he pursues a discovery. "Beauty is truth, truth beauty," said Keats, and science is the systematic search for truth. What tremendous emotions must have surged through Galileo when he saw for the first time through his telescope four tiny moons circling about Jupiter! Immediately his creative imagination saw demonstration of the lofty concept that the earth revolves around the sun, and therefore need not be considered the center of the universe.

This sweep and play of beauty extends throughout the whole of science. Consider the course of evolution. This concept, now well proved, has nothing to do with belief or absence of belief in God, though it has been upsetting in the past to some who were pained by the cracking of the carapace of inflexible theological dogma. The sublime prospect of the upward progress of life over millions of years stirs emotions equal to those produced by the most sublime poetry and art. Scientists who have seen the great paintings in the Sistine Chapel and the Louvre, and have felt that tingling in the spinal cord which comes from observation of truly great art, have received the same inner thrill from the realization that when a bird sits on a bough a tiny locking bone in his foot clamps his claws around the perch so that his muscles can relax without danger of his falling when asleep. The God who notes each sparrow's fall also built something into a proton that keeps the sparrow from falling.

Poets and other creative artists are intuitive, and the mystic is likely to feel superior to the scientist in his reliance on intuition. But the scientist must be intuitive as well. Intuition is the ability to integrate previous experience, without detailed analysis, to produce new awareness. Much of what is commonly called intuition involves merely a confusion of emotion and prejudice with thought, but true intuition consists of that leap forward in the dark, with no solid ground beneath, in which you end up in balance on your feet. Every scientific generalization is intuitive, for while the scientist may see a phenomenon just by looking, as at Newton's apple, he must use creative imagination and intuition to relate this apple to the moon and so discover the universal law.

Even this sketchy picture seems to me to indicate that we live in a universe which is progressing, and I hope it conveys a sense of the endless possibilities of this progress. The accumulation of experience results in an uneven but definite increase in the spiritual qualities which are of most importance to man – truth, justice, love, humility, integrity, and all the rest. Spiritual values distill slowly from the interaction of sensation, emotion, and thought, which we have seen depend in turn on man's physical body, which again is formed by his environment, which depends ultimately on the properties of matter. Science affects all of these. Even if you wish to picture the eternal verities as abstract concepts superposed on the character of man from without (and I do not quarrel with this, though I feel that it detracts from the beauty and integrity of the unified picture), man has demonstrated the power of developing them, and they are basically affected by his physical experience. This is codified and illumined by science, as by religion and art.

The phrase "You can't change human nature" springs from a short-range view. The shape of the human jaw and the size of the human brainpan change quite markedly in a hundred thousand years. The speed with which a thoroughbred can run a mile has been dropped from two minutes to one minute and thirty-six seconds in less than fifty years, by selective breeding. The patterns governing a young man's operation of his mental switches can be changed quite markedly in a few months. Human nature is not a static thing, for we live in a universe that is dynamic, which offers unlimited opportunity for change. Science teaches us that we can progress from being slaves of our environment to becoming masters of our destinies.

Two thousand years is only a flick of time in which to look for changes in man's intellect, but it is not too short a time to look for changes in his spirit. Take so fundamental a quality as empathy, the ability to put oneself in the other fellow's place. A century ago, even in America, one of the fundamental freedoms was the right to starve to death; a beggar could lie dying in the gutter and people would walk by unconcerned. Today, at least in lands where the standard of living has been raised by science to the point where the scramble to keep alive does not take up most of everyone's effort, empathy has developed to the point that no one is refused food or hospitalization. Over the ages, man's stimuli change, and gradually these change his thought processes and emotions, and through them his spiritual vigor.

The grandeur of human destiny becomes really manifest only when man is released, to some extent, from the battle for physical existence and learns that on a constantly widening scale he can become a small creator. "Build thee more stately mansions, O my soul" sang Holmes, and science aids religion and art in making this literally possible. The League of Nations was an example of a new kind of attempt at political co-operation, which had a type of experience probably not unlike that of the first swarm of bees. But a later swarm of bees had learned a little by experience, as has the United Nations. Social and political evolution, like that on all other levels, is continually going on, and those who do not believe that the progress is upward use too short a yardstick.

This brings me to the $64 question. Of what use is all this building of co-operative entities from simpler ones if the simplest materials of all are not stable? If scientists can arrange their protons and neutrons so that any man can blow us up, what becomes of progress? This view does not take into account the remarkable stability of nature, of science, and of man. Though evil things do happen, any individual evil, being destructive, eventually destroys itself. So there are many checks and balances on the release of nuclear energy, and I am confident that this will emerge as a great new beneficent force when its present political implications are forgotten. It is natural for man to be fearful in the presence of any great new power given him, but he has demonstrated in the past that he has an inherent stability which enables him to win through to ever higher levels of spiritual achievement. Remove science and you remove one of the principal factors in this stability.

The basic tenets of all great religions, the distilled spiritual wisdom of humanity (as distinguished from minor theological details, regarding which many thousands of existing creeds differ), represent closely what science is revealing. The universe is based on ordered progress, not on chaotic change. Man can improve his environment, his own nature, and his opportunities. Through co-operation new entities can be formed from lesser entities which give greater purpose and achievement to existence. There is direction to living, which gives stability in the midst of change. These things the ancient sages knew; science helps to make them apparent to us all.

QUESTIONS

1. How are Paragraphs 1–2, Section I, related to the title of the essay? What fears aroused by science are mentioned in these paragraphs? How is the phrase "the effect of science on the whole man" (Paragraph 4) related to the essay as a whole? Why should not Paragraph 4 be omitted?

2. In Paragraphs 5–10, Section I, show how the key words "unity" and "order" are used and in what ways they are connected. For what obvious reason does Harrison introduce in Paragraph 6 the "three forces of the

universe" and the "three basic particles"? How, in the third and second paragraphs from the end of Section I, does the author explain the importance of the Second Law of Thermodynamics?

3. How is the opening sentence of Section II connected with the thought of Section I and with the last paragraph of Section II? To what part of "the whole man" is Section II devoted? In what ways has science been an aid to man?

4. What is the unifying idea of Section III? Show that Harrison's methods of clarifying and developing the idea in this section are similar to the methods used in Section II. What mental qualities are emphasized, and what has science contributed to them?

5. Why are both the emotional nature and the spiritual nature of man included in Section IV? In what respects, according to Harrison, is science related to religion and art?

6. Why is "*Faith* and the Scientist" an appropriate title for this essay? At what point in the essay does faith become a significant topic? Has the author arranged his ideas in the order of increasing importance? What apparently is the controlling purpose of the essay as a whole?

VANNEVAR BUSH has been a professor, a vice-president, and a dean at the Massachusetts Institute of Technology. From 1939 until 1955, he was President of the Carnegie Institution of Washington. He has served on various advisory commissions of governmental agencies. The many honors and awards which he has received testify to the significance of his contributions to science and to society. He is especially at home in the subject matter of this essay, for Dr. Bush was the builder of a differential analyzer, a machine for solving differential equations. In addition to many scientific papers, he has also written *Modern Arms and Free Men* (1949). In 1957 Dr. Bush was elected chairman of the corporation of the Massachusetts Institute of Technology.

AS WE MAY THINK

by VANNEVAR BUSH

THIS has not been a scientist's war; it has been a war in which all have had a part. The scientists, burying their old professional competition in the demand of a common cause, have shared greatly and learned much. It has been exhilarating to work in effective partnership. Now, for many, this appears to be approaching an end. What are the scientists to do next?

For the biologists, and particularly for the medical scientists, there can be little indecision, for their war work has hardly required them to leave the old paths. Many indeed have been able to carry on their war research in their familiar peacetime laboratories. Their objectives remain much the same.

It is the physicists who have been thrown most violently off stride, who have left academic pursuits for the making of strange destructive gadgets, who have had to devise new methods for their unanticipated assignments. They have done their part on the devices that made it possible to turn back the enemy. They have worked in combined effort with the physicists of our allies. They have felt within themselves the stir of achievement. They have been part of a great team. Now, as peace approaches, one asks where they will find objectives worthy of their best.

I

OF WHAT lasting benefit has been man's use of science and of the new instruments which his research brought into existence? First, they have increased his control of his material environment. They have improved his food, his clothing, his shelter; they have increased his security and released him partly from the bondage of bare existence. They have given him increased knowledge of his own biological processes so that he has had a progressive freedom from disease and an increased span of life. They are illuminating the interactions of his physiological and psychological functions, giving the promise of an improved mental health.

Science has provided the swiftest communication between individuals; it has provided a record of ideas and has enabled man to manipulate and to make extracts from that record so that knowledge evolves and endures throughout the life of a race rather than that of an individual.

There is a growing mountain of research. But there is increased evidence that we are being bogged down today as specialization extends. The investigator is staggered by the findings and conclusions of thousands of other workers — conclusions which he cannot find time to grasp, much less to remember, as they appear. Yet specialization becomes increasingly necessary for progress, and the effort to bridge between disciplines is correspondingly superficial.

Professionally our methods of transmitting and reviewing the results of research are generations old and by now are totally inadequate for their purpose. If the aggregate time spent in writing scholarly works and in reading them could be evaluated, the ratio between these amounts of time might well be startling. Those who conscientiously attempt to keep abreast of current thought, even in restricted fields, by close and continuous reading might well shy away from an examination calculated to show how much of the previous month's efforts could be produced on call. Mendel's concept of the laws of genetics was lost to the world for a generation because his publication did not reach the few who were capable of grasping and extending it; and this sort of catastrophe is undoubtedly being repeated all about us, as truly significant attainments become lost in the mass of the inconsequential.

The difficulty seems to be, not so much that we publish unduly in view of the extent and variety of present-day interests, but rather that publication has been extended far beyond our present ability to make real use of the record. The summation of human experience is being expanded at a prodigious rate, and the means we use for threading through the consequent maze to the momentarily important item is the same as was used in the days of square-rigged ships.

But there are signs of a change as new and powerful instrumentalities come into use. Photocells capable of seeing things in a physical sense, advanced photography which can record what is seen or even what is not, thermionic tubes capable of controlling potent forces under the guidance of less power than a mosquito uses to vibrate his wings, cathode ray tubes rendering visible an occurrence so brief that by comparison a microsecond is a long time, relay combinations which will carry out involved sequences of movements more reliably than any human operator and thousands of times as fast — there are plenty of mechanical aids with which to effect a transformation in scientific records.

Two centuries ago Leibnitz invented a calculating machine which embodied most of the essential features of recent keyboard devices, but it could not then come into use. The economics of the situation were against it: the labor involved in constructing it, before the days of mass production, exceeded the labor to be saved by its use, since all it could accomplish could be duplicated by sufficient use of pencil and paper. Moreover, it would have been subject to frequent breakdown, so that it could not have been depended upon; for at that time and long after, complexity and unreliability were synonymous.

Babbage,* even with remarkably generous support for his time, could not produce his great arithmetical machine. His idea was sound enough, but construction and maintenance costs were then too heavy. Had a Pharaoh been given detailed and explicit designs of an automobile, and had he understood them completely, it would have taxed the resources of his kingdom to have fashioned the thousands of parts for a single car, and that car would have broken down on the first trip to Giza.

Machines with interchangeable parts can now be constructed with great economy of effort. In spite of much complexity, they perform reliably. Witness the humble typewriter, or the movie camera, or the automobile. Electrical contacts have ceased to stick when thoroughly understood. Note the automatic telephone exchange, which has hundreds of thousands of such contacts, and yet is reliable. A spider web of metal, sealed in a thin glass container, a wire heated to brilliant glow, in short, the thermionic tube of radio sets, is made by the hun-

* Charles Babbage (1792–1871), English mathematician. Inaccuracies of mathematical tables led him to attempt the construction of a calculating machine, which he never completed.

dred million, tossed about in packages, plugged into sockets – and it works! Its gossamer parts, the precise location and alignment involved in its construction, would have occupied a master craftsman of the guild for months; now it is built for thirty cents. The world has arrived at an age of cheap complex devices of great reliability; and something is bound to come of it.

II

A RECORD, if it is to be useful to science, must be continuously extended, it must be stored, and above all it must be consulted. Today we make the record conventionally by writing and photography, followed by printing; but we also record on film, on wax disks, and on magnetic wires. Even if utterly new recording procedures do not appear, these present ones are certainly in the process of modification and extension.

Certainly progress in photography is not going to stop. Faster material and lenses, more automatic cameras, finer-grained sensitive compounds to allow an extension of the minicamera idea, are all imminent. Let us project this trend ahead to a logical, if not inevitable, outcome. The camera hound of the future wears on his forehead a lump a little larger than a walnut. It takes pictures 3 millimeters square, later to be projected or enlarged, which after all involves only a factor of 10 beyond present practice.* The lens is of universal focus, down to any distance accommodated by the unaided eye, simply because it is of short focal length. There is a built-in photocell on the walnut such as we now have on at least one camera, which automatically adjusts exposure for a wide range of illumination. There is film in the walnut for a hundred exposures, and the spring for operating its shutter and shifting its film is wound once for all when the film clip is inserted. It produces its result in full color. It may well be stereoscopic, and record with two spaced glass eyes, for striking improvements in stereoscopic technique are just around the corner.

The cord which trips its shutter may reach down a man's sleeve within easy reach of his fingers. A quick squeeze, and the picture is taken. On a pair of ordinary glasses is a square of fine lines near the top of one lens, where it is out of the way of ordinary vision. When an object appears in that square, it is lined up for its picture. As the scientist of the future moves about the laboratory or the field, every

* The camera of the future will take pictures one tenth the size of those taken by present-day cameras, *i.e.*, one tenth the size of present pictures measured along one side; but it would take one hundred such pictures to equal the area of present-day pictures.

time he looks at something worthy of the record, he trips the shutter and in it goes, without even an audible click. Is this all fantastic? The only fantastic thing about it is the idea of making as many pictures as would result from its use.

Will there be dry photography? It is already here in two forms. When Brady made his Civil War pictures, the plate had to be wet at the time of exposure. Now it has to be wet during development instead. In the future perhaps it need not be wetted at all. There have long been films impregnated with diazo dyes which form a picture without development, so that it is already there as soon as the camera has been operated. An exposure to ammonia gas destroys the unexposed dye, and the picture can then be taken out into the light and examined. The process is now slow, but someone may speed it up, and it has no grain difficulties such as now keep photographic researchers busy. Often it would be advantageous to be able to snap the camera and to look at the picture immediately.

Another process now in use is also slow, and more or less clumsy. For fifty years impregnated papers have been used which turn dark at every point where an electrical contact touches them, by reason of the chemical change thus produced in an iodine compound included in the paper. They have been used to make records, for a pointer moving across them can leave a trail behind. If the electrical potential on the pointer is varied as it moves, the line becomes light or dark in accordance with the potential.

This scheme is now used in facsimile transmission. The pointer draws a set of closely spaced lines across the paper one after another. As it moves, its potential is varied in accordance with a varying current received over wires from a distant station, where these variations are produced by a photocell which is similarly scanning a picture. At every instant the darkness of the line being drawn is made equal to the darkness of the point on the picture being observed by the photocell. Thus, when the whole picture has been covered, a replica appears at the receiving end.

A scene itself can be just as well looked over line by line by the photocell in this way as can a photograph of the scene. This whole apparatus constitutes a camera, with the added feature, which can be dispensed with if desired, of making its picture at a distance. It is slow, and the picture is poor in detail. Still, it does give another process of dry photography, in which the picture is finished as soon as it is taken.

It would be a brave man who would predict that such a process will always remain clumsy, slow, and faulty in detail. Television equipment today transmits sixteen reasonably good pictures a second, and it involves only two essential differences from the process described above. For one, the record is made by a moving beam of electrons rather than a moving pointer, for the reason that an electron beam can sweep across the picture very rapidly indeed. The other difference involves merely the use of a screen which glows momentarily when the electrons hit, rather than a chemically treated paper or film which is permanently altered. This speed is necessary in television, for motion pictures rather than stills are the object.

Use chemically treated film in place of the glowing screen, allow the apparatus to transmit one picture only rather than a succession, and a rapid camera for dry photography results. The treated film needs to be far faster in action than present examples, but it probably could be. More serious is the objection that this scheme would involve putting the film inside a vacuum chamber, for electron beams behave normally only in such a rarefied environment. This difficulty could be avoided by allowing the electron beam to play on one side of a partition, and by pressing the film against the other side, if this partition were such as to allow the electrons to go through perpendicular to its surface, and to prevent them from spreading out sideways. Such partitions, in crude form, could certainly be constructed, and they will hardly hold up the general development.

Like dry photography, microphotography still has a long way to go. The basic scheme of reducing the size of the record, and examining it by projection rather than directly, has possibilities too great to be ignored. The combination of optical projection and photographic reduction is already producing some results in microfilm for scholarly purposes, and the potentialities are highly suggestive. Today, with microfilm, reductions by a linear factor of 20 * can be employed and still produce full clarity when the material is re-enlarged for examination. The limits are set by the graininess of the film, the excellence of the optical system, and the efficiency of the light sources employed. All of these are rapidly improving.

Assume a linear ratio of 100 † for future use. Consider film of the same thickness as paper, although thinner film will certainly be usable. Even under these conditions there would be a total factor of 10,000 between the bulk of the ordinary record on books, and its microfilm replica. The *Encyclopædia Britannica* could be reduced to the volume of a matchbox. A library of a million volumes could be compressed

* That is, the microfilm is one twentieth the size of the original along one side, but it would take four hundred such films to equal the area of the original.

† *I.e.*, in total area. See the two immediately preceding footnotes.

into one end of a desk. If the human race has produced since the invention of movable type a total record, in the form of magazines, newspapers, books, tracts, advertising blurbs, correspondence, having a volume corresponding to a billion books, the whole affair, assembled and compressed, could be lugged off in a moving van. Mere compression, of course, is not enough; one needs not only to make and store a record but also be able to consult it, and this aspect of the matter comes later. Even the modern great library is not generally consulted; it is nibbled at by a few.

Compression is important, however, when it comes to costs. The material for the microfilm *Britannica* would cost a nickel, and it could be mailed anywhere for a cent. What would it cost to print a million copies? To print a sheet of newspaper, in a large edition, costs a small fraction of a cent. The entire material of the *Britannica* in reduced microfilm form would go on a sheet eight and one-half by eleven inches. Once it is available, with the photographic reproduction methods of the future, duplicates in large quantities could probably be turned out for a cent apiece beyond the cost of materials. The preparation of the original copy? That introduces the next aspect of the subject.

III

TO MAKE the record, we now push a pencil or tap a typewriter. Then comes the process of digestion and correction, followed by an intricate process of typesetting, printing, and distribution. To consider the first stage of the procedure, will the author of the future cease writing by hand or typewriter and talk directly to the record? He does so indirectly, by talking to a stenographer or a wax cylinder; but the elements are all present if he wishes to have his talk directly produce a typed record. All he needs to do is to take advantage of existing mechanisms and to alter his language.

At a recent World Fair a machine called a Voder was shown. A girl stroked its keys and it emitted recognizable speech. No human vocal chords entered into the procedure at any point; the keys simply combined some electrically produced vibrations and passed these on to a loud-speaker. In the Bell Laboratories there is the converse of this machine, called a Vocoder. The loud-speaker is replaced by a microphone, which picks up sound. Speak to it, and the corresponding keys move. This may be one element of the postulated system.

The other element is found in the stenotype, that somewhat disconcerting device encountered usually at public meetings. A girl strokes its keys languidly and looks about the room and sometimes at the speaker with a disquieting gaze. From it emerges a typed strip which records in a phonetically simplified language a record of what the speaker is supposed to have said. Later this strip is retyped into ordinary language, for in its nascent form it is intelligible only to the initiated. Combine these two elements, let the Vocoder run the stenotype, and the result is a machine which types when talked to.

Our present languages are not especially adapted to this sort of mechanization, it is true. It is strange that the inventors of universal languages have not seized upon the idea of producing one which better fitted the technique for transmitting and recording speech. Mechanization may yet force the issue, especially in the scientific field; whereupon scientific jargon would become still less intelligible to the layman.

One can now picture a future investigator in his laboratory. His hands are free, and he is not anchored. As he moves about and observes, he photographs and comments. Time is automatically recorded to tie the two records together. If he goes into the field, he may be connected by radio to his recorder. As he ponders over his notes in the evening, he again talks his comments into the record. His typed record, as well as his photographs, may both be in miniature, so that he projects them for examination.

Much needs to occur, however, between the collection of data and observations, the extraction of parallel material from the existing record, and the final insertion of new material into the general body of the common record. For mature thought there is no mechanical substitute. But creative thought and essentially repetitive thought are very different things. For the latter there are, and may be, powerful mechanical aids.

Adding a column of figures is a repetitive thought process, and it was long ago properly relegated to the machine. True, the machine is sometimes controlled by a keyboard, and thought of a sort enters in reading the figures and poking the corresponding keys, but even this is avoidable. Machines have been made which will read typed figures by photocells and then depress the corresponding keys; these are combinations of photocells for scanning the type, electric circuits for sorting the consequent variations, and relay circuits for interpreting the result into the action of solenoids to pull the keys down.

All this complication is needed because of the clumsy way in which we have learned to write figures. If we recorded them positionally, simply by the configuration of a set of dots on a card, the automatic reading mechanism would become comparatively simple. In fact, if the dots are holes, we have the punched-card machine long ago produced by Hollorith * for the purposes of the census, and now used throughout business. Some types of complex businesses could hardly operate without these machines.

Adding is only one operation. To perform arithmetical computation involves also subtraction, multiplication, and division, and in addition some method for temporary storage of results, removal from storage for further manipulation, and recording of final results by printing. Machines for these purposes are now of two types: keyboard machines for accounting and the like, manually controlled for the insertion of data, and usually automatically controlled as far as the sequence of operations is concerned; and punched-card machines in which separate operations are usually delegated to a series of machines, and the cards then transferred bodily from one to another. Both forms are very useful; but as far as complex computations are concerned, both are still in embryo.

Rapid electrical counting appeared soon after the physicists found it desirable to count cosmic rays. For their own purposes the physicists promptly constructed thermionic-tube equipment capable of counting electrical impulses at the rate of 100,000 a second. The advanced arithmetical machines of the future will be electrical in nature, and they will perform at 100 times present speeds, or more.

Moreover, they will be far more versatile than present commercial machines, so that they may readily be adapted for a wide variety of operations. They will be controlled by a control card or film, they will select their own data and manipulate it in accordance with the instructions thus inserted, they will perform complex arithmetical computations at exceedingly high speeds, and they will record results in such form as to be readily available for distribution or for later further manipulation. Such machines will have enormous appetites. One of them will take instructions and data from a whole roomful of girls armed with simple keyboard punches, and will deliver sheets of computed results every few minutes. There will always be plenty of things to compute in the detailed affairs of millions of people doing complicated things.

IV

THE repetitive processes of thought are not confined, however, to matters of arithmetic and statistics. In fact, every time one combines and records facts in accordance with established logical processes, the creative aspect of thinking is concerned only with the selection of the data and the process to be employed, and the manipulation thereafter

* Herman Hollorith (1860–1929), inventor of electrical tabulating machines.

is repetitive in nature and hence a fit matter to be relegated to the machines. Not so much has been done along these lines, beyond the bounds of arithmetic, as might be done, primarily because of the economics of the situation. The needs of business, and the extensive market obviously waiting, assured the advent of mass-produced arithmetical machines just as soon as production methods were sufficiently advanced.

With machines for advanced analysis no such situation existed; for there was and is no extensive market; the users of advanced methods of manipulating data are a very small part of the population. There are, however, machines for solving differential equations — and functional and integral equations, for that matter. There are many special machines, such as the harmonic synthesizer which predicts the tides. There will be many more, appearing certainly first in the hands of the scientist and in small numbers.

If scientific reasoning were limited to the logical processes of arithmetic, we should not get far in our understanding of the physical world. One might as well attempt to grasp the game of poker entirely by the use of the mathematics of probability. The abacus, with its beads strung on parallel wires, led the Arabs to positional numeration and the concept of zero many centuries before the rest of the world; and it was a useful tool — so useful that it still exists.

It is a far cry from the abacus to the modern keyboard accounting machine. It will be an equal step to the arithmetical machine of the future. But even this new machine will not take the scientist where he needs to go. Relief must be secured from laborious detailed manipulation of higher mathematics as well, if the users of it are to free their brains for something more than repetitive detailed transformations in accordance with established rules. A mathematician is not a man who can readily manipulate figures; often he cannot. He is not even a man who can readily perform the transformations of equations by the use of calculus. He is primarily an individual who is skilled in the use of symbolic logic on a high plane, and especially he is a man of intuitive judgment in the choice of the manipulative processes he employs.

All else he should be able to turn over to his mechanism, just as confidently as he turns over the propelling of his car to the intricate mechanism under the hood. Only then will mathematics be practically effective in bringing the growing knowledge of atomistics to the useful solution of the advanced problems of chemistry, metallurgy, and biology. For this reason there will come more machines to handle advanced mathematics for the scientist. Some of them will be sufficiently bizarre to suit the most fastidious connoisseur of the present artifacts of civilization.

V

THE scientist, however, is not the only person who manipulates data and examines the world about him by the use of logical processes, although he sometimes preserves this appearance by adopting into the fold anyone who becomes logical, much in the manner in which a British labor leader is elevated to knighthood. Whenever logical processes of thought are employed — that is, whenever thought for a time runs along an accepted groove — there is an opportunity for the machine. Formal logic used to be a keen instrument in the hands of the teacher in his trying of students' souls. It is readily possible to construct a machine which will manipulate premises in accordance with formal logic, simply by the clever use of relay circuits. Put a set of premises into such a device and turn the crank, and it will readily pass out conclusion after conclusion, all in accordance with logical law, and with no more slips than would be expected of a keyboard adding machine.

Logic can become enormously difficult, and it would undoubtedly be well to produce more assurance in its use. The machines for higher analysis have usually been equation solvers. Ideas are beginning to appear for equation transformers, which will rearrange the relationship expressed by an equation in accordance with strict and rather advanced logic. Progress is inhibited by the exceedingly crude way in which mathematicians express their relationships. They employ a symbolism which grew like Topsy and has little consistency; a strange fact in that most logical field.

A new symbolism, probably positional, must apparently precede the reduction of mathematical transformations to machine processes. Then, on beyond the strict logic of the mathematician, lies the application of logic in everyday affairs. We may some day click off arguments on a machine with the same assurance that we now enter sales on a cash register. But the machine of logic will not look like a cash register, even of the streamlined model.

So much for the manipulation of ideas and their insertion into the record. Thus far we seem to be worse off than before — for we can enormously extend the record; yet even in its present bulk we can hardly consult it. This is a much larger matter than merely the extraction of data for the purposes of scientific research; it involves the entire process by which man profits by his inheritance of acquired knowledge. The prime action of use is selection, and here we are halting indeed. There may be millions of fine thoughts, and the account of the experience on which they are based, all encased within stone walls of acceptable architectural form; but if the scholar can get at only one a week by diligent search, his syntheses are not likely to keep up with the current scene.

Selection, in this broad sense, is a stone adze in the hands of a cabinetmaker. Yet, in a narrow sense and in other areas, something has already been done mechanically on selection. The personnel officer of a factory drops a stack of a few thousand employee cards into a selecting machine, sets a code in accordance with an established convention, and produces in a short time a list of all employees who live in Trenton and know Spanish. Even such devices are much too slow when it comes, for example, to matching a set of fingerprints with one of five million on file. Selection devices of this sort will soon be speeded up from their present rate of reviewing data at a few hundred a minute. By the use of photocells and microfilm they will survey items at the rate of a thousand a second, and will print out duplicates of those selected.

This process, however, is simple selection: it proceeds by examining in turn every one of a large set of items, and by picking out those which have certain specified characteristics. There is another form of selection best illustrated by the automatic telephone exchange. You dial a number and the machine selects and connects just one of a million possible stations. It does not run over them all. It pays attention only to a class given by a first digit, then only to a subclass of this given by the second digit, and so on; and thus proceeds rapidly and almost unerringly to the selected station. It requires a few seconds to make the selection, although the process could be speeded up if increased speed were economically warranted. If necessary, it could be made extremely fast by substituting thermionic-tube switching for mechanical switching, so that the full selection could be made in one one-hundredth of a second. No one would wish to spend the money necessary to make this change in the telephone system, but the general idea is applicable elsewhere.

Take the prosaic problem of the great department store. Every time a charge sale is made, there are a number of things to be done. The inventory needs to be revised, the salesman needs to be given credit for the sale, the general accounts need an entry, and, most important, the customer needs to be charged. A central records device has been developed in which much of this work is done conveniently. The salesman places on a stand the customer's identification card, his own card, and the card taken from the article sold — all punched cards. When he pulls a lever, contacts are made through the holes, machinery at a central point makes the necessary computations and entries, and the proper receipt is printed for the salesman to pass to the customer.

But there may be ten thousand charge customers doing business with the store, and before the full operation can be completed someone has to select the right card and insert it at the central office. Now rapid selection can slide just the proper card into position in an instant or two, and return it afterward. Another difficulty occurs, however. Someone must read a total on the card, so that the machine can add its computed item to it. Conceivably the cards might be of the dry photography type I have described. Existing totals could then be read by photocell, and the new total entered by an electron beam.

The cards may be in miniature, so that they occupy little space. They must move quickly. They need not be transferred far, but merely into position so that the photocell and recorder can operate on them. Positional dots can enter the data. At the end of the month a machine can readily be made to read these and to print an ordinary bill. With tube selection, in which no mechanical parts are involved in the switches, little time need be occupied in bringing the correct card into use – a second should suffice for the entire operation. The whole record on the card may be made by magnetic dots on a steel sheet if desired, instead of dots to be observed optically, following the scheme by which Poulsen * long ago put speech on a magnetic wire. This method has the advantage of simplicity and ease of erasure. By using photography, however, one can arrange to project the record in enlarged form, and at a distance by using the process common in television equipment.

One can consider rapid selection of this form, and distant projection for other purposes. To be able to key one sheet of a million before an operator in a second or two, with the possibility of then adding notes thereto, is suggestive in many ways. It might even be of use in libraries, but that is another story. At any rate, there are now some interesting combinations possible. One might, for example, speak to a microphone, in the manner described in connection with the speech-controlled typewriter, and thus make his selections. It would certainly beat the usual file clerk.

VI

THE real heart of the matter of selection, however, goes deeper than a lag in the adoption of mechanisms by libraries, or a lack of development of devices for their use. Our ineptitude in getting at the record

* Valdemar Poulsen (1869–1942), Danish electrical and physical research engineer; inventor of the telegraphone.

is largely caused by the artificiality of systems of indexing. When data of any sort are placed in storage, they are filed alphabetically or numerically, and information is found (when it is) by tracing it down from subclass to subclass. It can be in only one place, unless duplicates are used; one has to have rules as to which path will locate it, and the rules are cumbersome. Having found one item, moreover, one has to emerge from the system and re-enter on a new path.

The human mind does not work that way. It operates by association. With one item in its grasp, it snaps instantly to the next that is suggested by the association of thoughts, in accordance with some intricate web of trails carried by the cells of the brain. It has other characteristics, of course; trails that are not frequently followed are prone to fade, items are not fully permanent, memory is transitory. Yet the speed of action, the intricacy of trails, the detail of mental pictures, is awe-inspiring beyond all else in nature.

Man cannot hope fully to duplicate this mental process artificially, but he certainly ought to be able to learn from it. In minor ways he may even improve, for his records have relative permanency. The first idea, however, to be drawn from the analogy concerns selection. Selection by association, rather than by indexing, may yet be mechanized. One cannot hope thus to equal the speed and flexibility with which the mind follows an associative trail, but it should be possible to beat the mind decisively in regard to the permanence and clarity of the items resurrected from storage.

Consider a future device for individual use, which is a sort of mechanized private file and library. It needs a name, and, to coin one at random, "memex" will do. A memex is a device in which an individual stores all his books, records, and communications, and which is mechanized so that it may be consulted with exceeding speed and flexibility. It is an enlarged intimate supplement to his memory.

It consists of a desk, and while it can presumably be operated from a distance, it is primarily the piece of furniture at which he works. On the top are slanting translucent screens, on which material can be projected for convenient reading. There is a keyboard, and sets of buttons and levers. Otherwise it looks like an ordinary desk.

In one end is the stored material. The matter of bulk is well taken care of by improved microfilm. Only a small part of the interior of the memex is devoted to storage, the rest to mechanism. Yet if the user inserted 5000 pages of material a day it would take him hundreds of years to fill the repository, so he can be profligate and enter material freely.

Most of the memex contents are purchased on microfilm ready for insertion. Books of all sorts, pictures, current periodicals, newspapers, are thus obtained and dropped into place. Business correspondence takes the same path. And there is provision for direct entry. On the top of the memex is a transparent platen. On this are placed longhand notes, photographs, memoranda, all sorts of things. When one is in place, the depression of a lever causes it to be photographed onto the next blank space in a section of the memex film, dry photography being employed.

There is, of course, provision for consultation of the record by the usual scheme of indexing. If the user wishes to consult a certain book, he taps its code on the keyboard, and the title page of the book promptly appears before him, projected onto one of his viewing positions. Frequently-used codes are mnemonic, so that he seldom consults his code book; but when he does, a single tap of a key projects it for his use. Moreover, he has supplemental levers. On deflecting one of these levers to the right he runs through the book before him, each page in turn being projected at a speed which just allows a recognizing glance at each. If he deflects it further to the right, he steps through the book 10 pages at a time; still further at 100 pages at a time. Deflection to the left gives him the same control backwards.

A special button transfers him immediately to the first page of the index. Any given book of his library can thus be called up and consulted with far greater facility than if it were taken from a shelf. As he has several projection positions, he can leave one item in position while he calls up another. He can add marginal notes and comments, taking advantage of one possible type of dry photography, and it could even be arranged so that he can do this by a stylus scheme, such as is now employed in the telautograph seen in railroad waiting rooms, just as though he had the physical page before him.

VII

ALL this is conventional, except for the projection forward of present-day mechanisms and gadgetry. It affords an immediate step, however, to associative indexing, the basic idea of which is a provision whereby any item may be caused at will to select immediately and automatically another. This is the essential feature of the memex. The process of tying two items together is the important thing.

When the user is building a trail, he names it, inserts the names in his code book, and taps it out on his keyboard. Before him are the two items to be joined, projected onto adjacent viewing positions. At the bottom of each there are a number of blank code spaces, and a pointer is set to indicate one of these on each item. The user taps a single key, and the items are permanently joined. In each code space appears the code word. Out of view, but also in the code space, is inserted a set of dots for photocell viewing; and on each item these dots by their positions designate the index number of the other item.

Thereafter, at any time, when one of these items is in view, the other can be instantly recalled merely by tapping a button below the corresponding code space. Moreover, when numerous items have been thus joined together to form a trail, they can be reviewed in turn, rapidly or slowly, by deflecting a lever like that used for turning the pages of a book. It is exactly as though the physical items had been gathered together from widely separated sources and bound together to form a new book. It is more than this, for any item can be joined into numerous trails.

The owner of the memex, let us say, is interested in the origin and properties of the bow and arrow. Specifically he is studying why the short Turkish bow was apparently superior to the English long bow in the skirmishes of the Crusades. He has dozens of possibly pertinent books and articles in his memex. First he runs through an encyclopedia, finds an interesting but sketchy article, leaves it projected. Next, in a history, he finds another pertinent item, and ties the two together. Thus he goes, building a trail of many items. Occasionally he inserts a comment of his own, either linking it into the main trail or joining it by a side trail to a particular item. When it becomes evident that the elastic properties of available materials had a great deal to do with the bow, he branches off on a side trail which takes him through textbooks on elasticity and tables of physical constants. He inserts a page of longhand analysis of his own. Thus he builds a trail of his interest through the maze of materials available to him.

And his trails do not fade. Several years later, his talk with a friend turns to the queer ways in which a people resist innovations, even of vital interest. He has an example, in the fact that the outranged Europeans still failed to adopt the Turkish bow. In fact he has a trail on it. A touch brings up the code book. Tapping a few keys projects the head of the trail. A lever runs through it at will, stopping at interesting items, going off on side excursions. It is an interesting trail, pertinent to the discussion. So he sets a reproducer in action, photographs the whole trail out, and passes it to his friend for insertion in his own memex, there to be linked into the more general trail.

VIII

WHOLLY new forms of encyclopedias will appear, ready-made with a mesh of associative trails running through them, ready to be dropped into the memex and there amplified. The lawyer has at his touch the associated opinions and decisions of his whole experience, and of the experience of friends and authorities. The patent attorney has on call the millions of issued patents, with familiar trails to every point of his client's interest. The physician, puzzled by a patient's reactions, strikes the trail established in studying an earlier similar case, and runs rapidly through analogous case histories, with side references to the classics for the pertinent anatomy and histology. The chemist, struggling with the synthesis of an organic compound, has all the chemical literature before him in his laboratory, with trails following the analogies of compounds, and side trails to their physical and chemical behavior.

The historian, with a vast chronological account of a people, parallels it with a skip trail which stops only on the salient items, and can follow at any time contemporary trails which lead him all over civilization at a particular epoch. There is a new profession of trail blazers, those who find delight in the task of establishing useful trails through the enormous mass of the common record. The inheritance from the master becomes, not only his additions to the world's record, but for his disciples the entire scaffolding by which they were erected.

Thus science may implement the ways in which man produces, stores, and consults the record of the race. It might be striking to outline the instrumentalities of the future more spectacularly, rather than to stick closely to methods and elements now known and undergoing rapid development, as has been done here. Technical difficulties of all sorts have been ignored, certainly, but also ignored are means as yet unknown which may come any day to accelerate technical progress as violently as did the advent of the thermionic tube. In order that the picture may not be too commonplace, by reason of sticking to present-day patterns, it may be well to mention one such possibility, not to prophesy but merely to suggest, for prophecy based on extension of the known has substance, while prophecy founded on the unknown is only a doubly involved guess.

All our steps in creating or absorbing material of the record proceed through one of the senses — the tactile when we touch keys, the oral when we speak or listen, the visual when we read. Is it not possible that some day the path may be established more directly?

We know that when the eye sees, all the consequent information is transmitted to the brain by means of electrical vibrations in the channel of the optic nerve. This is an exact analogy with the electrical vibrations which occur in the cable of a television set: they convey the picture from the photocells which see it to the radio transmitter from which it is broadcast. We know further that if we can approach that cable with the proper instruments, we do not need to touch it; we can pick up those vibrations by electrical induction and thus discover and reproduce the scene which is being transmitted, just as a telephone wire may be tapped for its message.

The impulses which flow in the arm nerves of a typist convey to her fingers the translated information which reaches her eye or ear, in order that the fingers may be caused to strike the proper keys. Might not these currents be intercepted, either in the original form in which information is conveyed to the brain, or in the marvelously metamorphosed form in which they then proceed to the hand?

By bone conduction we already introduce sounds into the nerve channels of the deaf in order that they may hear. Is it not possible that we may learn to introduce them without the present cumbersomeness of first transforming electrical vibrations to mechanical ones, which the human mechanism promptly transforms back to the electrical form? With a couple of electrodes on the skull the encephalograph now produces pen-and-ink traces which bear some relation to the electrical phenomena going on in the brain itself. True, the record is unintelligible, except as it points out certain gross misfunctioning of the cerebral mechanism; but who would now place bounds on where such a thing may lead?

In the outside world, all forms of intelligence, whether of sound or sight, have been reduced to the form of varying currents in an electric circuit in order that they may be transmitted. Inside the human frame exactly the same sort of process occurs. Must we always transform to mechanical movements in order to proceed from one electrical phenomenon to another? It is a suggestive thought, but it hardly warrants prediction without losing touch with reality and immediateness.

Presumably man's spirit should be elevated if he can better review his shady past and analyze more completely and objectively his present problems. He has built a civilization so complex that he needs to mechanize his records more fully if he is to push his experiment to its logical conclusion and not merely become bogged down part way there by overtaxing his limited memory. His excursions may be more enjoyable if he can reacquire the privilege of forgetting the manifold things he does not need to have immediately at hand, with some assurance that he can find them again if they prove important.

The applications of science have built man a well-supplied house, and are teaching him to live healthily therein. They have enabled him to throw masses of people against one another with cruel weapons. They may yet allow him truly to encompass the great record and to grow in the wisdom of race experience. He may perish in conflict before he learns to wield that record for his true good. Yet, in the application of science to the needs and desires of man, it would seem to be a singularly unfortunate stage at which to terminate the process, or to lose hope as to the outcome.

QUESTIONS

1. In the third paragraph of the essay, Bush refers to "strange destructive gadgets." What purpose of the author's is suggested by his deliberate use of the word "gadgets" in this context?

2. What is the main problem, as Bush sees it, facing modern science in peacetime? Why does he refer to Leibnitz and Babbage in Section I?

3. Consider the opening sentence of Paragraph 1 of Section II. What is the relationship of this sentence to the rest of the essay? Point out the portions of the essay which particularize the three-part generalization of this sentence.

4. In Paragraph 6 of Section III, Bush distinguishes between "creative thought" and "essentially repetitive thought." How is this distinction related to his major intention in the essay?

5. What is the common feature which characterizes all of the various mechanical devices which Bush discusses in the essay up to Section VIII? How does the possibility of future development discussed in Section VIII differ from all the developments discussed earlier in the essay? Why does Bush emphasize this distinction?

HARLOW SHAPLEY, an astronomer and philosopher, was Director of the Harvard Observatory from 1921 until 1952. He is the Paine Professor Emeritus of Astronomy at Harvard University. Professor Shapley is a member of many scientific, professional, educational, and community societies and organizations. The recipient of numerous awards and prizes, he has written widely in all the fields of his interest. Among his publications are *Star Clusters* (1930), *Flights from Chaos* (1930), and *Galaxies* (1943). An outspoken critic and commentator, Professor Shapley originally prepared the material of " A Design for Fighting " as a speech before the American Association for the Advancement of Science, in September, 1944; the speech was published first in the *American Scholar* and was revised for publication in *The Atlantic Monthly*.

A DESIGN FOR FIGHTING

by HARLOW SHAPLEY

ONCE upon a time recently there was a great nation in a mess. The nation's ills were everywhere obvious. A great many poor people were hungry, while other citizens destroyed their surpluses; more than ten million were unemployed; the desires of the laborers for greater pay and prestige were doing badly; the women without higher education were submerged by custom and lack of opportunity; the people had no thrifty desires to accumulate savings — indeed they had nothing much to save; the young men and women received little systematic training in health or in patriotism; they had little opportunity to travel.

In this economically and spiritually confused country, diseases like measles, pneumonia, and syphilis were badly controlled, if at all; mosquitoes and flies were destined to be eternal pests and carriers of disease; the airplanes were relatively slow and weak (we continue to list the nation's ills); the researches in the physical sciences throughout the country were listless; the art of ship-building and ship-sailing had practically disappeared; and worst of all, there was little zest for life and liberty, no driving principle or policy to make the citizens from all the corners of the country proud to be citizens of that nation and brothers under a sun that might illuminate a hopeful future.

If I had, at that time, ventured to offer a remedy for all these ills, every one of them, by advising the afflicted nation to take active part in the greatest and bloodiest human war ever conceived – a war that destroys more property and brutally butchers more innocent people than the worst human butchers have ever enjoyed in their most gorgeous dreams; if I had recommended that mad procedure, guaranteeing the almost complete cure of all such ills within ten years, and the practical attainment of all the high goals I have implied, it is quite likely that both my advice and I should have been (to understate it) deplored.

Naturally, I did not make such a recommendation. Nevertheless, this nation did get into just such a war, and all those happy desiderata and many more have come about.

Probably never in the history of this country have its people, as a whole, eaten so well as during the past three years. There is practically no unemployment. The soldiers and sailors are the best paid and fed in the world. The nation is healthier. The people have rather willingly adopted healthful restraints, constructive collaboration, unified determination, a national spirit of worthy sacrifice.

Sensational advances in the treatment of certain diseases, new knowledge of food, new accomplishment in a million new home gardens, new and widespread instruction in world geography – all these have come also. Without the war, most of them would yet have been totally missing, and the others of slow maturing. The women in the offices, factories, and armed services have discovered abilities and self-assurance heretofore unrealized. Elementary applied sciences have been taught to about a million young men who would otherwise have been deprived of a practical training that is important in a civilization highly dependent on applied science. The political and social prestige of labor has increased remarkably in three years of war; and millions of citizens have billions in savings – establishing a policy heretofore unknown, unpracticed, or impossible.

With such manifold blessings to the majority of individuals and groups in America, and with such apparent social gain for the nation as a whole, who could sincerely regret this world war and who would take steps to prevent another one? Should we not praise those who precipitated it? Or is there a counteracting Design for Not Fighting – some substitute for Beneficent War?

War was long ago recognized as a good tribal business by certain savage and primitive people, but they fought for food, women, loot, and the joy of personal combat. These are not our American motives. We have food; we have, if anything, too many women; our individual property averages the most and best in the world; and the lust for personal combat has been pretty well bred out of us. (Even if it has not, modern war provides little opportunity for personal bloodletting, since it is about nine-tenths fought on the draftsman's board, in the machine shop, and by the remotely located ground forces.) Fewer than a tenth of our mobilized warriors in battlefields, factories, and farms ever smell the human enemy or grapple with him. The poetry and romance, the snorting rush of the foaming charger and the savage clash of sabers have been machined out of modern and future wars. Most of the thrills for most of us are vicarious. At the height of a hard-pressing crisis, we may work at the lathes some fifty-four hours a week – with time-and-a-half for overtime, of course.

Our material gains in war are therefore not so elemental as those which made war a national business for earlier tribes. It is now not so much for food, loot, and glory that we fight, as (if we judge by our successes) for the great social gains: for widely distributed prosperity, the education of the masses, large wealth for a new set of capitalists, the provision of work for everybody, and good pay for good work. Socially uplifting is this war, as well as materially profitable, for more than 100 million Americans.

Up to this point, it sounds as though it would be folly not to adopt world war as the national policy. The amazing advantages and dividends must be balanced somehow, or even written off in some way; otherwise we are at a loss to understand another equally amazing situation: namely, that practically everyone wants this beneficent war to end immediately, and fervently hopes, apparently, that there will never be another such war.

Undoubtedly there exist a few friends of war, scattered among the officers of the armed forces, the politicians and government officials, the magnified personalities of press and radio, and especially among profiteering businessmen – a considerable number altogether, who secretly hope that this war will continue and that others will come. These people must be watched, but I choose to consider them as low moral perverts, and not as a part of the American citizenry.

II

Why Not War as a National Business?

To enumerate briefly the chief objections to war, we note first that it is making nearly all our regularly trained army and navy personnel important, and perhaps overweeningly arrogant. The same is true for hundreds of Washington bureaucrats. It may be pretty hard to demobilize the pride and spirit and habits of many of the war-enriched, glory-inflated citizens.

The war is building a much greater American Legion – again, a two-edged sword, disadvantage and advantage.

The war has decreased the normal care of children, and probably their morale. The bull-market boom of the late twenties, of course, tended to do the same.

The usual type of college education has been interrupted for a few years for many boys. Presumably that should be listed as a disadvantage.

Although the war has improved the business of newspapers, of the radio, of manufacturers, of the transportation and communications industries, and of most small businessmen the country over, there were some enterprises temporarily ruined by the war (although the corresponding businessmen themselves have landed on their feet elsewhere). And the white-collar classes have, as usual, suffered disproportionately, because the take has lagged behind the increased outgo.

Some would list "the economic waste of war" as a frightful price to pay for our full employment and full stomachs and purses.

Finally, taxes have become atrocious; but hardly any of us regret that others pay the government heavily, to meet a part of the costs of the war and to help in moderating the inflation natural to the existence of prosperity. In fact, we almost cheerfully pay our own taxes as a part of the healthful national discipline.

It is obvious that I am reaching around desperately to find sufficient disadvantages of war; it must be discredited somehow.

As I see it, there are two major comments to be made on our aversion to adopting war as the best national or international business. One is obvious; the other leads toward hope.

We in America are on the winning side of this war, and from the first we have known that we are winning; also the war is not on the home grounds. Those obvious factors explain much. Practically none of the war advantages cited above have been available to the French, Dutch, Norwegians, Czechs, and other conquered states. Only a few temporary advantages (like full employment and perhaps unity of spirit) have been available to the now defeated Axis countries; and by no means all of our advantages have come to Great Britain and the Dominions. This time we have kept a winning war at a distance. It is relatively very profitable, and not all the profits are temporary. We have reasons to suspect, however, that a future war might eventuate otherwise.

It remains to make the hopeful comment that the basic reason why 130 million Americans and untold hundreds of millions of others want an end of this war, and of all similar world struggles, is that war is immoral. The moral values in the situation more than balance the immediate material and social advantages, more than balance the prosperity, the glory, the excitement – even for us, a winning nation. This is a fact of highest encouragement to all who are solicitous for the further evolution of the human race. It is inspiriting that we, who are temporarily gaining so many worth-while social and personal advantages, are nevertheless conscious of the cosmic error of it all.

We owe our present consciousness of the long-range tragic penalties of war to two widely different causes. One is the remarkably dramatic news coverage by press and radio, which has not concealed from Americans the bitter blood and tears. The other is the religious and secular education of past centuries, which has gradually built an intellectual heritage and a universal ethics that link peace with social justice, international good will, and human progress. Through moral education, peace has become an inherent human desire; it is almost an instinctive good, for educated men, and war an instinctive evil.

Possibly there are other important factors that tend to cancel or minimize the social and material gains of successful war at a distance – mass anxiety and regret over economic waste, for instance. But we also had deep pre-war anxieties. Personally I am content to accept the contention that the moral gain of abolishing war is the best reason for such a policy. The arguments based on economics and demography are too often specious and circular; usually they involve merely postponements and short-term compromises. The inherent moral antipathy, moreover, is a factor most clearly associated with the mental and spiritual development of mankind. I am gratified that we can rate it highly.

As the current strife draws to a conclusion that seems to be satisfactory for the continuance of a Western culture, we may profitably turn our thoughts first toward post-war peace plans. And when the world gets stabilized politically and economically, or even before then, we should begin planning for the next war. In the remainder of this article I hope to incite my readers to consider plans for new martial activities. It will then become clear why I have taken time to consider both the advantages of successful war and the moral and material costs thereof. We shall have standards of comparison.

III

Our Recent Inglorious Defeat and Humiliation

In 1918–1919 more than four times as many Americans were killed by Influenza as by our enemies of the First World War. Twenty million human beings perished of that ruthless disease. The economic loss in the world-wide battle with the influenza organism was also tremendous. Moreover, sad and shameful to say, we lost that war. Only when it became satiated with its successes did the savage foe recede into the invisible realms where it normally dwells, and from which it has at times made further minor forays with murderous and economically destructive results. Even yet, that adversary is not defeated; our defenses against it are permeable and insufficient.

Clearly we have right here a dangerous enemy for our next war. Why are we not all arming ourselves against this treacherous foe that does not hesitate to make sneak attacks and has no respect for armistice? There were several millions of us engaged in those influenza battles of 1918–1919; we are the casualties who recovered. I now wonder why in heaven we who returned from those battlefields did not form an American Flu Legion, don our old face masks and march in parades, brandish our voting strength, and influence Congressmen.

With our political power, under the leadership of General Doctor, Captain Laboratory Technician, and Lieutenant Nurse – all who fought valiantly with us millions of private sufferers in the great influenza war – we might have got the government to fortify research laboratories munificently, drill the citizens in epidemic prevention and control, enforce the care of body and mind, and turn the powerful mass psychology with a fervent patriotic assault on the enemies of mankind that have always been more deadly than the soldiers of European fanatics and tyrants. So prepared, when the next attack comes along, we should be ready for it. We could sell Health Bonds, pay taxes luxuriously, work like the devil, and perhaps, this time, win the war, conquer our great enemy, and keep him subjugated for as long as man remains civilized and sanitary.

But, alas, we did not organize. Medical investigators and public health officers continue to do their best, without much government or public support, while the undertakers year after year continue to tuck us away prematurely.

IV

Selecting Enemies for Coming Wars

But the Design for Fighting I want to sketch here is not so simple and obvious as would be a defensive war against some major decimating epidemic. To fight defensively means admission of intellectual defeat. I want to go deeper. We should remember that it is only the bodies of men and women that the grave-diggers inter and the cremators oxydize. Our influences, our contributions to knowledge and to the art and beauty of human living, — our spirits, if you will, — escape the mortuary. Our works live after us.

Let us, therefore, seek out some of the enemies that assail those human qualities that we group loosely under the term " civilization "; let us look up the opponents to the evolution of those human characteristics that seem to differentiate men from other animals and plants. We may discover that an enthusiastic warfare against such opponents, even if only partially successful, is a fair substitute for warfare against fellow men. At least it would emphasize the absurdity of world wars or national wars where life and property are wildly squandered, while these greater enemies — the enemies of the soul, mind, sometimes body — are almost completely ignored.

Instinctive and acquired human morality, as we have noted, opposes the promotion of man-kill-man war; but I believe this same inherent morality must unquestionably be vigorously pro-war, war to the death, if we define our enemies as those that obstruct or challenge the social and intellectual growth of man and of human society.

We could, of course, betray this innate evolutionary struggle, deliberately refuse to grow, and go turtling through the ages, dull and static; we could even regress, like a petered-out biological species, by way of recurrent world wars and social degradations. But it will be better cosmic sportsmanship to go to the top, to the limit of our abilities and aspirations; for there may be something at that rainbow's end that will make even the galaxies look incidental.

Whatever the postulates in which we clothe ourselves, whether our tailors are religious prophets, pagan philosophers, modern scientific cosmogonists, or the still striving spirits of jungle-born curiosity, the majority of Americans are already amply dressed for the uphill climb. This readiness of the citizen-soldiers is a challenge to those who venture to make plans. No boastful pacification of a restless island will suffice, no capture of a distant market for the enriching of a few traders, no gloating superiority in armored flying battleships. Those are goals unsuited to human dignity in this time of a New Renaissance.

No, it has to be good, this set of plans; and those whom we have trained to be the long-range social thinkers should heed well the ways and means, the details of joining battle with the real enemies. These new conflicts, moreover, must not be local wars, for a few scientific laboratories, or for one country or one county. The fight must be at least nation-wide. Perhaps over the borders are potential allies, willing, well armed, and similarly star-bent.

As a simple preliminary, I shall mention four national or international problems the resolution of which seems to lead in the right direction.

V

Illiteracy

Education, as we know, is well spoken of. Although it is perverted at times and in places into antisocial channels, it is by and large both good and necessary. It is indeed indispensable if democracy is to prevail and the dignity of the individual man is to be respected and enhanced. Literacy is basic for it. Notwithstanding the rapid rise of auditory education by way of the radio, and of pictorial education by moving pictures and oncoming television, there is no reasonable escape from the general necessity of knowing how to read and write. Even a tabloid requires a modicum of literacy, and the comic strips carry printed materials.

The point I am driving at is that Illiteracy can and should be wiped out. The basic equipment (reading and writing) for general and special education should be universally provided. It is not a job for schoolteachers alone. It is a national job, for the public and the local governments. Ten years from now the existence of illiteracy between the ages of ten and sixty should be reckoned as a community disgrace. The shame should be on the community, and not on the unfortunate individuals. In many communities volunteer teachers, performing a sympathetic rather than a patronizing task, could take care of this business without difficulty.

In Mexico, the enlightened president, General Manuel Avila Camacho, has requested educated adults to undertake, as a part of their national service, the elementary education of at least one unschooled neighbor. Must we lag behind in social progress? Must we wait for a presidential order? A command from the conscience of the community should suffice. The people can do this work with pleasure and with justifiable pride. And once the first battle for universal literacy has been won in the community, city, county, or state, the level can be raised and a further step taken toward an enlightened citizenry. The second goal might be: "Eighty per cent of those older than fifteen years to have a completed grammar school education"; and there should be a ceremonious bestowal, on the successful community, of an "E" for Excellent, or Education, or Evolving.

There may be, of course, an irreducible minimum of illiteracy of perhaps one per cent, because of the existence of insurmountable physical disabilities and the presence of illiterate transients. But the occurrence of foreign-language elements in a community should be no excuse for not undertaking or solving this problem; rather it should be a challenge – and an opportunity, by the way, for mutual education.

VI

Premature Senility

As a second martial enterprise, let us organize ourselves and declare war on Premature Senility. The more we study the life span and the death causes of Americans and Europeans, the more we realize that a few maladies and a few bad habits cut off too many useful people prematurely. Most of us say that we should dread the prolongation of useless old age; but who can object to the adding of ten years to the active lives of men and women to whom the years have brought augmented wisdom, and in whom experience has produced nobility of character?

I look forward to the time, perhaps in a century or so, when an adult caught with a communicable disease will be heavily fined, and one indulging in afflictions like cancer, tuberculosis, arthritis, and neuroses will be branded as a social pariah and put in jail. I hope that the names of some of those diseases will become so little known that one would find them only at the bottom of the dictionary page – "cancer: a rare disease, rampant in the dark ages, when, about 1940, it was killing 150,000 Americans annually." But my hope is perhaps too wild. Certainly there will need to be some hard fighting and heavy expense and further education before that Utopia dawns.

The Western world is not too crowded; there is useful work to be done, there are joys to be shared, fine thoughts to be meditated, sunsets for everybody. The proper balance for a diminishing but healthfully controlled birth rate could be the prolongation of adult life. Already the medical and health sciences have done astonishing work on the diseases of infancy. The average age has risen spectacularly in America and elsewhere. But mature men and women will live and work happily half a generation longer when, as the result of a sincere and widespread war, we conquer or control arthritis, cancer, nephritis, and diseases and disorders of the circulatory system, the respiratory system, and the brain. These six are the chief disablers. There is reason for the high hopes of continued advance against all of them.

The battles must be fought, to be sure, largely by the specialists, but in three ways the public can contribute notably; and without this public help, complete victory is impossible. We can inspire brilliant young scientists to enlist, preferably as volunteers, in this great war in the interest of human life and happiness. We can provide directly by gift, or indirectly through influencing governmental support, the necessary funds for the hospitals, research laboratories, and field studies. We can co-operate in controlling some of these scourges by care of personal health and by seeing to it that our communities are provided with appropriate health programs.

Let me comment briefly on each of the six: —

1. In the United States five million people suffer from the various forms of arthritis, and hundreds of thousands are prematurely disabled thereby. Yet, with minor exceptions, there are no appreciable funds for the basic study of this disease, and no specific research army or institution. Arthritis rarely finishes off its own victims; it prepares them painfully for the kill by some more lethal assailant. The average mildness of the malady is probably the reason it is commonly overlooked as one of man's great enemies.

2. Some further comments on the cancer war. The first eleven days of the critical and bloody invasion of Normandy took an average of three hundred American lives a day; cancer killed an average of four hundred Americans on each of those days. And it does not stop; it offers no armistice. In the next twelve months there will be the customary 150,000 deaths in America from this one source, preceded in general by great suffering, sorrow, and expense. Why are we not doing something about it? But we are! Yes, we spend *annually* in cancer research in all the universities and medical research institutions (not including the National Cancer Institute) a little less than the receipts of one major football game! For the current "War of the Tyrants" we spend 300 billion dollars of public money. For the war against cancer, the greater man-enslaving enemy, one-millionth as much!

Of course we need more research men and more ideas for the fight on cancer, but both will be forthcoming if ample funds are supplied for numerous *full-time* research positions in leading hospitals and medical schools. The cancer investigators must also explore the possibilities in neighboring fields, and the public should no more worry about efforts and money wasted in following faint trails than it now worries about the expense of exploratory scientific researches for the present war. Four hundred American lives a day justify an expensive fight.

3. Hard arteries and the associated consequences stop in midcareer too many important workers in business, in the professions, in public service. A career of high nervous pressure is tough on the circulatory systems of those men who respond too generously to the call of duty and opportunity. As yet we have no real defense — only worried sermons from harassed wives and family doctors. More than half a

million Americans die each year from diseases of the circulatory system; and of the people who are over ten years of age, more than half will die of these maladies unless something vigorous and drastic is done. How much do we spend in basic research on the ravages of this enemy? Practically nothing at all!

4. Tuberculosis is still a deadly enemy to those important people between the ages of twenty-five and forty years, notwithstanding modern progress in care of the afflicted; and also unsolved as yet is that other respiratory affliction, the expensive common cold.

5. Nephritis buries nearly 100,000 Americans a year. We lose the lives, but save a little money, for again there are negligible funds earmarked for research on kidney diseases.

6. But perhaps our greatest enemy among the major maladies is the group of physiological and psychological factors that disorder and spoil the human mind. Some of the many forms of mental diseases are already yielding to the various therapies. Epilepsy is pretty well under control. The depressions are better understood than formerly, and that new knowledge is a necessary preliminary to successful treatment.

The plight of the schizophrenics is no longer a hopeless mystery. The alarmingly large number of neuro-psychiatric cases coming out of the armed forces — approximately one half the total discharges for disability — emphasizes dramatically the great importance of fighting this ruthless enemy; fighting hard for the sanity of the race; fighting, also, for the prolongation of mental power. With the mind senile, a virile body is rudderless; the centenarian's closing days should be bright, but not balmy!

Without further documentation, let us acknowledge the need for a concerted national attack on the recognizable causes of premature senility — the ailment that sooner or later will be of personal interest to practically all of us. Would you like to have a tenth of one per cent of your future Federal income tax devoted to the elimination, or at least the great diminution, of the ills that prematurely weaken and destroy? That's all the cash it would require. There is a highly sponsored National Science Fund with committees that could administer grants for medical research.

Would you participate in a national " one meal fast " to pay for research on the major maladies? If all took part, and contributed the equivalent, about 15 million dollars, we should win both happiness and years, because several deadly diseases would die.

VII

Cultural Uniformity

Universal literacy is a goal the average citizen can help attain; longevity is a problem chiefly for the specialists to handle. I should like to isolate another conflict in which everybody can take part. We can name it the Fight Against Cultural Uniformity. It would take long to elaborate the need for this movement, and longer to specify sample procedures in detail. A brief summary must suffice here.

Life, I have found from experience, is the dullest thing one can live; and it would be vastly duller but for variety among the people one meets, diversity in their habits, manners, and intellectual reactions. To maintain and increase the diversity, to the end of enhancing the degree of satisfaction with life and the opportunity for intellectual and artistic growth, requires immediate fighting against real foes.

I assume people realize that a world state is in prospect for the near future – geologically near; perhaps not in this decade or generation, but soon. By world state I mean the organization of practically all terrestrial men. The quality and degree of the internationalism of the coming world state should be examined. Aviation and radio, and similar modern arts, force the unification. A world-wide economic association that encompasses all states that do business seems so inevitable, ultimately, that one wonders why we go ahead trying halfway substitutes.

And the unified political organization that will include all the present nations is also rapidly developing, notwithstanding some stubborn and perhaps bloody resistance, and in spite of the temporary dominance by political cartels of major powers. Some would probably predict that the political unity will be obtained and stabilized before the end of the present century; and others may hold out for a thousand years of strife and political individualism. But we all should probably agree, if put to it, that we either sink to savagery or rise, perhaps slowly, to a world unity, however drab this last prospect may appear.

But is a world-wide common culture an inevitability of the new order? I believe not. A political internation and a universal economic agreement need not lead to a sterile uniformity in the cultural world. Local languages perish slowly; and many local customs can persist because they are linked with local geography. Hills, valleys, deserts, mountains, the seashores, and the various belts of latitude will remain, notwithstanding the ingenuity and deviltry of man. And the climates, soils, waters, and scenery in these various types of geographical localities can and will have a basic effect upon the folkways of whatever inhabitants choose to remain, or are permitted to remain, in such relatively specialized domains.

That localized cultures change slowly (whether of man, plant, or animal), and with some care might be made almost permanent, is demonstrated in nearly all the large countries of the world by the present social and domestic differences in contiguous groups. Only if the world maintains these cultural human varieties, these endemic cultures, will it provide natural opportunities for evolution. I mean evolution in taste and art, as well as growth in industry and natural science. For it is well known to the biologist that a uniform population changes but little.

We must therefore oppose, if I am right, those tendencies that are working toward standardization and cultural homogeneity. We must strive against chain thinking and acting. As one contribution to this objective, the small community must continue to live, to play, and to think by itself. It must be our fervent hope that the local American community will grow in cultural self-sufficiency, not only for the delight of the people in being doers rather than in being done for, but also because of the importance of endemic cultures to general welfare.

We are quite willing to give over to international organization the responsibility of the larger political and economic management, if such delegation means peace, efficiency, and progress. But let us work toward a colorful new world through the development and maintenance of local customs.

And it is high time we got started on a program of deliberate cultivation of community life. For we must admit that much of our thinking and feeling has now been delegated to others through the predominance of chain newspapers, broadcasting syndicates, and motion picture theaters. It is alarming to realize how many of us hear the same news commentators, the same comedians and music analyzers; and to realize how many of us read the same comic strips, eat the same food, announce the same observations on passing events.

All this standardization and mental goose-stepping has gone so far that escape seems impossible. Chain thinking has linked our brains. The radio serves simultaneously ten million of us parrots. Originality of thought and expression has been sold down the river for the joy of hearing a hot gag.

Possibly we cannot retrace and start over; and most of us would not want to; we are mentally lazy, and too willing to follow leaders. But can we not counteract a little the deadening effect of this national centralized domination by emphasizing the activities and the contributions of localized natural communities?

Some of us have cheerful hopes about the more methodical encouragement of craftsmanship in country, town, and city. Already much is done, and it has been tremendously worth while. Art and science often blend in the craftsman. Local group work in the sciences is an entering wedge for community collaboration. In less than two years, the membership in Science Clubs of America has increased 600 per cent, and now we have some five thousand active groups that are doing things, with a maximum of inspiration and a minimum of centralized direction.

Much of the work of the Science Clubs, in the schools and among the adults, deals with the biology, topography, and archaeology of the community. Such interests foster pride in the community. Before long, many counties or valleys are going to be proud, for instance, that the herbarium of the home county valley is well known and has been related to the flora of larger regions and to the community's horticultural and agricultural problems.

The rise of small symphony orchestras and choruses, and the growth of amateur musical performances, are signs that we can develop loyalties to the home folk, and really enjoy their performances, notwithstanding the superior excellence that could be ours by the turning of a dial. These musical movements, especially when they can be related to the folk songs and folklore of the community, are a challenge for all of us who recognize the importance of the independent life of the community, and the heightened likelihood of the evolution of taste and intelligence if homogeneity is opposed.

In the contest against deadening centralized manipulation of the minds and mores of the people, we have a happy fight that all can join; and, paradoxically enough, nationally working artists and scientists can help to incite diversity and direct the development of local cultural projects; the radio and press syndicates can assist in spreading the gospel of community self-sufficiency.

VIII

The Tyranny of the Unknown

I come now to the fourth scheme for combat. I cannot escape the feeling that the human mind and human curiosity are significant in this world — even perhaps in the cosmos of geological time and intergalactic space. With this impression (or illusion) that the mind is the best of us, and the best of biological evolution, I cannot escape the feeling of a responsibility to glorify the human mind, take it seriously, even dream about its ultimately flowering into something far beyond the primitive muscle-guider and sensation-recorder with which we started.

It is, possibly, naïve to deduce that the acquiring of knowledge and sensations, and the judging and correlating of such knowledge and sensations, are a human necessity; and also rather elementary to observe that in the short time that the race has had for reasoning about things, it has been impossible to learn much. But pointing out such fundamentals gives us background, and perhaps modesty. Relative to the total surmisable extent of knowledge, we have advanced very little beyond the level of wisdom acquired by many animals of long racial experience.

We are, to be sure, no longer afraid of strange squeaks in the dark, or completely superstitious about the dead. On many occasions we are valiantly rational. Nevertheless, we now know " how much the unknown transcends the what we know." The unrevealed seriously oppresses us as men of mind. We are tyrannized by the unanswered more than by governmental restraints or social taboos. This tyranny shadows the brightness of the explored realms of nature and of man. To use again the battle cry of the cornered, the war slogan of the ardent social fighter, " Let's do something about it! " Let's exorcise these tyrannical spirits of the surrounding darkness. Let's declare a methodical and elaborate war on the Tyranny of the Unknown.

Already, in our quiet way, most of us are mildly opposing this tyranny. We do it in our spare time, sometimes apologetically, and sometimes with rather brave and hopeful sanction by our institutional chiefs. But, of course, except when we have war-urgency assignments, we do not let the fight get in the way of comfortable living, routine duties, and our ordinary neighborliness.

Now please do not get the impression that I have, with large words, simply advocated the continuity of research. That is not at all what I have in mind. I said " a *methodical* and *elaborate* warfare on the Tyranny of the Unknown."

It is time we quit treating the acquisition of new knowledge as the luxury of a special class, or as the precursor to profit-making new gadgets or nostrums. It is time we quit leaving the explorations beyond the horizons to the long-haired professors and the workers in a few government bureaus. The contest against the tyranny of the unknown is a job for the people of America, if they are going to keep up in the competition with other countries. It is their job if they are planning to participate in either the practical or the idealized progress of mankind. It should be the concern of the businessman, the labor union, the fruit grower, and the farmer. This war can be an affair for the Popular Front, if the proper leaders properly blueprint the campaign.

Practically every community in America that can produce an ensign or a sergeant could produce a boy or girl who could be trained to effective, even if modest, service in these new armies. Once the attack is briefed and the skills are sharpened, finding new facts and checking old interpretations are no more difficult than making an automobile from blueprints, or managing intership communications, or unraveling the mysteries of an income tax form. Yes, certainly the increase and spreading out of scientific and other research is a national concern, and, in making this a national issue, respect for fundamentals need not be sacrificed to the utilitarian. But how far we now appear to be from an aggressive governmental interest in this particular fight!

Over a year ago (on April 19, 1944), the British House of Commons debated " Sir Granville Gibson's motion calling for a bold and generous Government policy towards research. . . . The debate itself ranged over a wide ground, and no scientific worker could desire to have so many of his points made more effectively or trenchantly than was done in its course. The case for adequate remuneration of the scientific worker was pressed even more forcibly than in the House of Lords debate [the preceding July], and the arguments on this point . . . would have seemed incredible in a Parliamentary debate ten or twenty years ago. The credit for this change of outlook must be attributed in no small measure to the work of the Parliamentary and Scientific Committee, the reports of which have done much to prepare the ground for the debate." I am quoting from *Nature* for May 6, 1944. To me it seems that that particular session of Parliament was epochal, not only for science in Western civilization, but for the British Empire.

Can you imagine our own Congress sympathetically and understandingly considering research as a national issue of high importance? Almost inconceivable, you would say; and unfortunately there are smug scientists entrenched in Washington who would say, " Thank God, Congress is keeping out of this." And I fancy that many others would say, " Nonsense — this enlisting of the common people in a war against the unknown! They can't understand research, to say nothing of doing creditable creative work. They would only mess up the profession."

But fortunately only a few scientists feel that the increase of knowledge is for the elite alone. To the rest, I go on to say that we are not yet ready to open the systematic national or international campaign against Enemy Number One. There must be several preliminary preparations, all of which take labor, thought, and time: —

1. The crusade must be sold to the average citizen, through skill-

ful propaganda (or education, if you prefer that term). We must discover appeals to the imagination and the emotions. We need systematic research on the methods of creating understanding and sympathy for research. We must discover the way to make the fight against the tyranny of the unknown a national issue, like good government and individual freedom.

2. Local and national governments must be convinced of the merit of this cause, and of the importance of increasing official support for the mobilization of appropriate forces and resources.

3. The schools and colleges must recognize the importance of producing critical scholars and creative thinkers. They must see that one man fired with curiosity is worth much more than two solid and stolid citizens.

4. The Design for Fighting must be prepared. It must be outlined and published to the collaborating workers. It may require the leadership of a new institution – an Academy of Intellectual Exploration.

Among the citizens of America are several thousand who are the special agents of the people and of the civilization they compose. These agents or servants of society have been trained, mostly at the expense of the public, to know what is known and what is not.

It is to these several thousand servant-thinkers that I now put the question I set out to ask: Would it be advisable and possible to list *in extenso* for each of scores of special fields of knowledge the unsolved problems immediately before us?

The question requires elaboration. The proposed listing would be for technical specialists chiefly – and less directly, or only incidentally, for the non-specialist. Probably in all fields there are many able workers who for one reason or another do not have a grasp of neighboring areas, or even a full picture of their own subject. These workers may be young and as yet inexperienced, or they may be isolated scholars, away from discussion groups or large laboratories and libraries. Important fields often are thoroughly comprehended by only a few intense workers who have favorable temperaments and opportunities, and for such fields even highly competent investigators in adjacent areas are unacquainted with the problems solved and unsolved.

Everybody gains when the obstacles to enriched research – namely, the unclear pictures – are removed. Would not such detailed clarification through problem-listing be worth doing, for the benefit of beginner and professional? What are the immediate unknowns, practical and theoretical, which might be subdued if they were fully recognized and if there were an abundance of thinkers and resources available, in, for example, mammalian anatomy, in atomic structure, in the amelioration of insanity, in regional planning, in pre-Cambrian stratigraphy, in the history of printing devices, in the phylogeny of the anthropoids, in aeronautics, group tensions, meteorology, and the use of leisure?

I visualize a great impetus to research through the methodical listing of the problems. Several biologists and physicists have told me that the project should be both feasible and highly profitable in their own fields. No doubt in economics, sociology, administration, philology, and the like, it would be possible to prepare essays on the detailed problems that should be attacked. The evaluation of the unknowns would perhaps become more personal, and possibly less valuable, the farther one goes from the physical sciences. But surely, in almost any field of the humanities or the social sciences, there would be gain from an attempt to tell the world which unknowns (that time and intense study might liquidate) now seem most to bedevil the advance of knowledge and constructive theory. The various surveys could not well be homogeneous in formulation or presentation; and they need not be, to attain the desired end.

In practice, there would be the danger of narrow or personal views of the major and minor problems. And another handicap is the natural one that a scholar, forgetting his social responsibility, might hesitate to show his cards; he might want to reserve the brightest battles for a test of his own personal valor. He might be selfish. In the natural sciences a worker's connections with industrial research might stop him from presenting in detail some problems that have commercial value.

The campaign to list systematically, and with bibliographic reference, the visible problems in a special field will require the judgment and ingenuity of a leader in that area. Of this I feel sure. The work cannot be done by popular science writers. The big question then arises: Is the light worth the candle? Are the survey of the field, the guidance and acceleration of other investigators, worth the time and effort of the expert? Are we in America still young-minded enough, and socially-minded enough, to work in this way for a common national and human good? Or should we leave dreams such as this to those national groups where there is no hesitation in making five-year plans, social, economic, scientific — and where the plans are carried out and progress made premeditatively toward the transformation of a national culture?

The necessity has come to American scientists and other scholars of taking an active part in searching for intelligent substitutes for war. America and Americans will never retreat to the pre-war sociology and economics; need we retreat to the pre-war indifference of the academic specialist to the national social problems? To me that seems impossible, especially for scientists. There is not an officer or private, among the ten million in the Army and Navy, who does not know that we are winning this war, not alone through personal valor, but very largely because of our superior engineering and scientific activities.

We should be devoid of vision if we did not take advantage of these new contacts with practical science and of the new respect for it.

QUESTIONS

1. Why does Shapley begin his essay with a discussion of the social and material gains of World War II? Identify the tone of the opening sentence of the essay and show how this tone helps to reveal the intention referred to in the previous question. What is the general tone of the first section of the essay?

2. How does the author's emphasis on the immorality of war, in Section II, help to achieve the purpose of the first section?

3. What are the main differences which Shapley mentions between the war against Influenza (Section III) and the wars against the enemies mentioned in Section IV?

4. In discussing " The Tyranny of the Unknown," what distinctions does Shapley make between " the continuity of research " and the kind of warfare he has in mind? What details in this section suggest that " The Tyranny of the Unknown " possesses some of the same characteristics as the first three enemies mentioned?

5. What sort of response does Shapley expect from the reader, near the end of the essay, when he asks, " Are we in America still young-minded enough, and socially-minded enough, to work in this way for a common national and human good? " How does the language of this question help to produce the response which the author intends?

6. At the end of Section II, Shapley says, " In the remainder of this article I hope to incite my readers to consider plans for new martial activities. It will then become clear why I have taken time to consider both the advantages of successful war and the moral and material costs thereof. We shall have standards of comparison." In the light of the remainder of the essay, what " standards of comparison " have emerged?

STANLEY CASSON was a distinguished British archaeologist and for many years a Reader in Classical Archaeology in the University of Oxford. Casson (1889–1944) participated in many expeditions of excavation in the Near East. He served as Assistant Director of the British School in Athens and was Director of British Academy Excavations at Constantinople. In 1933–1934, he was a visiting professor at Bowdoin College in this country. Among his many books, the following list is merely a sampling: *Macedonia, Thrace and Illyria* (1926), *Progress of Archaeology* (1934), *The Discovery of Man* (1939), and *Greece Against the Axis* (1942). He was also a prolific contributor of scholarly articles to various journals of archaeology.

CHALLENGE TO COMPLACENCY

What Future Archaeologists Will Think of Us

by STANLEY CASSON

THE archaeologist has a cold and callous eye. It looks backward to the past and forward to the future and seldom pauses on the present. Walking down Fifth Avenue or Regent Street, I cannot help letting my imagination leap forward a thousand years or so. How, in that remote future, will these wide streets and concrete palaces look? What problems will they hold for the excavator of a new world that has prospered in some distant part of the globe, who has sent his reconnaissance expedition to investigate the enormous mounds, smooth and rolling and grass-covered, that will then mark the sites of capital cities of an almost-forgotten civilization?

You smile! Surely that can never happen, you say. And so smiled the Minoans of Cnossus, the ancient Indians of the vast city of Mohendjodaro in the Indus Valley, and the Mayas in their indestructible palaces of Yucatan. Yet they were forgotten for thousands of years, and only the chance of excavation brought them to light. Of course it will happen to us, yet we live in the unshaken complacency of an immovable belief that we are permanent — like those ancient Agrigentines of whom a Greek once said that " they live as if they were to die tomorrow, and build as if they were to live forever."

When the crash comes and civilization decides to shift elsewhere, when London and New York are as forgotten as was Athens after the fall of Rome, or as Persepolis after Alexander had burned it, how will the change come about by which London and New York are transformed into those delectable grassy hillocks that delight the eye of the prospective excavator?

Of course one must make assumptions. Cnossus or Persepolis did not perish overnight. A mighty sacking or conflagration is not fatal. London in 1666 started at once to recover and rebuild; Cnossus was sacked and ruined, but not reduced to a heap of rubble. Persepolis could have been remade and restored. One must assume certain political and social catastrophes that make it impossible for the inhabitants to return or to remake; some financial breakdown that forbids repair, upkeep, and restoration. And if in the dry and gentle climate of the Mediterranean, or in the dryer but hotter climate of India, several civilizations that in their bloom thought themselves as immutable as rock, as unforgettable as the sun, perished from the memory of man as utterly as if they consisted of mere squalid mud-hut villages, how much more shall London, New York, Paris, or Berlin be reduced to rolling hills of rubble under the impact of a climate that destroys with four times the speed of the climate of the Mediterranean or of India!

For what is the chief enemy of a great city, or, for that matter, of any building, but water? Water that seeps into cracks, water that freezes in those cracks and expands with a slow destructive force as great as dynamite, water that drips its way through ferro-concrete and oxidizes the immortal strength of iron and steel and reduces their power to heaps of red rust.

Let us look ahead. Imagine some devastating European-American war, a war in which the whole world is involved. Neglect grows as all energy is concentrated on the vigor of war. For a period of years there are no repairs done to cities and their buildings, no improvements, no strengthening, no painting of steel girders or refurbishing of stone surfaces. Imagine London or New York as was Vienna in 1919 – paint peeling from walls, plaster cracking, encompassing grime and mildew in holes and crannies and corners. And then imagine a financial crash more desperate, more irremediable than any that the world has suffered in the last few years, a crash from which there is no escape, for the cure of which no Roosevelt appears like a *deus ex machina*. Fortune is not always so obliging as to produce a magician to move every rock, and we must assume an accumulation of rocks with no magician at all.

The financial breakdown is followed by political chaos, political chaos by public insecurity. Out of this chaos only one element will emerge organized, and that is crime. The criminal elements will feed like parasites on a tottering fabric of civilization in a way far more deadly than ever in history, if only because crime can now obtain weapons which make its offensive quality more deadly. Failure of means of communication provides just the conditions most suitable for the growth of criminal organization, which in any case has its own channels of communication. Then famine and perhaps disease reduce the population to a minimum, and so in the end develops a situation in which mass emigration has become a necessity.

The climate of the Northern States of America would force a population thus swiftly deprived of its ordinary means of subsistence steadily to the south, whether to South America or to the Southern States does not matter. But in any breakdown of organized civilization a move to a climate where the essential comforts of a primitive mode of existence are more easily obtainable becomes obvious. And so from a by now barbarized North would move upon a still stable South a horde of people virtually indistinguishable from the barbaric Europeans who moved southward upon the stable culture of the Mediterranean at various periods of history. Thus fell Mycenae and Troy, and thus many attempts were made from the north upon Constantinople, which failed only because of the immensely superior defenses of that city.

A similar situation in England would be less easily evaded by mass movement. For in chaotic conditions the English Channel would prove a tremendous obstacle, only to be crossed by small numbers aided by a few enterprising craft, the property of pirates out for gain. Only the relatively rich would escape, and the remainder would die of starvation far more rapidly than in America; although, on the other hand, the rigors of the climate would not be so fatal to humanity as in America.

Such gloomy prognostications as these rise to my mind when I look at the neat complacent buildings of Regent Street or of the long alleys of New York. Perhaps I am a pessimist, but then I am not such a fool as to imagine that the particular kind of world I live in will go on for more than its fair share of time. Just as the average Londoner or New Yorker is incredulous that his city should not be there ten thousand years hence, so to me it is incredible that it should. And, indeed, London all but faded out of existence after the Roman departure from Britain, while New York faced catastrophe only three years ago! * And the ruins of Palmyra and Baalbek and Luxor cry loudly to the living that they are only leaseholders of property that will, after the 99 or

* The reference is, of course, to the economic depression of the early thirties.

999 or 9999 years' lease is up, revert once more to the ground landlord.

II

BUT let me get down to the grim archaeological details. Let us assume our New York, smitten by its financial catastrophe, its population denuded, its rich rapidly fled, its offices empty, its lovely skyscrapers rising unlit and gloomy at night over the twin waterways, now empty of shipping, silent and dark. A bare million of inhabitants, perhaps, still live on after the general bankruptcy that fell like a plague in the early spring of 2035 A.D. Somehow they live through the hot summer, consuming the accumulated provisions of the city, living on capital. The police, unpaid and without chiefs, have fled, the criminal elements usurp government. A fitful electric lighting service is maintained in a few places, a few automobiles ply at famine prices for traffic. Substantially, New Yorkers know nothing of what is happening outside New York, and very little of what is happening there. Those who were in England during the General Strike in 1926 will remember how the first result of dislocation of all transport was the complete isolation of every city; no one knew what was going on in the country as a whole.

Summer passes and an early winter falls with a crash in November. The population, now without adequate means of heating, perish rapidly from cold and from the ravages of influenza. New York gets emptier and emptier. As winter increases, the rain and sleet come in torrents. Neglected roofs begin to leak, unrepaired walls admit water through their cracks — and then comes a spell of that sub-zero temperature that even at the best of times causes damage and upset. The damp and water freeze to ice which expands with the remorseless strength of destiny. A few walls and houses fall, skyscrapers begin to show defects. The campaniles totter and the pinnacles are unstable. And thus begins that downward movement of a great city that ends in the grassy mounds which lure the eye of the archaeologist.

Slowly but inexorably the façades of towers and palaces flake off and fall to the ground. Round every mansion and every towering skyscraper is a steadily increasing circuit of accumulated fallings and droppings. For there is no one to clear it away or to repair the cracks and crevices. Like a ruthless crowbar of fate the frost peels off the outer cover of many a building and drops it crashing to the ground. In its fall the cover perhaps breaks through the roof of adjacent buildings. More ruin, more accumulations. Neglected water mains and pockets of gas burst the roadways upward into confused heaps. Every pull downward of this dreadful force known as gravity is followed by a convulsion, a push from below, just as if gravity were proving that it can act both ways.

Compared with London, New York would come to a swifter death, for New York is precariously balanced on its smooth rock. What the ice of the Glacial Age smoothed so cleanly into a platform designed for an imperial city, the ice of a post-glacial age, which still comes to sting you with the reminder that it was only a few moments of time ago that the glaciers retreated into Canada, will clear once more of impediments, though this time they will not be swept ruthlessly away, but merely left to crumble.

If you want to see the Glacial Age in New York, get on top of a bus at about 70th Street and ride down Fifth Avenue towards Battery Point. Look along the Avenue and you will see the roadway ahead undulating beautifully and harmoniously; the line of street lamps rises and falls like the rollers of the Atlantic.

The stranger seeing this for the first time is amazed. The more so if he is a Londoner, accustomed to the perfect level line of the lamps of Baker Street or of Oxford Street. Here is as voluptuous a series of curves as ever delighted an Oriental. And those are the curves worn out of your New York granite cliffs by the steady heave and grind of primeval ice in past ages, when the great face of the glaciers dropped its crashing fragments of ice into what is now New York Sound. Thus was New York forged, and the marks of its forging show today in that lovely line of undulating street lamps.

But tomorrow the vestiges of that ancient Glacial Age will clean the rock once more.

And so my dismal story works steadily to its conclusion. Among the shapeless heaps of rubble, concrete fragments, and red stone, amid the almost nightly crashes of falling buildings, there may still stand the vast height of the Empire State Building and the lovely knife edge of the Rockefeller tower. They are built of the most enduring of all modern materials. Yet they will not endure as has the Parthenon, for they have to face rigors of climate that Greece never even dreamed of. No ice or snow worth mention has shifted a stone of the Parthenon; no temperature of twenty degrees below zero, or worse, has driven its wedges into the cracks of any Greek, Persian, or Egyptian building. Nature has let them decline very, very gently.

After most of New York, except the newest towers, has tumbled into ruin, perhaps the twin heights of the two tallest skyscrapers will still remain, but not for very long. Soon their outer cover will flake and fall, and nothing will stand save the central cores of ferro-concrete. Slowly too this will wear and bend. Perhaps the Empire State tower will buckle and fall in one piece of its own weight; the Rockefeller building will come down in segments. But even if they lord it over the ruins for a year or two more, it is only a matter of time before they too are leveled. And where they fall what a grassy mound will rise!

On the rolling hillocks along the furrows that were once Fifth and Sixth and Seventh avenues, and the rest, will rise two vaster hills. The small advance party of excavators who are camped in tents near by will say at once, "Here were the principal palaces of this great capital. Here probably will be found the residence of the Chief of the ancient United States, believed to have borne the name of President. It was apparently an old family, for ever since the eighteenth century the Chieftain has always borne the same family name of President." Ultimately, when their supposed palaces of kings prove to be the Waldorf-Astoria or the Woolworth Building, immense volumes will be written to prove that, after all, America was a republic and not a kingdom, as her ruins might have suggested. The accurate planning of the reception office of the Waldorf-Astoria, the discovery of ancient hotel ledgers in steel safes that have been preserved under immense falls of concrete, and the general equipment of some of these palaces sites will ultimately prove to the world that New York was, after all, run on democratic lines — or at least that the palaces were open to all men.

Along the grassy edge of the New York island my excavators will find the crumbling relics of ancient quays, and in the accumulated mud of the harbor wharves the skeletons of ships. But the great ice jams of the Hudson that have broken through and swept the edges of the island will have left little to find. Their sharp edges will have shaved the outlines of the island almost back again to its Glacial Age contours.

And what of London? Here things will move more slowly, but not less certainly. Instead of a grassy heap of hillocks on a smooth rock, London will end more as an enormous waste of uneven ruins, rather like the vast cities of Turkestan, Merv,* or the ancient towns of the Gobi. But instead of lying gently in preserving sand, London of that distant future will be engulfed in mud and marsh. When the Thames Embankment falls, as it will do in a year or two after the final catastrophe, the tidal Thames will encroach and bite away the soft banks. And the piles of fallen masonry will be more formidable and more massive in some cases than in New York, because buildings like the

* A very ancient region (now called Mary) in the Turkmen Soviet Socialist Republic.

Houses of Parliament are far more solid and more massively constructed than the thinly made and largely hollow skyscrapers. Westminster will revert once again to the island in a marshy shore that it originally was, but on that island will rise a very vast mound of rubble, composed of the Victoria Tower and Big Ben Tower. For the rest, London will be in the main a low stretch of uneven mounds that will be partly sunk in the soft clay soil, while New York will lie above its impermeable rock foundation.

III

THE excavators of both London and New York will have considerable trouble with the enormous underground buildings and subways and tubes that penetrate everywhere. Some years ago, while excavating in Constantinople, I found the task of excavation made more complicated by finding endless systems of water supply. Apparently every third emperor had decided to enhance his reputation by installing new and more efficient water conduits. These we found at every level down to twenty-five feet. In London I can well imagine the chagrin of the excavators as they dig out Piccadilly Circus and get their sectional plans confused by the various Tube stations. And to have to clear the Grand Central Station after it had been completely silted up with mud and debris, and to pass all the earth excavated through a sieve in order to find the priceless documents preserved on the site of the Information Booth, are tasks which make me thankful that I explore only the cities of relatively simple folk.

Just as nineteenth-century history has today become far more burdensome a study than the history of the fourteenth century, partly because the enormous increase of population has produced more interesting individuals and more political and social activity, so the sites of the future will require at least ten times the number of excavators to handle them. Nor will those excavators be able to employ any new inventions for speeding up their excavation. Unfortunately the excavator must in all ages proceed at the speed of pick and shovel and at no faster rate. Nor can he employ any other than these primitive instruments.

In one respect the excavators of New York and London will be fortunate. Virtually all printed books and papers will have vanished as if they had never been. They will no more be found during the course of excavation than are papyri found in the slightly damp soil of Greece. The products of the printing press will have survived only in the dry climates. Perhaps, cynically enough, the only documents to be found during the excavation of London will be the *Codex Sinaiticus* * and other works recorded on tough and almost indestructible vellum. But one will always have to make an exception in the case of such documents as have been kept in safes, for safes will undoubtedly survive for a very long time.

Yet, imagine the reconstruction of English literature of the twentieth century based on the information obtained from safes! It will prove to be a blend of the sort of English to be found on legal conveyances and on the bogus prospectuses of dubiously promoted companies!

But the epigraphist will reap a rich harvest. From the shattered remains of tombstones and foundation stones of public halls and almshouses, from the pontifical inscriptions engraved on bronze tablets on churches, and from the war memorials of various wars, he will compose a disjointed history of our life and times that would freeze our marrow if we could but read it. What fun it will be for the archaeologist to compose lists of aldermen, mayors, and councilors, and attribute to them half the famous reforms of the age! To find stray fragments of Shakespeare and of Abraham Lincoln and of Emerson and of the Bible and of Mrs. Mary Baker Eddy, and to make out of them an anthology of our literature!

And what a task to classify the buildings that will be found! To fix the type of the church, the cinema, the night club, the prison, and the hotel of our day and then to identify buildings according to this classification. I can see the new Publishing House of the Christian Science movement at Boston being labeled as a night club, such is the glory of its interior and its plan; and Westminster Catholic Cathedral in London will probably be identified as a hotel on the lines of the Biltmore, while the Biltmore may be shown to be a church of some luxury sect. What fun it will all be, and what a pity we shall not be there to see!

In the abandoned countryside, things will be different. The more complex a city is, the more rapidly it will decay and fall to ruin. For all the services of a modern city are so interdependent that once one or two of these services fail the whole city is affected. In ancient Rome or Athens there was no municipal lighting or drainage or public health to speak of. If the system broke down, you carried on quite well without it. But today we are utterly dependent on the services of others. And if those others fail us we are helpless.

A modern city is the most vulnerable thing in the world. I have seen two modern cities left stranded and helpless — Salonika and Con-

* A fourth-century parchment manuscript in Greek of the Old and New Testaments, now in the British Museum.

stantinople. The first I saw burned to the ground in 1917, the second I saw in 1918 just after the Armistice. No words of mine can describe the complete chaos in each case.

In two hours Salonika was as helpless as any rubbish heap. After the fire had burned itself out, the masses of fallen masonry and charred ruins were well on their way to becoming a fine archaeological site. So complete was the ruin that the builders of the new Salonika a few years later merely pulled down what still-standing walls there were and leveled the rubbish to one uniform level; on this as a foundation they built their new city, so that today Salonika stands about six feet higher than it did before.

Constantinople in 1918 was a fully inhabited city, but then devoid of any public services for the inhabitants. There was no gas, no electricity except intermittently, no street cleaning, hardly any police, and an unsafe and erratic water supply. Yet the inhabitants somehow managed to survive until the army of occupation had set its engineers to rectify these breakdowns.

Had no one come to help, Constantinople would have died within a very few weeks. There would have been plague, famine, and massacre. Fires would have spread unchecked and crime would have been rampant. As it was, it was a common sight to see in the morning the corpses of those who had been shot by criminals during the night lying in the side streets. Dead horses lay in the gutters sometimes for days. The Turkish police, unpaid for months, could hardly be regarded as trustworthy guardians of law and order. Children starved and disease was rampant. And all this decline had taken place between November 11, 1918, and about December 31, 1918. Indeed, the resistance of a modern city to disintegrating forces is far lower than that of ancient cities, if only because the complexity of modern city life is based on the assumption that catastrophes do not occur. Simpler modes of life do not break down with that devastating swiftness with which our elaborate civilization may topple over the brink to destruction. Constantinople remains in my memory as a nightmare and as a warning. Imagine London or New York deprived of all its public services for a week only, and you will get some idea of the terrible swiftness with which decay will bring the whole organism to destruction.

IV

AND so it is to the countryside that we must look for the survival of some kind of semblance of the old order, when the great metropolitan centres have crashed into ruin. Probably for years after New York and

Chicago and Philadelphia and London and Edinburgh have been rendered uninhabitable the remote farmsteads of Maine and the Middle West and of Yorkshire and Cornwall will still show some kind of regular life and ordered existence. But it will be every farmstead for itself, every village its own master, every man armed, and every unit self-subsisting. The farmers will consume their own grain and their own stock; perhaps there will be a simple method of barter and exchange, though there will naturally be no further use for currency.

Some such state of affairs began to develop in the Caucasus in 1919, when from a chaos of revolution and disturbance there evolved five or six independent republican states, each about the size of a large English county. Each struck its own paper currency, which was not current or acceptable in any other republic. Each lived on its own capital and its own resources. Each was slowly dying, and only when all were incorporated in the Soviet Union did they show signs of renascence, based on a general interchange of commodities and a general discipline imposed by a central authority armed with the force to back it up.

For many years the relics of our old civilization will survive in rural regions and in small units. Slowly these units will become more and more isolated. Such was the condition of England after the Roman departure in the fifth century. Such was the state of affairs in Italy in the Dark Ages of the seventh and eighth centuries. Ancient Roman order existed in England in the Welsh and Cornish hills and moorlands until it slowly flickered out into Saxondom and a new order. Greece after the fall of the Mycenaean world was an aggregation of small units each of which hardly knew its neighbor. The immediate sequel to any universal crash has been this centrifugal tendency. As the great centres radiate an influence of decay and destruction, so the old order drifts toward the periphery, in so far as it is unable to emigrate en masse to some happier world.

The speed with which a fine system of roads will, by neglect and disuse, vanish slowly beneath the surface of the ever increasing and encroaching vegetation is astonishing. I have seen a fine system of roads which was built by the Allied armies in Macedonia gradually perish. For they corresponded, not to the natural requirements of the region, but only to temporary military necessity. Half of them have now almost faded away. Their culverts have broken, their bridges been swept away, their embankments have slipped down. The grass verge has gradually spread toward the centre of the metaling. Miniature ravines have been ploughed through the metaling here and there by torrents of winter rain. The peasants ride on their mules alongside the roadway, not on it, for the hard metaling is too much for the hoofs of their oxen and buffaloes and horses.

So the great Roman roads of Britain slowly sank out of sight and were mostly forgotten. So will the great cement turnpikes and parkways and arterial roads perish in a few years after the great catastrophe of the future.

Only the railways will remain, for the mighty embankments and cuttings have a longer life. Even so, the tunnels will fall in, the embankments will slip, and the cuttings will soon look much as the great Canal of Xerxes, through which he took his fleet, looks today. A few months only would let the Panama and the Suez canals fall into ruin if they are neglected. Many a time I have seen the Corinth Canal with its sides fallen in; the maintenance of it is a whole-time task, and there are constant falls. That small seaway would be rendered useless in perhaps a fortnight if its maintenance services were suspended.

England, after a hundred years of neglect following the great catastrophe, would revert almost to the same condition as that in which it was in neolithic times. The old marsh and forest areas, which then were impassable, and which archaeologists now faithfully plot on their maps, would be swamp and marsh and forest in one generation, and again impassable in two. Packs of wild dogs would rapidly degenerate into wolves, malaria would spread, and human habitations would be driven up on to the moors and downs where they started five thousand years ago. The ancient hill camps would be inhabited once again by melancholy and degenerate agriculturists who would have to eke out their thin crops with hunting. Weapons of the hunt would be as primitive as they were at the dawn of the Iron Age. The isolation of the downlands would make collaboration between settlements almost impossible. Fortification would be as necessary against marauding humans as against wolves.

I once saw a whole valley revert to this condition in a year. For military reasons we had in 1916 to evacuate all the inhabitants from the valley of the Struma in Macedonia. Their villages lay empty and undamaged. Their dogs remained behind and would not follow their masters. In a few weeks these village dogs left their villages and formed packs which lived in holes in the ground and came out at night to steal and kill. So dangerous were they to lonely patrols and isolated soldiers that it became necessary to hunt them down and shoot them. Swamp developed with incredible speed where had once been fertile maize and cotton fields. Malaria throve as it has never thriven before in those parts. Our own army lost 50 per cent of its effectives as a result.

V

FORTUNATELY in all these cases of incipient collapse there has been some organized power to prevent it spreading. But suppose there were no organized power left? Suppose a complete financial disaster robbed the authorities of the means to maintain any power at all!

I do not say that such a fate is imminent at this time in any part of the world, but I am quite certain that another world war would bring about the necessary conditions for collapse and it would be only by a miracle that the collapse would not follow. And a world-wide collapse of administration would entail a disaster compared to which the decline and fall of Rome or of Persia or of Egypt would be but a passing shadow. For the past is ready to leap upon us again. The more modern we become, the nearer we are to a neolithic or even to a paleolithic existence.

A newly created civilization is near enough to its origins to realize and to understand the dangers that surround it. It looks back only a short distance of time and sees and remembers those primitive conditions from which it emerged so recently. And it knows how to avoid the dangers which it has so recently overcome. The first Greek cities were small and easily managed. Intercommunication and association into groups started almost before the cities were built. The sea became the vehicle of communication before the sites were chosen or the colonial enterprises planned. The Greeks, and the Romans after them, built up their civilization solidly and step by step. And so Greece and Rome have not wholly perished yet.

But the Minoans of Cnossus achieved a precocious city life before it was due. At the height of its power, Cnossus perhaps held a hundred thousand inhabitants. War was not feared, because there was no enemy in Crete and none on the high seas worth consideration. And so there were no fortifications at Cnossus and no coastal fortresses. When the enemy came, the whole complex of city life vanished overnight, for the Minoans seem to have been a complacent folk who "built as if they were to live forever."

Today, with armies millions strong and with vast fleets waiting patiently in their harbors for purposes and enemies as yet unidentified, we still sit complacently in our palaces and let events carry us along on the tide. Yet whither the tide is taking us we do not trouble to inquire.

This is not an exposition of the horrors of war; still less is it a pamphlet for pacificism. I am writing a simple prophetic archaeological thesis. I am wondering what our proud cities will look like when curious scholars of a distant future come to collect the materials for the writing of a history of our times. I am enjoying the prospect of sitting on the edge of some furrow that was once East 60th Street or West 44th Street and wondering exactly how true a picture those future archaeologists will paint of the life that was once New York; how far they will be able to reconstruct that marvelous view which could once be seen from the middle of Queensborough Bridge. I am sitting on the top of a rough and high mound beneath which lie the tangled mechanism of Big Ben and the fragments of its brazen bells, and looking across the endless marshes to the North Sea, and I am wondering whether the precise and exquisite " Restored View of the Ancient City of London " will bear any resemblance at all to the London that we know.

I am really inquiring into the capacity of scholarship to reconstruct the past. And if, in the process, I sound a little pessimistic, that need not worry us. For all the great cities of the world pass in due course, only we tend, like the citizens of every city at every age of time, to think that we are immortal, that our metropolitan Babylons will live forever and change gently from generation to generation, growing ever statelier, more magnificent, and more civilized. They may, indeed they may go on forever; but no city has done so as yet, and the present condition of the world suggests that there is little likelihood of a very long life for any capital town or for our particular mode of life.

Again, I insist, I speak purely as an archaeologist. I know nothing of social developments or of political necessities. But I do know for certain that a dozen empires have passed away and a hundred cities vanished in the few thousand years during which man has become *Homo sapiens.* Only when he becomes *Homo sapientissimus* will there be less risk of cities vanishing into dust and of nations bleeding to death for reasons obscure and uncertain. And that *Homo sapientissimus* has at last emerged I see no hint or sign. On the contrary, at the moment there seems to have been a slight retrograde movement; man is *Homo insipiens.** We are hovering on the brink of a precipice, winding round that dizzy path up which we may ultimately reach the peaks of Wisdom, but off which we may so easily topple to destruction. Perhaps we shall meet others on the way, and, disputing the right of way, all fall over together. Perhaps we shall encounter friends who will help us to pull our burdens up the slope.

In any case, don't let us sit primly in our chairs admiring the view up Fifth Avenue or down Regent Street. For in how short a time will

* *Insipiens* means, literally, foolish or stupid.

that view be over rolling green hummocks and reed-grown wastes, with the sea or the river lapping at an empty shore!

QUESTIONS

1. Casson says in Paragraph 6, Section v, that his essay is "not an exposition of the horrors of war; still less is it a pamphlet for pacifism. I am writing a simple prophetic archaeological thesis." Again, in the next paragraph, he writes, "I am really inquiring into the capacity of scholarship to reconstruct the past." What evidence in the essay indicates that these apparently direct statements of aim or objective contain ironical suggestions of a different (or at least an additional) purpose? Show that Casson's intention is revealed as clearly by what he does not say as by what he does say.

2. What mood is evoked in Section II? (See page 80, Question 4 for definitions of mood and tone.) What specific words and phrases of this section contribute to the mood? Make a list of words and phrases in Paragraph 3 of this section which are especially rich in emotional power; then, with the aid of your dictionary, make a list of substitute synonyms which are more neutral in arousing feelings; and by contrasting the effects of the words in your two lists, show how the author's language contributes to his purpose in evoking the mood.

3. In Paragraph 1, Section III, the author anticipates, imaginatively, some of the problems future archaeologists will have in their excavations of London and New York. What is the dominant tone of this paragraph? What attitude toward contemporary civilization does the author reveal in this paragraph? How do the tone and attitude of this paragraph support the purpose of this section of the essay?

4. Using the same techniques suggested above in Question 2, analyze Section IV (and the language of the next to the last paragraph of this section).

5. Make a single-sentence summary of the topic of one section of the essay; then point out the topic sentence of each paragraph in that section (make one up if the paragraph does not contain an explicit topic sentence). Evaluate the resulting outline from the point of view of the author's intention in that section.

Freedom of Thought and Expression

WALTER LIPPMANN

ZECHARIAH CHAFEE, JR.

HOWARD MUMFORD JONES

JAMES S. POPE

GERALD W. JOHNSON

WALTER LIPPMANN, a member of the famous Class of 1910 at Harvard, took his degree a year early; since then he has had a distinguished career as a journalist, editor, and author. He has been Associate Editor of *The New Republic,* Editor of the New York *World,* and since 1931 has written his now famous column for the New York *Herald Tribune* and other newspapers. Mr. Lippmann's widely ranging interests in the fields of politics, diplomacy, morality, and freedom have borne fruit in many articles, essays, and books. Following is a highly selected list of book titles: *A Preface to Politics* (1913), *A Preface to Morals* (1929), *The Good Society* (1937), *U.S. Foreign Policy: Shield of the Republic* (1943), *The Cold War* (1947), *Isolation and Alliances* (1952), and *The Public Philosophy* (1955).

THE INDISPENSABLE OPPOSITION

by WALTER LIPPMANN

WERE they pressed hard enough, most men would probably confess that political freedom — that is to say, the right to speak freely and to act in opposition — is a noble ideal rather than a practical necessity. As the case for freedom is generally put today, the argument lends itself to this feeling. It is made to appear that, whereas each man claims his freedom as a matter of right, the freedom he accords to other men is a matter of toleration. Thus, the defense of freedom of opinion tends to rest not on its substantial, beneficial, and indispensable consequences, but on a somewhat eccentric, a rather vaguely benevolent, attachment to an abstraction.

It is all very well to say with Voltaire, "I wholly disapprove of what you say, but will defend to the death your right to say it," but as a matter of fact most men will not defend to the death the rights of other men: if they disapprove sufficiently what other men say, they will somehow suppress those men if they can.

So, if this is the best that can be said for liberty of opinion, that a man must tolerate his opponents because everyone has a "right" to say what he pleases, then we shall find that liberty of opinion is a luxury, safe only in pleasant times when men can be tolerant because they are not deeply and vitally concerned.

Yet actually, as a matter of historic fact, there is a much stronger foundation for the great constitutional right of freedom of speech, and as a matter of practical human experience there is a much more compelling reason for cultivating the habits of free men. We take, it seems to me, a naïvely self-righteous view when we argue as if the right of our opponents to speak were something that we protect because we are magnanimous, noble, and unselfish. The compelling reason why, if liberty of opinion did not exist, we should have to invent it, why it will eventually have to be restored in all civilized countries where it is now suppressed, is that we must protect the right of our opponents to speak because we must hear what they have to say.

We miss the whole point when we imagine that we tolerate the freedom of our political opponents as we tolerate a howling baby next door, as we put up with the blasts from our neighbor's radio because we are too peaceable to heave a brick through the window. If this were all there is to freedom of opinion, that we are too good-natured or too timid to do anything about our opponents and our critics except to let them talk, it would be difficult to say whether we are tolerant because we are magnanimous or because we are lazy, because we have strong principles or because we lack serious convictions, whether we have the hospitality of an inquiring mind or the indifference of an empty mind. And so, if we truly wish to understand why freedom is necessary in a civilized society, we must begin by realizing that, because freedom of discussion improves our own opinions, the liberties of other men are our own vital necessity.

We are much closer to the essence of the matter, not when we quote Voltaire, but when we go to the doctor and pay him to ask us the most embarrassing questions and to prescribe the most disagreeable diet. When we pay the doctor to exercise complete freedom of speech about the cause and cure of our stomachache, we do not look upon ourselves as tolerant and magnanimous, and worthy to be admired by ourselves. We have enough common sense to know that if we threaten to put the doctor in jail because we do not like the diagnosis and the prescription it will be unpleasant for the doctor, to be sure, but equally unpleasant for our own stomachache. That is why even the most ferocious dictator would rather be treated by a doctor who was free to think and speak the truth than by his own Minister of Propaganda. For there is a point, the point at which things really matter, where the freedom of others is no longer a question of their right but of our own need.

The point at which we recognize this need is much higher in some men than in others. The totalitarian rulers think they do not need the freedom of an opposition: they exile, imprison, or shoot their opponents. We have concluded on the basis of practical experience, which goes back to Magna Carta and beyond, that we need the opposition. We pay the opposition salaries out of the public treasury.

In so far as the usual apology for freedom of speech ignores this experience, it becomes abstract and eccentric rather than concrete and human. The emphasis is generally put on the right to speak, as if all that mattered were that the doctor should be free to go out into the park and explain to the vacant air why I have a stomachache. Surely that is a miserable caricature of the great civic right which men have bled and died for. What really matters is that the doctor should tell *me* what ails me, that I should listen to him; that if I do not like what he says I should be free to call in another doctor; and that then the first doctor should have to listen to the second doctor; and that out of all the speaking and listening, the give-and-take of opinions, the truth should be arrived at.

This is the creative principle of freedom of speech, not that it is a system for the tolerating of error, but that it is a system for finding the truth. It may not produce the truth, or the whole truth all the time, or often, or in some cases ever. But if the truth can be found, there is no other system which will normally and habitually find so much truth. Until we have thoroughly understood this principle, we shall not know why we must value our liberty, or how we can protect and develop it.

II

LET us apply this principle to the system of public speech in a totalitarian state. We may, without any serious falsification, picture a condition of affairs in which the mass of the people are being addressed through one broadcasting system by one man and his chosen subordinates. The orators speak. The audience listens but cannot and dare not speak back. It is a system of one-way communication; the opinions of the rulers are broadcast outwardly to the mass of the people. But nothing comes back to the rulers from the people except the cheers; nothing returns in the way of knowledge of forgotten facts, hidden feelings, neglected truths, and practical suggestions.

But even a dictator cannot govern by his own one-way inspiration alone. In practice, therefore, the totalitarian rulers get back the reports of the secret police and of their party henchmen down among the crowd. If these reports are competent, the rulers may manage to remain in touch with public sentiment. Yet that is not enough to know what the audience feels. The rulers have also to make great decisions that have enormous consequences, and here their system provides virtually no help from the give-and-take of opinion in the nation. So they must either rely on their own intuition, which cannot be permanently and continually inspired, or, if they are intelligent despots, encourage their trusted advisers and their technicians to speak and debate freely in their presence.

On the walls of the houses of Italian peasants one may see inscribed in large letters the legend, "Mussolini is always right." But if that legend is taken seriously by Italian ambassadors, by the Italian General Staff, and by the Ministry of Finance, then all one can say is heaven help Mussolini, heaven help Italy, and the new Emperor of Ethiopia.

For at some point, even in a totalitarian state, it is indispensable that there should exist the freedom of opinion which causes opposing opinions to be debated. As time goes on, that is less and less easy under a despotism; critical discussion disappears as the internal opposition is liquidated in favor of men who think and feel alike. That is why the early successes of despots, of Napoleon I and of Napoleon III, have usually been followed by an irreparable mistake. For in listening only to his yes men – the others being in exile or in concentration camps, or terrified – the despot shuts himself off from the truth that no man can dispense with.

We know all this well enough when we contemplate the dictatorships. But when we try to picture our own system, by way of contrast, what picture do we have in our minds? It is, is it not, that anyone may stand up on his own soapbox and say anything he pleases, like the individuals in Kipling's poem * who sit each in his separate star and draw the Thing as they see it for the God of Things as they are. Kipling, perhaps, could do this, since he was a poet. But the ordinary mortal isolated on his separate star will have an hallucination, and a citizenry declaiming from separate soapboxes will poison the air with hot and nonsensical confusion.

If the democratic alternative to the totalitarian one-way broadcasts is a row of separate soapboxes, then I submit that the alternative is unworkable, is unreasonable, and is humanly unattractive. It is above all a false alternative. It is not true that liberty has developed among civilized men when anyone is free to set up a soapbox, is free to hire a hall where he may expound his opinions to those who are willing to listen. On the contrary, freedom of speech is established to achieve its essential purpose only when different opinions are expounded in the same hall to the same audience.

For, while the right to talk may be the beginning of freedom, the ne-

* The reference is to "L'Envoi," by Rudyard Kipling (1865–1936); the poem may be found in *Rudyard Kipling's Verse, Inclusive Edition* (1892, 1893, 1899).

cessity of listening is what makes the right important. Even in Russia and Germany a man may still stand in an open field and speak his mind. What matters is not the utterance of opinions. What matters is the confrontation of opinions in debate. No man can care profoundly that every fool should say what he likes. Nothing has been accomplished if the wisest man proclaims his wisdom in the middle of the Sahara Desert. This is the shadow. We have the substance of liberty when the fool is compelled to listen to the wise man and learn; when the wise man is compelled to take account of the fool, and to instruct him; when the wise man can increase his wisdom by hearing the judgment of his peers.

That is why civilized men must cherish liberty — as a means of promoting the discovery of truth. So we must not fix our whole attention on the right of anyone to hire his own hall, to rent his own broadcasting station, to distribute his own pamphlets. These rights are incidental; and though they must be preserved, they can be preserved only by regarding them as incidental, as auxiliary to the substance of liberty that must be cherished and cultivated.

Freedom of speech is best conceived, therefore, by having in mind the picture of a place like the American Congress, an assembly where opposing views are represented, where ideas are not merely uttered but debated, or the British Parliament, where men who are free to speak are also compelled to answer. We may picture the true condition of freedom as existing in a place like a court of law, where witnesses testify and are cross-examined, where the lawyer argues against the opposing lawyer before the same judge and in the presence of one jury. We may picture freedom as existing in a forum where the speaker must respond to questions; in a gathering of scientists where the data, the hypothesis, and the conclusion are submitted to men competent to judge them; in a reputable newspaper which not only will publish the opinions of those who disagree but will re-examine its own opinion in the light of what they say.

Thus the essence of freedom of opinion is not in mere toleration as such, but in the debate which toleration provides: it is not in the venting of opinion, but in the confrontation of opinion. That this is the practical substance can readily be understood when we remember how differently we feel and act about the censorship and regulation of opinion purveyed by different media of communication. We find then that, in so far as the medium makes difficult the confrontation of opinion in debate, we are driven towards censorship and regulation.

There is, for example, the whispering campaign, the circulation of anonymous rumors by men who cannot be compelled to prove what they say. They put the utmost strain on our tolerance, and there are few who do not rejoice when the anonymous slanderer is caught, exposed, and punished. At a higher level there is the moving picture, a most powerful medium for conveying ideas, but a medium which does not permit debate. A moving picture cannot be answered effectively by another moving picture; in all free countries there is some censorship of the movies, and there would be more if the producers did not recognize their limitations by avoiding political controversy. There is then the radio. Here debate is difficult: it is not easy to make sure that the speaker is being answered in the presence of the same audience. Inevitably, there is some regulation of the radio.

When we reach the newspaper press, the opportunity for debate is so considerable that discontent cannot grow to the point where under normal conditions there is any disposition to regulate the press. But when newspapers abuse their power by injuring people who have no means of replying, a disposition to regulate the press appears. When we arrive at Congress we find that, because the membership of the House is so large, full debate is impracticable. So there are restrictive rules. On the other hand, in the Senate, where the conditions of full debate exist, there is almost absolute freedom of speech.

This shows us that the preservation and development of freedom of opinion are not only a matter of adhering to abstract legal rights, but also, and very urgently, a matter of organizing and arranging sufficient debate. Once we have a firm hold on the central principle, there are many practical conclusions to be drawn. We then realize that the defense of freedom of opinion consists primarily in perfecting the opportunity for an adequate give-and-take of opinion; it consists also in regulating the freedom of those revolutionists who cannot or will not permit or maintain debate when it does not suit their purposes.

We must insist that free oratory is only the beginning of free speech; it is not the end, but a means to an end. The end is to find the truth. The practical justification of civil liberty is not that self-expression is one of the rights of man. It is that the examination of opinion is one of the necessities of man. For experience tells us that it is only when freedom of opinion becomes the compulsion to debate that the seed which our fathers planted has produced its fruit. When that is understood, freedom will be cherished not because it is a vent for our opinions but because it is the surest method of correcting them.

The unexamined life, said Socrates, is unfit to be lived by man. This is the virtue of liberty, and the ground on which we may best justify our belief in it, that it tolerates error in order to serve the truth. When men are brought face to face with their opponents, forced to listen and learn and mend their ideas, they cease to be children and savages and begin to live like civilized men. Then only is freedom a reality, when men may voice their opinions because they must examine their opinions.

III

THE only reason for dwelling on all this is that if we are to preserve democracy we must understand its principles. And the principle which distinguishes it from all other forms of government is that in a democracy the opposition not only is tolerated as constitutional but must be maintained because it is in fact indispensable.

The democratic system cannot be operated without effective opposition. For, in making the great experiment of governing people by consent rather than by coercion, it is not sufficient that the party in power should have a majority. It is just as necessary that the party in power should never outrage the minority. That means that it must listen to the minority and be moved by the criticisms of the minority. That means that its measures must take account of the minority's objections, and that in administering measures it must remember that the minority may become the majority.

The opposition is indispensable. A good statesman, like any other sensible human being, always learns more from his opponents than from his fervent supporters. For his supporters will push him to disaster unless his opponents show him where the dangers are. So if he is wise he will often pray to be delivered from his friends, because they will ruin him. But, though it hurts, he ought also to pray never to be left without opponents; for they keep him on the path of reason and good sense.

The national unity of a free people depends upon a sufficiently even balance of political power to make it impracticable for the administration to be arbitrary and for the opposition to be revolutionary and irreconcilable. Where that balance no longer exists, democracy perishes. For unless all the citizens of a state are forced by circumstances to compromise, unless they feel that they can affect policy but that no one can wholly dominate it, unless by habit and necessity they have to give and take, freedom cannot be maintained.

QUESTIONS

1. In the last sentence of the opening paragraph of the essay, Lippmann uses the phrase " substantial, beneficial, and indispensable consequences." What differences of effect are produced by substituting synonyms for these words?

2. In the last paragraph of Section I, Lippmann refers to " the creative principle of freedom of speech." Identify this principle and outline the particulars of Section I which support it.

3. Why, according to Lippmann, is mere toleration of differing views not the same as real freedom of speech?

4. What distinctions does the author make in Section II between " incidental " rights and " the substance of liberty "?

5. In the next to the last paragraph of Section II, Lippmann distinguishes between self-expression as one of the " rights of man," on the one hand, and examination of opinion as one of the " necessities of man," on the other. Why does he emphasize this distinction?

6. According to the final section of the essay, what is the nature of the compromise without which freedom cannot be maintained?

7. Through a consideration of the specific details and the generalizations which they support, evaluate the success (or failure) of the author in achieving his principal purpose in the essay.

ZECHARIAH CHAFEE, JR., a native of Rhode Island, held degrees from Brown University and Harvard Law School, as well as several honorary degrees from various institutions. In 1916 Chafee (1885–1957) became a member of the Harvard law faculty, and in 1950 he became one of Harvard's University Professors. He served on committees of the American Bar Association and the United Nations, and was a delegate at the United Nations conference in Geneva in 1948. Among his significant books are *Freedom of Speech* (1920), *The Inquiring Mind* (1928), *Free Speech in the United States* (1941), *How Human Rights Got into the Constitution* (1952). "The Encroachments on Freedom" appeared subsequently as a chapter in his last book, *The Blessings of Liberty** (1956).

THE ENCROACHMENTS ON FREEDOM

by ZECHARIAH CHAFEE, JR.

WE HAVE been passing through very troubled years since Germany and Japan surrendered. Instead of returning to a happy period of unbroken homes and business as usual, for which everybody longed, we had to face almost immediately the threat of Communist power abroad, which broke into actual and protracted fighting in Korea. This unceasing tension in foreign affairs was aggravated by fears of Soviet sympathizers in our midst. It is not surprising, therefore, that influential persons and groups have urged various kinds of abridgments of liberty.

Were these sacrifices of freedom planned wisely? Did they really lessen the dangers from disaffection in the United States? Or were these restrictive measures often adopted in careless haste or out of personal vindictiveness and thirst for popularity? Such questions must be asked. The great ideals and traditions of liberty are in the Constitution because Englishmen and American colonists thought and worked, decade after decade, and were ready to risk prison and death. Shall we abandon them blithely?

In considering civil liberties in this country, I audaciously look forward to a future by no means wholly black. The recent segregation cases in the Supreme Court have begun the destruction of the last legal barriers against citizens who have a strain of color not white. The eventual disappearance of legal differentiations based on race or color will come not only by judicial nullification and legislative repeals but also — what is more important — through notable alterations in public opinion. Common sacrifices in war and other disasters and the experience of working and living together will make Americans regard themselves increasingly as a single people.

Other tangible rights acquiring greater solidity are those giving a fair trial to all persons who have to stand before judges and juries and face the possibility of being punished for crimes. Convictions obtained by mobs dominating the courtroom no longer stand. The Supreme Court has recently strengthened the right to counsel; and provisions for defenders paid out of taxes or community chests are making it easier to obtain a reputable lawyer without great pecuniary sacrifices. The presence of a lawyer in the courtroom greatly increases the practical value of all the constitutional rights of a prisoner on trial.

Abuses of an accused person's rights before trial such as the brutality called the "third degree" are likely to diminish with the striking progress in police organization and police methods. Even prolonged questioning of a person in custody may be subjected to more regulation.

I find much more cause for apprehension, however, when I think of the more subtle freedoms proclaimed by the First Amendment — those concerned with our believing, our thinking, our expression of our thoughts by voice and print, and our association with others to exchange or promote ideas.

Freedom of religion now appears safe for any man who holds any variety of faith, at least when it does not make it immoral for him to go to war. But what about the atheist or agnostic? The men of fluid beliefs who participated in the Constitution intended to protect him too. Although a churchman myself, I regard it as vital to our national life that a man's right to hold public office should never be affected by what he believes about his relation to the totality of being. The law may remain as now, but in practice atheists and agnostics are sometimes virtually ineligible as candidates for election or appointment to public office. Though no statute is likely to require church membership as a qualification for teachers in public schools, the same result can conceivably be attained by determined school committees.

When we go outside religion, freedom of thought and discussion about controversial issues will, I expect, have to be defended against frequent incursions for many years ahead. In our fear of domestic Communists and our eagerness to identify heterodoxy with spying and sabotage, we have developed vague legal concepts like "subversive" and "disloyalty" which will trouble us for a long time to come. Our present national policy of driving Communists underground will spread suspicion into new quarters.

Disputes about the proper ways to deal with radicals in our midst are largely caused by a sharp divergence of opinion about the extent of the danger. One group thinks the country to be in great peril. The other group has confidence in the heartfelt devotion of the American people to our form of government and in their ability to sift good ideas from bad ideas through their own intelligence and common sense without needing legislators and officials to do that job for them. Both groups are obliged to form their opinions without knowing badly needed facts. The basic question in every program of laws against domestic radicals is: How big a danger do they create, beyond what can be met by the ordinary processes of reasoning by voice and print? It is high time that some authoritative group of dispassionate persons gave us a trustworthy answer to that question.

II

WITHOUT expressing any judgment as to whether or not they were required by national safety, I shall list briefly several of the encroachments on the ideals of freedom of speech, press, and assembly which have taken place since 1945. I shall ignore issues of constitutionality. My only purpose now is to show what is going on.

McCarran Act

In 1950 Congress passed the Mundt-Nixon Bill, usually called the McCarran Act. It sets up a body of officials called the Subversive Activities Control Board, which on finding that groups have specified objectionable purposes can order them to register with the Attorney General and incur very disagreeable legal consequences. This law goes far beyond Communists. The machinery of the McCarran Act operated so slowly that, when nobody had registered by 1954, Congress jumped over the heads of the Board and, by the Communist Control Act, decided that the Communist Party of America had to register and made it an outlaw.

Aliens

Aliens are more and more made deportable by Congress for what they have said, or because of ideas expressed not by them but by other men in groups they have joined. It makes no difference how long an alien has been in this country or how deeply he has put down his roots. The laws began by throwing out anarchists and Communists, but since 1945 many new categories of objectionable ideas have been added.

The vital decisions are all made by government officials. These laws apply the same tests of orthodox thought to temporary visitors as to prospective settlers. Over and over again we have harmed ourselves by making it hard for distinguished scientists and scholars to obtain visas in order to give Americans the benefit of their knowledge in our universities and scientific conferences.

Passports

Officials can lock the frontier on both sides. They frequently deny American citizens a passport, which is indispensable for going to Europe but has been considered to be a gracious favor from the State Department, to be withheld whenever the Department did not like a man's mind. Recently the prospective traveler has been able to get help from the courts, if he wants to use the crowded weeks between engaging his passage and boarding the steamer for a lawsuit and pay a lawyer some of the money he had been saving for the Alps and Italy.

Books and magazines

The frontiers have also been closed by officials against books and magazines. The Customs Bureau has managed to by-pass the valuable law of 1929, which was intended to end its long practice of destroying at will whatever imported books and art it chose to consider indecent. It transferred the control to the courts and thus made possible Judge Woolsey's famous decision admitting Joyce's *Ulysses.* Afterwards the Treasury referred to Huntington Cairns, the secretary of the National Gallery in Washington, all cases where exclusion was possibly required by law. His wise rulings have been so satisfactory to all parties that it was unnecessary to call on the courts. Now, however, the customs officials have joined forces with the postal authorities and, with very dubious statutory authority, are freely seizing incoming material which is neither obscene nor revolutionary, simply because they think it undesirable " political propaganda " for Americans to read.

Investigations

Congressional investigations into radicalism were occasionally conducted after 1917 but became continuous in 1938 when the House Committee on Un-American Activities was organized. In 1945 it was changed from a special into a permanent committee. Hopes that the Senate was repelled from imitating what was going on in the House have been dashed since the end of the war. Indeed, the Senate now has two committees busy unearthing radicals. The Subcommittee on Internal Security in the Judiciary Committee seems adequate to guard the nation against real dangers, but that is not the view of the Permanent

Subcommittee on Investigations of the Senate Committee on Government Operations. This committee (until 1952 entitled Expenditures in the Executive Departments) is charged with all proposed legislation and other matters relating to budget and accounting measures (except appropriations); examining reports of the Comptroller General; studying the operation of government activities at all levels with a view to determining its economy and efficiency; reorganizing the legislative and executive branches; and studying intergovernmental relationships between the nation and states or municipalities, and between the United States and international organizations. One would suppose that these vast ramifications of public affairs would give the committee a gigantic task, but it prefers to spend much of its time investigating workers in private factories and teachers at Harvard.

These three congressional investigating committees have received more attention in the news than any other method by which our government has been restricting freedom of expression by American citizens, either singly or in groups. Some of their work has been devoted to the Communist Party and real Communists, but a great deal to so-called Communist-front organizations, subversive individuals, fellow travelers, and so on. For example, the most flamboyant and widely publicized hearings were held at Washington in October, 1947, to investigate the motion-picture industry. Representative Rankin, the moving force, spoke of "the loathsome, filthy, insinuating, un-American undercurrents that are running through various pictures." A notable film, *The Best Years of Our Lives,* was condemned because a banker hesitated to give a loan to a veteran (who eventually got it). If an occasional misleading radical photoplay gets past the gantlet of producers, banker pressure, the Hays-Johnston Office, and the Catholic Legion of Decency, will the harm be very great? We need creative art, not controlled art. Leave that to the U.S.S.R.

No doubt, bodies which hold so many sessions as these three committees do must occasionally run across something of value, but the voluminous press reports are mainly concerned with their resemblance to circuses and publish very little carefully considered information from them about the extent of the Communist danger. The impression is left that a large amount of the money of American taxpayers has been spent fishing in dirty waters for cast-off rubbers and battered tin cans.

The book-burnings

In the spring of 1953 the State Department, at the behest of staff members of a Senate investigating committee, took hundreds of books out of our very serviceable Information Libraries in foreign cities and junked them, not because of anything these books said, but because their authors were alleged to be subversive. It was considered perilous for foreigners to read books like Alan Barth's *The Loyalty of Free Men* and Dashiell Hammett's *The Maltese Falcon,* a thrilling crime story as remote from politics as Sherlock Holmes. While the State Department was thus alienating European lovers of liberty, President Eisenhower told the students at Dartmouth, "Don't join the book-burners." It is good to have a President who does not preach what his subordinates practice.

Loyalty programs

The loyalty and security-risk program came into extensive operation in April, 1947, through an executive order by President Truman. It called for every federal official to be investigated by the FBI and his superiors, so that disloyal or untrustworthy persons might be weeded out of the public service. There was a good deal to be said for screening men in sensitive positions like work for the Atomic Energy Commission, but the job did not stop there and it did not stop with possible Communists. Everybody had to stand before the searchlight and let it play over his whole life, his opinions, his family and friends, the books and magazines he read, and the opinions he held. Thus when it was discovered that the mother of a bootblack in the Pentagon had given $10 to the Scottsboro Defense Fund before he was born, seventy interviews by the FBI were required to find him worthy to shine the shoes of army officers.

After immense work and the outlay of millions of dollars, a very small percentage of the total number of officials were dismissed and the rest were cleared. Yet there were grave doubts whether the program had accomplished either of Mr. Truman's declared objectives in his order, that "[1] maximum protection must be afforded the United States against infiltration of disloyal persons into the ranks of its employees, and [2] *equal protection from unfounded accusations of disloyalty must be afforded the loyal employees of the government.*"

Mr. Truman's opponents showed no confidence whatever in the first objective. When Mr. Eisenhower came to the White House, he issued a different order and then pretty much the whole thing was gone through again. And some of the best men in public service have felt that the government is slighting the second objective of "protection from unfounded accusations of disloyalty." Dr. Vannevar Bush, the head of the Office of Scientific Research and Development in World War II, told the House Government Operations Committee in October, 1954, that the security-risk program had demoralized the scientific community and hindered the nation's program of research into weapons. He testified that the mutual respect between the military services and the scientific community achieved during World War II has been "almost destroyed, and one of the primary reasons was the security system." He added that although scientists are still continuing to serve the military department, their morale is so low that they are doing the job "without enthusiasm and without fruitful inspiration. They go on working, but they feel that they are not welcome; that they are regarded with suspicion; that some of the men who led them through the war are now being questioned and their security and loyalty are in doubt."

Apart from important questions as to procedure of the loyalty-security program, the main point for the government and the public to remember is that any possible risk from retaining a man who has performed good service in the past is not the sole consideration; it should always be balanced against the sure loss his dismissal will cause, by cutting off his future contributions to the national welfare. Most of the reasons given for denying J. Robert Oppenheimer access to classified information about nuclear physics related to events in his life before 1941. If the men who ousted him from public service in 1954 had been exercising authority at the time of Pearl Harbor, there would have been no danger from Dr. Oppenheimer and the United States would not have won the race for the atomic bomb.

The current satisfaction of politicians over the number of federal employees who have been dismissed for disloyalty is badly misplaced if in a considerable fraction of those cases the charges were improperly proved or insubstantial and the government has thrown out honest citizens. Somebody ought to count the number of devoted public servants who have resigned in disgust. Nobody can count the much larger number of able men who have decided not to enter government departments during the years since the loyalty-security program began because, as is the way of able men, they prefer to be part of an enterprise which is built on trust.

Subversive organizations

The Attorney General's list took shape under President Truman as an auxiliary to the loyalty-security program: —

Activities and associations of an applicant or employee which *may be considered* in connection with the determination of disloyalty *may include one or more of the following:*

> . . . f. Membership in, affiliation with or sympathetic association with any foreign or domestic organization, association, movement, group or combination of persons, designated by the Attorney General as totalitarian, fascist, communist, or subversive, or as having adopted a policy of advocating or approving the commission of acts of force or violence to deny other persons their rights under the Constitution . . . or as seeking to alter the form of government of the United States by unconstitutional means.

Although the executive order made this list only one piece of evidence against an official, it is not so treated in the administration of the loyalty program; instead it usually raises a prima-facie case of his disloyalty. Moreover, the list was compiled only to guide this federal program, and yet it has been widely employed by states and cities and even by private organizations as proof of the disloyalty of teachers and employees. The radio industry has accepted it as a basis for canceling the contracts of its performers. The list has accordingly become a powerful weapon for injuring any group there named or any individual who belongs to such a group.

Nevertheless, the reliability of this list is seriously undermined by the fact that most of the organizations on it were singled out by government officials as they pleased without giving the organization any notice or any hearing. Thus there was no chance for the heads of a group to state objections, to offer evidence, or to examine the Attorney General's evidence and argue against its trustworthiness or value.

Since the Attorney General's list is my only point of personal contact with contemporary restrictions on freedom of speech, some firsthand information may not be out of place. Occasionally somebody calls me a member of the Citizens Committee to Free Earl Browder, which is on this list as Communist. Hence I am said to be a bad security risk, next door to a Communist. Here is what happened. Around 1941, some people whose names I have forgotten wrote asking me to sign a petition to Attorney General Biddle for Browder's release from prison. I replied that I would not sign it because it said that Browder ought not to have been convicted. He had lied to his government on a passport application, and I believe that a citizen ought to tell the truth to his government. However, I thought four years in prison a very severe punishment. Browder had already served over two years, which seemed to me tough enough. I never knew Browder, but I was reliably informed that he was not a violent revolutionary and that his release would help our relations with the Soviet Union, then our ally, which were in a ticklish state. So I sent these views in a personal letter to Francis Biddle, whom I knew, who, as Attorney General, was charged by the Constitution with the duty of advising the President on legal matters. I do not know whether Mr. Biddle mentioned my request to Mr. Roosevelt; but I do know that the President, under Article II, section 2, of the Constitution, has "Power to grant Reprieves and Pardons for Offenses." And President Roosevelt did pardon Browder. If this be treason, make the most of it!

State laws

Thus far I have dealt only with restrictions by the national government on freedom of thought and speech. Meanwhile, the legislatures of numerous states have been imitating Congress by passing all sorts of anti-Communist laws and setting up their own investigating committees. It is an important question whether the time has not come for state legislatures to give up concerning themselves with subversive activities and entrust the whole matter of the safety of the nation to the government of the nation. Obviously, nobody has the slightest chance of overthrowing the government of Massachusetts by force and violence unless, at the same time, he succeeds in overthrowing the government of the whole United States. Although Senators and Representatives with large powers to cut down our fundamental freedoms are a serious cause for anxiety, the petty imitators who follow in their train are even worse.

Objectionable ideas

Combined national and state attacks on objectionable ideas have produced a mass of restrictions which reach into almost every human activity. Loyalty oaths have been required of candidates for election, occupants of public offices, teachers in public schools, labor union officials bargaining under the Wagner Act, students in state colleges and universities, applicants for unemployment compensation, and prospective jurors. California requires such oaths from all institutions seeking exemption from taxes. Congress has excluded from federal housing projects "a person who is a member of any organization designated as subversive by the Attorney General," and thousands of occupants have been required to furnish certificates of non-membership. One court had difficulty in seeing how the efforts of subversives would be combated "by compelling them to live in slums."

Pennsylvania denies poor relief to persons actively seeking to change the form of government by unconstitutional means, perhaps thereby making unhelped paupers see the benefits of the existing system. California tried to prohibit the use of public schoolhouses by "subversive" groups, though opening them for other meetings. The Georgia Board of Education allows local school authorities to revoke, perhaps for life, the license of any teacher who supports the idea of non-segregated schools or agrees to teach in such a school. In 1953 the legislature of Alabama and Texas required all school textbooks to bear certificates stating that the authors were not Communists or ex-Communists and whether they had belonged to an organization on the Attorney General's list. Any schoolboy in Louisiana who advocates the violent overthrow of the government will be expelled.

Recently, after Albert Sprague Coolidge, Harvard chemist and skilled amateur musician, had been asked to succeed his mother as trustee of a fund for chamber music which she had given to the Library of Congress, the appointment was withdrawn for security reasons. Because he had joined years ago an organization opposed to the totalitarian dictatorship of Franco, his judgment on string quartets might be infected with disloyalty.

As a striking example of what is going on, a doctor was suspended from practicing medicine in New York because he had served six months in jail for failing, on advice of counsel, to produce papers to the House Un-American Activities Committee relating to the activities of his organization in rescuing and healing victims of the totalitarian government of Spain. So the New York State authorities reduced him to idleness for six months more. The highest court in New York and the Supreme Court of the United States were helpless to give him relief. But Justice Douglas observed: —

> So far as I know, nothing in a man's political beliefs disables him from setting broken bones or removing ruptured appendixes safely and efficiently. . . . When a doctor cannot save lives in America because he is opposed to Franco in Spain, it is time to call a halt and look critically at the neurosis which has possessed us.

III

THE zeal of those in power to protect the nation from ideas they detest has imperiled more than the First Amendment. It has weakened great policies which underlie several other parts of the Constitution.

The strongest safeguard of human rights in the Constitution is the habeas corpus clause. It protects the liberty of the person by usually enabling a judge to release an imprisoned man at once, unless he has been convicted or ought to be held to stand trial for a crime. Thus it prevents officials from jailing anybody because they think he might possibly commit a crime someday. The Constitution specifies only two emergencies which will justify the suspension of habeas corpus — " Rebellion or Invasion." The McCarran Act of 1950 by-passes this clause. It produces the effect of suspending habeas corpus by allowing American citizens who have committed no crime to be shut up in a concentration camp in any war, even if it be a localized conflict thousands of miles from our shores without the slightest danger of an invasion.

The President and the Attorney General can imprison any person "as to whom there is reasonable ground to believe that [he] probably will engage in acts of espionage or sabotage" or will conspire with others for that purpose. Other officials can review this decision, but there is very little likelihood that any court can reverse it. In 1942 civil and military officials tore scores of thousands of American citizens of Japanese descent from their homes because, so the officials asserted, they might commit sabotage and spying. Yet "not one person of Japanese ancestry was accused or convicted of sabotage after Pearl Harbor while they were still free." Here is a sample of official reasoning: "The very fact that no sabotage has taken place to date is a disturbing and confirming indication that such action will be taken."

Officials whose minds work like that will easily find a "reasonable ground to believe" that anybody whose views they happen to dislike is a potential spy or saboteur.

In the Fifth Amendment, we are departing from the tradition that no person shall "be twice put in jeopardy" for the same offense. Technically, of course, the clause applies only to criminal prosecutions. Still, the human values are just as great when any other serious penalty is involved. You get a happier civilization if a man who has been forced to go through a grueling legal proceeding in order to keep his job can say, after being acquitted of wrongdoing, "That's over," and then go back to untroubled work. Serenity is impossible if he knows that he may have to rebut the same charges and go through all the agony again, perhaps even many times. Yet that is the situation under the loyalty program. Nobody is ever really cleared. In a recent case reported to the Hennings Committee, a naturalized Austrian was dismissed by the State Department for close association with his wife, although he had been cleared on substantially the same charges the year before. This man had been officially cited for standing up under Nazi tortures, from which he escaped through barbed wire. There is no lasting escape through red tape.

We have been creating a new kind of second-class citizen out of naturalized Americans. More and more they are denaturalized and then deported. The final step was to strip citizenship from native-born Americans. In 1954 Congress turned everybody convicted under the Smith Act * into a Man Without a Country.

* The Alien Registration (Smith) Act of 1940 makes it a crime 1) to teach or advocate the overthrow of any government in the United States by force or violence; 2) to organize, or help to organize, any group advocating such violent overthrow; 3) to become a member of such a group "knowing the purposes thereof."

Finally, where the radical opinions of citizens and their affiliations are concerned, we are abandoning the American ideals of a fair trial, proclaimed by the Sixth Amendment. Of course, it begins " In all criminal prosecutions," and hence its provisions are not constitutionally applicable to congressional investigations or the loyalty program. Nevertheless a loyalty board can deprive a public employee of his livelihood, and a congressional committee frequently takes away a man's good name and perhaps his job too. These consequences may be worse than a fine or a jail sentence. Conclusions which are so damaging to a citizen ought to be reached with the utmost care to determine the truth.

Proper safeguards for a fair trial are embodied in the Sixth Amendment. They are essentials of decent procedure in any inquiry which may result in punishment. Consequently, even though this amendment is not binding in a departmental or legislative inquiry, it is wise that the same essentials should be substantially observed in order to prevent unfairness and grievous mistakes.

Two principles in the Sixth Amendment are especially desirable in departmental or congressional inquiries into a man's loyalty. First, he ought " to be informed of the nature of the accusation." Many trials before the Star Chamber and other groups of bishops and royal officials show the intensity with which our ancestors objected to answering roving questions. Second, it is of the highest importance that the suspected man should " be confronted with the witnesses against him." Perhaps the most besetting sin in non-judicial trials is for the deciding officials to make use of information which is not communicated to the person whom they have power to condemn. For instance, in the Dreyfus* case the army officers on the court-martial read secret army papers which were kept back from Dreyfus.

One important benefit from confronting the suspect with his accusers is the opportunity to cross-examine them and rigorously test any dubious statement. Add to that the old-fashioned value of putting people face to face out in the open. An honest witness may feel quite differently when he has to repeat his story looking at the man whom he will harm greatly by distorting or mistaking the facts. He can now understand what sort of human being that man is. As for the false witness, the tribunal can learn ever so much more by looking at him than by

* Alfred Dreyfus (1859–1935), a Jewish officer in the French army, was convicted in 1894 of betraying military secrets and was condemned to imprisonment on Devil's Island. His conviction became a *cause célèbre* and those who believed him innocent (like Émile Zola, who wrote a pamphlet, *J'Accuse,* in 1898, attacking the conviction) finally got the first trial annulled in 1899. Dreyfus was retried and condemned again, but was soon pardoned. In 1914 he was declared innocent and completely exonerated.

reading an FBI abstract of his story. The pathological liar and the personal enemy can no longer hide behind a piece of paper.

No doubt, police are helped by concealment of the names of the men who supply evidence used by congressional committees and loyalty boards. Still, the question is whether official secrecy excuses unjust condemnations. No such excuse for hiding spies and taletellers will be listened to by a judge in a criminal prosecution. Either the informant must take the stand and be cross-examined, or what he said cannot be used in the trial at all. Is an inquiry which may take away a man's lifetime job or his good name really different?

My great confidence in the American people, in their love of liberty and their good sense, makes me believe that their fit of tantrums about disloyalty among our fellow citizens will end before long. Even though relations with the Communist countries continue strained, as seems probable, we may appreciate the advantages of a united nation and stop increasing suspicion of one another. And, in government as in any sensibly run business, we may learn to trust the judgment of the men who select officials and the wisdom of the superiors who are in close contact with the work of subordinates day in and day out. Once more we shall be content to meet bad talk not with force but with plenty of good talk. The blessings of liberty, though weakened, are ours if we want them, to hold and make strong.

QUESTIONS

1. Why does Chafee believe that the future of civil liberties in this country is not wholly black? What specific aspects of civil liberties give him cause for apprehension?

2. Note carefully what Chafee says in Paragraph 1, Section II. What kind of response does Chafee hope to create in the reader by such statements as the concluding sentences in Paragraphs 4, 6, 7, 8 and 9, in Section II? Do these statements constitute expressions of judgment? Are there other statements in this section which are intended to create similar responses?

3. What evidence is there in Section II that Chafee's statement in Paragraph 1, that his " only purpose now is to show what is going on," is an understatement?

4. In what specific ways does Chafee believe the loyalty program abandons the American ideals of a fair trial?

5. What reforms in the loyalty program does Chafee imply are necessary?

HOWARD MUMFORD JONES. For biographical headnote, see "Undergraduates on Apron Strings" on page 12. "How Much Academic Freedom?" was adapted from a lecture that Jones gave to the students at Wellesley College.

HOW MUCH ACADEMIC FREEDOM?

by HOWARD MUMFORD JONES

UNIVERSITIES have been under attack for many reasons in many times. They have been attacked for religious heresy, for economic heresy, for poltical heresy, for moral heresy, and for philosophical heresy. Across the years they have been thought to be centers of atheism, free love, materialism, sectarianism, pedantry, and ignorance. The creative artist looks down upon the humanistic scholar, who seems to him to reduce art to learning and joy to dreary discipline. The businessman, stern, practical creature that he is, inclines to regard professors as dreamers, except on those occasions when he wants something from them, or when he discovers that they have led his son or his daughter into an independent intellectual life differing from his own. Religious persons are also frequently critical of the colleges — institutions, they think, where one loses one's faith; places which deny the possibility of belief; centers no longer dominated by theology and no longer dedicated to the service of the Lord. Mothers are fearful about the morals of their daughters, and fathers are fearful about the companions of their sons. In short, when one considers the variety of persons who find fault with the colleges, it is wonderful that these wicked institutions survive — not only survive, but increase in numbers and importance as the decades go by.

The kinds of faultfinding I have enumerated are familiar; and though they do occasionally seriously interfere with the life of the college, though the makers of these complaints have now and then managed to reduce legislative appropriations or diminish the gifts of alumni or hamper the trustees or even, on occasion, get professors fired, experienced administrators know how to deal with these patterns. The threat to the good life of an academic institution by the use of, or the withholding of, funds is something the colleges and universities can, I think, manage on their own. When Mr. Frank B. Ober of Maryland wrote to President Conant of Harvard some four years ago that he would not subscribe to the Law School Fund unless Mr. Conant got rid of two members of the Harvard faculty Mr. Ober did not approve of, Mr. Grenville Clark, then a member of the Harvard Corporation, wrote a lengthy reply, from which I quote because it seems to most of us in the colleges to state the plain sense of the matter.

Said Mr. Clark: "I want to add a comment on your decision not to subscribe to the Law School Fund. As Mr. Conant wrote you, it has happened before that subscriptions have been withheld because of objections to the acts or opinions of professors or because of disapproval of University policy. This is natural and normal, I think; and it is certainly the right of anyone not to aid an institution with which he is as out of harmony as you now seem to be with Harvard. But it is also true, I am sure you will agree, that Harvard cannot be influenced at all to depart from her basic tradition of freedom by any fear that gifts will be withheld.

"An interesting test case on this point," continued Mr. Clark, "came up during the first World War. It related to Professor Hugo Münsterberg, who was a German and very pro-German, and is described in Professor Yeomans' biography of President Lowell. It appears that the press reported that a certain Harvard man had, in Professor Yeomans' words, 'threatened to annul a bequest to the University of $10,000,000 unless Münsterberg was immediately deprived of his professorship.' Thereupon Professor Münsterberg wrote [a letter] to the Harvard Corporation offering to resign if the graduate would immediately remit $5,000,000 to the Corporation. The Professor's letter was returned and the Corporation issued, as Professor Yeomans puts it, 'one of its rare public pronouncements,' as follows: 'It is now officially stated that, at the instance of the authorities, Professor Münsterberg's resignation has been withdrawn, and that the University cannot tolerate any suggestion that it would be willing to accept money to abridge free speech, to remove a professor or to accept his resignation.'"

II

TODAY the colleges and universities are again under attack — a severe attack, extending over years and reaching from the University of Washington and the University of California on the Pacific coast to New York University and the New York municipal colleges on the Atlantic seaboard. The substance of the attack is nothing new. It is alleged or whispered or surmised that the colleges are the breeding places of radicalism; that many, or most, or some, or one of the professors is a Communist, or a proto-Communist, or a crypto-Communist, or a fellow traveler.

Proof, when it is offered, tends to be of three sorts. The first kind appears when the teacher confesses that he has been a member of the Communist Party — no one, I think, has so far admitted to being a member of the party now. The second is that a former Communist testifies that Professor So-and-so was, or is, a member of the party, or was, or is, sympathetic to its aims. The third is a little more difficult to state, but it arises from a series of inferences. From lists of organizations and names not commonly available to the public, it is inferred that Professor So-and-so now belongs, or has belonged, to one or more of the seven hundred organizations listed by the attorney-general of the nation as subversive — I take my figure from hearsay, and cannot be sure of the exact total except that it is too large to have meaning. Therefore Professor So-and-so is a radical.

Or else it is alleged that because Professor So-and-so by public utterance has declared, or seemed to declare, a likeness of view between his own opinions and the opinions or programs of these organizations, or of the Communist Party, he must therefore be either a secret member of the party, or tantamount to a member, or — a rather unflattering third alternative — a fool; that is, an impractical, dreamy person who doesn't know the facts of life and is drawn into subversive or allegedly subversive organizations innocently. There has always been a lurking suspicion that teachers, queer fellows that they are, are a radical group; and this suspicion has been confirmed in the minds of some observers by the fact that now and again, among the witnesses appearing before one or another investigating committee, teachers have appeared. I may say that inasmuch as Communism seems to find its best breeding ground in areas of economic insecurity, and since on the whole teachers are economically insecure, the surprising thing to me is not that there are a few teachers who are Communists, but that they are so few. I think it a great tribute to the patient patriotism of a much maligned profession that this is so.

A second observation seems to be pertinent. As nearly as I can make out from the figures of the Bureau of the Census, there were in 1952 about 1,200,000 teachers in the United States, not counting teachers in schools for the blind, reform schools, stenographic schools, and other schools not a part of our formal educational system. We do not know the present size of the American Communist Party, but I have seen estimates that allot it 40,000 members, which is high, and others of 20,000, which is low. In April the FBI estimated the membership of the party at 24,796. Let us say the number is 30,000. I think it a fair guess that the Communists would be happy if they could find 500 teachers among this number. I doubt that the number is that high, but I may of course be wrong. But even if 500 teachers in the United States were members of the Communist Party, they would amount to only one twenty-four hundredth of our total teaching staff. I cannot regard this as a very frightening situation.

But perhaps the situation is frightening. Perhaps teachers are trembling on the verge of becoming the radicals legend paints them as being. How likely is this?

I have been a college professor all my life. I have taught in about twelve states of the Union. I am also a member of various national organizations of teachers and scholars, so that I am reasonably well informed about American college professors. I think I can testify that the professors are very much like the rest of the population except in two particulars: their professional training and their rather conservative social views. I think there may be a connection between these two attributes. The training of scholars and scientists, by and large, tends to make them cautious in judgment; and though I do not say there are no radicals or neurotics or visionaries among them, they are not as a group any more visionary than are other Americans — for example, businessmen, some of whom have seriously consulted fortunetellers, or invested their money in Florida real estate, or suffered mental breakdowns, or run off with the stenographer, or argued seriously that you can simultaneously increase your trade with the rest of the world and also boost tariff barriers. I do not seem to read about college professors going to jail in the proportion in which I read about politicians or gamblers or — dare I say it? — businessmen going to jail. They do not customarily falsify their income tax returns. They do not usually go on binges with wild, wild women. When they have a vacation, they do not spend it on soapboxes in Columbus Circle in New York City inciting laboring men to riot; they do not conceal bombs having time fuses in the local post office, despite their professional knowledge of chemistry; and they have not as yet taken to assassinating their opponents. They spend their free time in the Christmas recess soberly attending professional conventions almost as dull as the conventions of the national salesmen of this or that, and they commonly spend their summers teaching or writing a book.

It is true there is a vague, floating fear they have been indoctrinating somebody with something. I have not observed any large companies of little Republicans or little Democrats, little Communists or little Fascists, pouring out of anybody's classroom. Sometimes I think that what the profession needs is instruction in the technique of indoctrination — life would be simpler if teachers were more successful in getting their goods across the counter. Meanwhile I find it difficult to see that radicalism has in any dangerous way taken root in the profession.

III

THE other preliminary matter I wish to touch upon is this: that the investigating committees do not in theory wish to interfere with something they call academic freedom. I say " in theory " because some of the investigating committees, especially those set up by some of the state legislatures, seem to regard academic freedom as a false front erected by hypocritical professors. So-and-so is a Commie, isn't he? Away with him! The taxpayers are footing the bill, aren't they? They gotta right to hire and fire, haven't they? Off with his head! And I am extremely sorry to say that some boards of trustees and some college presidents have by their actions endorsed this summary proceeding.

Fortunately the present chairman of the House Un-American Activities Committee has taken an opposite view. Whether as a result of public pressure (as some allege), or because he sees that you cannot possibly secure good teaching from an intimidated profession (as it is nobler to believe), he has been careful to make it clear that his committee does not desire to investigate classroom procedures. He does not want to damage academic freedom. And other members of the committee take the same position. In examining Professor Robert Gorham Davis, Congressman Clardy expressly stated this: ". . . we will at no time attack teachers as teachers, schools as schools, churches as such, nor any of the other groups."

It is, however, also — and regrettably — a matter of record that other chairmen and other members of committees, senatorial, congressional, or legislative, have not been thus scrupulous about academic freedom. Appearance before one of these committees is not a court procedure — the witness, as one of the members of Congressman Velde's committee said, is not on trial — and the consequence has been in the past, at any rate, that the committee has done pretty much what it pleased. The tone and nature of its procedures inevitably vary from witness to witness and from session to session.

It was not so long ago that some notes were literally snatched out of the hands of a very distinguished scientist while he was testifying before such a committee. It is probably also true that legislative committees of investigation, of which we have had examples in Washington, California, Illinois, and other states, have not always shown the courtesy and intelligence of Congressman Velde and his associates.

Some witnesses, it is true — including, I regret to say, teachers — have proved recalcitrant and roused the ire of the committee; and some committee members — including, I regret to say, Senators of the United States — have been rather unscrupulous, not only in their examination of witnesses, but also in subsequent statements to the press.

In most cases the friendly witness before an investigating committee seems not to have endangered his professional career. But the witness who, for whatever reason, refuses to answer any and every question put to him by some member of an investigating body is in a very different situation. If he attempts to draw around himself the protection of the Fifth Amendment, which says, among other things, that no one "shall be compelled in any criminal case to be a witness against himself," three things happen. In the first place he puts himself, so to speak, into the midst of a criminal proceeding, whether he intended to or not, by the very fact that he has claimed the protection of the amendment, a protection that mostly concerns the Federal courts. It is also to be noted that appeal to this amendment has not always protected the witness.

In the second place, despite the legal maxim that guilt is by no means to be inferred from appealing to the amendment, popular opinion does infer guilt, so that the witness sustains serious damage in the community.

And in the third place, and most important matter of all, many boards of trustees and many college presidents have now taken the view that the professor's plain duty is to answer the questions of the committee and that failure to do so is grounds for dismissal from the teaching post. They have, in other words, substituted their official consciences for the private conscience of the witness.

Now it is likely that there are cases wherein witnesses have taken refuge in the Fifth Amendment for hypocritical reasons, just as criminals have taken refuge in it for hypocritical reasons. But I am sure that other teachers called before investigating committees have suffered agonies of conscience in the effort to determine what is right and what is wrong — that is, ethically right or wrong. Some have taken the line that, since they are no longer members of the Communist Party, they are justified not only in confessing their own past acts, but also in implicating others. Some have taken the line that although they were quite willing to answer questions concerning themselves, they had no moral right to implicate others, especially in view of the powerful emotions the charge of Communism evokes today. And some, after studying the history of these committees, the history of court cases growing out of testimony before such committees, and the confused state of legal opinion concerning the rights and duties of witnesses, have decided that the only safe thing for them to do, both with respect to themselves and with respect to their obligation to other persons, was to refuse to answer any question, or at the least any leading question, put to them by the committee. Such persons have usually been guided by the advice of counsel; and it should be said to the credit of the present congressional committee that its members have encouraged witnesses to consult counsel before answering important questions.

Unfortunately, the advice of counsel, however respectfully treated by the investigating committee, has had little effect upon trustees and presidents who have incontinently discharged professors or suspended them, despite the fact that they were following legal advice. Presidents and trustees who have done this have in fact said by their actions that they were wiser than counsel before the committee. This seems to me both a shocking and an arbitrary act. It means that the witness does not have even the protection extended him by the committee which has encouraged him to seek counsel and to follow it. Let me say flatly that I see no justification in law and none in ethics for such procedure.

Indeed, it is here, and not in the mere response of witnesses to the committee questions, that the true threat to academic freedom lies. This is, in fact, more than a threat to academic freedom. It goes deeper. I am alarmed by the common acceptance of a situation in which responsible and intelligent administrators not only place the morality of the state above the rights of private conscience, but go beyond the state in depriving witnesses both of their immediate jobs and of any prospect of future jobs in the profession for which they have been trained. Without prejudice to any witness who has appeared before any committee — and these witnesses may, indeed, have been speaking as much from conscience as those who refused to answer particular questions — the situation thus developed by administrators inevitably puts a premium upon the informer and penalizes him who does not believe it right to endanger the fortunes of other persons in the profession.

If the state were in any real danger because of the infiltration by Communists into the teaching profession, there might be some pragmatic reason for insisting upon this rigid duty to the state. We are, fortunately, in no such dilemma. It is not pretended by the congressional committee, for example, that there is any real danger to American education. The committee members, or some of them, have expressly said the committee does not propose to investigate teachers as teachers. They have said that they do not intend to investigate schools as schools.

So far as my reading goes, no testimony yet elicited before any investigating committee has indicated that any attempt has been made to indoctrinate any body of pupils or students in the classroom. The investigations are understandably confined to discovering who the members of the Communist Party are and what they do, or have done, as party members. If there is any clear and present danger to education as such from the Communist Party, no investigator has made it clear that the danger is clear and present.

In saying this I do not deny that the American Communist Party would gladly seize the government if it could, but the immediate question does not concern this large issue; the immediate question is the relation of these investigations to academic freedom in the United States.

IV

ACADEMIC freedom, it is agreed, is a precious possession. It is so precious a possession that the congressional committee wishes to protect it; so precious that the American Association of University Professors wishes to protect it; so precious that even presidents and boards of trustees deny they are violating it – and yet professors get fired or are suspended, even though they follow sound legal advice when they appear before the committee.

What is really alleged by administrators is not that the offending instructor is romantically a conspirator against the peace and dignity of the United States; what is usually now said is that, by virtue of being a member of the Communist Party, the offending instructor has a closed mind and is therefore no longer fit to teach.

This is very attractive doctrine. It carries considerable weight and immensely simplifies the administrative problem. It gives the administrator a great moral advantage, and takes every advantage, both moral and intellectual, away from the man who is fired. He has no possible retort. If you are classified as belonging to a category of citizens whose minds are closed, it is clear that you do not belong in the academic community, where minds are supposed to be open. But I strongly infer from my own experience and observation, after a lifetime of teaching, that the first criterion of an open mind is not to make absolute statements about men.

The one sure fact in the general uproar is that very few persons are going to admit to being Communists. What, then, is the administrator to do, if he is to avoid closed minds? There is, of course, the loyalty oath; but if anything is clear from experience with loyalty oaths, it is that they do not automatically produce loyalty. Or is the administrator to refer every teaching appointment to the FBI? I imagine the FBI would be the first to complain. Or shall he hire some private detective agency paid out of college funds donated by the alumni?

Moreover, it is not merely the known Communist (if you can discover him) who is to be denied appointment because he has a closed mind; it is the potential Communist who is not going to be hired – that is, anybody upon whom somebody else can, as we say, hang something. Even the conservative New York *Times*, in the articles on education which appear in its Sunday issues, recently noted how the intellectual life of our campuses has declined in vigor with the growth of investigations into education, government, science, and what not. Students, especially as they near the time they must go into the army or into employment, find it is a whole lot wiser not to express dangerous thoughts. Fear of being suspected of leanings towards the left has closed the mind and shut the lips of youth in our time. As a young friend of mine was told the other day by an older student: "Don't join anything – then they can't get you into trouble ten years from now."

The simple principle that you can, a priori and arbitrarily, distinguish a whole class of persons whose minds are permanently closed on all subjects, and set them apart from other persons, whose minds are not closed, seems to me so mischievous a principle, so laden with eventual disaster, that I vigorously dissent from it. Here, as in other areas, circumstances alter cases; here, as in any other crucial problem of academic life, the individual case must be studied; here, as in all matters of appointment and promotion, we must take into account the totality of components in the personal problem – professional training, teaching skill, personality, promise. It is this coming back to the individual and studying him in his professional context that has made the American college or university a great institution as compared with what it was when, for example, economic or theological orthodoxy was made the primary test for teaching in the universities.

How quickly we forget! As late as 1897 President Andrews of Brown was forced to resign because he had a closed mind on the gold standard. It is true, he was later reinstated, whereas Dr. Weinberg of the University of Minnesota, acquitted of perjury by a trial jury in March, has been informed that he will not be reinstated because he refused to co-operate with Federal authorities! What good is acquittal in such cases if the academic world refuses to recognize the implication of law?

What *is* academic freedom? Whatever it is, we shall not nourish it, we shall not protect it, by laying down the rule that such and such persons are unemployable by reason of their past associations or their present interests. We shall neither nourish it nor protect it by exalting the morality of the state above the morality of the individual conscience. We shall not nourish it, we shall not protect it, by assuming that all members of a party we hate are wicked and evil persons. We shall not nourish it, we shall not protect it, by abandoning, even in this day of the cold war, the traditional wise doctrine of toleration for persons whose views we detest and whose practices are almost invariably wrong. Annoying as Communists are, baffling to the democratic process as their tactics have proved, right though it be to trace out and bring to publicity their devious ways, I for one rest defiantly upon the great paragraph of Mr. Justice Holmes in his dissenting opinion of 1918, when five Russian-born Communists were sentenced to imprisonment for distributing leaflets in New York City – leaflets which a majority of the Supreme Court found to be incentives to bring about a change of government by force and violence. Justices Brandeis and Holmes could not agree that there was any clear and present danger in this act, and Mr. Justice Holmes wrote these memorable words: –

"When men have realized that time has upset many fighting faiths, they may come to believe even more than they believe the very foundations of their own conduct that the ultimate good desired is better reached by free trade in ideas – that the best test of truth is the power of the thought to get itself accepted in the competition of the market, and that truth is the only ground upon which their wishes safely can be carried out. . . . I think that we should be eternally vigilant against attempts to check the expression of opinions that we loathe and believe to be fraught with death, unless they so imminently threaten immediate interference with the lawful and pressing purposes of the law that an immediate check is required to save the country."

I am not persuaded by anything I have read or know that the presence of a few Communists among the teaching profession in this country constitutes an emergency; I cannot agree that the refusal to incriminate one's self before an investigating committee is *per se* proper ground for wrecking the professional life of a teacher, however foolish I may think he is; and I only regret that I cannot put my faith into more impressive words. Unless some unforeseen turn of events should alter the present posture of affairs, I believe that long-run wisdom in the United States is to leave reason free to combat error.

QUESTIONS

1. How is the topic of the opening paragraph developed? What word in the last sentence adds a touch of irony? In the Harvard incident what does the withholder of funds imply about his own understanding of educational policy? What, exactly, was the result which the university officials wished to avoid?

2. In Paragraph 6, Section II, how does Jones' defense of teachers develop into an attack? Of what does Jones appear to be skeptical in the next paragraph?

3. Section III mentions for the first time the issue of " academic freedom." How does Jones make the transition from the threat of communism to this issue? In Section III, what does Jones list as three results of a teacher's invoking the Fifth Amendment? Why does he give special attention to the third result? In this connection, note particularly the last five paragraphs of this section.

4. In connection with the " closed mind " in Section IV, examine Paragraphs 2, 3, 5, and 6. Why is the last sentence of Paragraph 3 a significant one? How is the point made in Paragraph 5 related to the discovery and dissemination of truth?

5. Jones does not formally define academic freedom. What meaning of the term is implied in the last two paragraphs of the essay? Which phrases are especially helpful in suggesting a definition?

6. Is the purpose of the author mainly intellectual, or emotional? Does he rely wholly on reasoning and evidence? Would a professor, a college president, or a chairman of an investigating committee probably be angered by the criticism?

JAMES S. POPE, a native of Georgia, attended Emory University. For fourteen years, starting in 1926, he served as reporter, city editor, and managing editor of the Atlanta *Journal,* and from 1940 to 1952 was managing editor of the Louisville *Courier-Journal.* Among the journalistic distinctions he has achieved are the Elijah Lovejoy Fellowship (1952) and the Distinguished Service Fellowship of Sigma Delta Chi (1953). Having served for several months in the Office of Censorship in Washington (1943–1944) and having been chairman of the Committee on Freedom of Information which he mentions in the following essay, he is well qualified to discuss the suppression of news.

THE SUPPRESSION OF NEWS

by JAMES S. POPE

IF ONE condition for a democracy can be set ahead of all others, it is this: the people, being the rulers, must receive complete and accurate information. But within the past year a sharp and critical disagreement has been found to exist between the country's newspaper editors and the officeholders who contrive much of its news. How much should the people know?

Of course, every newspaperman is used to a nominal tussle over news that reflects some discredit on elected or employed public officials — whether they operate in the city hall, the county courthouse, the state capitol, or in Washington. If the story is going to make the governor or the mayor or the county judge, or the major general, squirm with embarrassment, then the reporter expects to dig a little harder than usual to get it. This is a conflict as old as government and news of government.

But the conflict has gone far beyond that simple ceremonial. Only recently have most editors begun to realize that these familiar little guerrilla skirmishes now are part of a broad-scale offensive against freedom of information — against the basic principle of the citizen's right to know, so that he may govern himself.

The truth is that many men in office now propagate a contrary creed, which holds that it is dangerous for news of government to leak out in any natural, unprocessed form. The fountainhead of this cult is Washington, but devotees dot the land.

No concept in our ideology is more important and more widely misunderstood than Freedom of Information. It is not by any means Freedom of the Press. It is an implication, but little more, of that primary freedom. The right to publish journals of news without government interference was guaranteed in the First Amendment. Freedom of the Press exists. It is tangible, dynamic, well protected in general by courts and by public opinion.

But Freedom of Information is just an idealistic first cousin. It is a hope. If we forget it for a while, it can be stolen away, because it has never been nailed down. It is chiefly an inference; an inference that if the Founding Fathers wanted government to keep its hands off the press, they expected that government to be conducted openly. Otherwise, a free press would be unable to serve its intended purpose.

Few public officials would dare challenge Freedom of the Press, yet they can weaken and perhaps eventually destroy it if they are allowed to strangle Freedom of Information. The truth is that we can have a completely legalistic Freedom of the Press and at the same time lose a vital part of the information which gives this freedom any meaning. We can lose it through a combination of guileful concealment and coloration by public servants, and just plain apathy among the workers of the press.

In the ultimate, Freedom of Information is just about this: the freedom to fight for it. This conclusion, coupled with a warning that it is past time to start the fight, was presented to the American Society of Newspaper Editors a few weeks ago by its Committee on Freedom of Information. This committee could not escape learning how widespread curtailment of information has become. It received appeals for aid against secretive officialdom from papers large and small; from the little editor being denied basic information by his police chief to the big editor who got bruised by the Bureau of Internal Revenue.

The committee is still carrying on a heavy correspondence with scores of editors and public officials, probing, discussing, expounding, disputing. Out of this exchange, two significant factors in the war for knowledge have assumed clear shape. They are new factors in several respects, but certainly in the sense that they have far outgrown their image in the public mind. One is the spreading philosophy that the inside man, the head of a department or agency, knows better than anyone else what the public should be told, and must screen his records accordingly. The other is the technique of news control itself, which now enlists more than 50,000 workers in the Federal Government alone. This is a competent estimate. *Editor & Publisher* said in its issue of April 7, 1951, that the exact number of publicity agents in the Federal

Government is not known, and that the Bureau of the Budget had declined the job of finding out unless given a special appropriation from Congress.

If it is questioned whether these twin forces really are new, a good witness is Harold L. Cross, the noted newspaper lawyer who has been retained by the A.S.N.E. to make the first comprehensive survey of laws and decisions affecting access to public records. He said in his interim report: —

> This Society . . . had well served the profession of journalism for a quarter of a century before need arose to create a committee with the prime function to strike down barriers to access to public records and proceedings. For a decade longer I practiced newspaper law without encountering a serious case of refusal of access. Now scarcely a week goes by without a new refusal. The last five years brought more newspaper lawsuits to open records than any previous twenty-five.

II

THERE is just cause for concern, not only about the national government but about the grass roots of state and community news. The Governor of Arizona became worried about criticisms of his Land Commissioner and asked the Attorney General to investigate. The Attorney General's report so moved the Governor that he fired the Land Commissioner; but he refused to let the *Arizona Daily Star* or any other representative of the public take a look at the report. The state claimed this report was not a public record, though it was made by, on, and to a public official. The *Star* took up the challenge and is still fighting for a court decision which will pry open this official secret.

There has been trouble in New England. A public school board has a peculiarly vital public function, yet the board in Torrington, Connecticut, repeatedly denied admittance to its meetings or access to its minutes to a reporter for the Waterbury *American*. Court action forced the minutes out, but it may well be asked: In what atmosphere of medieval repression does a public body reside when it compels its public to go to court to obtain basic information?

The trouble is that many small papers do not have the resources, the self-confidence, the legal assistance needed to fight successfully for news rights that are denied by men of influence in the community. Not all editors by any means are in a position to antagonize a board of education. That is why the battles which are fought and won are so important: they go into the record and into the psychology of free information.

Yonkers, New York, offers the interesting problem of what is meant by "vital" when dealing with vital statistics. The City Clerk does not consider them vital to the people of the community. Marriage licenses, especially, are guarded jealously by the Clerk. In March the *Herald-Statesman* complained editorially: —

> We find that in January the City Clerk's office issued a total of 123 marriage licenses. The number published by the Herald-Statesman (all the paper could get) was 63. In February, the official total was 40; our total for publication was 15. This means that 62.5 per cent of the marriage licenses were withheld from the public last month.

In Norwich, Connecticut, the Police Commission decided to close its records. The Norwich *Bulletin* learned of a car theft, recovered the car, and printed a story about it before the police had admitted that a car was gone. This is known as the Page One method of breaking up news blocks, and requires no wasted time in court. The police commissioners had red faces and soon hoisted a white flag.

Direct defiance of secretive practices is almost invariably effective. The Iowa State Tax Commission issued regulations that reporters must file requests for information in writing, and all department heads must submit the material to the commission for approval before release. Such delaying actions, which frequently survive the timeliness of the news, are greatly cherished by such commissions. The avowed purpose was to ensure that "the public be correctly informed."

Led by Kenneth MacDonald, Executive Editor of the Des Moines *Register and Tribune,* Iowa newspaper editors protested to the commission that "the effect of your order will be to establish news censorship over all the activities of an important branch of our Government." The Commission Chairman proposed a conference "to develop a satisfactory and adequate press policy," to which Mr. MacDonald astutely replied: "I feel the proper course is to do away with the rules instead of conferring about them." They were done away with.

The Supreme Court of Rhode Island in, as Harold Cross put it, "its second opinion redolent of musty technicalities," dismissed a proceeding in which the Providence *Journal* has for more than two years sought access to the most public of all information: tax-abatement records in the city of Pawtucket. It took a resounding decision of a federal court, which ignored the musty technicalities and went back to the freshness of the Bill of Rights, to break the barrier. But Pawtucket has appealed this decision.

Now let it not be assumed that the enemies of free information are tongue-tied, unable to explain and justify their tampering with the structure of American freedom. Reasons are given for most secrecies. In the Pawtucket case for example, a member of the City Council declared: —

> No Republican councilman will repudiate The Providence Journal because The Providence Journal and the Republican Party are synonymous. As long as there is a fighting Democrat left in Pawtucket we will fight The Providence Journal Company.

The Attorney General of Michigan, Stephen J. Roth, is another public servant who understands why information is concealed; and he explained it with some eloquence to a Michigan Editorial Conference: —

> I think the less concern you have with what you are entitled to under the law the better off you're going to be; because I think you'll discover or have discovered in your experience that public officials unless they are interested in political suicide are going to be pretty circumspect on letting you take a good look at what public business is being conducted.

The virtues of candor are understood also by Jim Hagerty, guardian of information in Governor Dewey's office. When asked at a New York State Associated Press meeting if one purpose of off-the-record conferences was not to tie up news, he replied "Oh, sure." The "when" is as important as the "what" to the manipulators of information. If reporters get too close to a story the executive considers premature, he gives them part of it "off the record," thus damming the news until he is ready to open the gates himself. Besides off-the-record conferences, the tools of control include handouts (the Hoover Commission put the cost to the Federal Government, for research and printing of booklets and bulletins, at $74,829,000 in 1946; current estimates are over a hundred million), directives, regulations (which enforce secrecy without statutory authority in many cases), classifications, executive meetings at which the press is barred, and similar devices.

III

THERE are many sincere and competent men in the huge information force in Washington, but not many refute the axiom that no man is going to release data which will displease or discredit his boss.

Among Washington correspondents, there is remarkable agreement about the departments that do a good information job and those which do not. Of course, their opinion is not beyond challenge. Many correspondents are too lazy to check deeply into stories, and they admire government employees who give them enough to satisfy the home office.

But for what it is worth, a recent survey among some Washington reporters turned up a general endorsement of the Department of Agriculture as having the best information service in the Capital. Compliments were plentiful for the Departments of State and Defense (though both of them suppress vast quantities of information for inadequate reasons). The Justice Department and the Bureau of Internal Revenue won the unpopularity awards. They are wrapped in mantles of inviolability, partly woven by an indulgent Congress and partly self-created. They dislike inquiries and habitually rebuff them.

As one correspondent summed it up succinctly: "Justice: this joint is lousy. It's worth your life to try to pry anything out of officials there. The same goes for the Bureau of Internal Revenue." And the same goes, by general agreement, for the Reconstruction Finance Corporation in recent years. It is no accident that R.F.C. has bred some scandals; secrecy almost invariably breeds them.

The burgeoning executive departments and agencies within the District of Columbia have increased their employees since 1930 from 71,237 to 173,662. In that time, the Washington press corps has increased too; but most of the newcomers have been in the processing field — those who write or broadcast news and comment — rather than in the news-digging field. The miners are still greatly outnumbered. For that reason, dependence on handouts has increased to an alarming extent. It may be that newspapers have far too few reporters to hope to cover all the recesses where news can be hidden. It is a danger the press must acknowledge.

All federal offices have constantly before them an inspiring example of news control. The citizens of that lovely village on the Potomac not only cannot vote; they cannot look while their masters, appointed by Congress, transact what elsewhere would be called public business. The Commissioners of the District of Columbia are not required, as is practically every city council in the free world, to hold open sessions — so they hold them in secret. Outside the Iron Curtain, Washington is one of the few world capitals where the right of the people to know is scorned.

Some federal agencies have created vast areas of secrecy with the blessing of statutes, but many others make their own ground rules as they go.

The Louisville *Courier-Journal*, interested in the parole from a federal prison of a Louisville character who had been serving a term for income-tax fraud, asked the U.S. Board of Parole for the names of the endorsers of the parole. Apparently these good citizens were willing to help a friend but did not want their friendship known. The Parole

Board refused the information. When the A.S.N.E.'s Committee on Freedom of Information asked for a reason, the board relented and supplied the names. Then George G. Killinger, chairman of the board, wrote: —

In the future . . . desired information will be supplied if, in our opinion, such information is compatible with the welfare of society.

Now that is a ringing phrase, but a very foolish one. The men who created our free institutions put no such restrictions on information, designated no guardians of the public mind. Mr. Killinger's credo, widely embraced in government, is the altruistic complement of the ultimatum delivered by Attorney General Roth. But whether the intent is good or bad, the public loses. The Committee on Freedom of Information wrote Mr. Killinger: —

Who is to decide what is compatible with the welfare of society? It is decided very easily in the nations which maintain control of all information, and we are sure you do not advocate our adopting their system. The Bill of Rights did not make exceptions to be applied to public officials who might be honest.

Another example of the I-know-better-than-the-people policy was expressed for the Bureau of Internal Revenue by its chief counsel, Charles Oliphant. It happened that a good many bars in Albany, New York, had formed the habit of adulterating their whisky, and the *Knickerbocker News* reasonably thought the names of these bars should be known in the community. But the Alcohol Tax Unit, which had investigated and compromised the charges with fines, refused the paper any information, claiming the protection of a departmental regulation. Mr. Oliphant, asked by the Committee on Freedom of Information why these deals were not a public record, expressed the opinion that Congress had given the department the authority to control such information by regulation, adding that "the transaction is primarily of interest to the individual and to the bureau."

That, of course, was poppycock. Any adulteration of food or drink is of concern primarily to the public. And Internal Revenue's attitude underlines a curious and seldom-challenged Washington practice of creating a special class of law violators: those who offend against the Federal Government. If someone stole your wallet in a bar, you would have him arrested and tried; and he would have no way of suppressing the news about it. But the bartender can rob you in his subtle way, buy immunity from federal officers, and you never know what happened. It is a sort of official blackmail, doubtless encouraging the payment of fines, but not open and honest government. The practice is widely used, of course, in the handling of cases of income-tax evasion, and probably in numerous other transactions of which the public hears nothing — or, for that matter, of which the newspapers hear little or nothing.

The editors who served on the Committee on Freedom of Information were disturbed most, not by any single case of news suppression they discovered but by the suspicion that each one was but a tiny facet of our ignorance, one scrap of evidence of things not known. They wondered if perhaps the widespread unawareness of concealment, of its scope and variety, was not a bigger story than any of the stories being concealed. Being blind to news-blindness could be fatal to any democracy.

For example, who has seriously challenged the proceedings of the Board of Governors of the Federal Reserve System? Those gentlemen deal with that vital part of our economy, management of money. But they never hold open meetings. Most federal commissions — Trade, Power, Communications — do hold open hearings part of the time. Because the Reserve Board of Governors do not, as an experienced Washington observer has just reminded the Committee on Freedom of Information, "nobody really knows just what the arguments were on which they based their decisions regarding the rediscount rate, or the revising of reserve requirement for banks, or the buying and selling of government securities. The end result is that the Washington correspondents probably know less about our monetary problems than about any of the other problems in Washington. Yet [they are] the most crucial."

A method of news suppression in the Capital that has proved disturbingly effective, because it is paved with good intentions, is the so-called advisory censorship of the Department of Commerce for businessmen and manufacturers. The service was conceived to protect secrets that might be of value to a potential enemy in case of war. Any definition of security gets to be so broad as to proscribe practically any free-flowing news; but the Commerce Department does not pretend to confine its advice on news suppression to elements of military security. Its advice takes the form of a blunderbuss to shoot down all intelligence about our mobilization, and shows little awareness of the dangers of public ignorance at a time of crisis. A department bulletin thus defines the scope of its service: —

> Information falling within the scope of this program includes unclassified [which means no security is involved in the remotest degree] technical data on: advanced industrial developments, production know-how and technology, strategic equipment, special installations.

Depending on any one man's interpretation of these sonorous phrases, you have there a formula for blacking out all news about defense production. It is the formula of a timid soul, too ignorant or too lazy to narrow his definitions down to actual security items, and completely unconcerned about the right of the people who fight the war, and pay the bills, to know what goes on.

How foolish can our fear of news become? One Chamber of Commerce was advised to leave out of a local defense roundup "any information in connection with the national-defense effort." It has more the sound of dictatorship than of well-meaning government muddling.

The Department of Defense is guilty, too, of failing to think through its security needs, and of using an indiscriminate smoke screen instead. The Mohawk Carpet Mills circulated a handout reporting an order for heavy duck. However, "due to limitations imposed by the military," they were not free to list either the yardage or the price. The military, challenged by the Committee on Freedom of Information, did not claim the price of duck involved any security. In a tone of self-pity, security experts told their Director of Information that it was a troublesome problem, and they hoped to get "more reasonable rulings" sometime soon. In the meantime, the flow of information is being controlled in this and innumerable other cases by arbitrary and unjustified "rulings," with no impetus whatever within the government to break these blockades. Outside the field of atomic energy, there is no law forbidding publication of any news about the war any editor can get, if he just has the determination to get it.

IV

IN ONE large field, becoming more controversial every day, there is a law. The Federal Government donates monies to the states for public welfare: aid to the aged, the needy blind, and dependent children. A federal statute requires that these welfare rolls be kept secret, and no state can get federal funds without preserving such secrecy. This secrecy provision was legislated back in the fervor of the Rooseveltian reform era. Its greatest weakness, now it is being attacked, is that it was not attacked on any such scale before. In short, there was no adequate public debate on it. In consequence, many citizens and state legislators now are peering at it with suspicion, as something hatched secretly.

Actually, there were some respectable grounds for keeping welfare rolls confidential. As the Federal Security Agency says: —

[The restriction] is designed to prevent the use of such information for political and commercial purposes; to insure efficient administration and to protect recipients from humiliation and exploitation.

This reasoning is based, of course, on a dubious faith that if relief rolls are not made public, Statehouse and county politicians will not know who is on them, and cannot bring pressure for political support.

There are certainly social arguments in favor of protecting relief clients. On the other hand, here is more than $2,000,000,000 a year being disbursed, and no reporter can check on all the reports of fraud that every newspaper receives. Sentiment seems to be growing that the necessity to guard an increasingly huge sum from grafters takes precedence over the right of personal privacy. Indiana has repealed her secrecy law, risking loss of $22,000,000 of federal funds. Legislatures in Tennessee, Georgia, Illinois, Florida, and other states have expressed great dissatisfaction with the present policy. Two bills which would destroy the confidential status have been introduced in Congress. If this area of secrecy, which has some justification, is opened up to the public view, the effect will be profound in other agencies which have no law to sanction their concealments.

The Bureau of Unemployment Security keeps its rolls secret by "regulation," lacking specific statutory direction. Here again, there are some valid reasons; and there is also the urgent need for more intensive checks against fraud than the administrative agency itself is likely to provide. Again, more than a billion and a quarter dollars a year is being disbursed, and the public is told just not to worry.

When expenditure of public monies is considered along with secrecy, one agency looms gigantically over all others — the Atomic Energy Commission. It has more money and more secrecy than our concept of government can comfortably tolerate. And if press and public are somewhat indulgent about areas of perfectly legitimate information which are being sealed off, it is little wonder they prostrate themselves ridiculously before the august enigma of the atom.

The Committee on Freedom of Information embraced a one-man subcommittee — Paul Block of the Toledo *Blade* — which did a hard-headed and yet imaginative job of inspecting the realm of atomic secrecy. In brief, Mr. Block's report said: —

1. Secrecy is intrinsically a dangerous and corrupting thing; it is highly probable that it already has hampered research and development and that it has cost the taxpayers millions in wasted expenditures. While the press must recognize the necessity of some military secrecy, it also must constantly review and question the validity of the A.E.C.'s decisions on what is to be withheld.

2. The reporting of the purely scientific aspects of atomic energy . . . is being done adequately by science writers.
3. The press, however, has been guilty of inadequate reporting of many aspects of the atomic energy program not behind official curtains of secrecy. This is because of an awe amounting almost to superstition. A touch of robust scepticism and the ruthless persistence of the police reporter are badly needed.

A robust scepticism is needed in the approach to the whole problem of freely flowing public information. It has been strangely dormant of late, but there are signs of regeneration.

QUESTIONS

1. In the first four paragraphs of the essay, how does Pope indicate the importance of his subject? What is his *basic* assumption, and where is it stated?

2. How does Pope distinguish in Section I between "Freedom of the Press" and "Freedom of Information"? Why does he make these distinctions at this point in the article?

3. What sentence contains the principal generalization in Section II? How is the idea supported? What use of irony is made in the last three paragraphs of the section? What is the meaning of "off-the-record" conferences and "handouts"?

4. In organizing the material, how has the author distinguished between the examples placed in Section II and those included in Section III? In Section III, what has the author done in addition to *stating* the examples? (Consider, for instance, the paragraphs on page 401 beginning "Another example of . . ." and "That, of course, was poppycock.")

5. In the first sentence of Paragraph 6, Section III, what is the effect of the word "inspiring"? What point is made about "welfare of society," in the two paragraphs on pages 400–401 beginning "The Louisville *Courier-Journal* . . ." and about "security," in the last four paragraphs of Section III? Of what importance is the phrase "unawareness of concealment" in the paragraph on page 402 beginning "The editors who served . . ."? How is this idea related to the next paragraph?

6. What two kinds of federal expenditure form the basis of Section IV? Show how the author gives the impression of being objective (unbiased) here. How does this impression aid the author in achieving the controlling purpose of his essay?

GERALD W. JOHNSON, after his graduation from Wake Forest College, began a distinguished career as a journalist. His principal contributions have been in the writing of editorials for the Baltimore *Sunpapers* and in the production of outstanding histories and biographies. Among the latter are *Andrew Jackson* (1927), *Roosevelt: Dictator or Democrat?* (1941), *Woodrow Wilson* (1944), and *This American People* (1951). He lives in Baltimore, has been a free-lance writer since 1943, and in 1954 received the Peabody Award for his work as a news commentator on television. His most recent book is *The Lunatic Fringe* (1957).

THE MONOPOLY OF NEWS

by GERALD W. JOHNSON

THE final going down of the New York *Sun* is said to have thrown twelve hundred newspaper workers out of employment. The individual tragedies involved in this catastrophe are justly regarded as of more than local concern; they have a large social significance as evidence of the constricting limits of one field of human endeavor, that of daily journalism. Daily newspaper work, if not a dying profession, is certainly a shrinking one, which is a matter of concern to newspapermen everywhere, not merely in New York City.

But the figure has another significance, not for newspapermen only, but for every citizen of the United States. It takes twelve hundred men to get out a daily newspaper in New York, and that by no means the largest.

This statement portrays a change in American journalism, not only in degree but also in kind, since the time when the New York *Sun* was founded. It means that the newspaper proprietor of 1950 is not the same kind of man that he was in 1833 and earlier, and this invalidates some forms of traditional thinking. It was in 1787 that Thomas Jefferson wrote to Edward Carrington * that if he had to choose between government without newspapers and newspapers without government "I should not hesitate a moment to prefer the latter," and perhaps he would have repeated the assertion as late as 1833; but it does not necessarily follow that he would say the same thing in 1950. In 1787 Jef-

* Colonel Edward Carrington (1749–1810), soldier in the Colonial Army, friend of Washington, and member of the Continental Congress.

ferson undoubtedly would have said that he preferred a horse to a car for getting about the country; but he would not say so now. Yet the meaning of the word " car " has changed hardly more since his time than has the word " newspaper."

If you doubt it, consider the origin of the newspaper whose death last January threw twelve hundred persons out of employment. The New York *Sun* began in a saloon that flourished just off Newspaper Row in the eighteen-thirties. There four cronies sat together after work nearly every day and discussed the state of the world over tankards. Three of them were printers – honest, hard-working men without a doubt, but certainly no earthshakers – named Benjamin H. Day, William Swaim, and Arunah S. Abell. These were youngsters, all in their twenties. The fourth member of the group was in his forties, an amusing fellow, but a notorious ne'er-do-well, always out at elbows, and probably regarded by steady-going artisans as little better than a bum. His name was James Gordon Bennett.

Day alone was his own master. He was the proprietor of a small job-printing establishment. Swaim and Abell were compositors, and Bennett was a reporter at those relatively infrequent times when he had a job. But they are not so remembered. Historians recall them today as the founders, respectively, of the New York *Sun*, the Philadelphia *Public Ledger*, the Baltimore *Sun*, and the New York *Herald*, four newspapers that revolutionized American journalism.

Day brought out the first issue of the *Sun* in September, 1833, with the assistance of one reporter and two carrier-boys, and it was a success from the start. The last issue was brought out with the assistance of twelve hundred people, and it was a failure. Another Day, to start another newspaper that would be instantly recognized as better than any existing in New York, would probably have to start with a couple of thousand people. Marshall Field employed hundreds to get *PM* going in New York and it eventually gave up the ghost. He has had a very difficult time with the Chicago *Sun*. In short, the only kind of man who can start a big-city newspaper in 1950 is one with many millions at his command, and even he has no assurance of success.

The explanation is that the collection and dissemination of news in 1950 requires such tremendous equipment and such vast numbers of people that it can be undertaken only by men in control of immense capital resources. Yet it is a necessity – in fact, the prime necessity – for the successful functioning of the sort of government we have developed. Jefferson's remark requires adaptation, without essential change; we cannot have our kind of government without newspapers, and excellent newspapers, at that.

Remember that next November we shall have to choose the members of the Eighty-second Congress, which will determine – if only by the method of blocking – the policy of the United States for the next two years; and upon the policy of the United States depends the destiny of a large part of the world. The selection of representatives competent to deal with the problems that will confront that Congress is therefore of supreme importance. But the gravest of those problems will take shape as a result of what is now happening, not in the next county, but on the other side of the world. What you and I know about what is happening there is what the press tells us. Under the best circumstances our decision in November may be the wrong one; but if the information on which the decision is based is false, then the decision is bound to be false. We are hostages of fortune who will inevitably be sacrificed if the press fails to keep faith.

II

ACCURATE news is not merely a prime necessity in a representative democracy: it is *the* prime necessity. Nothing takes precedence over it.

But when any article is a necessity and when that article cannot be supplied except by an immense organization at vast expense, the business of purveying it becomes a natural monopoly. Communication is such a necessity. No rational man dreams that the public interest would be served by setting up a competing post office in every town. We did try competing telephone companies for a while, but the system didn't work. Water is a necessity, but supplying it is a natural monopoly, and to have two sets of water mains in every street would be sheer insanity.

News is rapidly assuming the status of water, communication, and electricity. Supplying it calls for an immense, and increasing, capital investment and very large daily expenditures. Whether it comes through newspapers, by radio-television, or through the movies, it involves the employment of millions of money and thousands of men; and only great capitalists, usually in the form of great corporations, can undertake it. This means that supplying news assumes every day more of the nature of a natural monopoly.

It is already collectivized to a high degree. The Associated Press, the United Press, and the International News Service are all essentially co-operatives, even when, as in the case of INS, they preserve the form of private ownership. The local newspaper is simply an outlet, as is the individual member of a co-operative chain-store group. As regards the purity of the product, this has worked well. Even if one newspaper wished to adulterate the news, it would have little chance to do so when nine hundred and ninety nine others draw from the same source, and many of them would object to any adulteration proposed.

But such tremendous technological changes have certainly altered the nature of the institution, and when the very nature of an institution alters, its position in the social structure calls for reconsideration. A car, in Jefferson's day, was a horse-drawn vehicle, usually clumsy and always slow. The invention of the internal-combustion engine changed its nature. Not only were the horses discarded, but the whole attitude of society toward the vehicle changed and an entirely new field of law and an almost entirely new field of engineering were created to express that attitude.

A newspaper, in Jefferson's day, was a journal of opinion as well as a disseminator of information. It not only published the news, but it interpreted it in comment expressing the opinion of the newspaper editor. When editorial opinion expressed the views of such people as Day, Abell, Swaim, and Bennett, it reflected pretty faithfully the opinion of the masses, for even when these men had become successful and comparatively rich they were not far removed from their origin.

It is interesting to remember that when Day, within four months, was selling four thousand copies of the New York *Sun* at a cent apiece, the other three rushed out and set up penny papers of their own – Bennett in New York, Swaim in Philadelphia, Abell in Baltimore. An enterprise that could take in the prodigious sum of forty dollars a day from circulation alone was, in their estimation, colossal. But a man who can manage successfully an enterprise taking in forty thousand dollars a day differs widely, in most of his attitudes and ways of thinking, from a man who is impressed by receipts of forty dollars a day. His opinions, therefore, are not likely to reflect faithfully the opinions of the masses.

The accuracy of this inference is attested by the fact that for the past eighteen years the majority of the American press – among big-city newspapers, the overwhelming majority – has opposed the party in power. At the same time, the majority of the voters – in the big cities the overwhelming majority – has supported that party. Thus it is evident that whatever opinion the newspapers reflect, it is not the opinion of the majority.

This is no proof that newspaper opinion is wrong, but it is proof that it is not popular opinion. So the question arises, Should this opinion, plainly not acceptable to the majority, be inseparably attached to a necessity – to wit, news?

If we are to live without excessive inconvenience in a modern city, telephones we must have, gas and electricity we must have. Hence it is unavoidably necessary to admit into our homes telephone repairmen, meter readers, and inspectors. But if these employees of the telephone company and of the gas and electric companies should take advantage of that necessity to instruct us how to vote next November, think of the howl that would go up! Why, then, should the purveyor of another necessity, news, be allowed the privilege of thrusting upon us unwanted and unacceptable advice? Why should the function of disseminating news, now that it approaches the status of a monopoly, continue to be bound to the function of interpreting news, which is distinctly different and which, under no circumstances, should be monopolized?

This is not an assertion that corporations engaged in this essentially monopolistic enterprise should be forbidden to form and express opinions on public men and public affairs. Not only are they guaranteed that right by the First Amendment to the Constitution, but the whole history of ideas supports the theory that the truth is most likely to prevail where every variety of opinion may be published without let or hindrance. To forbid a newspaper to publish an opinion on any subject, even though it is the composite opinion of a corporation, not that of any of the men who write the newspaper, would be a step away from liberty and, as I believe, away from truth.

The question is this: Should a corporation enjoying a monopolistic position in the distribution of a necessity be permitted to use that position to give its own opinion a preferred position over any other by attaching that opinion to the necessary product it purveys? We do not allow it to radio, which, by reason of the limited number of channels available, is also a natural monopoly. The Federal Communications Commission requires a radio corporation, if it expresses a controversial opinion, to give equal time to the expression of opposing opinion. If that is just as regards radio, why is it unjust as regards any other medium of communication?

As a matter of fact, many American newspapers have already seen the point and have taken, on their own initiative, steps to fortify their position. In one-newspaper towns it is a common practice for the journal enjoying the monopoly to print every day comment diametrically opposed to its own views; and few reputable newspapers will refuse to print a letter to the editor because it takes issue with the paper's stand on a matter of public interest. Some journals not only reprint opposing comment from other sources, but go to considerable expense in buying from syndicates signed columns written by men known to be of an opposing political or economic faith.

But this is at most a plea in confession and avoidance. It attests an honorable disposition on the part of the press to play fair, and acquits it of a determination to accomplish by monopoly what the government is forbidden to do by law — namely, to abridge freedom of speech. However, it does not affect the relation of the institution to society. It proves only that American opinion has an intelligent and, on the whole, a benevolent master, not that it has no master. Opinion is free only when nobody can monopolize it, not when nobody does monopolize it.

III

It is widely believed that certain popular columnists, not always the more intelligent ones, swing more votes in every election than the greatest newspaper in the United States. The returns for the past eighteen years certainly suggest it.

Within the craft this may be taken as another brutal assault on that favorite target of every sniper, the editorial writer. If it were so, it would be inexcusable, for I have been an editorial writer myself, and know the virtues of the breed. Editorial writing is, or ought to be, journalism's final and best contribution to society and the state. In view of the immensity and complexity of the volume of news now poured upon the American public, careful and skillful interpretation of the significance of that news is more important and more valuable today than it ever was before. An interpretation made by a detached observer with wide information and, above all, long experience in reading newspapers can lead the average man to the truth in a fraction of the time it would take him to get there himself by floundering through the news with no guidance.

What the country needs is not the abolition of editorial writers, but more, many more, and better ones. But as daily newspapers decrease in numbers there are fewer positions open to such men; and as the corporate form grows vaster and more complex, their independence is more and more restricted. My suggestion is that the editorial writer is badly placed on a daily newspaper, and that his position grows worse with every newspaper that collapses. He deals, not so much with events, as with the ideas that spring from events, and in the battle of ideas one's weapons are burnished and sharpened by the clash of contending opinions — and the number of contending opinions has been reduced by 40 per cent since 1929, by the disappearance of daily newspapers in that proportion.

Unfortunately, we have not developed in this country any place for this kind of worker that can serve as an alternative to the daily newspaper. With us, the journal of opinion is still rudimentary. The *Nation* and the *New Republic* have existed precariously, even as weeklies; a daily devoted to the propagation of ideas is unknown and, to most American newspapermen, unimaginable. Pre-war Paris, to be sure, could manage thirty-one, but not New York; and it is true enough that only a handful of the Parisian dailies were genuinely interested in ideas. The rest were pretty much scavengers.

Nevertheless, although the French may never have pulled it off, it is possible that they had the right idea, and it is conceivable that in time we may take it over and make it work better. That the American daily press is in a period of transition is plain to the dullest. In speed it has already been superseded; the radio can outdistance it so easily that the old-time extra long ago disappeared, and the scoop is now practically unknown. Added to economic giantism, this plainly points to the day when most cities will rely for news of record on one huge journal, issued twice — and in large cities possibly three times — a day.

But no one will look to it for opinion any more than people now look to the telephone or the electric light company for opinion. That will be supplied by a multitude of four-page sheets sold for a cent but written by exceptionally alert and well-informed men. Not being burdened with responsibility for millions of other people's money, as a conscientious executive of a large newspaper is, they will say what they think, and they will usually think accurately. The monopolistic newspaper will continue to tell the world what happened yesterday; but small, fugitive sheets will tell it what is going to happen tomorrow. Many will guess wrong, and perish, but others will appear to replace them, for it will not take a Marshall Field to start one; any fairly prosperous job-printer, such as Benjamin H. Day, can do it, and when one comes along who pretty consistently guesses right, he will flourish. He will never be able to build another San Simeon * to rival Hearst's, or endow the Metropolitan Museum of Art, as Munsey † did, but he will take in forty dollars a day, and may even net that much after he has paid off his printer and a couple of writing hands.

That would be an income of twelve thousand dollars a year, which is mere pocket-change to a big modern publisher. But this lad would collect something else. Assuming that he really understood the news and knew how to explain it, and assuming that he actually did so, considering only the interest of the average man, not that of any corporation or class or political party, it would not be long before everybody in town would be reading his sheet and in addition to his forty dollars he

* Fabulous estate of over 200,000 acres located in California and developed by the American publisher William Randolph Hearst (1863–1951).

† Frank Andrew Munsey (1854–1925), publisher of various magazines and newspapers in New York, left most of his fortune to the Metropolitan Museum of Art.

would be taking in something else – he would be acquiring influence to an incredible extent.

Some men like that better than money, and such men include many of the best newspaper workers. Suppose the monopolistic journal continued to roll up millions for its owners but, if it thundered at all, continued to thunder for the current Landon, with the traditional result – eight electoral votes. And suppose some owner of a journal of opinion, able to compile his income tax return on the short form, was also able to look over mayors, and governors, and Congressmen, and say to one go, and he goeth, and to another come, and he cometh – well, I know plenty of men who would not hesitate for an instant to take the short income with the long reach. They would not impress bankers, but they would have a wonderful time.

Be that as it may, the ordinary voter in this country should prepare himself to consider some startling arguments over the rights, privileges, and duties of the American press, and that within a short time. For the trend toward monopoly is irreversible. It was not planned by malefactors of great wealth, or by malefactors of any kind. Most of the caterwauling about the "capitalistic press" and its sins is sheer bosh. If it is a menace to liberty it was made so by its virtues, not by its sins. Its very excellence as a purveyor of news has made it so expensive that it can no longer reflect, much less mold, the opinions of the impecunious majority; yet that expense has put it into the position of a natural monopoly.

The result is that free opinion must find some other channel. What that channel will be, only the seventh son of a seventh son is competent to guess. But it will be found. To doubt it would be to doubt the final perseverance of intelligence.

QUESTIONS

1. The origin of four great newspapers may be of interest in itself, but what additional purpose does the topic serve in Johnson's essay? Explain the importance of the last paragraph in Section I.

2. What two functions of a newspaper form the basis of Section II? What is the author's distinction between the expression of opinion in the newspapers of Jefferson's day and the expression of opinion in the press of our time? How is the point illustrated?

3. In Section II, both the paragraph on page 409 beginning "This is no proof . . ." and the paragraph on page 410 beginning "The question is this:" ask the same question. By considering the structure of the question and the context in which it appears, show what is gained by this repetition. To what preceding material is the last sentence of Section II related?

4. Section III concentrates upon the columnist and the editorial writer. How does the trend toward monopoly affect these newspapermen? What prediction about the purveying of opinion is a major point in this section?

5. To what phrases, ideas, or references introduced in Section I does the author return in the other sections? What results are achieved by this device?

6. Do the subject matter and the diction of the essay indicate that the author is alarmed over the monopoly of news? Does he try to appeal emotionally as well as intellectually to the reader? What is the effect of the comparisons with other "natural" monopolies?

Values

IRWIN EDMAN

ARCHIBALD MACLEISH

VANNEVAR BUSH

CLARENCE B. RANDALL

CURTIS CATE

IRWIN EDMAN's death, in 1954, removed from the literary scene "one of the foremost American practitioners of the increasingly rare familiar essay." For over thirty years a professor of philosophy at Columbia University, he influenced the thinking of generations of undergraduates. Himself an urbane and polished man of the world, he was a skillful writer of light verse, an accomplished conversationalist, and a wise commentator on the American scene. In addition to contributing reviews, essays, poems, and articles to numerous magazines and journals, Professor Edman also edited the works of Plato and Santayana. Among his many books, the following is but a brief list: *Poems* (1925), *Four Ways of Philosophy* (1937), *Philosopher's Holiday* (1938), *Arts and the Man* (1939), and *Philosopher's Quest* (1947).

A REASONABLE LIFE IN A MAD WORLD

by IRWIN EDMAN

THAT the world is mad has been the judgment of self-denominated sane philosophers from the Greeks to the present day. It is not a discovery of our own age that both the public and private lives of human beings are dominated by folly and stupidity. Philosophers pressing the point have brought such charges not against human nature only – that is, the world of human relations – but against that larger universe in which the world of human relations is set. As far back as the Book of Job and probably much further back, for there must have been at least gruntingly articulate Jobs in prehistory, it is not only men who have been declared mad: by any standards of rationality the universe itself has been called irrational, pointless, meaningless, with incidental, unintended overtones of cruelty and injustice.

With the provincialism of each generation, ours imagines that the causes of cynicism and despair are new in our time. There have, of course, been modern improvements and refinements of stupidity and folly. No previous generation has been by way of organizing itself with insane efficiency for blowing the whole race to smithereens. It does not take a particularly logical mind at the present moment to discover that the world is quite mad, though a great many critics apparently think that the cruel absurdity of technical efficiency combined with moral bankruptcy is a discovery that it took great wit on their part to turn up.

Reputations are being made by reiterating, to the extent of four or five hundred pages, that collective modern man is a technical genius merged with a moral imbecile.

The first encouragement I can bring is the reminder that the kind of madness which we all realize to be the present state of the world is not something new. It is, just like everything else in the modern world, bigger and more streamlined, if not better. It is a pity some of the great satirists are dead; Swift and Voltaire would have given their eye-teeth for the present situation. And Aristophanes would scarcely have believed it. But the essential charges they would bring against the present time and the essential absurdities they would show up are not different in essence now from what they were.

Neither nature nor man appears reasonable by reasonable human standards. So acutely does this seem to many people to be true that in almost exuberant desperation they decide to march crazily in the insane procession. Existentialists make a cult of anxiety and despair and find a kind of wry comfort in saying, Since the world is absurd, let absurdity and irony be our standards. There are others who say – and the currency of an ersatz theological literature shows how epidemic they are – that since the world and mankind at present seem so palpably absurd it simply can't be true, and history, as Toynbee * now assures us, moves delightfully and progressively to fulfillment in the Church of God – a kind of quiet, English Church incorporating the best features of Islam, Buddhism, Confucianism, and a little, even, of the Hebrew prophets and the secular sciences.

The excitements and confused urgencies of the present time may seem to make hysteria or mystical narcosis or hedonistic excitement tantamount to a philosophy. But the still, small voice of rationality persists. And the question still remains the same as that propounded by the Greeks long ago: How, in a world certainly not at first acquaintance rational-appearing, is it possible to lead a rational life?

It seems mad now to say that anyone could believe, as the Fabians did (including such unsentimental people as George Bernard Shaw and Sidney and Beatrice Webb and Graham Wallas * and later H. G. Wells), that the world could be transformed into a livable, beau-

* Arnold J. Toynbee (1889–   ), English historian; author of the monumental *A Study of History.*

† Graham Wallas (1858–1932), English author and political scientist; wrote *Fabian Essays* (1889). The Fabians (whose Society was founded in 1884) took their name from Quintus Fabius Maximus (d. 203 B.C.), whose military tactics of wearying and exhausting the enemy earned him the surname "the Delayer." The Fabians hoped to reform society gradually over a long period of time and to avoid the revolutionary methods of the Marxists. The Fabians helped to establish the British Labor Party, and the Fabian Society is still active.

tiful, reasonable place by the co-operation of reasonable men. It is not simply that the violent external events of the past generation have revealed to us how precarious were security and comfort, and for how few it obtained at all.

But the psychological sciences have revealed to us the deep sources of violence, confusion, hysteria, and madness in ourselves. What perhaps a generation ago seemed a melodramatic aphorism when Santayana uttered it seems now to be a hitting of the nail on the head: " The normal man holds a lunatic in leash." The definition needs to be amended. In the light of the past twenty-five years, the normal man no longer *does* hold a lunatic in leash. The fact that even talk about a third world war has become standard has practically made lunacy respectable. It is now become a stamp of madness to talk as if one seriously believed that a peaceful and just world were possible.

And yet the sentiment of rationality persists and the hope persists also that it is not impossible, at least in imagination, to dream and in organized effort to work for what seems, though almost ridiculously familiar to common sense, " an ordered, coherent world society." The most ardent workers for such a world, however, realize that there is plenty of madness left, out of which a third world war may come.

II

THE persistence of power politics, the greed for privilege, the insane clutching of wealth, the pathological tribalisms of nations, of class, and of race; it is this world in which we are actually living, and the human problem for anyone in it is to discover what is a reasonable life in such a world.

Is it to forget as far as possible and to live only in the moment and to make that moment as brief and bright as possible? Is it to surrender any hope for pleasure or happiness now and give one's dedicated and ruthless devotion to work for a more reasonable world? Is it to seek Nirvana or to seek some salvation in another world? There seems to be some sense in each answer, but which answer one chooses will depend ultimately on how one answers a basic question: Is the world always and necessarily mad? Is it completely mad now, and is it possible even now to understand the madness and, through understanding, to endure or change it?

Let us try as simply as possible to deal with some of these questions. First, is the world always and necessarily mad? By " the world," of course, one means both the processes of nature and the activities of human beings. For " world " in the first sense one had perhaps better use the word "universe." A thoroughly rational universe would be one which was achieving a purpose set down in advance, a purpose which in human terms made sense and which by human standards made moral sense. A rational universe might be one such as the Deists conceived in the eighteenth century, in which nature was simply reason incarnate or reason embodied in the vast machinery of things.

In one respect at least the advance of knowledge of the physical world has not made the world seem more irrational. It has made it seem orderly and regular. But in another respect an understanding of the causes and consequences of nature by conventional standards made nature seem wholly irrational. "I am what I am," said Jehovah in the Old Testament, as if that announcement were sufficient explanation of his wrathful ways. "It is what it is and it does what it does" may be said to be the conclusions of empirical physical science. It is maddening to rational creatures to discover they were born into a world which is not particularly interested in human purposes, which perhaps permits and sustains these purposes but is innocent of any solicitude concerning them. The rain notoriously falls on the just and the unjust, and the just feel highly put upon. Death is no respecter of persons; plagues fell the virtuous. The most generous and devoted enterprises are washed away by floods along with the conspiracies of the sinister and hateful.

Theologians have spent a good deal of time trying to gloss away the irrationalities of the universe, explaining that God moves in a mysterious or at least salutary way, his morally therapeutic wonders to perform. Job was not greatly impressed by his comforters, and neither are we. But if exasperated humans have criticized the world in general, they have been especially critical of the madness of their fellow men. Voltaire found his greatest weapon of satire in treating cruelty, barbarism, and superstition not as evil but as absurd.

The most serious and damaging charge we can bring against civilization is that by the very standards of civilization it is a ridiculous failure. It takes a high degree of sophistication and technical resources to make such an international shambles as we seem fated to do. It takes something like genius in folly to have millions starving in the midst of plenty, to have technological magic whose fruits are poverty, squalor, anarchy, and death; it takes a refinement of absurdity to use the most generous aphorism of the highest religions to justify or rationalize intolerance, violence, and our established international disorder.

Now about the first irrationality: that of the universe itself. Perhaps the only reasonable attitude is that of resignation and endurance of it. Perhaps it is only the persistence of our childhood wishes and expectations that has led us to an assumption that the universe must conform to human purposes and that it is shockingly unreasonable of it not so to conform. We can, within the limits of a world not made for us, make it conform to ideals and values which flower out of nature itself. Part of the life of reason is a contemplation of the unchanging and unchangeable elements in the world of nature; part of it is a sedulous attempt to discover the ways of changing the world in the interest of human values.

With respect to the world of human activities there has been an accelerated desperation at the present time. In the old days when humor could still flourish in Central Europe it used to be said that the difference between the temper of Berlin and Vienna could be stated as follows: In Berlin when things went wrong it was remarked: " The situation is serious but not hopeless "; in Vienna with smiling deprecation the Viennese used to say: " The situation is hopeless but not serious." The Berlin version seems of late more greatly to have impressed the world.

Though Existentialism may be said to describe the world as being both hopeless and trivial, if one so conceives the realm of human affairs the Epicurean prescription for a reasonable life is perhaps the best that one can find. However clouded and uncertain the future, there is at least possible for the lucky and the prudent a brief, bright interval in which they may find luster and to which their refined sensibilities may give luster. In a world without meaning they may find exquisite nuances of meaning in the arts, in friendship, in love.

The trouble with the Epicurean solution and abdication is that it is always haunted by a scruple of conscience and the shadow of despair. There is something already tarnished in a brightness that declares itself both ultimately meaningless and transient. Sorrow and inhibition and regret dog the footsteps of the Epicurean in a world where folly is no longer a joke but a terrifying threat to all mankind.

There are those, therefore, in our own age who jump to the other extreme. One insists that one *must* give up any hope for present happiness and give one's dedicated and ruthless devotion to work for a better world. I have friends, especially in social or government work or in the social sciences, who regard humor, irony, urbanity, or relaxation with something of the same moral impatience with which a missionary might watch the natives of the Fiji Islands dance or lounge in the sun. There is so little time; it is later than you think; there is no time for comedy. Urbanity is a form of evasion, and laughter is a form of bourgeois or decadent callousness. Let us gird our loins and work together rapidly for the common good or we shall all in common be destroyed.

The psychiatric departments of hospitals number among their patients a good many people who in their earnest haste to save the world from destruction ended up by destroying their equilibrium and almost themselves. The tension of moral earnestness, the refusal to permit the enjoyment of even such goods as are possible in a chaotic world, is one of the diseases of our civilization, not a sign of its health. If Epicureanism leads to dismay, unrelieved moral dedication leads to fanaticism. Neither the playboy nor the zealot is a true or adequate incarnation of the life of reason.

Those who recognize the disillusion of a pleasure philosophy or the destructiveness of a moral fanaticism have begun in our age, as they have in other ages, to turn to otherworldly philosophies. They have tried to seek an inward light unquenchable by external circumstances. They have tried in spirit to follow the Indian saint into the wilderness or the monk into his cell or the mystic into his remote meditation. They have sought Nirvana, or a Oneness with the One, or an Aloneness with the Alone. The follies of society are not cured by the incantations of pure mysticism, and the search for oblivion is really a pathological attempt simply to become oblivious to the actual and remediable conflicts and disorders in society.

There are still others than the pleasure-lovers, the Nirvana-seekers, the devotees of such mystics, who have sought to make a prescription for a reasonable life. Among those others now epidemic are followers of historians and zoologists who with the theological wave of a wand discover that a palpably absurd world is somehow moving toward a cozy fulfillment where, as I heard Mr. Toynbee say, "God is Love." It would seem a strange moment to detect the course of history as the operations of universal love when the world is being filled with universal hate.

No, I do not think any of these ersatz solutions will do. The pressure of events simply confirms again what the life of reason does consist in: a brave contemplation of what things are discoverably like and a resolute attempt to improve the lot of man in the conditions into which he finds himself born. The life of reason must always have a stoic element because there is no sign that either the follies of humanity or the uncaring order of nature will ever be magically transformed.

The life of reason must also contain an element of hope, for it is quite clear, as the history of every improvement in man's estate has shown us, that human intelligence accompanied by human goodwill may profoundly improve the life of mankind. The life of reason must include the pleasure principle also, for what else gives life meaning if not joy and delight of life, and what a folly it would be not to cherish and embrace, not to nourish then, even in a sick society, that which yields the fruit of a quickened, multiplied awareness, the substance of vision and of joy. The universe may be pointless, but there are many good points in it. Our urgencies may be intense, but the world does not end with us or even with our own civilization; nor, if we do not quench intelligence and generosity in ourselves, is it a foregone conclusion that our civilization must end. And the best insurance, perhaps, of maintaining both is to reaffirm the quality of life itself, of its possibility of beauty and its intimations of order and of justice.

QUESTIONS

1. What is the specific purpose of the opening paragraph of the essay?

2. What evidence of a satiric intent on the author's part is to be found in Paragraph 2, Section I? Does the single sentence of Paragraph 3, Section I, deserve a separate paragraph?

3. What distinction does Edman make between the attitude of the Fabians (Paragraph 7, Section I) and the attitude of his own contemporaries (the next paragraph)? Why does he emphasize this distinction?

4. How does Edman answer the question: " Is the world always and necessarily mad? " What does he recommend as perhaps " the only reasonable attitude " toward the irrationality of the universe?

5. What, according to Edman, are the values and limitations of " the Epicurean prescription " for a reasonable life?

6. What is Edman's criticism of " moral dedication " as a way of meeting irrationality in the world of human activities? What is his attitude toward mysticism as a cure for the world's madness?

7. Why does Edman call the various prescriptions for a reasonable life " ersatz solutions "?

8. Summarize the conception of the life of reason which Edman presents in the last two paragraphs of the essay. Is Edman's conclusion justified by the details and particulars of the rest of the essay?

ARCHIBALD MACLEISH, although trained professionally at Harvard Law School, preferred writing poetry to practicing law. He has received the Bollingen prize, the National Book Award, and the Pulitzer prize twice — in 1932 and 1935. From 1939 to 1944 he served as Librarian of Congress. Also, he has held important posts in the Office of War Information (1942–1943) and in the State Department (1944–1945), and was active in the organization of UNESCO. Since 1949 he has been Boylston Professor of Rhetoric and Oratory at Harvard University. A challenging political thinker and writer as well as an outstanding contemporary poet, MacLeish frequently has been attacked for his liberal views. During the past forty years he has produced more than twenty-five volumes of verse and prose.

HUMANISM AND THE BELIEF IN MAN

by ARCHIBALD MACLEISH

THE end of the war will present two great questions — a question of government for the governors and a question of education for the teachers. There will be other questions as well. There will be bankers' questions for the bankers, and food questions for the farmers, and traders' questions for the traders, and military questions for the generals and the admirals. But the two great questions will be the questions of government and of education.

How do you govern in the new world with its invisible frontiers? And how do you educate the new people with their new possibilities of creation and destruction?

These two questions are serious. We can perhaps get along if the bankers fail to find an answer to the question of money — or refuse to accept the answer someone else finds for them. We can probably get along somehow whether or not the farmers find an answer to the question of food, and whether or not the traders learn how to trade, and the generals and admirals how to police the isthmuses and the oceans and the islands. But unless the governors — which means those who are governed as well — and the teachers — which means also those who are taught — can find out how to govern the new world and how to educate men and women to live in it, we are quite literally lost. Lost not in rhetoric: lost in truth.

We used to say twenty-five years ago that the world couldn't survive another war. We thought we were making speeches. We know now that we were stating fact. The only parts of the world which will survive this war, except as ruins and fragments and remains, will be the parts of the world over which the war has not been fought. Next time, as the Nazis have obligingly shown us, there will be no margins. Planes which flew a few hundred miles with a few pounds of explosives in 1918 now fly thousands of miles with tons of explosives. Robot projectiles which now carry a ton of explosives a couple of hundred miles will increase both range and load in much the same way.

The lesson we have learned over the last few years is the lesson that "there are no neutrals in this war." In the next war — if there is a next war — the lesson we shall learn will be the lesson that there is no part of the world which is not a battlefield. Which means, not as a figure of speech but as a statement of fact, that what we understand by "the world" will not survive that war. Which means, in turn, that if there is another war our world is lost. Which means, finally, that we have no future worth thinking about unless we can learn, and learn quickly, to govern the world in such a way, and to educate its people in such a way, that another war will not occur.

When anyone talks about the crisis of humanism at the war's end, he is talking, if he is serious, about the answer humanism has to give, or ought to have to give, or ought to be allowed to have to give, to these two inescapable and desperate questions of government and education. He is not talking, that is to say, about the sad plight of the classics in the modern college, or the overemphasis on science in the current curriculum, or the lamentable discovery, in universities which had previously terminated all literature with the last rock on Land's End, that an American literature also exists. He is not talking, that is to say, in terms of academic politics or academic prestige or his own future as a professor. Above all, he is not talking about the effect of the Army training program on the academic economic system.

He is talking about the most urgent and most critical decisions to be taken in his time. And he is saying that a certain approach to these problems, a certain tradition of thought, a certain discipline, has something of importance to offer to their solution. He is saying that the tendency of the practical men among his contemporaries to exclude that approach and that discipline is dangerous. He is saying that it is dangerous, not to him and his academic fellows only, but to the practical men themselves — and to the world they share with us.

The serious question in all this discussion of the humanities, in other words, is the question whether the humanists and their discipline have, in fact, anything to offer to the solution of the two great moral and intellectual and political problems we must solve or perish. If they have not, if the humanists can claim no more than a decorative function in the preparation of young men for dinners-in-hall, then their disputes with their academic rivals, however brilliantly managed and however learnedly expressed, are hardly worth the present attention of living men. For one thing, living men have other and more urgent business to attend to. For another, they have every reason to remark that a philosophy of the education and life of man which has nothing to say to mankind about its life and education at the most critical moment in its recorded history is not a philosophy of man at all but a dilettantism with a pretentious name.

Both problems clearly fall within the field of humanist concern. Certainly the question of the role of education in the crisis of our time is a question on which the humanists can be expected to speak and by which they should expect to be judged. Humanism is at bottom a theory of the education proper to man and cannot therefore avoid judgment upon its position in the most solemn examination of educational theory the modern world has been obliged to undertake. On the contrary, humanism might well protest, and bitterly protest, its exclusion from that great assize.

The same thing is true, or so it seems to me, of the problem of government. Humanists, I realize, have not claimed the right in recent years to speak with authority of the art of government. Some of them may even decline that right today. Some of them, thinking of humanism as though it were something in a university catalogue, may perhaps refuse to hold opinions on the art of government – on the ground that government is taught in the courses on political science and that the courses on political science are not usually given in the departments of humanities.

Others, taking a less curricular view, might conceivably renounce all right to be heard on the issue of government, and might decline to be judged by their contribution to its solution, on the ground that humanism is concerned with men solely as individuals and not with men in their relation to each other, or on the ground that humanism looks inward, not outward, or on the ground that humanism looks backward, not forward.

Philosophers of the ancient world would consider these to be strange limitations, I submit, upon the spiritual jurisdiction of a school which concerns itself with *humanitas* – with those things in man which are most manlike. Aulus Gellius * defined *humanitas* by saying that earnest

* Lived in second century A.D. Student of law in Rome and of philosophy in Athens. Author of a collection of essays called *Attic Nights*.

students of the liberal arts are most highly humanized because the knowledge they pursue is " granted to man alone of all the animals." Of the various forms of knowledge granted to man alone of all the animals, knowledge of the art of government is surely not the least.

Nor was it the least regarded in the past. It was not believed in Athens and Rome that the best education for man was an education unrelated to his practice of the art of government. On the contrary, it was assumed that a philosophy which thought in terms of the whole man, of the man in whom the manlike qualities were most developed, must necessarily have views not only on the training of those qualities but upon their exercise as well, and above all upon their noblest exercise — which would have included, in that time and in those cities, their exercise in government.

II

BUT there are other reasons than reasons of logic and history for the extension of humanistic jurisdiction, and therefore of humanistic responsibility, to the art of government. There are reasons of a practical nature. The humanistic renunciation of the public world has been happy neither for the public world nor for humanism. Humanism has become pallid with the pallor of all things grown within ivory walls; and government, once considered a noble art, has become at best a kind of profession and at worst a business. The recent uproar about Henry Wallace makes the point with an unintentional but appalling pertinence. Henry Wallace, said a characteristic article by one of the best-known American journalists, is an exceptionally fine human being. He has a feeling for the tendency of things to come. But he is not at home and at ease in " the real world " and he is therefore, under the circumstances of the election, unacceptable for the Vice-presidency.

Whatever may be said of the opinion of Henry Wallace, the view of statesmanship there expressed is one a humanist might challenge and, in my opinion, should. Indeed both humanism and statesmanship would be healthier today if the humanists had challenged the businessman's view of the art of government before it produced the generations of leaders " at home in the real world " which conducted Western civilization through so much of the nineteenth century and the twentieth to the situation in which we find ourselves today. It would be difficult to prove that there would have been more Lincolns and Jeffersons if the humanists had not forsaken the public world, but it must be obvious that there would almost certainly have been fewer Coolidges and Tafts.

I propose to assume, therefore, and for the purposes of this discussion, that humanism can be expected to supply an answer to the two critical questions of how to govern and how to teach. It remains therefore to consider whether the answer humanism can be expected to offer is or is not entitled to a better hearing than it has had.

But that consideration turns, of course, upon the nature of the humanist answer. There are almost as many definitions of humanism and the humanities as there are men who have written them. If one assumes, for example, that the humanities are what Webster calls "the branches of polite learning," especially belles-lettres and the ancient classics, and that humanism is merely a scholarly devotion to these studies, there will be some difficulty in persuading a tortured world that humanism and the humanities have much to say to it.

Polite learning, it will be objected, is all very well for a polite age, and knowledge of the ancient classics and of beautiful letters is a charming embellishment in a serene and spacious time; but for us, bewildered and frightened in a chaotic and savage world in which all the landmarks are lost and all the assurances washed away, the book beneath the classic bough is a mockery and a delusion. We have First Things to learn again before we can learn Last Things. We must learn again how to survive — how to keep the peace; how to restrain the wild beasts and the violence. Keep your culture, the world might well say, until we can build a quiet room to house it in — until we can be certain that the house of culture will stand at least for a generation at a time; until the skies are quiet again and a place for stars, not for the most terrible and insensate death and the swiftest destruction.

And there will be much the same objection if you define your humanist as the perfect type of intellectual aristocrat, living a life of reflection and criticism above the battle and the common dust. You will be told that such a man, if he does not make himself a prig in the process, may well become an ornament in a world which has room for ornaments, but that we, who must buttress and rebuild our lives before chaos engulfs them, have no time to think of such luxuries as a natural aristocracy of learning and of taste.

So again if you adopt the definition of humanism which describes it as a form of intellectual discipline — the discipline of the intellect for its own sake rather than for the sake of proficiency in some art, or craft, or profession. Rude persons will tell you that to cultivate the mind for its own sake one must first have leisure, and that to have leisure one must be able to foretell the time, and that in our world a man cannot foretell the time since the time is already past and nothing is sure and each day is more dangerous than the last and a man can only prepare himself for disaster or survival.

It will be the same, too, even if you take the more generous definition in which humanism appears as that method of education and that practice of life of which the purpose is to free the faculties of men for their fullest exercise and their finest development. To free the faculties of men for their fullest exercise is a noble purpose. But its end, as someone will be unkind enough to point out, is not a free man, — a man committed to freedom as well as possessed of it, — but rather a *freed* man — a man freed of all commitments, including the commitment to freedom itself.

III

SUCH an end, however enchanting it may seem in a peaceful time when men can afford the after-dinner sport of questioning everything and giving themselves to nothing, has an irresponsible and even a frivolous look to a generation which has been compelled to think of freedom as something you were either prepared to die for or prepared to lose. To be free of every prejudice, including the prejudice of freedom, may make a man superior, but it can hardly endear him, for the moment at least, to those who have offered their lives precisely to defend the prejudice that freedom has a supreme and absolute worth. Moral eclecticism looks curiously out of place among the dead wreaths and the fading cotton flags of the soldiers' cemeteries. It is particularly out of place when the certainty of the soldier's grave that freedom was worth dying for is the only certainty men have to hold to. To offer to teach the men of such a generation how to avoid the pitfalls of prejudice and excessive belief is indeed to offer stones to those who starve for bread.

The fact is that the humanism of these various definitions is a humanism which finds its reason in the fifteenth century rather than our own — in the fifteenth century and in those later centuries in which, as in the fifteenth, the sickness of the soul was dogma and superstition. Humanism considered as an intellectual discipline-for-discipline's-sake, or as a regimen to free the mind of prejudice and infatuation, or as an aristocratic training of the taste, or as a cult of the classic past, or as the appreciation of fine arts and beautiful letters, is a prime specific for such ills as bigotry and puritanism and Jesuitry and vulgarity and Victorianism and the complacency of the bourgeois mind. But humanism so conceived has little if anything to say to a time in which the spiritual sickness is not excess of belief but lack of belief. And ours, if we understand the ills we suffer from, is such a time.

We have valued liberty enough to fight for it, and we know very well what enemy we detest, but the affirmative cause, not only of the war but of our lives, escapes us. When we debate, as we have debated endlessly, the question of what we are fighting for, we have sometimes thought it was what we are living for we needed most to know. The weakness is not in the time, we think, but in ourselves. We have seen whole peoples deliver their lives and purposes and wills to tyrants they themselves have invented out of a loud voice and a blathering mouth and a ridiculous uniform to satisfy the hunger of their fear. We have seen others who cried out for a great conversion of the world, a vast revival, a wind from beyond the planet and the stars, to fill us in spite of ourselves, and without our effort, by some miracle of faith, like the miracle they imagine to have happened when Christianity first took the world, or when the religion of the Prophet took it.

Everywhere in our time there are the signs and indications of a passion to believe, a passion to escape from the sense of human inadequacy which spreads and deepens as science and the mechanical arts disclose the enormous scale and the terrible potentialities of a universe vaster and more dangerous than men, before our generation, had imagined. The natural sciences open fissures in the skin of the earth and the cover of the sky which lead beyond human meaning. The specialists press their narrow drills of research outward and away from the human center of experience. The libraries overflow with a flood of printed pages, and knowledge has become too vast for men to know.

The world, we say to ourselves, is too large for us, too difficult to understand, too savage to restrain, too swift to master. It is no longer a world to be measured in distance by a man's foot, or in time by a man's sleeping and waking, or in danger by a man's strength or an animal's. It is a world beyond the capacity of men to control — a world that needs gods or men like gods. And so we long for the men like gods, or for the gods, to believe in.

Humanists may regret this hunger to believe, but they will be foolish, notwithstanding, if they ignore the longing of their generation; and worse than foolish if they do not see the significance of that longing to themselves and to their cause. For the meaning of our longing for belief is this: that we have lost our sense of the place of man in the universe.

It is to a generation which has lost this sense that the humanists now must offer what they have to teach. If they do not understand the significance of that fact to the philosophy they protest; if they persist in declaring that what they have to teach is a method only, a gymnastic, or at the best an antidote, a cleansing salt, an antiseptic; if they are unwilling to turn their questions into answers for a time that needs their answers — then they have themselves to thank, and not the blunders of the Army and the Navy, or the blindness of their colleagues in the universities, for the indifference of which they now complain.

IV

FOR there is a definition of humanism by which humanism becomes a belief in the one thing in which man has greatest need now to believe – himself, and the dignity and importance of the place he fills in the world he lives in. There is a definition of humanism by which humanism becomes precisely the belief of man in his own dignity, in his essential worth as a man, in what Ralph Barton Perry calls "his characteristic perfection": a belief not in the potentiality of man, but in the actuality of man; a belief not in the classic perfection of the beautiful letters men have written in the distant past, but in the human perfection of the men who wrote those letters and of others like them, whether writers or others than writers, and whether living in the past or in the present or not yet born; a belief not in the thing a man may become if he reads the right books and develops the right tastes and undergoes the right discipline, but a belief in the thing he is.

No one has put this better than Professor Perry in his superb *Definition of the Humanities.* "The reference to man in the context of the so-called 'humanities,'" he says, "is . . . not descriptive or apologetic, but eulogistic; not 'human – all too human,' or 'only human,' but human in the sense in which one deems it highest praise to be called 'a man.'" The answer humanism has it in its power to make to the two great questions, how to govern and how to teach, is the answer of belief in man, "in the sense in which one deems it highest praise to be called 'a man.'" If the world can be taught to believe in the worth of man, in the dignity of man, in the "characteristic perfection" of man, it can be taught not only to survive but to live. If the world can be governed in belief in the worth of man, in the dignity of man, it can be governed in peace.

These propositions need no proof. They speak for themselves. If government throughout the world were directed by a convinced belief in the dignity of man as man, in the worth of man as man, so that decisions of government were everywhere made in consonance with that belief and in furtherance of it, no one can doubt that the world would be well governed and that peace would be as nearly certain as peace can be in a variable universe. It is lack of faith in the essential dignity and worth of man which corrupts and weakens democratic governments, substituting for a government by the people in the people's interest, which is peace, a government of rulers in the rulers' interest – which may be war. It is doubt of the dignity and worth of man which opens the road to the tyrannies and dictatorships which have no choice but war. It is cynical contempt for the worth and dignity of man which makes the wars of the dictators wars of slavery and subjugation.

If the fundamental proposition upon which the government of the world was based were the proposition that man, because he is man, and in his essential quality as man, has worth and value which governments exist to serve and to protect, regardless of race and regardless of color or religion, there would be little room for the play of international politics which, under color of realism or under color of necessity, puts power first or oil first or gold first, and men second or nowhere, preparing thus for the wars of power or of oil or gold. If the first business of government everywhere were man, the whole man of the humanists; if the first object of government everywhere were the good of man, man "in the sense in which one deems it highest praise to be called 'a man'"; if the first principle of government everywhere were the principle that government exists for man and not man for government, there would be no place for the governments of which the first business is business, or for the governments of which the first object is economic advantage, or for the governments of which the first principle is power.

But to govern in this way it is necessary first of all to believe, and not merely to declare that one believes, in the fundamental worth and value of man and to practice that belief and never to cease to practice it. It is necessary to believe in man, not only as the Christians believe in man, out of pity, or as the democrats believe in man, out of loyalty, but also as the Greeks believed in man, out of pride.

V

THE same thing is true of the question how to teach. If education were informed with a belief in the dignity and worth of man; if the purpose of education were an understanding not only of the weaknesses of man and the sicknesses of man and the failures of man but of the essential nobility of man also, of his "characteristic perfection," men would be able again to occupy their lives and to live in the world as the Greeks lived in it, free of the bewilderment and frustration which has sent this generation, like the Gadarene * swine, squealing and stumbling and drunk with the longing for immolation, to hurl themselves into the abysses of the sea.

If science were taught, not as something external to man, something belittling of man, but as one of the greatest of the creations of the human spirit; if economics were taught not as a structure of deterministic laws superior to man and controlling his conduct, but as one

* At Gadara, in ancient Palestine, Jesus cast the evil spirits out of two men "possessed" and into a herd of swine, which reacted in the manner indicated by MacLeish. (See Matthew 8:28–32.)

of the many mirrors man has constructed to observe the things he does; if history and descriptive literature were taught not as peepholes through which the unworthy truth about mankind may be observed but as expressions of man's unique ability and willingness to see and judge himself; if belief in man and in his dignity and worth became the controlling principle of education, so that the people of the world were taught to respect the common principle of humanity in others and in themselves, and to believe that their lives would be shaped and their future determined not by some law of economics, or by some formula of science, or by some regimen of the subconscious, but by their own wills and on their own responsibility — if these things could be accomplished, who will doubt that the sense of irresponsibility and frustration which has driven so many millions of our contemporaries down the blind steep of slavery into war could be corrected?

The task education must accomplish, if free societies are to continue to exist, is the re-creation of the sense of individual responsibility — which means the re-establishment of the belief of men in man. Fascism is only another name for the sickness and desperation which overcome a society when it loses its sense of responsibility for its own life and surrenders its will to a tyrant it, and it alone, has invented. But the sense of responsibility in a nation is a sense of responsibility in the individuals who compose that nation, for the sense of responsibility is always a charge upon the individual conscience and vanishes when many share it. And to re-create the sense of individual responsibility it is necessary to restore the belief of men in man — the belief that man can direct his destiny if he will.

It is impossible to charge the consciences of men with responsibility for the world they live in without convincing them that they can act upon their world — that the power to decide and act is theirs. No one knew that better than Abraham Lincoln, who knew many things about the human soul. When it became necessary for him, in the terrible December of 1862, to drive home to the Congress a sense of its responsibility, he used these words: "Fellow citizens, we cannot escape history. We of this Congress and this Administration will be remembered in spite of ourselves. No personal significance or insignificance can spare one or another of us. The fiery trial through which we pass will light us down, in honor or dishonor, to the latest generation. . . . We — even we here — hold the power and bear the responsibility."

What education in the free countries must drive home, if the free countries are to survive, is the conviction that we — even we here — hold the power and bear the responsibility. The task is in part a task beyond the power of the schools as such, for the sense of individual responsibility and power involves a sense of individual participation, and a sense of individual participation is only possible in a society in which individuals can make themselves felt directly and not through agglomerations of money or people. There must be social changes as well as educational changes. But the educational changes come first. Not until men believe that the responsibility can be theirs to bear, and therefore should be theirs to bear, will they make it theirs. To teach men to believe in themselves therefore is to teach them responsibility and so to assure their freedom.

VI

THESE, as I understand humanism, are the answers the humanists have it in their power to give to their time and to the questions their time has asked of them. They are answers which seem to me to be true and to dispose, once and for all, of the question whether humanism has anything to say to the generation to which we belong. Any school, any philosophy, which can go as close to the root of the essential sickness of our time has a right to be heard, and may claim that right, and may denounce fairly and justly those who deprive it of that right, pretending that other points of view are more practical and therefore more important.

But these answers are not the answers, as I read the record, which the humanists — all the humanists at least — are willing to give. On the contrary, many humanists would reject them, and reject them for a reason which goes very deep. They would reject them because the dignity of man in which they believe is not the dignity implicit in these answers — is not, that is to say, a dignity which men possess because they are men, but only a dignity which men may earn by undergoing certain disciplines and acquiring certain characteristics.

Man, to these humanists, is not born with worth, but may acquire worth. Until he has earned it he has no right or reason to believe in himself, nor should a belief in man determine the attitude in which he is to be ruled. Humanism to these humanists, in other words, is not a democratic doctrine on which a practice of self-government can be founded, but an aristocratic doctrine which, because its concern is inward, has little to say of government of any kind. It is, if anything, a doctrine opposed to democracy and to theories of the universal worth of man, because excellence, not equality, is its goal and purpose.

It would be a mistake to dismiss these humanists as dwellers in towers, or their definitions as definitions of refuge. The passion for excellence can be a sword as well as a sanctuary. Committed to the love of the arts and the great books and the monuments of unaging intellect, as Yeats so wonderfully called them, and the courtesies and graces and perceptions of a civilized and generous life, the worshipers of excellence have waged war, and noble war, against an increasing vulgarity which has won its greatest triumphs in our time, having found the mechanical means at last to intrude its coarseness into every hour, however private, and every chamber, however secret, of our lives.

Those to whom humanism is the worship of excellence do not admit, as they look around them in the streets and trains and hotel lobbies of our world, that all men have dignity and worth. They do not believe, as they look back across the centuries to the world they imagine to have existed in Athens and in Rome that all men are able to govern themselves or should be allowed to. They do not agree, as they face the crisis of our time, that freedom is the answer to everything. They do not necessarily hold with public freedom. The freedom they seek is inward in the large and lofty world of enlightened intellect where learning paints the various landscape and a trained and delicate taste selects the road. That there must be peace and quiet outside the mind, if a man is to journey within it, they readily admit. But the peace without, they say, is not their business.

VII

IT IS understandable enough that men should love what these men love, and hate what they hate. Their ideal of the truly civilized man is in every way admirable. Their contempt for a world in which taste is determined in advertising agencies, and intelligence is measured by the answers children give to questions on the air, is a contempt which later generations of Americans will not find strange. But what is not understandable is their choice of the word humanism to describe their inward and selective life. Humanism as a word cannot cut itself off from its root or forget its derivation. Humanism, to deserve the *humanitas* from which it comes, must incorporate some notion of things appropriate to every man as man — things worthy of man in every man.

It must incorporate, that is to say, some notion of a universal dignity which men possess as men and by virtue of their manhood. The dignity of man upon which a philosophy of man, a school devoted to man, is based cannot be a rare and sought-for attribute which only the school can teach man to acquire and only the philosophy aid man to deserve. You do not construct out of the airy goal at which you hope to arrive the solid ground from which you depart. You do not derive the dignity of man on which your philosophy is founded from the dignity which those few who practice your philosophy can claim to possess. The dignity of man is either here and now or it is never. It is either in mankind or it is nowhere.

One can no more make an aristocracy of human dignity than one can make an aristocracy of human love or human curiosity, or any other fundamental human characteristic. Some men will develop their manlike qualities farther than others. Some will be more learned, have surer taste, livelier imagination, greater gentility — will be, in brief, more civilized than others. But whatever the degree of their development, the qualities with which the true humanist is concerned are the manlike qualities — the qualities which men possess because they are men; the qualities, therefore, which all men possess to one degree or another. It is man whom the humanist values, and man is in all men — *is* all men.

To limit humanism, therefore, — to put a narrower construction upon it than this, — is quite literally to deprive it of its fundamental meaning. It is as though a select association of superior and cultivated people were to call themselves the association of mankind. The word mankind, in such a context, would have an ironic meaning or have none at all. So humanism, if its concern is not man, and therefore all men, has only an ironic meaning or has none. But founded on the universal human basis which its root implies, the name becomes a noble and intelligible word with meanings which our time needs more than any others.

This war is a war against those who, in contempt of man and in despair of man's power to direct his life, have surrendered their lives into the hands of tyrants they themselves have created. It is a war against the philosophy of contempt for man and despair of his future which those who have surrendered their lives have invented to justify themselves, or have accepted from their masters. It is a war therefore in which the issue is, in last analysis, the issue of man — of the concept of man which is to shape and control our time; of the idea of man which governments are to reflect and societies to mirror.

We, on our side, have found it easy to put our cause into negative words, into words of resistance. We are opposed to the philosophy of contempt for man and to those who accept that philosophy: we have seen what it does to those who practice it and to those upon whom it is practiced also. But we have not found it easy to put our cause into the affirmative words of our own purpose. And for this reason: that the affirmative statement of our cause is a declaration of belief in man, and we have not been altogether ready and willing to make that declaration, since we too have felt the winds of fear and doubt which turned our enemies to disbelievers. More than anything else, we need a rebirth of belief in ourselves as men. If humanism will make itself the instrument of that renaissance of man, its place, not only in the universities but in the world, is sure. For if it will make itself that instrument it will give our time its cause.

QUESTIONS

1. In Paragraph 1, Section I, MacLeish states clearly two questions which he intends to consider. How is this intention justified in Paragraphs 3, 4, and 5? How does the first sentence of the paragraph on page 425 beginning "The serious question . . ." indicate the scope of the essay? What do the style and diction of Section I reveal about the mood and purpose of the writer?

2. In Section II, Paragraph 4 to the end of the section, what definitions of humanism (or humanist) are mentioned? Why, in MacLeish's opinion, is each of these definitions inadequate? How is this reason related to the thought of Paragraph 2, Section III?

3. Of what importance in the selection is the first sentence of Paragraph 1, Section IV? In the second sentence, how does the context suggest the difference between "classic" perfection and "human" perfection? How is Paragraph 2 in this section related to the essay as a whole?

4. In the second sentence of Paragraph 4, Section IV, note that the clauses in parallel structure are related to the phrases in parallel structure toward the end. How does this sentence resemble in structure the one long sentence in Paragraph 2, Section V? How does it differ?

5. Point out the unifying idea and the supporting statements in Section VI. Note that in the last paragraph of Section VII MacLeish insists that a positive rather than a negative attitude is needed. With which of these two attitudes has Section VI dealt?

6. Is the main appeal of the author in this selection intellectual, or emotional? In arriving at your answer, consider tone, diction, and subject matter.

VANNEVAR BUSH. For biographical headnote, see "As We May Think" on page 308.

CAN MEN LIVE WITHOUT WAR?

by VANNEVAR BUSH

NEARLY fifty years ago William James wrote an essay which he called "The Moral Equivalent of War." Since then many things have happened: there have been two world wars, a crippling depression, and now a phenomenal burst of fairly solid prosperity. The whole art of war has been profoundly altered by the application of science. A new kind of empire has arisen, rigidly controlled and avowedly bent on world conquest. The old colonial empires have disintegrated, and a new spirit of nationalism pervades lands that were once inarticulate. Most important of all, there is a growing understanding of what war may mean, and a deep yearning among all peoples for peace. It is proper, therefore, to review the arguments which James advanced and to do so in the light of the new circumstances.

James foresaw, with a clarity which was remarkable, that war would sometime end. At a time when warfare and the applications of science were poles apart, he said, "And when whole nations are the armies, and the science of destruction vies in intellectual refinement with the sciences of production, I see that war becomes absurd and impossible from its own monstrosity."

And so he turned to what might follow, with evident apprehension that men would become soft — that the virility which had brought the race thus far would give place to flat insipidity.

He first stated the case of the apologists for war, better than they themselves had stated it, repeating the only alternatives they offered: "a world of clerks and teachers, of co-education and zo-ophily, of 'consumers' leagues' and 'associated charities,' of industrialism unlimited, and feminism unabashed. No scorn, no hardness, no valor any more! Fie upon such a cattleyard of a planet!"

With this extreme point of view he evidently had a genuine sympathy, for he added: "So far as the central essence of this feeling goes, no healthy minded person, it seems to me, can help to some degree partaking of it. Militarism is the great preserver of our ideals of hardihood, and human life with no use for hardihood would be contemptible. Without risks or prizes for the darer, history would be insipid indeed; and there is a type of military character which every one feels that the race should never cease to breed."

But when he then sought a moral equivalent for war he was far from convincing. His alternative was the struggle with nature as a substitute for the struggle between men and nations. Rugged though the struggle with nature sometimes is, we can hardly believe that it would fully serve to keep the red blood flowing hot in our veins, and to release the adrenalin which is the messenger between a virile mind and a fighting body. For the conquest of nature today involves only relatively few of us, and it is becoming an intellectual effort rather than a matter of brute strength. So James left me, at least, disappointed with his alternative and bewildered. Let us review his line of argument, in the present setting, and see whether there may be a way out of the dilemma.

His first point may indeed now be underlined. We strive for peace today with conviction and intensity, for great wars must cease if we are to pursue further the path of progress. And our striving is by no means hopeless. If great wars are outlawed – not by treaty, perhaps, but by a general realization of their absurdity – secondary wars will go on for a time by conventional means, and nations will maintain their postures of readiness to fight. But the end of all war is now definitely in sight for the first time in human history. No nation can today attack its prepared neighbor with the expectation of profiting immensely and securing a place in the sun, as has been attempted twice within our memory. The result today would be devastation for all, cities utterly destroyed, populations killed and maimed, starvation and disease rampant. That this is the brute fact is now obvious to the most obtuse. Nor can a tyrant or ruling clique, by bringing on a war, hope to advance their private interests or provide a diversion from popular discontent; no modern all-out war will leave in power anywhere those who perpetrated it.

War might, to be sure, come by accident, and this we must guard against assiduously. Little wars with the foolhardy use of weapons of mass destruction could lead to a great war; and if tempers rise, we shall need to curb the trigger-happy fools among us. Were we so gullible as to let down our guard too soon and invite a surprise mass attack which would prevent our retaliation and end the conflict at a single stroke, the invitation might be seized upon by those who still think of conquering the world by force of arms. It is not impossible that a group of desperate men could pull the temple down on all of us.

But the conditions and concepts which brought on most of the great wars of history have now disappeared. We are all on notice, if we can read or listen, that indulgence in all-out war would be suicide. Self-preservation is a very powerful primary urge, and an understanding of the present monstrosity of war is increasing among the masses of people in spite of both iron and bamboo curtains. There is certainly more chance than ever before that we may now look forward to peace. In fact, we may conclude that we can have peace if we are not utterly gullible or careless.

II

THE second point made by James also deserves emphasis. The main argument of the apologists for war has vanished as science has stepped into the picture. Whatever else may happen, the glamour of war is gone.

Where do the virtues of war lie today? Is courage needed to watch a radar screen or adjust a guided missile? Where is the daring of the soldier when the folks at home encounter equal risks? When one man guides a plane that can destroy a city, what becomes of the infectious influence of comradeship, the sense of being engaged with many others in a common hazardous campaign, the identification of self with a group which could inspire, or was supposed to inspire, even the common soldier with ideals and courage? Great war has become complex and must now be fought at a distance, if at all. It has lost forever those qualities that once had a real appeal for the red-blooded man.

Do we then look forward to some sort of Utopia? James had little use for Utopias, for he wrote in "The Dilemma of Determinism": —

> Why does the painting of any paradise or utopia, in heaven or on earth, awaken such yawnings for nirvana and escape? The white-robed harp-playing heaven of our sabbath-schools, and the ladylike tea-table elysium represented in Mr. Spencer's Data of Ethics, as the final consummation of progress, are exactly on a par in this respect, — lubberlands, pure and simple, one and all. . . . If *this* be the whole fruit of the victory, we say; if the generations of mankind suffered and laid down their lives; if prophets confessed and martyrs sang in the fire, and all the sacred tears were shed for no other end than that a race of creatures of such unexampled insipidity should succeed, and protract . . . their contented and inoffensive lives, — why, at such a rate, better lose than win the battle, or at all events better ring down the curtain before the last act of the play, so that a business that began so importantly may be saved from so singularly flat a winding-up.

We need have little fear of any such dismal outcome. Struggles will not cease even if armed conflict ends. Between nations there will continue to be political jockeying for position and very intense economic competition. We shall still need to cope with penetration and subversion and face the difficult task of guiding our friends among the younger nations to positions of true independence and stability.

Nor will struggle and conflict end in our internal affairs. We shall have much to quarrel about.

Our racial antagonisms have by no means vanished. We hope we have learned to avoid great depressions, but on this score we should by no means be sanguine. Whether we can maintain full employment without forcing inflation remains to be seen. The division of our product between capital, labor, and management can still lead to paralyzing strikes. We have narcotics, juvenile delinquency, defiance of law. The preservation of our liberties demands eternal vigilance. If we are easygoing, a swollen bureaucracy will certainly regiment us. Our political contests can still be embittered and sordid.

If war ceases, it will be a different sort of world; and the apologists for war usually overlook one of its primary attributes, the ending of which might greatly influence our lives in subtle ways. During the past two decades this country has forged ahead at an unprecedented rate until it stands as the unquestioned leader of the free world, powerful, disciplined, even wise as it attempts to press further by lifting its neighbors with it. War and the fear of war produced this result – produced also our present great prosperity. And this did not occur because of war profits; for there are no such things as war profits for a country as a whole; war merely wastes man's goods and man's labor. In many nations the waste has overbalanced all else, but we were fortunate. Our advance has come about because the nation became internally united and went to work, because secondary quarrels were submerged or tempered in the common cause, because public opinion forced the channeling of all effort in a single direction, because men's spirits rose and their blood ran hot as they faced together an enemy that all could recognize. Where would we now be had there been no such cement to hold us together during the past twenty years – if we had worked at cross-purposes, occupied ourselves with petty quarrels, or succumbed to the vices of intrigue and treachery?

Does this mean that, if peace comes and the fear of war is lifted, we shall again return to all the old quarrels and become a nation divided, split into factions with animosity and petty intrigues paramount? Does it mean that we shall lose the vision of a happy and prosperous nation, brought about by our own unity and determination, in which we can approach our disagreements objectively and in a spirit of relative good will? Does it mean that we shall forget how to battle with one another vigorously and with full conviction and determination, but standing up, and shall again thrash about in the mire of mutual suspicion? Do biting and kicking have to take the place of honest blows given and received?

III

THE citizens of this country have shown that they take most of the guarantees of the Bill of Rights for granted, that they see no real danger to our primary liberties or any need to be keenly on the alert to preserve them; and in this complacency lies danger. But there is one element of the free life that is not taken for granted at all, that is highly valued, and that men are willing to fight for, if necessary, without question. This element is the opportunity for an individual to rise as far as his talents, health, and determination will take him, without artificial barriers of any kind.

We have by no means reached perfection in this regard. There are still artificial barriers of race, birth, and resources. Nor would we banish the paternal instinct, forbid the father to aid his son to make a good start in life, or frown on any effort of a man to help one of his fellows. There is a fundamental difference between this mutual aid — even the banding together of groups with mutual interests for mutual advancement — and the throwing of artificial obstacles in the path of a young man struggling to rise by his own efforts. We shall always have with us those who will drift, who will refuse to pull their weight in the boat, to whom opportunity means nothing; but the problem of their place in society is not one that concerns us here. It is the artificial obstacle in the path of the ambitious and able that we would banish, and this has not as yet been fully accomplished.

But we have proceeded much farther toward the ideal than ever before in any country at any time. The workman at the bench recognizes the artificial limitations that surround him; and his own ambitions may be ended. But he knows, too, that for his son, his neighbor's son, or the bright attractive boy down the street there are genuine opportunities to rise to positions of influence and satisfaction. Luck, the caprice of men in high places, loyalty to dependents, an insidious bacterium or virus — any one of these may stop him in his tracks. Only a few will have the ambition to rise and the skill and personality that must go with it. But the opportunity is there, and it is real. The son of a tailor on the east side may become the honored surgeon, respected by men of power, loved by patients who owe their lives to him. The peddler of bananas may come to rule an industrial empire he has built. The painter's helper may become a labor leader and treat on equal terms with the captains of industry. The haberdasher may become president. It has happened. The bans and taboos are less than they ever were before. This is the land of opportunity, and we had better keep it so and enhance this central aspect of our liberty.

It is this which may yet bind us together in the ideal of brotherhood among men, not as a vague generality to which we pay lip service but as a living reality, exemplified by the opportunity for all to develop their talents to the utmost for their own benefit and the benefit of their fellow men.

We look forward to living in a new sort of world. The flowering of science, which has rendered war absurd, is also giving us wealth, comfort, and freedom from disease of the body or the mind. Our contests for position in the intricate fabric of society need no longer require that the unsuccessful shall suffer want and distress.

When individual progress is artificially barred, when men are divided into classes with impenetrable barriers, when men are serfs or slaves, or fettered by false restraint so that they cannot move, struggles on any subject are bound to be bitter. When a man knows that if he loses out, in competition with his fellows, those he loves will be ill-nourished and neglected, he must fight too desperately to care for the conventions of fairness and decency.

But when artificial barriers are gone, and men may rise if they have what it takes — when there is a floor beneath which no man need fall, a floor that will ensure a decent life — then the contests of men with one another may well be on a different plane. The key is the preservation and enhancement of individual opportunity in all its forms. Few will rise, for few are the places to fill at the top. But all will have dignity and satisfaction; and those who prefer for any reason to remain in humble and peasant status will do so by choice.

We can have peace. And with it we can have prosperity, greater than the world has ever seen, with a distribution of its blessings that preserves the necessary order of an industrial society while avoiding both arrogant opulence and cringing poverty. As we attain these things, whenever we do, shall we return to petty bickering and strife, sordid intrigue, and bitter recriminations? Or shall we tackle our problems as men, vigorously, with courage and convictions, pulling no punches, but with decency and fairness? We may, indeed, be able to rise to the latter if we keep our senses and our objectivity — and, above all, if we open the door of opportunity wide so that we battle as free men, in the pride and dignity to which only free men may aspire.

Here, indeed, may be an acceptable equivalent for war, preserving and enhancing in our people those virile attributes which conquered the old frontiers and built an industrial civilization beyond compare. When the foolhardy nature of international combat is fully recognized and great wars are banished, we may still struggle with nature and with one another and thus keep the vitality of the race from being sapped by insipid ease. If we do so as free men, independent, proud, seizing our opportunity in an open field from which artificial barriers have been removed, we may find that struggle, so necessary for the health of our race, can be entered upon in decency and dignity, and the vulgarity of war may give place to strife for worthy causes conducted with fairness and good will.

Yet, having said this, we have not come to the end of the matter. Man needs to exercise his virile attributes — in sport, in coping with the hazards of the wilderness, in honest and decent conflict with his fellows for just and worthy causes. No man has fully lived who has not experienced the fear, the exultation, of meeting great odds and struggling to prevail. But no man has fully lived who has not also experienced the joy of close association with worthy fellows or who has not known the thrill of individual creation. He who can say honestly to himself that he has discovered a set of facts or a relation between phenomena not known to any man before him in all history, and that by his insight and skill he has made them comprehensible to the human intellect — such a man experiences the same uplift of spirit as the one who first climbs a high mountain or first runs a mile in four minutes. And when the accomplishment results not from the lonely acts of individual genius but from the efforts of a team or group having mutual trust and confidence, supplementing one another's skills, compensating for one another's weaknesses, carrying the unfortunate over the rough places, heartening the leader by steadfast support — then all members of the group enjoy a satisfaction transcending that of accomplished creation, a satisfaction of success in their margin of effort to attain something that was beyond the capacity of any individual.

If war ends, we must still have outlets for our inherited energies; we need only attempt to render them dignified and worthy. But we shall also have increased opportunities for other satisfactions, not so intense but far more lasting and substantial. The unifying bond of war will be gone, but it can give place to a nobler bond, less universal, far more genuine and strong. This can appear in the midst of diverse careers. To me, naturally, the field of science stands out uniquely in its opportunities.

The country will be full of struggle and conflict as diverse causes are fought over. As individuals and citizens we enter if our consciences and inclinations so dictate. And by entering we may help to raise the level of the contests and render them worthy. But research centers such as the Carnegie Institution stand aside from all this.

Within the institutions dedicated to scientific research lies opportunity for the individual. They do not care about a man's origins—his country, race, or religion. They seek men who have an ambition to rise to the heights in their scientific professions, and insist, moreover, that among their talents should be a large measure of ability to rise by effective collaboration with others. They want men of generous instinct, and men who are devoted to science because they believe that the life of a scientist yields more satisfaction than any other career on earth and contributes more genuinely to the public weal. When they find a young man of this sort they welcome him with open arms. After that no artificial barrier stands in his path. He can rise as rapidly and as high in his profession as his own effort, judgment, and skill will carry him. He will be judged only according to the estimation in which he is held by fellow scientists—his peers. The requirements are rigorous, but the opportunity these institutions offer is real and complete. We must always keep it so.

No more war? Peace is indeed in sight if we are wise. But not an end of contest or struggle. And certainly not an end of opportunity, which may render the lives of those who follow us not insipid but virile, not belligerent but creative.

QUESTIONS

1. How does the author justify his use of the essay by William James? What is the meaning of the phrase "apologists for war," in Paragraph 4, Section I? What value of war is stressed in Paragraph 5? To what extent is the belief of Bush (as revealed in Section I) similar to that of James?

2. Show how the phrase "glamour of war" (Paragraph 1, Section II) is related to Paragraphs 4–5, Section I, and Paragraph 2, Section II. List the various kinds of conflicts which might continue even if war ceases. What is the primary attribute referred to in the first sentence of the next to the last paragraph in Section II?

3. Which of the three sentences in Paragraph 1, Section III, is most essential to the development of the author's thought? Explain. Why is the word "artificial" used so frequently in Section III? According to Bush, what is the distinctive function of science and, more specifically, of a research center such as the Carnegie Institution?

4. What key words or phrases in Section III—in addition to "artificial barriers"—bring out the principal idea Bush leaves with the reader?

5. Bush does not emphasize the horrors and the catastrophic nature of another world war. What does this fact reveal about the author's purpose in the essay? Does he appeal to the emotions of the reader?

CLARENCE B. RANDALL completed his formal education at Harvard University in 1915; then he practiced law in Michigan for ten years. For over thirty years, starting in 1925, he was associated with the Inland Steel Company, of which he became president in 1949 and chairman of the board in 1953. Although chiefly an industrialist and financier, he has found time to serve on the boards of two major universities – Harvard and Chicago – and to act as chairman of President Eisenhower's Commission on Foreign Economic Policy in 1954. After his retirement from Inland Steel in 1956, he became the President's special adviser on economic relations with other countries. In his writing, Randall has concerned himself with basic national problems, as the following titles indicate: *Civil Liberties and Industrial Conflict,* written with Roger N. Baldwin of the American Civil Liberties Union (1938), *A Creed for Free Enterprise* (1952), and *Freedom's Faith* (1953).

FREE ENTERPRISE IS NOT A HUNTING LICENSE

by CLARENCE B. RANDALL

THESE are very sobering days for the American businessman. The world as we have known it is falling to pieces around us. The relentless and paralyzing creep of socialism day by day draws nearer to the things in which we most deeply believe.

The other evening I happened to be at the home of a friend of mine in one of our Chicago suburbs which is very remote, and as I sat there in his lovely country home, I said, "What do you do around here when the house catches fire?"

He said, "Perfectly simple. We know exactly what to do. We get on the telephone immediately. All the neighbors rush over and watch the house burn." We mustn't be that way in the business field today.

Or to put another metaphor to you, think of the villagers who live on the side of Vesuvius. Suddenly they see the top of the mountain blow off. The hot lava starts flowing relentlessly down the side of the mountain, burning here a bush and there a tree, and they wonder whose house will be first. They stand idly by with a sense of desperate futility because they don't know what to do about it. That must not be true with us. And in my judgment it need not be true with us. This avalanche can be stopped.

I have searched my mind as to why it is, as businessmen, we seem so paralyzed with fear these days, and so certain that we are going down the chute. We know that socialism is a failure. If ever the people of the world needed a laboratory experiment to disprove the theories of the Fabian socialists, they have it in the conditions in England. And it is no mere accident that the one nation strong enough to bear the troubles of the whole world is the last citadel of free enterprise.

Across the seas we have seen our Anglo-Saxon cousins try the experiment which is offered now to us, and have seen them go down close to complete bankruptcy and destruction. I have watched it with my friends in the British steel industry. Because of my service in the Marshall Plan I have come to have wide acquaintance with men in the steel industry in Europe.

I once talked with an officer of one of the great steel companies of England, and he told me: "I say to you something I have said to no countryman. I don't think I can take it. I think I must stop. All the things that I believed in are gone. I have no incentive to go forward. If I win, nobody will give me credit; if I lose, I will be blamed. I think I must stop."

Now, what can that mean in the economic stagnation of a country? What will it mean if the men who should be the national leaders suddenly feel they can't take it, that they have to stand aside?

That great laboratory experiment in socialization is before the world; and yet, in the face of it, disguised socialization is offered to us day by day in myriad forms, and we know it, are disheartened, but are not certain what to do about it.

I have searched my mind as to what may be the reason why the American businessman today is not making headway against this trend with the same vigor, the same determination, that he ought to have, and I am afraid I am led rather sorrowfully to this conclusion: that in his own natural circle of influence the American businessman today is not looked to as the leader. I say that sadly, but I am afraid it is true. Yet if we in our own individual circles of influence are not the natural leaders of the people, we cannot collectively form public opinion.

Now, it was not always thus. A hundred years ago, when our prairies were being broken into civilization, the businessman was the leader. He formed the communities. He built the churches and the schools and established the courts; he participated in the territorial and then the state government; he went to Washington; when war threatened, he raised the company of volunteers; it was he who formed public opinion, and it was toward him that people looked for guidance and leadership.

That was still true fifty years ago in my boyhood, and I think of a figure in the village I lived in in New York State who typified the things I am talking about. In my little town of less than 800 people, a farming community, my father kept the general store. We had just one industrialist in that town, and he was the blacksmith.

Now, he was the best blacksmith in all those parts. There were other blacksmiths in the villages near by, but whenever there was a tough job it came to our man. He had a good forge, good tools, he was absolutely tops in his craft; but that wasn't why he was the leader in our village. Without that he could not have qualified, but he knew that when he went home at night from the forge, having been a good craftsman all day, his job wasn't done. In addition, he was the superintendent of our Sunday School; he was the one under whom I learned the Ten Commandments and the Sermon on the Mount, and learned to sing the beloved old hymns. But that wasn't enough. He was also the president of our school board, and when I graduated from high school, he handed me my diploma. As his fame spread from our village to the surrounding villages, he came to be widely known in the county, and we sent him to the legislature as the representative of all the people.

II

FOUR things about that old blacksmith typify the qualities needed today in business leadership. The men in the steel industry and the forging industry are the lineal descendants of that early blacksmith, spiritually speaking. We must be tops in our job. We owe it to American production to let no man excel us in competence in our business jobs, but we have no right to think that that in itself establishes us as leaders in our communities, because it doesn't.

Who among us is superintendent of a Sunday School or is having a part in some other character-forming agency? We decry double morality in government and corruption in high places; yet what as businessmen are we doing to form sturdy characters in the young men and women who will bear those responsibilities in another twenty years? We turn to the universities for the best brains they have to bring into our businesses. We seek them avidly. What are we doing about maintaining those educational institutions? We know perfectly well that with a privately endowed institution the student's tuition pays less than half of the cost of that education. Are we willing to take that education as a gift to us and do nothing to perpetuate those institutions that mean so much to us? Who among us seeks out the principal of the local high school and brings him home to dinner for a chat, and who invites the professors of the colleges and universities to his business places that they may understand firsthand his business problems?

Who among us takes the active part in the day-to-day political life of our nation that he should? We shrug that off, assuming that somewhere there is a group of wise and able men with lots of leisure to perform those tasks. We cry out for the best of leadership in American life, but who among us has run for office, who has gone down to Washington, who has left his business desk to stand at Charles Wilson's side to help bear the burden of government in this crisis?

Those are heart-searching questions, my friends, but they bear directly upon this problem of business leadership. I have the feeling that as businessmen we worship production too much. That is a strange thing for me to be saying. I am tremendously proud of the job of production that the steel industry has done. When I look back at what steel capacity was when the other war began, and what it is today, it seems to me unbelievable that in the state of advancing costs that we have faced, the steel industry has brought about the miracle of increase in production that it has.

All of the steel production of the free world outside of the United States is, of course, less than ours; and yet, as I say, I think we can go too far in polishing our own ego by telling ourselves over and over again what great big wonderful men we are in production. After all, production is not an end in life. Production is a tool. God didn't put man on this earth just for industrial production. He put man on this earth to live the good life, the rich, full life, to develop the powers of his mind and the powers of his spirit, to make the world a better place because he has lived in it. We must keep production in its place as we think about life.

The people in your community, frankly, aren't terribly excited just because you have increased your production 50 per cent since 1945. That leaves them just a little cold. They would like to know what is going to happen to the pavement in front of their house; they would like to know how long you are going to stand by and see gambling places open to their high school seniors. They want to know how long the hospital in your town is going to be unable to take in the desperately ill, and so on through the whole gamut of community and civic services which are your job as well as theirs.

Whenever an industry goes into a new, remote place, what does it do? What has the oil industry done since it has gone into Venezuela? The first thing the oil people do is to build a modern community. They recognize that it is their job to see that there are good housing, good churches, good schools, good entertainment and recreation, and everything that goes to make the good life for the American. That job is your job as much when you live in a congested city as it is when you operate in the remote place, only you don't quite see it.

Only by re-establishing ourselves in leadership in the things that mean something to the people, and not merely in production, will they turn to us for guidance on these social and economic questions with which we think the country is threatened.

III

Now, when people lose the respect of those about them, several things ordinarily account for it. One of the first is always the question of integrity. No man can have an important part in forming public opinion if there is the slightest question about his integrity. I don't mean vulgar things like stealing money or juggling accounts, but I think we may well do some heart-searching on various aspects of our business creed on the subject of intellectual honesty. We dislike people in government who talk out of both sides of their mouths. We must, however, be very careful that we, ourselves, don't talk out of both sides of our mouths.

The first and obvious question is whether we have genuine, vital, honest competition one with the other. The free-enterprise system is not just a hunting license to you to get all that you can get without restraint. The free-enterprise system is a way of life which brings the greatest good to the greatest number, but it must be policed by the free market. The two are inseparable.

We resent price controls. We say that price controls are not required because the operation of natural laws, supply and demand, will themselves adjust prices. The thing we dislike about it is that those natural laws are suspended by government. Now, if that be true, and if those natural laws are what guarantees to the public the integrity of the free-enterprise system, we have no right as private individuals to suspend them. We have no right as honest men to tamper with that automatic control mechanism.

My friends of the British steel industry tried it and they got nationalization. They wanted price rigging; they would rather have the guaranteed price than freedom. They took price fixing under government control, and thereby created the handy tool which government needed and used to nationalize them, and I say we can't have it both ways. We can't have the freedom of free enterprise and not assure to the American people a free market.

The second thing that bears upon our intellectual honesty is our understanding of the sources of capital. The free-enterprise system must perpetuate itself; it must find the capital for expansion in the savings of the people. If we can persuade enough new people to become partners with us in industry, we shall simultaneously find our required new capital and solve our public relations problem. We have no choice but to turn boldly toward the mass savings of the two most powerful political groups in America — the worker and the farmer. That the worker and the farmer have in the aggregate sufficient savings to relieve the capital stress in heavy industry seems to be clear from every authoritative survey. But it is equally clear that at present neither of these groups is devoting its savings to the purchase of common stocks.

One thing is certain, and that is that there must be no employer pressure. Our job is to explain and to create an atmosphere of understanding, but the action must be voluntary on the part of the worker. He must take the risk because his self-interest is aroused, but he must do it with his eyes open.

I know of no reliable statistics on this subject, but as nearly as I can guess less than 2 per cent of the men and women employed in the production of steel own stock in their respective companies. And one of the most revealing figures is the low percentage of officials and supervisors who buy the stocks of their companies. They buy new automobiles and television sets, but not common stocks. As their future has become more secure through the operation of pension plans, they have tended to live more and more right up to the limit of their current incomes. They show little understanding of their personal relationship to the perpetuation of the industry that provides their livelihood.

We have help at hand where self-interest is very much at stake. The security exchanges and security dealers across the country sense this problem keenly and would welcome support from the industry.

Some think that the best medium is the open-end investment trust, designed specially for the farmer or the worker. The thing that might be lost there is the sense of ownership and stake in a particular enterprise. The worker and the farmer do pay insurance premiums, and insurance companies lend money to companies, but the process is so diluted that the ultimate investor does not know our successes or fear our losses.

To these and similar questions I have no specific answers. But twenty-five years ago neither did the engineers who were struggling with continuous rolling. They saw a job to be done and did it. And because they were determined and resourceful, vast new areas of usefulness to the public were opened up to the steel industry. This new challenge is different. It is abstract. It is intangible. But its possibilities are likewise vast. When we reach every responsible segment of the American public through the time-honored method of joint venture, we shall find our future expansion adequately financed.

We shall have the public with us instead of against us.

Unless we can bring into industry the mass savings of the workers, we shall not have sufficient capital for the further development of industry. We have to teach the American public the profit-and-loss system of risking for gain. And we must not take the easy way out, of asking government for capital. I say integrity is involved when any advocate of the free-enterprise system turns to government for anything, whether it be money or a special law or a special regulation.

We must be tough; we must recognize that if we believe in free enterprise we have to accept its limitations in order to get its values.

Now, this takes me straight to this point: the time has come when every American businessman must have his own thoughtful, personal philosophy. He has to know what he believes and why. We sometimes think that we have put in a terrific day because we have worked so many hours or kept so many appointments.

I am a little tired of hearing how hard men work, in terms of the hours they put in and the number of places they have rushed to by automobile or airplane. It isn't the number of hours you put in in a day, it is the number of ideas you have in a day, that counts now.

We are in a conflict of ideas, and the forces of darkness are well equipped with men who understand ideas and how to use them. I know a man in business who has a very responsible job, and thinks he is a great success, who to my knowledge hasn't read a book in twenty-five years. He wouldn't know what to do with a book if you gave him one.

We need time to think; we need time to reflect and to understand and to do the heart-searching that I have been talking about. We must have opinions on the questions that are perplexing these friends of ours who are in government. We must understand the problems of business. We must also get to the top level and try to understand the implications of the foreign problems of our country. As we approach those difficult questions, we must study, have patience and honest discussion with those who differ from us. We must consciously try to forge a philosophy that is clear in our own minds.

That is all necessary if we are to be restored as leaders in America. Having once formed that philosophy, we must do something about it. We must communicate those ideas to those about us on every conceivable occasion, by every medium at our disposal.

Take the worker. Why should the worker be barred from knowing what the opinion of the boss is about taxes, about Korea, about politics? If the worker is barred from our leadership, it is by our default.

Now, I would be the first to insist that no management plan intrude upon the proper function of labor leadership in such things as collective bargaining. It is right that the worker who is organized should turn to his leaders in the subject matters that deal with employment, but there is no reason at all why he should turn to those leaders any more than to you for guidance and for wisdom in the great social, political, and economic questions of the day. And I have a sneaking opinion he would rather know your opinion than he would the other fellow's. He honestly thinks you know more about these things than his labor leaders and you aren't telling him, you aren't doing a thing about it. And in that connection you are certainly overlooking the distaff side. What the woman thinks is awfully important today, and it seems to me not only proper but compelling that the employer have views on these important questions and from time to time, in personal meetings or by letters to the home or any other means of communication, tell the workers and their wives what he thinks.

If we honestly believe that the free-enterprise system is God's greatest gift to man, why can't we believe in it so deeply and understand it so clearly that we talk about it everywhere we are, to everybody who comes within the sound of our voice? We have to use the written and the spoken word to expound and develop and promote a clear philosophy, but I don't advise you to start talking until you have begun thinking. It is no good opening the tap if there is nothing in the tank. There are people who do that. You have to have a head of steam before you release it, and that means you must take time out from the busy, bustling worries of your life and make up your mind what it is you think. Then when you know what you believe, you can convince anybody of it if you believe it deeply enough.

What is the essence of freedom in business? It is not the right to do as we please. It is not the right to do all that we want to do, for ourselves. We are restrained, but by what? The essence of the American way is not restraint by law, but restraint by conscience. It is the self-imposed restraints that are the essence of the free-enterprise system. We may press our advantage to the full, but we must stop short of damaging others, and we are to be the judges of when to stop short. It is the abuse of that freedom that creates law. It is when men do not impose the restraint their conscience dictates that we turn to government, and the more we fail in self-restraint and the more we turn to government, the greater is the likelihood that we will go the socialist way.

We must on the one hand preserve the great drive that comes from freedom. In some forms of society, man is kept to his job by the whip. Under our system we are kept to our job because we know that our interest parallels that of society, but when the time comes that those lines cross, and we press our advantage to where we are causing damage to the common good, law is necessary. Therefore, the greater our abuse, the more the law and the inevitability of socialization.

The freedom that we enjoy in the free-enterprise system is the last strength of civilized man. It is for us to preserve it and develop it. We do that by understanding it and, with scrupulous integrity, maintaining it.

QUESTIONS

1. In the opening paragraphs, how does Randall make clear his attitude toward the " paralyzing creep of socialism "? In Paragraphs 6 and 7, why does the author refer to his personal experiences in England and Europe? What group of readers is he addressing?

2. What are the " four things about that old blacksmith " (Paragraph 1, Section II), and where are they mentioned specifically? How does Randall use them in developing the thought of Section II?

3. What purpose is served by Paragraphs 4–6 in Section II? What attitude of Randall toward the reader is evident here? Is this tone or attitude consistent with the tone of the article as a whole?

4. In Paragraph 1, Section III, what does " integrity " mean as Randall uses the term? What synonym does he offer for it? How is the term related to the title of the article? What implications about businessmen and industrialists are contained in the title?

5. How does Randall make his transition from Section II to Section III? How many of the " several things " (Paragraph 1, Section III) does he discuss? Which one does he emphasize especially?

6. What does the author try to accomplish in the latter part of Section III (beginning with the paragraph on page 452 which starts " Now, this takes me straight to this point: " and continuing to the end of the essay)? List the principal ideas in these paragraphs. How does Randall convey the impression that he is not *merely* " a practical, hard-headed man of business "? Would it be accurate to say that in this article Randall has tried to enlarge the concept of " free enterprise "? Consider especially, in this connection, the third paragraph from the end.

CURTIS CATE was born in 1924 in Paris and received his early education in France and England. He is the holder of three University degrees — a B.A. degree in History from Harvard (1947), a degree in Russian from the School of Oriental Languages in Paris (1949), and an M.A. degree from Oxford in Philosophy, Politics, and Economics (1952). He spent a year in the Middle East, 1953–1954, writing articles for *Visión*, the *New York Herald Tribune*, and the *Christian Science Monitor*. He joined the staff of the *Atlantic Monthly* in August, 1954. Articles of his have appeared in the *Reporter*, the *Canadian Forum*, and the French quarterly *Tour d'Horizon*.

GOD AND SUCCESS

by CURTIS CATE

WHETHER or not the historians of the future will agree with Norman Vincent Peale's verdict that "America is the first great nation in history to be established on a definitely religious premise," it is perhaps a little premature to say. But when they come to bend their magnifying glasses over the confusing paradoxes of the present, there is one symptom at least which they are likely to single out for special study as constituting, for better or for worse, an unquestionably American innovation in the field of contemporary religion. This is the new style, or perhaps one should say the new pace, which has been set by those rugged captains of faith, by those trail-blazing religionists, who have sought in the last ten years to give a new and unprecedented impetus to religious predication in this country.

The American *religionist* — the title is a relatively recent one — has no exact counterpart in any other country. He is not a saint or a holy man, with his staff and his bowl, as we have been brought up to imagine them. There is none of the monk or the mystic about him, though there is quite a touch of the missionary. He is not a man of meditation but an activist; not a man of faith and prayer himself so much as a man who assiduously instructs others in how to acquire faith and how to pray. A religionist, in fact, does not even need to be a clergyman at all — an immense advantage in this age of growing scarcity — for it has been pretty well proved that his functions can be performed by a doctor, a psychiatrist, or a successful businessman. His essential mission is simply to popularise and sell religious health. He is a zealous promoter of psychic comfort, a tireless booster of peace of mind, a super-salesman of salvation who has revolutionized the traditional methods of propagating piety by learning to peddle faith with all the *élan* of a Madison Avenue advertiser plugging a new barbiturate.

Reinhold Niebuhr put his finger on the nub of this revolutionary change when he remarked that today "the 'Unknown God' of Americans seems to be faith itself." The new faith, however, has little to do with the old-fashioned faith as Saint Paul conceived it – the faith of the contrite Christian humbly imploring the mercy and guidance of the Almighty to fight off sin and temptation. That is a negative approach to faith which our pioneer religionists have repudiated as unworthy of the Century of the Common Man. The new faith is a positive faith in man's power to have faith and to use it to conjure up the coöperation of God; it is a confident faith in the latest "prayer techniques" that are guaranteed to get results; it is a streamlined faith in the tried and tested spiritual formulas that will win us those earthly rewards which the Baptist faith-healer, Oral Roberts, assures us are our due, because, as he has put it, "Christ has no objection to prosperity."

One of the easiest ways of acquiring this new, twentieth-century approach to religion is to dip into a few of the inspirational books which have added such a luster to the literary output of recent years. What distinguishes them all and makes them such inspiring reading is their positive character, which shines brightly on every page and even glows fiercely in the title itself. Lay hold of the master key to the life within you, Marcus Bach recommends, in a recently published book, and you will acquire *The Will to Believe.* Just learn to think well of yourself, Dr. Hyman Schachtel urges, and you will get *The Life You Want to Live,* unless you prefer to sample *The Real Enjoyment of Living,* which was the title of his previous faith-booster. You can achieve spiritual sovereignty, Dr. Roy Burkhart assures us, by acquiring *The Freedom to Become Yourself.* Harness *The Magic Power of Your Mind,* Walter Germain encourages us, and you can live twenty-four hours a day. Learn to pray while at work, George Murran insists, and you will find that *There Is a Place for God in Business.* Forget the "if's" in your life and you will discover, according to Alexander Lake, that *Your Prayers Are Always Answered.*

It is true that the last three authors are not gentlemen of the cloth, but as I have suggested, religionists form a broad category that brooks of no rigid lines of demarcation. Mr. Germain is a former Michigan

Police Inspector who has made a specialty of juvenile delinquent psychology; Mr. Murran is a New York business consultant and the founder of the Spiritual Guide for Business Institute; and Mr. Lake has been an African big-game hunter and guide as well as a writer. But each may be said to be a religionist *malgré lui,* for what each is offering is in effect an ABC course in psychic self-help, a beginner's reader in "Faith without Tears" (in twenty easy lessons) – which is what religionism really amounts to.

But I have overlooked the most important source books of the new faith, which are, of course, the great classics of Dr. Norman Vincent Peale. Of these there are already more than half a dozen to draw on, and if the output of recent years is any criterion, we may confidently expect this number to grow as the years advance. Get rid of your inferiority complex, Dr. Peale urges us, and you will possess *A Guide to Confident Living.* Learn to believe in yourself and you will find that *You Can Win* and that you can enjoy *The Art of Living.* With Dr. Smiley Blanton (Dr. Peale's coauthor and psychiatrist colleague at the Marble Collegiate Church in New York) you will discover that *Faith Is the Answer* to all your problems, and you will develop *The Art of Real Happiness.* Learn to break that worry habit and you will be able to tap the miraculous reserves of hidden energy stored up in *The Power of Positive Thinking.*

The latest masterpiece in this impressive series has just been published by Prentice-Hall under the confident title *Stay Alive All Your Life.* Like its predecessors, it is an anthology of success stories. Its author assures us that it goes even further than *The Power of Positive Thinking* in "emphasizing how to achieve well-being, vitality, enthusiasm, and effectiveness in life."

II

REDUCED to its essence, Dr. Peale's philosophy is this: the mind of man is like an eight-cylinder motor. If it feeds on "defeat thoughts," it splutters and chokes, like a Cadillac that has been filled with bad gasoline. Weighed down by negative thoughts, man loses his self-confidence and his power to act. Everything in him turns gloomy, somber, sour. The sourer he gets, the more he alienates his friends and associates, thus exacerbating his initial feeling of rejection and insecurity. To escape this vicious cycle, he must cleanse his mind of negative thoughts and inject new positive ones. This will act on his spiritual metabolism like high-octane gasoline on a coughing engine, turning his mind into a "power-producing plant." And how do you go about getting these "positive thoughts"? The answer is simple: by praying (prayer is an essential ritual in the "power-producing process"), by going to church (going to church also ensures a longer life), and above all by dipping into the Bible.

"The words of the Bible," says Dr. Peale, "have a particularly strong therapeutic effect. Drop them into your mind, allowing them to 'dissolve' in consciousness, and they will spread a healing balm over your entire mental structure." For example, as you get up in the morning, repeat the following Biblical phrase three times: "This is the day which the Lord hath made; we will rejoice and be glad in it." (Psalms 118:24.) And the Doctor adds: "Only personalize it and say: '*I* will rejoice and be glad in it.' . . . If you repeat that one sentence three times before breakfast and meditate on the meaning of the words, you will change the character of the day by starting off with a happiness psychology."

There is, of course, nothing radically new about this kind of morale-boosting technique, variants of which can be found in a number of our religious cults. It is reminiscent of the technique of "conscious auto-suggestion" which was popularized just after the First World War by Dr. Émile Coué. But the method prescribed by the genial French doctor from Nancy had almost no religious overtones, and it contained suspicious symptoms of negative thinking. You could, if you wished, add the phrase "By the Grace of God" after you had made the ritual incantation (twenty times repeated) of "Every day in every way I am getting better and better," and thus turn it into a prayer. But this addition was not essential to the success of the formula. Furthermore, Dr. Coué's pocket reader, *Self Mastery Through Conscious Auto-Suggestion,* is studded with negative warnings, like the fine print in an insurance contract. "Of course, the thing [desired] must be within your power," or "Don't discuss things you know nothing about, or you will look ridiculous."

When we move from Dr. Coué's modest book to those of Dr. Peale we move from a timorous to a confident universe. There is no place here for lily-livered caveats and scruples that are typical of the negative approach to life of Europeans. Dr. Peale's many formulas are altogether positive and guaranteed to work for all sorts of situations, and above all, for hard-pressed business executives down on their luck. Get rid of your negative-thinking friends and learn to have faith, and you will soon be moving mountains of dollars. Invoke God's divine assistance through "deep prayers that have a lot of suction" and you will get what you want in life, or at any rate you will *potentially* be in a position to get what you want. (This is, fortunately, the only shadow of negative thinking haunting Dr. Peale's books.)

A typical case cited by the Doctor as an example of the success of this method is that of a saleswoman who has been unable to sell vacuum cleaners. One day she breaks down and pours out her tale of woe to a sympathetic customer, who, taking pity on her, gives her this encouragement: "Repeat this formula before every call. Believe it and then marvel what it will do for you. This is it. 'If God be for us, who can be against us?' [Romans 8:31.] But change it by personalizing it so that you say, 'If God be for *me,* who can be against *me?* If God be for me, then I know that with God's help, I can sell vacuum cleaners.'" The upshot of this story is that the saleswoman goes out and sells vacuum cleaners. And Dr. Peale concludes: "Now she declares, 'God helps me to sell vacuum cleaners,' and who can dispute it?"

The beauty of this moving story lies, of course, in the ingenious way in which Saint Paul's exhortation to his fellow Christians in their desperate struggle against the pagan authorities of Rome has been "personalized" and adapted to the everyday usage of the harassed saleswoman. The new formula is thus ready-made for secular use and has no religious implications whatsoever. This is, indeed, the signal originality of Dr. Peale's works. They are great religious books with a minimum of religion in them. You can search their pages in vain for moral injunctions or guidance as to the kind of good or bad actions you should or should not undertake in life. These books are not much concerned with morality; their essential concern is success. What matters is that you should get what you want. This is what makes them such up-to-date, twentieth century books, worthy of an author who is chairman of the Horatio Alger Committee of the American Schools and Colleges Association.

The almost total absence of any old-fashioned morality in Dr. Peale's works makes them some of the most revolutionary books ever written by a clergyman. We can appreciate this better, I think, merely by comparing *The Power of Positive Thinking* with a book like Giovanni Guareschi's *The Little World of Don Camillo,* a book written only a few years ago, but which our religious pioneers must consider a basically negative and reactionary work. The author of this book is an Italian journalist, who wrote it to be entertaining rather than religious; yet there is ten times more old-fashioned religion and morality in it than in *The Power of Positive Thinking.*

Yes, Dr. Peale's God is a radically different deity from Guareschi's. We almost never find Him restraining, rebuking, disciplining, or punishing. These are all negative attitudes that have no place in Dr. Peale's world. His is, happily, a confident, positive God, ever ready to contribute that extra burst of divine power that we poor under-carbureted mortals need for the long, uphill climbs. God figures prominently in Dr. Peale's works because His name is the key word in the magical incantation, in the Abracadabra of success. His name is the glorious sesame that will open every door, and above all, the closed door of the corporation president's office. Invoke God's aid and you will succeed in whatever you attempt. This is the talismanic formula that will never fail, and, happily, there is no sign of failure in Dr. Peale's confident books. They are a heartening anthology of success stories, according to the tried and tested formula we love so much in the comic strips. Like Prince Valiant and Superman, his heroes and heroines always win in the end.

This new, confident approach to religion has been objected to by some theological traditionalists on the ground that it inevitably implicates God in the seething ebb and flow of human fortunes. It is all very well to say that if you have faith in God, He will never let you down. But what happens if your good luck fails to materialize or suddenly ends? Are you to conclude that God has broken His part of the bargain? To this objection our forward-looking religionists, like Dr. Peale, have a ready answer: you simply didn't try hard enough. Go out and try again. They are equally unperturbed by such judgments as this one of Henry L. Mencken's: "All great religions, in order to escape absurdity, have to admit a dilution of agnosticism. It is only the savage, whether of the African bush or the American gospel tent, who pretends to know the will and intent of God exactly and completely." Mencken was notoriously one of the most negative thinkers this century has produced, and his past pontifications have simply been ignored by our pioneer religionists, even supposing they have ever bothered to read them.

The new fashion, on the contrary, is to see God everywhere and at least potentially succoring everyone in his secular pursuits – except, of course, Communists and fellow travelers. Today the idea of partnership with the Divine is no longer seriously contested, except perhaps in a few last strongholds of resolutely negative thought. Everywhere else it is expanding and triumphing prodigiously. In Dr. Peale's books we find God everywhere, lending a hand in the most mundane occupations. We find Him helping to sell vacuum cleaners and running a beauty parlor; we find Him on the football field, the athletic field, and out on the golf links; above all, we find Him in the business office, helping the enterprising to get ahead in the world. For nothing succeeds better in business, Dr. Peale assures us, than "effecting a merger with God." God is everywhere in the universe, the source of all energy, like a cosmic battery that any believer can plug into with the live wire of faith.

This, of course, is pantheism – a new breezy kind of pantheism in suede shoes and a gray flannel suit. The new cult has gone to the extreme of sporting a rakish-looking zoot suit, as happened last July when the International New Thought Alliance held its annual convention in Washington, D.C. I doubt if there has been a religious convention in modern times that has been as positively inspired as this one. For before it was over, the delegates had swept away all the old distinctions between God and Mammon, celebrated the mystic marriage of the Cross and the Dollar, and plunged into ecstatic dithyrambs over the distribution of a pamphlet, written by one cleric present, which bore the electrifying title: *Money Is God in Action!*

There is little mystery as to why it is that this new form of pecuniary pantheism is enjoying such a vogue in this country. Dean Inge once said that "a religion succeeds, not because it is true, but because it suits its worshippers" – a statement that Dr. Samuel Shoemaker has recently brought up to date by assuring the members of the Pittsburgh Golf Club that "God loves snobs as well as other people." The most far-seeing of our religious pioneers, like Dr. Peale, who is, as it happens, a good friend of Dr. Shoemaker's, have grasped the essential fact that getting God into the business office, and even out on the golf links, is the surest way of making Him popular in a period of prosperity. It is the easiest way of divesting Him of his former aloof, paternal attributes, of "bringing Him down to earth" and "democratizing" Him, in order to make Him more palatable to the success-seeking, Freud-ridden, leisure-loving generations of the present.

Thanks to our pioneering religionists, we can now take comfort in a new God shaped "in the image of Man"; a really friendly, companionable, democratic God, who doesn't mind having His back slapped in a spirit of pious partnership; a God who, as Jules Masserman* has put it, has become "man's omnipotent slave."

The underlying intent of this *avant-garde* trend is easy to discern. It is to give religion an unprecedented popularity in these times of prosperity and plenty by removing from its cultivation all those stuffy old notions and practices that make it at all rigorous, demanding, restraining, or remotely painful. These are vestiges of the negative past that must be swept away. In the brave new religion that we are being promised for tomorrow no ascetic discipline or special marks of contrition will any longer be required. It will have none of that gritty

* Jules H. Masserman (1905–), professor of neurology and psychiatry at Northwestern University, director of the National Foundation of Psychiatric Research; author of *Behavior and Neurosis* (1943), *The Principles of Dynamic Psychiatry* (1946), and *The Practice of Dynamic Psychiatry* (1955).

old morality in it. It will be a delicious, soothing kind of religion that you can suck in with pleasure through a straw. It will be a hot-water bottle form of piety. It will be a brand of faith that has been synthesized, vitaminized, homogenized, and capsulized, and it will be as ready-made for effortless consumption as that magically bleached, cottony, crustless, already sliced white bread which is the symbol of the modern American's massive superiority over the pagan bushwacker.

Did I say tomorrow? I was being overcautious and almost guilty of negative prognostications. For our boldest pioneers have already left even as enterprising a religionist as Dr. Peale far behind. A harbinger of the great things to come was the recent Gospel Boogie craze, in which jazzed-up fragments of the New Testament were offered to jam-packed audiences munching popcorn and sipping soda pop. Another is the wave of religious songs that has recently swamped the juke boxes with such immortals of sentimentalized piety as "It Is No Secret What God Can Do," "Are You Friends with the King of All Friends?", "If Jesus Came to Your House," and "The Man Upstairs."

Some of the verses in these songs are, it is true, a trifle sticky; and referring to God as "The Man Upstairs" may be hard to swallow for the old fashioned among us. But this is the sacrifice we must all be prepared to make in the name of religious progress. It is the price we must pay for the privilege of bringing God into the drug-store as well as the business office. And in viewing the radiant future ahead of us, who can predict to what new heights this bold, new trend may not be carried? Only the backward looking, I think, need be concerned by Reinhold Niebuhr's somber anathema: "Religion *qua* religion is naturally idolatrous, accentuating rather than diminishing the self-worship of men by assuring them of an ultimate sanction for their dearest wishes." The good Doctor alas! seems incorrigibly wedded to retrograde and negative ideas. But the rest of us know what our dearest wishes are, and we can all rejoice, with Dr. Peale and his fellow pioneers, that the Good Lord has heard the call and condescended with such debonair grace to be One of the Boys, A Hundred Percent American, and a valued member of the Team.

QUESTIONS

1. As indicated in the opening paragraph, what specifically is the occasion for the writing of this essay? Why is it appropriate that the first sentence includes a quotation from Dr. Peale? What is meant by " religionist," and what methods are used to define the term in the second paragraph?

2. How is the mood of the author revealed in the opening paragraphs? Note, for example, " trail-blazing religionists," " promoter of psychic comfort," and " supersalesman of salvation." Are these and other phrases from the language of advertising and selling appropriate for the author's purpose?

3. What do the titles in the last four paragraphs of Section I have in common? What does the author achieve by mentioning so many of them and by including numerous quotations in Section II?

4. For what purpose is the name of Dr. Coué introduced (Paragraph 3, Section II)? In what ways do the methods of the contemporary religionists differ from those of Dr. Coué? Show that Dr. Coué, Dr. Peale, and " our boldest pioneers " (next-to-last paragraph of the essay) represent three successive steps in the development of an idea. Is the order in which these steps are arranged appropriate for the author's purpose? Why, or why not?

5. What, according to the dictionary, is " pantheism "? How is the meaning of the term related to the title, *Money Is God in Action*?

6. This essay informs the reader of an " American innovation in the field of contemporary religion." What else does the author try to do? How would you describe the total effect of the essay? (Consider the material chosen, the arrangement, the diction, and such devices as titles, quotations, and slogans.) What is implied about the *readers* of the books mentioned by the author?

EDUCATION IN COLLEGE

George F. Kennan (1904——) "Training for Statesmanship," May, 1953

Howard Mumford Jones (1892——) "Undergraduates on Apron Strings," October, 1955

Oscar Handlin (1915——) "Yearning for Security," January, 1951

Lynn White, Jr. (1907——) "Educating Women in a Man's World," February, 1950

Allen Jackson (1927——) "Too Much Football," October, 1951

Harold W. Stoke (1903——) "College Athletics: Education or Show Business?" March, 1954

LANGUAGE AND THE ARTS

Jacques Barzun (1907——) "English as She's Not Taught," December, 1953

Alice Hamilton, M.D. (1869——) "Words Lost, Strayed, or Stolen," September, 1954

E. M. Forster (1879——) "The Ivory Tower," January, 1939

W. T. Stace (1886——) "The Snobbishness of the Learned," December, 1936

George F. Whicher (1889–1954) "Out for Stars: A Meditation on Robert Frost," May, 1943

Al Capp (1909——) "The Comedy of Charlie Chaplin," February, 1950

Edward Weeks (1898——) "The Meaning of Literary Prizes," October, 1935

PERSONALITIES

*Bertrand Russell (1872——) "Mahatma Gandhi," December, 1952

Gamaliel Bradford (1863–1932) "Mark Twain," April, 1920

†C. W. Ceram (1915——) "The Man Who Found Troy," November, 1951

Judge Charles E. Wyzanski, Jr. (1906——) "Brandeis," November, 1956

Rollo Walter Brown (1880——) "'Kitty' of Harvard," October, 1948

A TOUCH OF HUMOR

Richard Gordon (1921——) "The Common Cold," January, 1955

Robert Lynd (1879–1949) "Objections to Laughter," March, 1930

Philip Wylie (1902——) "Science Has Spoiled My Supper," April, 1954

SOCIAL PATTERNS AND PROBLEMS

Ralph Barton Perry (1876–1957) "Domestic Superstitions," August, 1921

David L. Cohn (1896——) "Do American Men Like Women?" August, 1946

James Howard Means, M.D. (1885——) "Government in Medicine," March, 1953

Judge Elijah Adlow (1896——) "Teen-Age Criminals," July, 1955

Albert Jay Nock (1873–1945) "Utopia in Pennsylvania: The Amish," April, 1941

AS THE SCIENTIST SEES IT

George R. Harrison (1898——) "Faith and the Scientist," December, 1953

Vannevar Bush (1890——) "As We May Think," July, 1945

Harlow Shapley (1885——) "A Design for Fighting," August, 1945

Stanley Casson (1889–1944) "Challenge to Complacency: What Future Archaeologists Will Think of Us," July, 1935

FREEDOM OF THOUGHT AND EXPRESSION

Walter Lippmann (1889——) "The Indispensable Opposition," August, 1939

*Zechariah Chafee, Jr. (1885–1957) "The Encroachments on Freedom," May, 1956

Howard Mumford Jones (1892——) "How Much Academic Freedom?" June, 1953

James S. Pope (1900——) "The Suppression of News," July, 1951

Gerald W. Johnson (1890——) "The Monopoly of News," September, 1950

VALUES

Irwin Edman (1896——) "A Reasonable Life in a Mad World," March, 1949

Archibald MacLeish (1892——) "Humanism and the Belief in Man," November, 1944

Vannevar Bush (1890——) "Can Men Live Without War?" February, 1956

Clarence B. Randall (1891——) "Free Enterprise Is Not a Hunting License," March, 1952

Curtis Cate (1924——) "God and Success," April, 1957